Fast Food and Junk Food

Advisory Board

Fast Food and Junk Food

AN ENCYCLOPEDIA OF WHAT WE LOVE TO EAT

VOLUME II: K–Z

Andrew F. Smith

GREENWOOD

AN IMPRINT OF ABC-CLIO, LLC
Santa Barbara, California • Denver, Colorado • Oxford, England

Library of Congress Cataloging-in-Publication Data

Smith, Andrew F., 1946–
    Fast food and junk food : an encyclopedia of what we love to eat / Andrew F. Smith.
        p. cm.
    Includes bibliographical references and index.
    ISBN 978-0-313-39393-8 (hardback) — ISBN 978-0-313-39394-5 (ebook)
    1. Convenience foods—Encyclopedias.   2. Junk food—Encyclopedias.   I. Title.
    TX370.S635   2011
    642'.1—dc23

                                                                                    2011037658

ISBN: 978-0-313-39393-8
EISBN: 978-0-313-39394-5

16 15 14 13 12   1 2 3 4 5

This book is also available on the World Wide Web as an eBook.
Visit www.abc-clio.com for details.

Greenwood
An Imprint of ABC-CLIO, LLC

ABC-CLIO, LLC
130 Cremona Drive, P.O. Box 1911
Santa Barbara, California 93116-1911

This book is printed on acid-free paper ∞
Manufactured in the United States of America

This encyclopedia is dedicated to America's youth—particularly Meghanne, Reilly, Ethan, and Owen.

May you make wise decisions as you balance your food and beverage choices throughout your lives.

Contents

List of Entries

List of Entries by Topic

Bakery Goods

Bagels

Bakery Goods

Cakes

Chips Ahoy!

Chocolate Chip Cookies

Cinnabon

Cookies

Crackers

Croissants

Cupcakes

Deep-Fried Junk Food

Doughnuts/Donuts

Dunkin' Donuts

Entenmann's

Famous Amos

Fortune Cookies

Girl Scout Cookies

Hostess Brands

Keebler

Krispy Kreme

Little Debbie

Moon Pie

Mrs. Fields Famous Brands

Muffins

100-Calorie Snack Packs

Oreos

Pancakes

Pepperidge Farm

Pie

Pop-Tarts

Snack Foods

Twinkies

Waffles

Winchell's Donut House

Beverages

A&W

Barq's Root Beer

Beverages

Cadbury Schweppes

Canada Dry Ginger Ale

Carbonation

Chocolate Beverages

Coca-Cola Company

Coffee

Cola

Cola Wars

Convenience Foods/Drinks

Diet Soda

Companies and Corporations

Organizations

K

Karcher, Carl N.

Carl N. Karcher (1917–2008) was born near Upper Sandusky, Ohio. His father was a sharecropper and the family moved regularly. Karcher dropped out of school and worked long hours on the farm. An uncle in Anaheim, California, offered him a job in 1936, and he accepted. When he arrived in southern California, he was amazed at the number of hot dog stands on many major street corners. He concluded that operating such a stand could be profitable, so he borrowed $311 and purchased a hot dog cart. It was so successful that he bought a second one. By the end of World War II, he owned four. In January 1945 he purchased a restaurant, which he named Carl's Drive-In Barbecue. His business soared after the war.

During the 1950s, Karcher visited the McDonald brothers' restaurant in San Bernardino, California. His visit convinced him to open his own fast food restaurant. The first Carl's Jr. opened in 1956, and Karcher quickly opened many more outlets in California. Ten years later the company incorporated as Carl Karcher Enterprises, Inc. (CKE). In the 1980s it went public and began selling franchises nationwide. In 1988 Karcher and his family members were charged with insider trading; he agreed to a settlement. The 1990s were a difficult time for CKE, and the company ended up in debt. At that time, Karcher proposed making a deal with Green Burrito, a Mexican restaurant chain in California. The CKE board opposed the deal and ousted Karcher in 1993. Nine months later, he engineered a takeover and had the Green Burrito plan adopted. The corporation turned around in 1997 and Karcher purchased Hardee's, making CKE the fourth-largest hamburger chain in the world. Karcher died in 2008 and CKE Restaurants, Inc., was sold to Apollo Management in April 2010.

See also Burrito; Carl's, Jr.; Chains; CKE Restaurants; Entrepreneurs; Fast Food; *Fast Food Nation*; Franchising; Hamburger; Hardee's; Hot Dog; McDonald's; Mexican American Food

For Further Information:

Karcher, Carl, and B. Carolyn Knight. *Never Stop Dreaming: The Story of Carl Karcher Enterprises*. San Marcos, CA: Robert Erdmann Publishing, 1991.

Knight, B. Carolyn. *Making It Happen: The Story of Carl Karcher Enterprises*. Anaheim, CA: C. Karcher Enterprises, 1981.

Schlosser, Eric. *Fast Food Nation: The Dark Side of the All-American Meal*. New York: Houghton Mifflin Company, 2001.

Keebler

Godfrey Keebler opened a neighborhood bakery in Philadelphia in 1853. By the beginning of the twentieth century Keebler products were distributed regionally, and it slowly expanded its operations. It combined with other bakeries to become the United Biscuit Company. By 1944, the company consisted of sixteen bakeries located from Philadelphia to Salt Lake City. In 1966 Keebler Company became the official corporate name and the brand name for all of its products, and Ernie Keebler and the Elves became company symbols and represented snacks baked in the Hollow Tree. The Keebler jingle went, "Man, you never would believe where the Keebler Cookies come from. They're baked by little elves in a hollow tree. And what do you think makes these cookies so uncommon? They're baked in magic ovens, and there's no factory. Hey!" The Elves, known for making "uncommonly good" products in a "magic oven," are among the best-recognized advertising characters in America. In 1996 Keebler acquired the Sunshine brand, makers of Hydrox cookies. Keebler decided to change Hydrox's flavor and rename the cookie Keebler Droxies. Through its Little Brownie Bakers subsidiary, Keebler is also a leading licensed supplier of Girl Scout cookies. Keebler's brands include Cheez-It, Chips Deluxe, Famous Amos, Fudge Shoppe, Keebler, Plantation, Sunshine, and Town House. Keebler was acquired by the Kellogg Company in 2001. It is the second-largest cookie and cracker manufacturer in the United States.

See also Advertising; Cookies; Crackers; Famous Amos; Girl Scout Cookies; Kellogg Company

For Further Information:

Keebler Web site: www.kelloggs.com/keebler

Kellogg Company

John Harvey Kellogg established the Battle Creek Toasted Corn Flake Company in 1906. He named his younger brother, Will K. Kellogg, president of the new company, but John Harvey Kellogg was unwilling to advertise the company's products. The brothers clashed and Will Kellogg gained control. To enhance sales, Will added sugar and other additives to the cereal. In its first year, the company shipped 175,000 cases of Corn Flakes. Within a few years, Kellogg's Corn Flakes had become a household name and could be found in nearly every kitchen in the United States. Will Kellogg expanded operations into Canada and Australia in 1924, followed by Europe and Asia. The name of the company was changed in 1922 to the Will K. Kellogg Company and then subsequently shortened to the Kellogg Company.

Kellogg created many products, including All-Bran (1916), Rice Krispies (1928), Sugar Pops (1950), and Frosted Flakes (1952). The Kellogg Company began producing snack foods based on their cereal line, such as Rice Krispies Treats (1995). In 2001 the Kellogg Company acquired the Keebler Company, makers of Famous Amos cookies, Cheez-It, and many other junk foods.

Globalization

Kellogg Company began operations outside the United States early in the twentieth century. It began operating in Australia, Canada, and South Africa in 1920s, and in the United Kingdom in the 1930s; after World War II the company constructed twenty manufacturing factories outside the United States, and the company has continued to expand abroad ever since. As of 2011, the Kellogg Company was the world's largest-selling cereal manufacturer with a 33 percent global market share. The Kellogg Company is headquartered in Battle Creek, Michigan.

See also Cereals; Cookies; Famous Amos; Keebler; Sugars/Sweeteners

For Further Information:

Bruce, Scott, and Bill Crawford. *Cerealizing America: The Unsweetened Story of American Breakfast Cereal*. Boston: Faber and Faber, 1995.

Carson, Gerald. *Cornflake Crusade*. New York: Rinehart & Company, Inc., 1957.

Kennedy and Crown Fried Chicken

Kennedy Fried Chicken was founded in 1979 in New York City, probably by an Afghan immigrant. Today, it is a collection of independent fast food restaurants that share a common name but not a common menu, other than fried chicken. Crown Fried Chicken, which is not affiliated with Kennedy Fried Chicken, is precisely the same—an independent collection of restaurateurs with different menus. Many Kennedy and Crown outlets are owned and managed by minorities and recently arrived immigrants, especially from Afghanistan, and many stores are located in inner-city neighborhoods. Their fried chicken is often called "ghetto chicken."

According to their Web sites, restaurants bearing each name "have been carefully and objectively reviewed" and provide their customers with quality food at fair and economical prices. As of 2011, there were about 200 Kennedy Fried Chicken and 145 Crown Fried outlets in New York, New Jersey, Pennsylvania, and Rhode Island. There are several hundred additional restaurants in inner cities that share the name and the purpose, but are not associated with the national groups.

See also Chicken; Deep Fried; Fried Chicken; KFC

For Further Information:

Crown Fried Chicken Web site: CrownFriedChicken.com

Kennedy Fried Chicken Web site: www.kennedyfriedchicken.com

Ketchup

The word "ketchup" derives from the Amoy dialect of Mandarin and originally meant a pickled fish or fermented sauce. British colonists brought ketchup recipes to North America and Americans continued to experiment with it, using a variety of additional main ingredients, including beans and apples. Tomato ketchup may have originated in America. It was widely used throughout the United States in the early nineteenth century.

Small quantities of tomato ketchup were bottled in the 1850s. After the Civil War, commercial production of ketchup rapidly increased. One commercial producer was the H. J. Heinz Company, which first sold tomato ketchup in 1873. At that time it was not among Heinz's important products. By 1890, Heinz hit upon the now world famous combination of the keystone label, the neck band, the screw cap, and the octagon-shaped ketchup bottle. This bottle has become a culinary icon throughout the world. Shortly after the turn of the century, the H. J. Heinz Company was the largest tomato ketchup producer, and it remains so today.

Ketchup on a hamburger with fries. (Dreamstime.com)

Another ketchup manufacturer was the Del Monte Corporation of San Francisco, which began bottling ketchup by 1915. It rapidly expanded production during the 1940s. Yet another manufacturer was the Hunt Brothers Packing Company, which began producing ketchup during the 1930s. Today, Heinz, Del Monte, and Hunt's are the three largest ketchup producers in the world.

Initially, ketchup was used as a cooking ingredient for making savory pies, sauces, and as a condiment for meat, poultry, and fish. In about 1900, ketchup became mainly a condiment with the invention of three major host foods: hamburgers, hot dogs, and french fries. Ketchup has expanded along with the ever-growing fast food chains, where it is dispensed in single-serve packets or from large plastic containers with push-pumps. Overall, Americans purchase 10 billion ounces per year, averaging out to about three bottles per person. Worldwide, more than 840 million 14-ounce bottles of Heinz ketchup are sold annually.

By the end of the twentieth century, ketchup was used the world over. Mainly owing to the expansion of fast food chains, the use of ketchup spread rapidly throughout Latin America, Europe, Australia, and East and Southeast Asia. Few other sauces or condiments have transcended local and national culinary traditions as has tomato ketchup. Some denounce it as an American culinary atrocity, and others condemn it as a promoter of global homogenization. Still others view it as the Esperanto of cuisine.

See also Condiments; French Fries; Hamburger; Hot Dog

For Further Information:

Smith, Andrew F. *Pure Ketchup: The History of America's National Condiment.* Columbia: The University of South Carolina Press, 1996.

Kettle Foods

Cameron Healy became a Sikh in 1971 and changed his name to Nirbao Singh. He engaged in food manufacturing and distribution, but his first business failed. In 1978 he tried again by creating the N. S. Khalsa Company in Salem, Oregon. He started by selling minimally processed nuts, cheese, and trail mix. In 1982 the company expanded to producing potato chips made from potatoes grown in Oregon and seasoned with "natural" flavorings. The chips were made in individual batches in large kettles, so the company called them kettle chips. At the time, they were the only handmade potato chips sold in America. They were thicker and had a harder surface than potato chips sold by other manufacturers. They also contained more oil and calories. They became popular as a natural food in the last two decades of the twentieth century. As the company became more successful, Singh changed his name back to Cameron Healy, and he changed the name of the company to Kettle Foods in 1988.

Kettle Foods greatly expanded their product line to include twenty-eight types of flavored potato and tortilla chips. According to the company, their Kettle Brand Baked Potato Chips are "the only baked potato chip to be made with whole slices of real potatoes, and not potato starch, potato flour or dehydrated potato pulp molded, extruded or popped into the shape of a chip." They also popularized batch production of their chips, and this encouraged other potato chip makers to develop lines of chips made in the same way.

In 1988 Kettle Foods opened a branch in the United Kingdom, where their chips were called "crisps." The company expanded sales to Canada, the European Union, and the Middle East. In 2006 the company was sold to a private British equity firm, Lion Capital LLP, and four years later, it was sold again to San Francisco–based Diamond Foods, owner of Emerald Nuts, Pop Secret, and Diamond of California snacks and nuts.

See also Diamond Foods; Nuts; Potato Chips

For Further Information:

Diamond Foods Web site: www.diamondfoods.com

International Directory of Company Histories. Vol. 48. Chicago: St. James Press, 2003.

Kettle Foods Web site: ww.kettlebrand.com

KFC

Harland Sanders devised his formula for making fried chicken at his restaurant in Corbin, Kentucky. He continued to develop it, and by the early 1950s he believed that he had a successful formula that could be franchised. He attended a foodservice seminar in Chicago where he met Pete Harmon, who operated a hamburger restaurant in Salt Lake City. Harmon became the first franchisee for what would become Kentucky Fried Chicken (KFC). Sanders' chicken was the most successful item on Harmon's menu—accounting for 50 percent of his entire sales—and he urged Sanders to sell his recipe and methods for frying it nationwide. When Sanders' own restaurant failed in 1955, he went on the road selling franchises. Lacking money to promote his company, he dressed in a distinctive white suit and a black string neck tie, which set off his white hair and white goatee (the Colonel Sanders image). He charged no fee, but franchisees paid him a few cents on each chicken sold. Franchisees were required to display KFC signs and his likeness. It was a good formula for commercial success. By 1963, Sanders had six hundred restaurants under license, all of which sold his chicken but had little else in common.

In 1964 Sanders sold KFC to John Y. Brown and Jack Massey for about $2 million, plus an additional salary of $40,000 per year for life to act as a spokesperson for the company. Brown and Massy stopped licensing existing restaurants.

KFC Fried Chicken. (AP/Wide World Photos)

In 1966 they required a uniform structure for every franchise. They changed their franchising agreement so that royalties were based on a percentage of sales, and franchisees were required to purchase some goods and seasonings from the parent company. In addition, franchisees were charged an annual advertising fee, and the company launched a major promotional blitz that cultivated a family image. Brown and Massey quickly expanded franchises. By the late 1960s, KFC's sales exceeded those of McDonald's. In 1970 KFC had more than six thousand franchise agreements. It dominated the fast food chicken market and during the early 1970s became the nation's largest commercial foodservice operation.

KFC had an influence upon other fast food chains. Dave Thomas was a KFC regional manager who worked closely with Harland Sanders. Thomas used the $1 million he generated through KFC to launch his own fast food chain, Wendy's, in 1969. When KFC began opening outlets in New Orleans, Al Copeland was encouraged to launch his own chicken chain, which he called Popeyes. McDonald's saw the KFC sales figures and created Chicken McNuggets to compete in the chicken line. Burger King launched a similar product, and KFC finally developed a finger food of its own to compete with McNuggets.

In 1971 Brown and Massey sold KFC to the Heublein Company for a reported $280 million. Heublein was purchased by R. J. Reynolds in 1982, which sold it to PepsiCo in 1986. Over the years, KFC lost its first-place position among commercial foodservice operations, and it was in need of rejuvenation. Owing to the public's deep concern with anything fried, the company changed its name from Kentucky Fried Chicken to just KFC, in order to eliminate the word "fried" from its name. However, American outlets later revived the original name.

Globalization

KFC began opening outlets in other countries, which have fared extremely well. KFC was the first American fast food chain in Japan. From its start in 1970, it was a joint venture with Mitsubishi Trading Company, which encouraged development of a local menu, such as *yaki-musubi* (grilled or toasted riceballs), that would appeal to Japanese customers.

In 1987 KFC was one of the first fast food chains in China, and today it is the most-recognized foreign brand in China. It has localized its food offerings, such as Shrimp & Chicken Sandwich and Egg Tarts (pastry cups filled with egg custard). As of 2011, KFC housed 3,700 stores in China with an expected increase to 20,000. The company makes more money in China than it does in the United States. KFC has opened restaurants in other Asian countries, including Sri Lanka, where it offers Chicken Buriyani (fried chicken, buriyani rice, and curry gravy), and Cambodia in 2007. KFC is one of the leading fast food operations in South Africa with more than 600 restaurants, and the company plans to expand this to 850 by 2014. It plans to open outlets in Nigeria, Ghana, Angola, and Zambia; by 2014, the company plans to have 350 restaurants in the rest of Africa. KFC is also the leading American fast food chain in Southeast Asia, with more than 570 restaurants in Malaysia, Singapore, Brunei, Cambodia, and India.

Today, KFC has outlets in forty-five countries and has more restaurants outside the United States than within it. It has been so successful in its operations abroad that the term "Chickenification" has emerged to refer to the phenomenon.

World Hunger

In 2009 KFC teamed up with the United Nation's World Food Programme to raise money for food assistance programs in Somalia, India, Rwanda, Colombia, and Ethiopia. It is the world's largest private sector hunger relief effort, spanning 110 countries, 36,000 Yum! Brand restaurants, and their more than one million employees. The effort generated $20 million to alleviate hunger.

Double Down

The Double Down is a recent addition to the KFC menu that was released on April Fools' Day in 2010. It is a sandwich-like food with two deep-fried chicken breasts serving as a bun, with bacon, two types of cheese, and sauce between the two pieces of chicken. When it was released it sparked a media frenzy, and it was subsequently criticized for its excessive calories, fat, and salt content.

Corporate

PepsiCo used KFC and other restaurant chains as outlets to sell its soft drinks. Other large fast food chains, such as McDonald's, refused to dispense Pepsi beverages owing to competition with the PepsiCo-owned restaurants. PepsiCo divested itself of KFC and other restaurant subsidiaries by creating Tricon Global Restaurants, later renamed Yum! Brands. These restaurants, however, all have continued to sell PepsiCo beverages.

See also Chicken; China; Fried Chicken; PepsiCo; Popeyes; Sanders, Harlan; Secret Formulas; Yum! Brands, Inc.

For Further Information:

Darden, Robert. *Secret Recipe: Why KFC Is Still Cooking after 50 Years*. Irving, TX: Tapestry Press, 2004.

Jakle, John A., and Keith A. Sculle. *Fast Food: Roadside Restaurants in the Automobile Age*. Baltimore: Johns Hopkins University Press, 1999.

Liu, Warren. *KFC in China: Secret Recipe for Success*. Singapore; Hoboken, NJ: Wiley, 2008.

Pearce, John Ed. *The Colonel: The Captivating Biography of the Dynamic Founder of a Fast-Food Empire*. Garden City, NY: Doubleday, 1982.

Sanders, Harland. *Life as I Have Known It Has Been Finger Lickin' Good*. Carol Stream, IL: Creation House, 1974.

Kids' Meals

In 1973 Burger Chef, a small, regional hamburger chain, began offering a kids' meal promotion. The kids' meal was a success, but the chain failed. The success of Burger Chef's kids' meal encouraged McDonald's to launch its brightly colored Happy Meals in 1978. Their success convinced McDonald's—and other fast food chains—that their most important customer was children.

McDonald's, Burger King, and other fast food chains developed a vast array of kids' meals accompanied by toys and other premiums. In 2006 the fast food industry spent more than $360 million on toys to sell more than 1.2 billion meals to kids.

For the past decade, critics have questioned the nutritional content of these meals. In 2010 the Rudd Center for Food Policy & Obesity reported that researchers had studied 3,039 possible kids' meal combinations, from a host of fast food restaurants, using nutritional criteria developed by the Institute of Medicine, the health arm of the National Academy of Sciences. Its Committee on School Meals concluded that preschool-age kids' meals should not exceed 410 calories and 544 mg of sodium per meal, while a meal served to older children should not exceed

650 calories and 636 mg of sodium. For both groups, less than 10 percent of the calories should be from saturated fat. The researchers found that only twelve combinations for preschoolers met the criteria regarding saturated fat, sugar, sodium, protein, and calories, and only fifteen did so for older kids.

The report identified potential kids' meal combinations offered at Subway and Burger King as among the best. The best combination identified by researchers was Subway's Veggie Delite sandwich with wheat bread and no cheese, accompanied by apple slices and a 100-percent-juice drink. It had 285 calories, no saturated fat, and only 295 mg of sodium. Burger King's macaroni and cheese, accompanied by apples with no caramel sauce and fat-free milk, was a runner-up with 285 calories, 490 mg sodium, and only 14 calories from saturated fat. At the bottom of the list was Dairy Queen's cheeseburger accompanied by fries, a full-sugar soft drink, and a chocolate Dilly Bar. This combination had 973 calories, 171 of which were from saturated fat, and 1,450 mg of sodium. Runner-up for the worst kids' meal was KFC's popcorn chicken, biscuit, Mountain Dew, and string cheese with 840 calories, 1,610 mg sodium, and 99 calories from saturated fat.

In addition, the study found that even when healthy foods were available, employees did not offer children those options. When children's meals were ordered at McDonald's, which offers apple slices and skim milk as possible side dishes, more than 80 percent of the time employees did not offer the apples or the milk, but automatically put french fries and soft drinks with the order. During 2008–2009, a study by the Center for Science in the Public Interest (CSPI) found that only 5 percent of children ordered fruit and only 14 percent ordered plain milk or 100-percent juice at fast food restaurants.

The National Restaurant Association responded to the report with a statement that claimed that the number one food trend in fast food restaurants was the increasing number of healthful options and nutritious offerings in kids' meals.

See also Burger King; Calories; Center for Science in the Public Interest (CSPI); Dairy Queen; Fat, Dietary; Hamburger; Happy Meals; McDonald's; National Restaurant Association; Obesity; Rudd Center for Food Policy & Obesity; Sodium/Salt; Subway

For Further Information:

Harris, Jennifer L., et al. "Fast Food FACTS: Evaluating Fast Food Nutrition and Marketing to Youth" New Haven, CT: Rudd Center for Food Policy & Obesity, 2010, as at: www.fastfoodmarketing.org/media/FastFoodFACTS_Report.pdf

Marketing Food to Children and Adolescents: A Review of Industry Expenditures, Activities and Self-Regulation. Washington, D.C.: Federal Trade Commission, 2008, as at: www.ftc.gov/os/2008/07/P064504foodmktingreport.pdf

Rudd Center for Food Policy & Obesity FACTS Web site: fastfoodmarketing.org

Killer at Large

Killer at Large is a 105-minute documentary film about America's obesity epidemic. It begins with the story of 12-year-old Brooke Bates who weighed 218 pounds. Her solution was liposuction because she wanted to be popular. The movie graphically shows the medical procedure that removed thirty-five pounds of fat. A few weeks later, surgeons removed another ten pounds. Within months, she had gained considerable weight back and sought more surgery.

From here the film proceeds to discuss the nationwide obesity crisis, including discussions of actions (or inactions) that the American government has taken over the past sixty years that have contributed to American obesity. As Richard Carmona, the U.S. surgeon general during the George W. Bush administration, proclaims in the film, "Obesity is the terror within. It is destroying us; it's destroying our society from within."

The film features interviews with a wide variety of others concerned about obesity in America, including former president Bill Clinton, Ralph Nader, Kelly Brownell, Marion Nestle, Michael Pollan, and many more. *Killer at Large* was produced and directed by Steven Greenstreet and was released by Shinebox Media Productions in 2008.

See also Brownell, Kelly D.; Obesity; Pollan, Michael

For Further Information:

Killer at Large. DVD, 2009.

Killer at Large Web site: www.killeratlarge.com

Kit Kat

Combination bars had proved unsuccessful in the United Kingdom when Forrest Mars arrived and produced the Mars Bar in 1932. Mars' success encouraged the British company Rowntree's of York to develop the first successful English combination bar, called the Chocolate Crisp, which was released in 1935. It consists of layers of crème-filled wafer covered in smooth milk chocolate. Two years later, Rowntree changed its name to Kit Kat, which quickly became the company's most popular and successful chocolate candy.

In 1969 the Hershey Company of Hershey, Pennsylvania, licensed the rights to manufacture and sell Kit Kat bars in the United States. Hershey engineers could not figure out how to manufacture it, so Rowntree's had to send its engineers to the United States to help set up the manufacturing process. Rowntree's was acquired by Nestlé, which has dramatically expanded the Kit Kat line to include a wide variety of flavors, ingredients, and shapes, such as Kit Kat Chunkies (1999) and Kit Kat Kubes (2003). In the United States, the Hershey Company worked with 7-Eleven to produce Kit Kat Bites that could fit in car cup holders, so drivers could eat them while traveling.

The Hershey Company continues to manufacture the Kit Kat bar in the United States, and Nestlé continues to produce the Kit Kat bar throughout the rest of the world. They remain extremely popular in the United Kingdom, where an estimated forty-seven Kit Kat bars are consumed every second.

See also Candy; Chocolate; Hershey Company; Kit Kat; Mars Bar; Rowntree's of York; 7-Eleven

For Further Information:

Kit Kat Web site: www.kitkat.com

Klondike Bar

The Klondike Bar consists of a vanilla ice cream square encased in a layer of hard chocolate. It was invented in about 1922 by the Isaly family, who owned the Mansfield Pure Milk Company in Mansfield, Ohio. The bar is believed to be named after the Klondike River in the Canadian Yukon territory that was made famous by the gold rush of the 1890s. The bar was initially made on a stick and included several different flavors. It was made by hand at the family's store near Youngstown, Ohio, and later by the Isaly Dairy Company of Pittsburgh, founded in 1931. In 1967 the company's operations were consolidated in Pittsburgh.

Until the 1970s, Klondike Bars were sold only in Ohio, western Pennsylvania, and West Virginia. In 1972 the company was sold to a group of investors, and five years later the Clabir Corporation purchased it and expanded distribution to Philadelphia, Florida, New York, and New England. In 1982 the company began a national advertising campaign featuring the jingle, "What would you do for a Klondike Bar?" It quickly became America's best-selling novelty ice cream bar. In 1993 the Isaly Klondike Company was acquired by Unilever and it was folded into a subsidiary, which also sold Good Humor Bars and Breyers ice cream.

See also Breyers; Chocolate; Good Humor; Ice Cream

For Further Information:

Butko, Brian. *Klondikes, Chipped Ham & Skyscraper Cones: The Story of Isaly's.* Mechanicsburg, PA: Stackpole Books, 2001.

Klondike Web site: http://www.klondikebar.com/

Kool-Aid

Kool-Aid, a powdered, fruit-flavored beverage, was created by Edwin Perkins, head of the Perkins Products Company of Hastings, Nebraska. The firm manufactured a wide array of products sold through mail order. In 1920 Perkins marketed his first soft drink concentrate, Fruit Smack, a bottled syrup intended to be combined with water and sugar. Fruit Smack was successful but the bottles were heavy, which increased mailing expenses, and the bottles often broke in transit, which upset customers and required the company to refund money. Inspired by the tremendous success of Jell-O dessert powder, Perkins designed a powdered beverage concentrate that could be sold in paper packets, thus reducing expenses. Customers were only required to combine the powder with water and sugar. He called his product Kool-Ade, which was later changed to Kool-Aid.

In 1927 the packets were first sold through the mail for 10 cents apiece. The original six flavors were cherry, grape, lemon-lime, orange, raspberry, and strawberry. As the sales of Kool-Aid increased, Perkins phased out the company's other products and focused on marketing Kool-Aid. Rather than only sell it by mail,

Kool-Aid Packets. (AP/Wide World Photos)

Perkins began an aggressive campaign to sell Kool-Aid through grocery stores. By 1929, it was sold throughout the United States. During the Depression, Perkins lowered the price of Kool-Aid to a nickle a packet and launched a major national advertising campaign aimed at children. Perkins tried to expand his Kool-Aid product line with pie fillings and ice cream mixes, but they were never as successful as his powdered beverage. During World War II, sugar was rationed and the manufacture of Kool-Aid was limited, but after the war Kool-Aid sales took off. By 1950 the company was manufacturing one million packets a day, and sales increased during the following years.

In 1953 Perkins sold his company to General Foods, which introduced the famous "Smiling Face Pitcher" advertising campaign in 1954. General Foods added additional flavors, such as Root Beer and Lemon, in 1955. Presweetened Kool-Aid was first marketed in 1964.

In 1988 General Foods merged with Kraft Foods, which launched new product lines, such as Kool-Aid Slushies and ready-to-drink Kool-Aid Splash. When Kool-Aid celebrated its seventy-fifth anniversary in 2002, the Museum of Natural and Cultural History in Hastings, Nebraska, installed a permanent exhibition of the company's memorabilia and history.

For many Americans, Kool-Aid evokes images of childhood, innocent summer fun, and cool refreshment. Its longtime advertising image, a smiling face drawn in the condensation on an icy pitcher of Kool-Aid, has become a national icon.

See also Advertising; Beverages; General Foods Corporation; Ice Cream; Jell-O; Kraft Foods; Powdered Mixes; Root Beer; Sugars/Sweeteners

For Further Information:

Hastings Museum of Natural and Cultural History's Web site: www.hastingsmuseum.org

Kosher

Kosher (or more accurately, Kashruth) are the Jewish dietary laws outlined in the Hebrew Bible. Any food that has been handled, processed, or packaged must be subject to strict rabbinic supervision. The laws fall into three basic categories: prohibition of the consumption of blood, prohibition of the consumption of certain categories of animals (such as pork or shellfish), and prohibition regarding combinations of milk and meat products. The Union of Orthodox Jewish Congregations is the most well-known certifier of kosher foods in the United States. Foods certified by this group are identified with the symbol of a letter U inside a letter O. Many junk foods have been so certified, and the symbol can be found on their packages.

In Israel, most American fast food chain outlets, such as those of Burger King, KFC, McDonald's, and Sbarro, have kosher restaurants. In the United States, some

Kosher Coke

In 1915 Coca-Cola wanted kosher certification. It showed an Atlanta rabbi the "secret formula," under the condition that the rabbi swore never to reveal it. He gave Coke certification after the Coca-Cola Company removed a tallow-derived glycerin from its formula.

chains have kosher certified outlets. Many Baskin-Robbins outlets are kosher, but a few flavors served at kosher outlets are not, and each store has a sign indicating which flavors are not kosher. Dunkin' Donuts, Krispy Kreme, Nathan's, and Subway have some kosher outlets. Most are located in areas with large Jewish populations, such as New York City.

See also Baskin-Robbins; Burger King; Coca-Cola Company; Dunkin' Donuts; Israel; KFC; Krispy Kreme; McDonald's; Nathan's Famous; Pork; Sbarro; Subway

For Further Information:

Fishkoff, Sue. *Kosher Nation: Why More and More of America's Food Answers to a Higher Authority.* New York: Schocken, 2010.

Kraft Foods

Kraft Foods dates back to the early twentieth century, when James L. Kraft (1874–1953) started selling cheese out of the back of a wagon on the streets of Chicago. Kraft, born in Ontario, Canada, immigrated to the United States, where he engaged in a variety of pursuits. One of his jobs was with the Buffalo Cheese Company, where he learned the business. Kraft arrived in Chicago in 1903 with $65 in his pocket. He bought a wagon and a horse to pull it, and fifty pounds of cheese, which he peddled on the streets. Sales were slow until Kraft came up with the idea of packaging the cheese in portions in advance, rather than weighing out and wrapping pieces to each customer's specification. He was joined in the business by his four brothers, and the firm grew. The brothers incorporated the company in 1909 as J. L. Kraft & Bros. They differentiated their cheeses from others on the market by prominently labeling them with the company name, and also began an aggressive marketing campaign in the Chicago area. In 1914 the Kraft brothers opened their first cheese-making plant. At that time they were selling thirty-one different cheeses and had expanded their market throughout the upper Midwest. In 1915 they began to package their cheese in tins. The following year the company patented the first processed cheese made from milk solids, along with emulsifiers, salt, and food colorings. The advantage of processed cheese was that it could be made with by-products of regular cheese production and it had a longer shelf life than did natural cheese.

By 1917, Kraft's earnings were $2 million. When the United States entered World War I, Kraft received a major contract to produce cheese in tins for the Army. In 1920 Kraft purchased a Canadian firm, MacLaren's Imperial Cheese Co., Ltd., and Kraft began selling its products in Canada. By 1923, the company's annual sales had reached $22 million. During the 1920s, Kraft began to expand abroad, opening its first office in London in 1924, and one in Germany three years later. Also during the 1920s, Kraft began to create and manufacture new products, such as Velveeta, which debuted in 1927.

In 1928 Kraft merged with the Phenix Cheese Company to create the Kraft-Phenix Cheese Company. Phenix had been formed by a group of New York dairy farmers who, around 1880, had created and marketed Philadelphia Cream Cheese. Both Kraft and Phenix were early producers of processed cheese, but Kraft was the first company to patent such a product. Together, the two companies soon controlled 40 percent of the nation's cheese sales. Thomas Henry McInnerney, president of the National Dairy Products Corporation, bought the Kraft-Phenix Company in 1930. National Dairy Products acquired several other firms, including the Breyers Ice Cream Company. By 1931, the company had plants in thirty-one states and several foreign countries. During the 1930s, the company debuted several more new products, including Miracle Whip (1930), the Kraft Macaroni and Cheese Dinner (1937), and Parkay Margarine (1940).

During World War II, Kraft supplied cheese to the American armed forces and Allies abroad. Kraft Kitchens, a division established in the home economics department in 1924, devised and disseminated recipes to help Americans at home cope with food restrictions. In 1945 the Kraft Cheese Company changed its name to Kraft Foods Company. In 1951 the postwar economic boom drove National Dairy's gross sales over the $1 billion mark.

Kraft Foods packaged the nation's first processed cheese slices in 1950, and then introduced Cheez Whiz (1952) and Cracker Barrel Cheese (1954). One reason for the company's success was its savvy use of national media for advertising. To promote Miracle Whip, the company sponsored the Kraft Music Program on NBC radio in 1933; when television emerged as a national advertising tool, the company invented the Kraft Television Theatre, beginning in 1958.

In 1969 the National Dairy Products Corporation changed its name to KraftCo, and in 1976 changed it again, to Kraft, Inc. In 1988 Kraft was acquired by the Philip Morris Companies, which had acquired the giant General Foods three years earlier.

General Foods was an outgrowth of the Postum Cereal Company, founded by C. W. Post in 1895. When C. W. Post committed suicide in 1914, his daughter, Marjorie Merriweather Post, inherited the company. She married the financier Edward F. Hutton in 1920, and he took over Postum Cereal. During the 1920s, Hutton went on a buying spree, acquiring fourteen other brands, including Jell-O, Swans Down Cake Flour, Minute Tapioca, Baker's Coconut, Baker's Chocolate, and Log Cabin Syrup. In 1928 Maxwell House Coffee was absorbed into Postum. The following year, Hutton acquired Clarence Birdseye's General Seafood Company and then named the new conglomerate General Foods. After the Depression and World War II, General Foods went on another buying binge, this time acquiring companies such as Perkins Products, the maker of Kool-Aid, in 1953.

In 1981 General Foods acquired Oscar Mayer & Co. The original Oscar Mayer was a German immigrant who started out working for a Detroit meat market before moving to Chicago, where he worked in the stockyards. In 1883 Mayer joined his brother, a sausage maker and ham curer, in opening a small retail butcher shop in a German neighborhood on Chicago's Near North Side. In 1904 the Mayers took the bold step of putting their own name on their products and began selling America's first brand-name meats. When the Meat Inspection Act was signed into law in 1906, Oscar Mayer was one of the first companies to voluntarily comply with the provisions of the new law. In 1929 Oscar Mayer further distinguished its products by placing a yellow paper band around its hot dogs. The company became famous for its Wienermobile, a hotdog-shaped vehicle that has traveled about the United States since 1936.

In 1989 Philip Morris merged its two food divisions—General Foods and Kraft—to form Kraft General Foods. In 1993 Philip Morris acquired the ready-to-eat cereals division of RJR Nabisco. Philip Morris' food companies were merged and reorganized under the name Kraft Foods, Inc. In 2000 Philip Morris acquired the rest of Nabisco, which it folded into Kraft Foods. Nabisco was formed in 1898, when the American Biscuit Company, composed of forty bakeries in the Midwest, merged with the New York Biscuit Company and the smaller United States Biscuit Company to form the National Biscuit Company (NBC), which operated under the brand name Nabisco. The merged company became famous for many products, including Fig Newtons, introduced in 1891; Uneeda Biscuits (1898), the first nationally advertised cracker in America; Graham Crackers (1898), of which Sylvester Graham would have disapproved, since they are made with sugar; Barnum's Animal Crackers (1902); Triscuits (1903); Oreos (1912); Ritz Crackers (1934); and Chips Ahoy! (1963).

Nabisco acquired the Shredded Wheat Company in 1928 and the Cream of Wheat Company in 1962. In 1981 Nabisco merged with Standard Brands to form Nabisco Brands. Standard Brands was created when three nationally known brands—Fleischmann's Yeast, Chase & Sanborn Coffee, and Royal Baking Powder—came together in 1929. Standard Brands became one of the largest suppliers of grocery goods to supermarkets. In 1961 Standard Brands acquired Planters Nut and Chocolate Co., which had been formed in 1906 by two Italian immigrants. It also acquired the Curtiss Candy Company, makers of Baby Ruth and Butterfinger candy bars.

Nabisco Brands also acquired Life Saver Candies from the E. R. Squibb Corporation in 1981. Life Savers mints were created in 1912 and were sold at bars and tobacco shops to freshen the breath of drinkers and smokers. In 1913 the Life Savers brand was acquired by the Mint Products Company, which spun off the Life Savers Corporation in 1926. In 1956 Life Savers merged with Beech-Nut, makers of chewing gum, candy, and baby food, to form Beech-Nut LifeSavers, Inc. It merged with E. R. Squibb & Sons in 1968.

At about the same time that Philip Morris acquired General Foods, in 1985, R. J. Reynolds Industries acquired Nabisco. Like Philip Morris, R. J. Reynolds had already acquired some food companies in an effort to diversify its operations as the specter of antismoking sentiment and litigation loomed ahead. In 1968 Reynolds bought the Chun King Corporation, which produced Chinese-style packaged foods, and established a subsidiary, R. J. Reynolds Foods, for other nontobacco acquisitions. It had previously acquired Patio (Mexican-style foods), Hawaiian Punch (fruit punch), College Inn (broth and boned chicken), Brer Rabbit (molasses), and My-T Fine Desserts. In 1979 Reynolds acquired Del Monte Corporations.

In 1986, the year after its merger with Nabisco, R. J. Reynolds Industries changed its name to RJR Nabisco. Three years later, Kohlberg Kravis Roberts & Co. (KKR) acquired RJR Nabisco in the largest leveraged buyout in American history. To pay off its debts, KKR began selling assets, including Chun King, Hawaiian Punch, Brer Rabbit, Patio, and My-T-Fine Desserts. The leadership of the Del Monte subsidiary acquired what was left—about half of the original Del Monte company—through another leveraged buyout in 1990. RJR Nabisco sold its cereal foods to Philip Morris Industries in 1993, and finally sold the remainder of Nabisco to Philip Morris in 2000.

The merger between Nabisco and Philip Morris Industries was approved by the Federal Trade Commission, provided that Philip Morris divest the merged company of Jell-O, Royal brands, Life Savers mints, and others. Its products ranged from Starbucks Brand Coffee to Oreos. In 2006 executives made the decision to sell the remaining stock in the company's food division, and thus on March 30, 2007, Kraft Foods became completely independent—and became America's largest food company, the second largest in the world.

The company has continued to acquire and grow. For instance, in 2010 it acquired Cadbury, a British confectionary maker. It also has spun off some of its operations. For instance, it combined Post Cereals with Ralcorp Holdings, a manufacturer of breakfast cereals, cookies, crackers, chocolate, snack foods, and peanut butter, and set up a new company called Post Foods. It also sold its Tombstone and DiGiorno's frozen pizza to Nestlé in 2010.

As of 2011, Kraft Foods was a $40 billion company with 97,000 employees. It was America's largest confectionary and food company. In August 2011 the company made the decision to split its grocery products—such as DiGiorno Pizza,

Jell-O, Tang, and Kool-Aid—from its snack foods—such as Oreo cookies, Trident gum, Cadbury, and Toblerone. The snack food products company will be spun off.

See also Baby Ruth; Butterfinger; Cadbury; Cheez Whiz; Chips Ahoy!; General Foods Corporation; Jell-O; Kool-Aid; LifeSavers; Nabisco; Oreos; Post Foods; Ritz Crackers; Starbucks; Tang; Toblerone; Tombstone Pizza

For Further Information:

Allen, Gary, and Ken Albala, eds. *The Business of Food; Encyclopedia of Food and Drink Industries*. Westport, CT: Greenwood Press, 2007.

Kraft Foods Web site: www.kraft.com

Smith, Andrew F. *Eating History: Thirty Turning Points in the Making of American Cuisine*. New York: Columbia University Press, 2009.

Krispy Kreme

In 1937 Vernon Rudolph launched a doughnut shop in Winston-Salem, North Carolina, which became known as Krispy Kreme. He sold doughnuts to local grocery stores and to customers through a window in his small factory. During the 1940s, Rudolph opened other outlets for his doughnuts, particularly in the southeast. Rudolph died in 1973 and Beatrice Foods purchased the company in 1976. A

Krispy Kreme doughnuts. (AP/Wide World Photos)

small group of investors purchased the chain from Beatrice in 1982. Krispy Kreme rapidly expanded its operation, opening its first outlet in New York in 1996 and in California in 1999. Krispy Kreme also sells doughnuts in grocery stores. In 2005 they were the largest-selling doughnut in this category.

Chef Chandler Goff of Decatur, Georgia, reportedly came up with the idea of placing a hamburger patty between two Krispy Kreme doughnuts. He called his invention the Luther Burger. In 2006 the Gateway Grizzlies, a baseball team in Illinois, began selling the Grizzlies' Burger with hamburger, bacon, and cheese between two Krispy Kreme doughnuts. Cooking television star Paula Deen added an egg to it and popularized this combination throughout the nation. In 2010 a vendor at the Wisconsin State Fair launched the Krispy Kreme Cheeseburger, a burger with cheese and bacon sandwiched between two Krispy Kreme doughnuts. It weighed in with more than one thousand calories.

Krispy Kreme began to expand abroad, opening its first international outlet in Canada in 2001; subsequently outlets have opened in seventeen other countries, including Australia and Japan. In 1976 Krispy Kreme became a wholly owned subsidiary of Beatrice Foods. Franchisees purchased the company in 2003. It is headquartered in Winston-Salem.

See also Doughnuts/Donuts; Fair Food

For Further Information:

Krispy Kreme Web site: www.krispykreme.com

Mullins, Paul R. *Glazed America: A History of the Doughnut*. Gainesville: University Press of Florida, 2008.

Kroc, Ray

Raymond Albert Kroc (1902–1984), who created the fast food empire of McDonald's, was born in Oak Park, Illinois. He held various jobs, including selling beans, sheet music, Florida real estate, and an instant beverage. He became a Lily Cup salesman and later sold restaurant supplies. These positions gave him a broad knowledge of soda fountain and restaurant operations. In 1938 he became an agent for the Multimixer, a machine that could make several milkshakes simultaneously. A few years later he purchased the company. After World War II, the company thrived by selling Multimixers to operators of ice cream chains such as Dairy Queen. When the Dairy Queen franchisees created a national trade association in 1948, Kroc attended their first meeting. Through his association with Dairy Queen franchisees, Kroc learned how franchising worked and came to understand the many problems facing franchisees.

During the early 1950s, the sale of Multimixers began to slide and Kroc began looking for ways to increase sales. Most restaurants bought a single Multimixer, but Kroc noted that a small fast food restaurant in San Bernardino, California, had bought several. When Kroc read advertisements and articles about Richard and Maurice McDonald's fast food operation, Kroc decided to pay them a visit. Kroc liked what he saw and he struck an agreement with the brothers to sell franchises nationally. Kroc opened his first McDonald's in Des Plaines, Illinois, in 1955, the same year he launched McDonald's Systems, Inc.

Kroc's relationship with the McDonald brothers was stormy from the beginning. The brothers wanted to maintain the quality of the chain that bore their name, and therefore required that all McDonald's outlets be precisely the same as their own. They were inflexible on this matter, and this meant that Kroc could not change or improve upon their model. In 1961 Kroc borrowed $2.7 million and bought the company from the brothers. At the time it had 228 outlets. The McDonald brothers insisted on keeping their San Bernardino restaurant, which was renamed the Big M. Eventually, Kroc opened a McDonald's restaurant across the street and ran the Big M out of business; the building eventually burned down.

Kroc took McDonald's national, creating a fast food empire. To do this, Kroc developed a three-tiered business system composed of corporate managers, franchisees, and suppliers. He was a strong believer in K.I.S.S.—"Keep it simple, Stupid." His goal was to simplify all activities in the restaurants and reduce the level of complexity and the range of responsibilities for each of his employees. His organizing concepts were: "Quality, Service, Cleanliness, and Value."

In 1972 Ray Kroc gave an illegal personal contribution of $250,000 to the presidential reelection campaign of Richard Nixon. It was uncovered during the Watergate scandal in 1974. Although it was a personal contribution, it turned out to be a public relations disaster for McDonald's. Kroc retired from managing the company in 1977. When he died in 1984, there were more than 7,500 McDonald's outlets.

See also Chains; Dairy Queen; Entrepreneurs; Fast Food; Franchising; French Fries; Hamburger; Ice Cream; McDonald's; Milkshakes, Malts, and Ice Cream Sodas

For Further Information:

Funderburg, Anne Cooper. *Sundae Best: A History of Soda Fountains*. Bowling Green, OH: Bowling Green State University Popular Press, 2002.

Kroc, Ray, with Robert Anderson. *Grinding It Out: The Making of McDonald's*. Chicago: Henry Regnery Company, 1977.

Langdon, Philip. *Orange Roofs, Golden Arches: The Architecture of American Chain Restaurants*. New York: Knopf, 1986.

L

Lance

In 1913 Philip L. Lance founded the Lance Packing Company in Charlotte, North Carolina. They sold roasted peanuts and peanut butter to local merchants. He spread the peanut butter on crackers as samples for customers. This was successful so he began selling packaged peanut butter and cracker sandwiches. During World War I the company began selling peanut brittle, and subsequently the company added crackers, cookies, granola bars, and packaged cheese cracker sandwiches to its product line. The company expanded its sales area first to the southeastern United States, and then nationally.

In 2009 Lance acquired the Stella D'oro Biscuit Company. In 2010 Lance, Inc., merged with Snyder's of Hanover to form Snyder's-Lance, Inc.

See also Cookies; Crackers; Granola; Peanut Brittle; Peanut Butter; Peanuts; Snyder's-Lance, Inc.; Snyder's of Hanover; Stella D'oro

Latin America

American fast food companies operate throughout Latin America and the Caribbean. KFC, McDonald's, Burger King, and Dominos all have franchises in Latin America. McDonald's restaurants are the largest American fast food chain, followed by Burger King with its 1,138 outlets. Quiznos has a presence in eight Latin American countries or territories, and it plans to boost its presence in Argentina, Chile, and Ecuador.

American junk food companies have also expanded to Latin America. Ritz Crackers were exported to South America, as was Tang and Cheetos. Soft drink companies, such as Orange Crush, Pepsi, and Coca-Cola, expanded aggressively into Latin America

---

Pollo Campero

Pollo Campero is the largest restaurant chain in Guatemala and the largest chicken fast food chain in Latin America. In 2002 Pollo Campero opened a franchise in Los Angeles, its first restaurant in the United States. As of 2010, Pollo Campero had more than fifty restaurants in the United States.

In Argentina, McDonald's and Burger King have a strong presence. These chains have encouraged the growth of indigenous hamburger chains, such as Carlitos de Gesell, which sells a large variety of hamburgers. Argentina supplies beef for hamburger outlets throughout the world. Argentinean companies such as Quickfood and Finexcor (a subsidiary of the U.S. multinational Cargill) specialize in manufacturing super-frozen hamburger patties of precisely uniform size, weight, and fat content. The vacuum-packed, frozen patties are shipped throughout the world.

After the end of Chile's dictatorship in 1990, American fast food operations, such as KFC, McDonald's, Burger King, and Domino's, began to open outlets there.

See also Brazil; Burger King; Domino's Pizza; KFC; Mars, Inc.; McDonald's

Lawsuits

The junk food and fast food industries are no stranger to lawsuits, which fall into three broad categories: most frequently corporation(s) filing suits against other corporation(s); on occasion corporations filing suits against one or more individuals; and more frequently, individual(s) filing suits against corporations.

Corporation vs. Corporation

Corporations engage in lawsuits against other corporations for a variety of reasons. These include claims of trademark infringement or restraint of trade and false advertising claims. For instance, White Castle sued White Tower for trademark infringement. White Castle claimed that White Tower had used its architecture, slogans, and other concepts in an effort to lure customers who intended to enjoy White Castle. The court ruled in favor of White Castle. White Tower was ordered to change its name and all resemblances to White Castle in its appearance and slogans so as not to confuse would-be customers. White Tower maintained its name and operations by paying White Castle a large sum of money.

Pepperidge Farm, makers of Goldfish, sued Nabisco for trademark infringement when the latter manufactured CatDog crackers, an orange-colored cheese snack, some of which were shaped like fish. Pepperidge Farm won. When Mars tried to launch a version of M&M's Peanuts that copied the coloring and styling of Hershey's Reese's Pieces, Hershey sued, claiming that Mars was trying to capitalize on Hershey's goodwill and investment in Reese's Pieces. Hershey's won. When Burger King claimed that its hamburgers were more popular than either McDonald's or Wendy's, both companies sued Burger King for false advertising and Burger King settled for undisclosed terms out of court.

Corporation vs. Individuals

In an unusual case, a company filed suit against two individuals, Helen Steel and Dave Morris, who passed out leaflets in front of McDonald's outlets in London.

McDonald's claimed that the leaflet libeled them. Dubbed "McLibel," the lawsuit ended up being the longest case in British history. While technically the court agreed with McDonald's on some of its charges, it was a tremendous public relations disaster for the company. McDonald's also sued an Italian newspaper critic for an uncomplimentary reference the critic made to the company's french fries.

Individuals vs. Corporation

Another category of lawsuits related to fast food and junk food are individuals bringing suit against corporations. In many cases they are class action lawsuits—a legal action undertaken by one or more plaintiffs with common claims who represent others and sue as a group.

A well-known individual suit was by 81-year-old Stella Liebeck, who bought a cup of coffee at a McDonald's drive-thru window in Albuquerque in 1992. When she removed the lid, the coffee spilled onto her lap, causing third-degree burns. Her suit, filed in state court in Albuquerque, claimed the coffee was "defective" because it was scalding hot and McDonald's had ignored warnings from others who had been similarly injured. The jury awarded her $2.9 million, but the judge reduced the amount to $640,000. It was eventually settled out of court for a reported $600,000. As a result of the lawsuit, McDonald's decreased the temperature of its coffee and placed signs warning customers that the coffee was hot.

Beef Tallow and Transfats

In 1989 some customers complained that McDonald's fries were prepared using an animal product, and were therefore a problem for vegetarians and for those customers concerned with their cholesterol. In 1990, with considerable fanfare, McDonald's announced that they had switched to "100% vegetable oils" with "added natural flavorings." In 2001 it was revealed that the natural flavorings included beef tallow; vegetarians launched five different lawsuits against McDonald's. The following year McDonald's paid out $8 million in damages to vegetarians and devout Hindus living in the United States.

In 2003 Steven Joseph sued Nabisco (a subsidiary of Kraft Foods) over the presence of transfats in their Oreo cookies. Joseph believed that transfats were a danger that was not commonly known by most consumers, especially children, who Nabisco had targeted in its advertising. As a result of adverse media coverage and mounting evidence about the possible negative health consequences of transfat consumption, Nabisco agreed to reduce or eliminate transfats from their products and Joseph dropped the suit.

When McDonald's shifted from a frying medium with animal fat to one containing only vegetable oils, it began using transfats, which at the time were considered healthy. As problems with transfats emerged, McDonald's announced that it would end their use in 2003. Steven Joseph, a lawyer, filed a lawsuit against McDonald's when it continued to use transfats without adequately notifying its customers. In

2005 McDonald's eliminated its use of transfats and settled the lawsuit, agreeing to pay $7 million to the American Heart Association, and to expend another $1.5 million for a public advertising campaign alerting the public to the dangers of transfats. In 2007 the Center for Science in the Public Interest (CSPI) brought suit against Burger King to stop using transfats. Burger King pledged to phase out their use of transfats by November 1, 2008.

Other lawsuits have been initiated against Frito-Lay, Inc., for its inclusion of olestra (Olean) in some of its so-called light snack foods. Olestra, a fat substitute, can cause diarrhea, stomach cramps, and other symptoms in some people. As these problems emerged in 1996, the Food and Drug Administration (FDA) required that foods containing olestra carry the warning label: "This product contains olestra. Olestra may cause abdominal cramping and loose stools. Olestra inhibits the absorption of some vitamins and other nutrients. Vitamins A, D, E, and K have been added." In 2003 the Food and Drug Administration dropped this requirement. In 2006 the Center for Science in the Public Interest (CSPI) threatened to sue Frito-Lay over the unlabeled inclusion of olestra in its light junk foods. This was resolved by an out-of-court settlement in which Frito-Lay agreed to include a large label on the fronts and backs of packages saying that they contained olestra.

Obesity Lawsuits

In 2002 the guardian of Ashley Perlman, a child under the age of eighteen, and others commenced a class-action lawsuit against a McDonald's franchise in New York. The plaintiffs alleged that McDonald's engaged in deceptive advertising and fraud about the nutrition and healthfulness of their products. The plaintiffs claimed that the company injected its products with additives without informing customers and that the additives changed their nutritional content. The plaintiffs also alleged that their everyday consumption of food served at the restaurant made them fat and had led to related health problems. After several hearings, the attorneys for the plaintiffs concluded that it was just too difficult to create a cause and effect relationship between obesity and fast food. This lawsuit and the threat of others, however, may have encouraged fast food chains to rethink their menus and add more healthy selections.

To protect itself against such lawsuits, the National Restaurant Association led the effort to pass the Personal Responsibility in Food Consumption Act in Congress to exempt fast food chains from lawsuits related to obesity. In 2004 the bill passed in the House but was not voted on in the Senate. Several states, however, have passed "cheeseburger laws" to prevent people from suing fast food restaurants or food manufacturers on grounds that their food is to blame for causing obesity or related illnesses such as heart disease, diabetes, or hypertension. In December 2010 CSPI filed a class-action suit against McDonald's on behalf of Monet Parham, a mother of two children residing in Sacramento. CSPI alleged that

McDonald's used the toys in its Happy Meals as "bait" to lure children into gorging on "unhealthy junk food." Michael Jacobson, the executive director of CSPI, claimed that "multi-billion-dollar corporations make parents' job nearly impossible by giving away toys and bombarding kids with slick advertising."

Energy Drinks

In 2007 the Center for Science in the Public Interest (CSPI) announced that it would sue Beverage Partners Worldwide, a joint venture of Coca-Cola and Nestlé, for claiming that their tea-flavored soda, Enviga, burns calories. CSPI claimed that this was unsubstantiated. Jacobson declared that "if the Food and Drug Administration were at all credible, major corporations like Coca-Cola and Nestlé wouldn't try to take consumers to the cleaners like this."

States have their own consumer fraud statutes and regulatory acts and will often take action to halt fraudulent or deceptive claims if the Federal Trade Commission chooses not to. Enviga claims interested the attorneys general of several states, who commenced their own lawsuit. In 2009 Beverage Partners Worldwide agreed to stop making the claim, to pay a total of $650,000 to the states and add disclosures to Enviga's packaging.

Seasoned Beef

In 2011 an Alabama law firm, Beasley, Allen, Crow, Methvin, Portis & Miles, filed a class-action lawsuit against the Taco Bell chain for false advertising. What Taco Bell calls "seasoned beef" was actually just 36 percent meat, according to the law firm's analysis. The rest consisted of extenders, binders and preservatives, including wheat oats, water, modified corn starch, sodium phosphate, soy lecithin, autolyzed yeast extract, maltodrextrin, soy bean oil, flavorings, and other ingredients. If true, it would violate U.S. Department of Agriculture guidelines that require beef products to contain at least 70 percent meat. Taco Bell denied that their advertising was misleading and claimed that their seasoned beef was 88 percent beef, and the rest was a "secret formula" consisting of water, sugar, and spices. Taco Bell has threatened to countersue the law firm and its client.

Escherichia coli (E. coli)

In January 1993 Jack in the Box distributed undercooked hamburger patties that contained fecal matter to its Pacific Northwest restaurants. The E. coli O157:H57 in the meat caused six hundred customers to become ill and four children died. The company was served with hundreds of lawsuits, most of which were settled out of court. A nine-year-old girl who suffered kidney failure, for instance, received $15.6 million. In addition to its legal costs, the company lost $44 million in 1993 largely owing to bad publicity. As a result, Jack in the Box completely redesigned its restaurants and changed its policies to avoid future problems. It also sued the supplier that had sent the infected meat to the company's restaurants.

Hoax

Food companies are not immune from lawsuits that seek to enrich fraudsters. One ploy is to claim that the presence of a foreign object in their food caused great distress. On March 22, 2005, Anna Ayala of San Jose, California, reported finding a one-and-a-half-inch fingertip in a bowl of chili served at Wendy's. She hired a lawyer with the intention of suing Wendy's, but in the days following she decided not to do so. Wendy's hired private investigators, who found no evidence that the finger had any connection with the company. Wendy's claimed that the incident decreased sales by an estimated $2.5 million and offered a $100,000 reward for information leading to the finger's original owner. On April 22, Ayala was arrested, and a month later San Jose police reported that the finger, which had been lost in an industrial accident, had belonged to an acquaintance of Ayala's husband, to whom she paid $100 for his fingertip. In September 2005 Ayala and her husband pled guilty to conspiring to file a false claim and attempted grand theft; they were sentenced to several years in prison.

In May 2005 David Scheiding found a three-quarter-inch-long slice of human flesh in his Arby's chicken sandwich. It was believed that this was another hoax inspired by Anna Ayala's fraud, but on investigation it was found that the manager had sliced his thumb while shredding lettuce. Scheiding sued the franchisee for more than $50,000 and won.

See also Advertising; Burger King; Center for Science in the Public Interest (CSPI); Cheeseburger Laws; Coca-Cola Company; Coffee; *Escherichia coli*; Frito-Lay; Goldfish; Jack in the Box; KFC; Mars, Inc.; McDonald's; "McLibel"; Nabisco; National Restaurant Association; Nestlé; Obesity; Oreos; Pepperidge Farm; PepsiCo; Taco Bell; Transfats; Wendy's; White Castle; White Tower

For Further Information:

Alderman, Jess, Jason A. Smith, Ellen J. Fried, and Richard A. Daynard. "Application of Law to the Childhood Obesity Epidemic." *Journal of Law, Medicine & Ethics.* Northeastern University Public Law & Legal Theory Research Paper No. 17 (Spring 2007): 90–112.

"Ban Trans Fat: The Campaign to Ban Partially Hydrogenated Oils" Web site: BanTrafsfat .com

Brownell, Kelly D., and Katherine Battle Horgen. *Food Fight: The Inside Story of the Food Industry, America's Obesity Crisis, and What We Can Do about It.* Chicago: Contemporary Books, 2004.

Charatan, Fred. "Lawyers Poised to Sue US Junk Food Manufacturers." *British Medical Journal* 324 (June 15, 2002): 1414.

Frank, Theodore H. "Taxonomy of Obesity Legislation." *University of Little Rock Law Review* 28, no. 3 (2006): 427–41.

Fried, Ellen. "Obesity: The Sixth Deadly Sin." *Gastronomica* 7 (Winter 2007): 6–11.

Levenson, Barry M. *Habeas Codfish: Reflections on Food and the Law.* Madison: University of Wisconsin Press, 2001.

Vidal, John. *McLibel: Burger Culture on Trial*. New York: The New Press, 1997.

Williams, Elizabeth M., ed. *The A–Z Encyclopedia of Food Controversies and the Law*. Santa Barbara, CA: Greenwood, 2010.

Licorice

Historically, licorice (or liquorice) was made from a sweet substance in the roots of about twenty species of *Glycyrrhiza*, a small, leguminous shrub native to Europe, Asia, and the Americas. The wild American licorice, *Glycyrrhiza lepidota*, was not commercialized during colonial times, but European licorice (*Glycyrrhiza glabra*) was imported into America and used as a sweetener, as it was fifty times sweeter than sugar. It was also considered as a medicinal plant and was used to treat a number of diseases.

Licorice-flavored candy was one of the earliest confections sold in stores. The plant's long, thick roots and rhizomes contain an aromatic sweet liquid that tastes bitter owing to other substances. Beginning in the eighteenth century, sugar was mixed with licorice extract, along with flour thickeners to give it a pliable texture. Historically, licorice was considered a medicine and was used to make comfits. It was also used as a flavoring and coloring in gingerbread, beers, and liquors.

Licorice candy was sold in grocery stores, and licorice was added as an ingredient to other junk foods. In 1884 Thomas Adams added licorice to gums to create Black Jack gum. Candy-coated licorice forms the base for Good & Plenty, first marketed in 1893. Twizzlers, another common licorice-flavored candy, were first made in 1929 by Y & S Candies, which originated as Young and Smylie in 1845. In 1870 the company adopted the trademark of Y & S. In 1904 Y & S merged with two other candy companies to create the National Licorice Company. Y & S Candies was acquired by the Hershey Company in 1977. Today, Twizzlers come in a variety of sizes, shapes, and flavors, including strawberry, cherry, and chocolate. Similar in appearance to Twizzlers are Red Vines, which are made by the American Licorice Company of Union City, California.

Today, most licorice is mass-produced with synthetic ingredients flavored with anise. This is probably for the best, as there are some health risks for consuming too much licorice, which may affect the balance of sodium and potassium in the body and may affect blood pressure and fluid retention.

See also Good & Plenty; Gum; Hershey Company; Sugars/Sweeteners

For Further Information:

Hershey Company Web site: www.hersheys.com/twizzlers

Mason, Laura. *Sugar-Plums and Sherbet: The Prehistory of Sweets*. Devon, UK: Prospect Books, 2004.

Richardson, Tim. *Sweets: A History of Candy*. New York: Bloomsbury, 2002.

LifeSavers

Clarence Crane, a chocolate confectioner in Cleveland, Ohio, had a problem—the pure chocolate that he used in his shop melted during the hot summer months. He began experimentation on a hard candy that he could sell during warm weather. He saw a druggist using a hand-operated pill-making machine and concluded he could use a similar machine to make candies. In 1912 he had created a small, round mint candy with a hole in the middle. Because they resembled ships' floating lifesavers, he named them accordingly. Crane packaged his LifeSavers in cardboard boxes, but the boxes' glue seeped into the candy and grocers refused to stock them. In 1913 Crane sold the manufacturing rights to Edward Noble, owner of the Mint Products Company of New York. To solve the glue problem, Noble repackaged the mints, wrapped them in tinfoil wrappers, and sold them for a nickle. Owing to their previous experience, grocers still refused to stock them, so Noble sold them to bars where displays were installed next to the cash registers. The mint candy served as a "lifesaver" to those who frequented bars but did not want others to know they had been drinking. In 1915 the United Cigar Store chain placed the displays in their many stores, and LifeSavers became successful. They are considered the first impulse food item.

LifeSavers were made by hand until 1919, when machinery was acquired to manufacture them in bulk. Noble marketed them to drugstores, grocery stores, and other retail stores, encouraging proprietors to place them by the cash register. For ten years, the company only made Pep-O-Mint LifeSavers; later, it added fruit-flavored candies without the holes. By 1929, the fruit-flavored LifeSavers acquired holes and, five years later, the five flavors were combined to form the Five-Flavor LifeSavers Roll. LifeSavers were manufactured in Canada by 1920; by 1969, the company's plant in Hamilton, Ontario, produced a score of different flavors and more than a billion LifeSavers annually. In 1956 LifeSavers Candies acquired Beech-Nut, makers of gum and baby food. LifeSavers Candies in turn was acquired by Kraft Foods, which in 2004 sold LifeSavers to the Wrigley Company.

See also Gum; Kraft Foods; Wrigley Co.

For Further Information:

Broekel, Ray. *The Great America Candy Bar Book*. Boston: Houghton Mifflin Company, 1982.

Hine, Thomas. *The Total Package: The Evolution and Secret Meanings of Boxes, Bottles, Cans, and Tubes*. New York: Little, Brown and Company, 1995.

Richardson, Tim. *Sweets: A History of Candy*. New York: Bloomsbury, 2002.

Limited Time Offers

Limited time offers (LTO) is a traditional sales technique that encourages customers to buy a product that may not be available later. LTOs are a commonly used technique in both fast food and junk food businesses. They are frequently versions of a company's core products or new products intended for either long- or short-term sales. LTOs have two additional advantages—they gain high visibility, far beyond the company's advertising, and companies can test-market new products to determine if they should be added to their regular menu.

Fast food LTOs include McDonald's McRibs, which were marketed in 2005 as a "Farewell Tour"; McRibs have subsequently had additional "Farewell Tours." In 2010 Burger King responded with its own LTO of real BBQ ribs. In 2010 Burger King introduced an LTO Sprout Surprise Whopper, with a fried brussels sprout patty and Emmental cheese, in selected stores in England. From a sales standpoint it was not a success, but it gained large amounts of free advertising owing to the unusual ingredients. Along with a major advertising campaign, in January 2011 Burger King in the United States released an LTO called the Stuffed Steakhouse Burger with bits of jalapeño peppers and cheddar cheese, topped with creamy poblano sauce and other condiments .

In the junk food world, many companies introduce variations of popular products as test-marketing ploys. Mars, for instance, introduced a mint version of its famous Milky Way bar. The company also has produced special packages with red-and-green M&M's at Christmastime. Oreos, typically made with a white-cream center, have occasionally been produced with mint-green fillings. Other LTOs are intended to gain visibility. Heinz, maker of America's most popular ketchup, once produced ketchup colored green and purple.

See also Burger King; Ketchup; M&M's; Mars, Inc.; McDonald's; Milky Way; Oreos

Lindt & Sprüengli

In 1845 David Sprüengli and his son owned a small confectionery shop in Zürich, Switzerland. They added a small factory to make dark chocolate candies. In 1899 the company incorporated, acquired the chocolate factory of Rodolphe Lindt in Bern, and changed its name to Lindt & Sprüengli. Lindt invented the conching machine, which breaks down and blends the chocolate, producing an excellent high-end product—one that was comparatively expensive.

After World War II, Lindt & Sprüengli began to sell its chocolates in the United States. The company also opened specialty shops, many of which were closed in 2009 owing to the economic downturn.

In 1998 Lindt & Sprüengli acquired Ghirardelli Chocolate Company, based in San Francisco. It was a chocolate maker that primarily sold in the western United States, but Lindt expanded its reach into the international market.

See also Chocolate

For Further Information:

Ghirardelli's Web site: www.ghirardelli.com

Lindt USA Web site: www.lindtusa.com

Little Caesars Pizza

In the 1950s Mike Ilitch began making pizza in the kitchen of a Detroit nightclub. At the time, pizza was a minor fast food. Ilitch's operation, however, proved so successful that in 1959 Mike and Marian Ilitch opened a pizza restaurant, called Little Caesar's Pizza Treat, in a strip mall in Garden City, Michigan. From the beginning, the Little Caesar logo was part of the operation.

Little Caesar's Pizza's carry-out operation was one of the chain's claims to fame, because its promotion campaign offered two pizzas for the price of one. This was the basis for the Little Caesar mascot and his famous advertising line, "Pizza! Pizza!," which the company trademarked. The company quickly expanded and by 1987 was operating throughout the United States and in parts of Canada. As of 2011, the company had outlets in twenty-six other countries.

Little Caesars remains a privately owned company. It claims to be the world's largest carry-out pizza chain. Little Caesars ranks eleventh among restaurant chains in America, and it is the fourth-largest pizza chain. It is headquartered in Detroit.

Feeding the Hungry

In 1985 the company created the Little Caesar's Love Kitchen, a big-rig truck that provides meals for the homeless and disaster survivors. Since then, it has fed more than 2 million people in the United States and Canada.

See also Advertising; Ilitch, Mike; Pizza

For Further Information:

Helstosky, Carol. *Pizza: A Global History*. London: Reaktion Books, 2008.

Little Caesars Web site: www.littlecaesars.com

Little Debbie

According to tradition, the Little Debbie logo was inspired by a photo of the four-year-old granddaughter of O. D. McKee, the founder of McKee Foods. Pearl Mann, an Atlanta artist, did the original artwork for the Little Debbie brand, which made four-year-old Debbie look older. It was not until after the first cartons had been printed in 1960 that Debbie's parents found out that their daughter's name and likeness were used on McKee Food's Oatmeal Creme Pie.

By 1964, the company was manufacturing fourteen different products, and all had Little Debbie's image. By 2010, Little Debbie products included brownies, cakes, crackers, cookies, doughnuts, and pies—a total of more than sixty different products. Its best-selling Little Debbie products included Swiss Cake Rolls, Nutty Bars Wafer Bars, Oatmeal Creme Pies, and Fudge Brownies.

The company also licenses Little Debbie–style Barbie Dolls and Little Debbie Hot Wheels car sets. McKee Foods Corporation is a privately held company headquartered in Collegedale, Tennessee. As of 2011, Little Debbie cakes manufactured by McKee Foods were the best-selling cakes in America.

See also Bakery Goods; Cakes

For Further Information:

Little Debbie Web site: www.littledebbie.com

Lobbying

Lobbying—the act of trying to influence government officials—has become a major activity of fast food chains and junk food manufacturers, as well as of advocacy groups and nonpartisan organizations.

The late nineteenth and early twentieth century was a period of intense political ferment regarding food. Large corporations maintain their own lobbyists in Washington, D.C., or they hire firms to represent their interests. Corporations also join associations, which also lobby for or against legislation.

Many makers of confections adulterated their products by including colorings and flavorings that were harmful to consumers. The National Confectioners Association (NCA) was formed in 1884 to foster industry self-regulation and lobby against adulterants. The NCA lobbied for passage of state pure food laws and, with its support, legislation was passed in New York State in the late nineteenth century.

During World War II, the NCA lobbied to ensure that candy would be declared an "essential food," thus ensuring that at least some members of the association received sugar rations. The NCA maintains a full-time lobbyist who has weighed in on NCA issues, such as excise taxes on confections, sugar and peanut price supports, nutritional labeling laws, and issues related to international trade.

Corporations also have established alliances that support particular positions, such as the recently created American Council on Fitness and Nutrition, which has lobbied against national standards for school food.

In addition to formal lobbyists, fast food and junk food manufacturers have also contributed to political campaigns. Such contributions have not always been legal. In 1972, Ray Kroc, founder of McDonald's, secretly gave $250,000 to President Richard Nixon's reelection campaign, which was against the law. To avoid detection, he divided his contribution into smaller donations, which he gave to different Republican agencies. During the Watergate scandal, these contributions came to light. At the time, McDonald's and other fast food chains were lobbying Congress to pass the so-called McDonald's bill that would allow employers to pay 16- to 17-year-old employees less than minimum wage. It was believed that Kroc made his contribution to buy the Nixon's administration's support for the legislation. The legislation did not pass.

Similarly, many grassroots groups organized to support the passage of pure food and drug acts in state legislatures and at the federal level. This effort achieved success with the passage of the Pure Food and Drug Act in 1906. Nonprofit and advocacy groups have lobbied for many issues. The Center for Science in the Public Interest, for instance, has lobbied on matters related to food safety and nutrition.

See also Center for Science in the Public Interest (CSPI); Kroc, Ray; McDonald's; National Confectioners Association; Nutrition; School Food

For Further Information:

Nestle, Marion. *Food Politics: How the Food Industry Influences Nutrition and Health.* Berkeley: University of California Press, 2002.

Schlosser, Eric. *Fast Food Nation: The Dark Side of the All-American Meal.* New York: Houghton Mifflin Company, 2001.

Locations

As with other retail businesses, one of the most important decisions an owner must make is the location for fast food chain outlets. Beginning with the first fast food chains, such as White Castle and its imitator, White Tower, site selection for outlets was crucial: they selected urban areas near mass-transit stops (train, trolley, subway, or bus stops). As automobiles became more common during the 1920s, drive-ins began constructing their outlets along highways, intersections, and in places where property values permitted them to buy, rent, or lease inexpensive space for large parking lots.

Thomas Carvel, founder of the Carvel Corporation, thought that the best place for ice cream stores was on secondary highways with free-flowing traffic moving along at a slow speed (25 mph or less). The problem with major highways was that automobiles sped by too fast and drivers were unable to stop. Likewise, highways where traffic was frequently snarled were not ideal, because potential customers were more interested in getting through the congestion than stopping for an ice cream. There also had to be a large enough permanent population in an area so that the store could generate repeat customers. Carvel brought in "location engineers" when he was in doubt; they used counters to determine the number of cars and people who passed by a given location.

After World War II, when families began to flee inner cities and buy homes in the suburbs, new criteria for site locations were used. Ray Kroc of McDonald's was one of the first to recognize the importance of this shift. He refused to build outlets in major urban areas, and he carefully selected sites in fast-growing suburban communities. The chain bought satellite photos, which they used to predict suburban sprawl and determine locations for their outlets. Kroc personally selected many of the early McDonald's locations, occasionally traveling by helicopter to select the best location for an outlet. While Kroc may have been able to accurately predict areas that would grow, his successors employed a computer software program called "Quintillion—A Geographic Information System" for projecting suburban growth and identifying good potential site locations. Other fast food chains, such as Burger King, have used similar systems to select their sites.

During the 1950s and 1960s, suburban locations made sense. These areas were rapidly growing, particularly with families, and McDonald's and other fast food chains had concluded that their real target was children. In addition, crime and civil unrest were endemic to many inner cities, while suburbs tended to have less crime. Finally, fast food outlets were oriented toward automobiles because the outlets had few indoor eating areas in them until the late 1960s. As soon as indoor eating areas became common, fast food chains reexamined their decision not to open outlets in urban areas. In the 1970s McDonald's, Burger King, and other fast food chains reversed their long-held policy of staying out of urban areas. By the end of that decade, virtually all national fast food chains were present in large cities.

Some chains have used different strategies. For instance, A&W, Hardee's, and Dairy Queen have intentionally selected small towns as their preferred locations for outlets. Still others have selected particular venues as profitable. For instance, Orange Julius targeted shopping malls and Cinnabon targeted airports.

Location around Schools

The fast food industry identified children as a major target consumer in the 1970s. From then on, many fast food outlets have tried to locate around schools. Several studies have been conducted with regard to location of fast food establishments. A 2005 study of fast food locations in Chicago found that 78 percent of the city's schools had at least one fast food restaurant within easy walking distance, and that there were three to four times as many fast food restaurants within a mile of schools "than would be expected if the restaurants were distributed throughout the city in a way unrelated to school locations." The conclusion of those researchers was that "fast-food restaurants are concentrated within a short walking distance from schools, exposing children to poor-quality food environments in their school neighborhoods."

During the late twentieth century and early twenty-first century, a number of other changes occurred. Owing to the acquisition of many different restaurant chains by single owners, such as Yum! Brands, co-branding, multibranding, and bundling have become common. In these locations, a single site will feature two or more different types of noncompeting fast foods, such as pizza, hamburgers, and ice cream. In addition, several fast food establishments have begun co-branding with other businesses, such as K-Marts, Walmarts, and service stations. For instance, Blimpie co-branded with Texaco and many Texaco gas stations now have Blimpie restaurants.

The fast food industry is considered mature in the United States, and placement of new outlets has become more difficult. Most fast food companies, however, have been rapidly expanding in other countries, and different location criteria are needed for development in each nation.

See also A&W; Automobiles; Blimpie International; Branding; Burger King; Carvel Corporation; Chains; Cinnabon; Crime; Food Courts; Food Trucks; Franchising; Hamburger; Hardee's; Kroc, Ray; Service Stations; Walmart; White Castle; White Tower; Yum! Brands, Inc.

For Further Information:

Austin, S. Bryn, et al. "Clustering of Fast-Food Restaurants around Schools." *American Journal of Public Health* 95, no. 9 (2005): 1575–81.

Davis, Brennan, and Christopher Carpenter. "Proximity of Fast-Food Restaurants to Schools and Adolescent Obesity." *American Journal of Public Health* 99 (March 2009): 505–10.

Funderburg, Anne Cooper. *Chocolate, Strawberry, and Vanilla: A History of American Ice Cream*. Bowling Green, OH: Bowling Green State University Popular Press, 1995.

Jakle, John A., and Keith A. Sculle. *Fast Food: Roadside Restaurants in the Automobile Age*. Baltimore: Johns Hopkins University Press, 1999.

Boone-Heinonen, Janne, et al. "Fast Food Restaurants and Food Stores; Longitudinal Associations with Diet in Young to Middle-aged Adults: The CARDIA Study," *Archives of Intern Medicine* 171(13) (2011):1162–1170, as at: http://archinte.ama-assn.org/cgi/content/short/171/13/1162

Schlosser, Eric. *Fast Food Nation: The Dark Side of the All-American Meal*. New York: Houghton Mifflin Company, 2001.

Lollipops/Suckers

Lollipops are a hard candy made mainly of sugar or treacle. They first appeared in England in the late eighteenth century. References to them appear in the works of Charles Dickens, and they were popularized at the 1851 Great Exposition in London. When sticks were added by hand in the late nineteenth century, lollipops, also called suckers in the United States, became an important early commercial candy in America. An early manufacturer of lollipops was George Smith, owner of a confectionery business called the Bradley Smith Company in New Haven, Connecticut.

Whistle Pops

Whistle Pops were lollipops with a hole; when you blew into the hole, it made a whistle noise. Despite this novelty, the Whistle Pop was discontinued. Chupa Chups, a Spanish company, has reintroduced Melody Whistle Pops, which are now available in many stores in the United States.

Samuel Born, a Russian immigrant, founded the Just Born Candy Company in New York. He is credited with inventing the Born Sucker Machine, which automatically inserted sticks into lollipops. This invention revolutionized the sucker industry. Many companies began producing stick candy with various names during the twentieth century. The Akron Candy Company of Bellevue, Ohio, for instance, manufactured suckers beginning in 1922. They manufactured Dum Dum Pops two years later. The James O. Welch Company introduced caramel-covered Sugar Daddies in 1926, followed by Sugar Babies in 1935. They are manufactured today by Tootsie Roll Industries.

Rainbow lollipop. (Dreamstime.com)

See also Candy; Caramels; Just Born; Sugars/Sweeteners; Tootsie Roll Industries

For Further Information:

Richardson, Tim. *Sweets: A History of Candy*. New York: Bloomsbury, 2002.

Spangler Candy Company Web site: www.spanglercandy.com

Long John Silver's

In 1969 Long John Silver's Fish 'n' Chips was launched by Jerrico, Inc., of Lexington, Kentucky. Its name was derived from a character in Robert Louis Stevenson's *Treasure Island*. Its first outlet proved successful and franchising began the following year. Its first restaurants were small and the architecture was intended to resemble a building from an early American fishing village.

Long John Silver's sign. (AP/Wide World Photos)

Initially, Long John Silver's featured battered, fried fish and grilled fish, along with french fries and coleslaw. Its menu has evolved and now includes seafood, chicken, sandwiches, salads, and desserts.

In 1989 senior management and a New York investment firm acquired Jerrico and its subsidiaries in a leveraged buyout. Long John Silver's had difficult times and went bankrupt in 1998. The following year it was merged with A&W to form Yorkshire Global Restaurants, based in Lexington, Kentucky. Yorkshire Global Restaurants, in turn, was purchased by Tricon Global Restaurants (now Yum! Brands) in 2002. In 2011 the chain was acquired by franchisees. As of 2011, there were more than 1,100 Long John Silver's restaurants and more than four hundred other points of distribution in multibranded restaurants. It is the largest fast food fish chain in America.

See also A&W; Architecture/Design; Chicken; Fish; Fish and Chips; French Fries; Salads; Sandwiches; Yum! Brands, Inc.

For Further Information:

Jakle, John A., and Keith A. Sculle. *Fast Food: Roadside Restaurants in the Automobile Age*. Baltimore: Johns Hopkins University Press, 1999.

Long John Silver's Web site: www.ljsilvers.com

M

M&M's

During the 1930s, Forrest Mars, the son of the founder of Mars, Inc., established a chocolate manufacturing company in Chicago along with Bruce Murrie, the son of the president of the Hershey Company. Because both of their last names started with M, they called their new company M&M. In 1940 they launched their first product, which they named M&M's Chocolate Candies. These were small, colorful, round, candy-covered chocolates. They were packaged in paper tubes, which made them easy to carry.

Mars, Inc., tradition has it that the idea for M&M's was based on Forrest Mars' visit to Spain during the Spanish Civil War (1936–1937). He saw soldiers eating chocolate candies covered with a layer of hard sugar. It is more likely that Forrest Mars acquired the idea from Smarties, which are small, round, colorful, sugar-coated chocolates that had been introduced in England by Rowntree's of York in 1937. Smarties were packaged in paper tubes. Forrest Mars later claimed that he had encouraged Rowntree's to produce candy bars and Smarties, which could well have been true.

The original M&M colors were red, yellow, green, orange, brown, and violet. These have been changed over the years, with some colors added and others removed. M&M's candies were popularized during World War II, when they were included in soldiers' rations. In 1948 M&M's were packaged in brown plastic bags, and later the company introduced M&M Peanut Chocolate Candies, which were packaged in yellow plastic bags. After the war, the relationship between Mars and Murrie became strained, and in 1949 Forrest Mars bought out Murrie for $1 million. He subsequently changed the name of M&M to Food Manufacturers, Inc., and it later merged with Mars, Inc.

During the 1950s, Forrest launched a major advertising campaign in national newspapers and magazines, radio spots, and billboards. By 1949, annual sales had increased to $3 million. The slogan for M&M candies was an immediate success: "The milk chocolate that melts in your mouth, not in your hand." Cartoon characters, Mr. Plain and Mr. Peanut, went along with the advertisements in 1954. Another commercial featured M&M's jumping into a pool of chocolate. The advertisement ran on television on the *Howdy Doody Show* and the *Mickey Mouse Club*. By 1956, M&M sales topped $40 million, ranking them the most popular candy in America.

In 1976 the Food and Drug Administration released a study correlating cancer with red dye food coloring. Even though M&M's did not include this dye, Mars pulled the red candies to avoid consumer misperception. Ten years passed before Mars reintroduced red M&M's.

Over the years, the company has made many additions to the M&M's product line. It released Peanut Butter M&M's to compete with Reese's Pieces, but their sales peaked in 1991. In 1996 it produced M&M Mints, which were sold in tubes. Other additions include Almond Chocolate Candies, M&M Pretzels, and MINIS Mega Tubes. In 2005 Mars released a limited edition of M&M's as a tie-in with the release of the Star Wars movie *Star Wars Episode III: Revenge of the Sith*.

In 2000 the name of plain M&M's was officially changed to M&M's Milk Chocolate Candies. Peanut M&M's are America's most popular confection and M&M's are also sold around the globe, generating annual revenue of more than $2 billion. In 2010 Harris Interactive's Youth EquiTrend study ranked M&M's first on brand recognition among 8- to 24-year-olds.

Recently, Mars has opened theme stores, such as the M&M World in Las Vegas, Orlando, and New York. These sell candy, clothing, and other ephemera connected with Mars candies.

See also Advertising; Candy; Cartoon Characters; Chocolate; Food and Drug Administration (FDA); M&M's; Mars, Forrest; Mars, Inc.; Peanuts; Pretzels; Radio; Rowntree's of York; Sugars/Sweeteners; Television

For Further Information:

Brenner, Joël Glenn. *The Emperors of Chocolate: Inside the Secret World of Hershey and Mars*. New York: Broadway Books, 2000.

M&M Web site: www.m-ms.com

Pottker, Janice. *Crisis in Candyland: Melting the Chocolate Shell of the Mars Family Empire*. Bethesda, MD: National Press Books, 1995.

Schremp, Gerry. *Kitchen Culture: Fifty Years of Food Fads, from Spam to Spa Cuisine*. New York: Pharos Books, 1991.

Mad Cow Disease

Bovine spongiform encephalitis (BSE), commonly known as Mad Cow disease, is a fatal disease affecting the bovine central nervous system. BSE was first discovered in the United Kingdom in 1986, but it was thought that it could not be transmitted to humans. It infected cattle that had consumed a protein-rich diet of remnants of rendered carcasses and bones of sheep, cattle, pigs, horses, chickens, and dogs and cats from animal shelters. However, it is an infectious, degenerative disease that can be transmitted to humans, causing an illness similar to Creutzfeldt-Jakob disease (CJD), although the relationship between the two diseases remains unclear. An epidemic of BSE hit England, France, and Italy in the mid-1990s; 157 people are known to have been infected and all died. It is acquired by eating infected beef that has not been cooked long enough. By 2005, six BSE-infected cows were identified in North America; there were no known human illnesses related to these incidents.

There is no known cure for BSE and the only known solution is prevention—not feeding cattle the rendered meal obtained from butchered animals, and cooking beef properly.

See also Beef; Foodborne Illnesses

For Further Information:

Carlson, Laurie Winn. *Cattle: An Informal Social History*. Chicago: Ivan R. Dee, 2001.

Connor, Elizabeth. *Internet Guide to Food Safety and Security*. New York: Haworth Information Press, 2005.

Ferreiro, Carmen. *Mad Cow Disease (Bovine Spongiform Encephalopathy)*. Philadelphia: Chelsea House Publishers, 2005.

Gratzer, Walter. *Terrors of the Table: The Curious History of Nutrition*. New York: Oxford University Press, 2005.

Mallomars

Mallomars are chocolate cookies consisting of a biscuit base (similar to a Graham cracker), topped with marshmallow, and coated in pure dark chocolate. They were first manufactured by Nabisco in 1913. They are made seasonally, especially for metropolitan New York, where 70 percent are sold. They are not made during the summer, as the heat melts the pure chocolate.

All American Mallomars are made in Canada, but they are only sold in the United States. Mallomars are similar to Whippets, made in Montreal, Canada, which are made year-round owing to different climatic conditions and different formulae for the chocolate. Mallomars have the same general ingredients as do many other junk foods, including S'Mores, which have been a Girl Scout favorite since 1917.

See also Canada; Chocolate; Cookies; Girl Scout Cookies; Marshmallows

For Further Information:

NabiscoWorld Web site: www.nabiscoworld.com

Man v. Food

Man v. Food is a television series hosted by Adam Richman. It is broadcast on the Travel Channel and premiered in December 2008. Each episode includes an eating contest, which Richman sometimes wins and other times loses. In one episode,

Richman and a group of eaters near Detroit tried to beat a Guinness World Record by consuming a 190-pound hamburger; in this case, the food won.

See also Hamburger

For Further Information:

Trailer for the 190-pound hamburger episode on YouTube Web site: www.youtube.com/watch?v=edvqgN4gmGA

Marketing to Children

There are more than 56 million Americans under the age of fourteen in the United States. Children themselves have little buying power, but they do have "pester" or "nag" power. Research indicates that nagging spurs about one-third of family trips to fast food restaurants or to stores to purchase junk food. In addition, advertisers believe that childhood experiences will be remembered throughout their lifetime.

Brand loyalty begins early in life. As Wayne Chilicki, an executive at General Mills, which markets cereal to children, proclaimed: "When it comes to targeting kid consumers, we at General Mills . . . believe in getting them early and having them for life." This is a marketing strategy followed by many junk food and fast food companies. Studies have shown that by the time American children are three years old, they recognize an average of one hundred brand logos, most of which are for fast food or junk food products. There are good reasons for this recognition: the majority of advertisements on children's television programs is for products that contain massive amounts of calories, fat, or sodium, and are low in good nutritional components. One estimate attributed 40 percent of childhood obesity to junk food and fast food marketing.

Targeting Children

Children have been targeted by junk food and soda manufacturers since the early twentieth century. The Cracker Jack Company, for instance, inserted toys in their product boxes, and gum manufacturers placed baseball and other sports cards in their packages. Since then, junk food and fast food makers have targeted kids: their advertising aimed at children is ubiquitous and extremely effective. McDonald's, for instance, has heavily marketed its Happy Meals to young children and adolescents. According to *Advertising Age*, the company's promotion for the Happy Meal alone accounts for 8–10 percent of all measured-media spending in the United States.

Food companies expend almost $12 billion to reach children and young adults, who are exposed to 40,000 television commercials every year—half of which are for food, most of which are high in calories, fat, and sodium, and less than 3 percent are for healthy foods. Of the more than 8,000 ads aired during children's shows, none advertised fresh fruits or vegetables. Advertising has particularly expanded on children's television, where approximately 15 percent of all commercial children's programing is devoted to advertising.

During the past twenty years, there has been a dramatic increase in the number of commercials and money spent on advertising. This increase is largely owing to the expansion of commercial cable television channels and the increase in the number of programs targeting children. Approximately two-thirds of junk food advertising falls within three product categories: cereals, candies, and fast food restaurants. According to the Federal Trade Commission, cereal companies alone spent 97.5 percent of their advertising budgets in 2006 on marketing to children and youth. Many studies have offered evidence that children exposed to commercials for products in these three categories prefer the product that was advertised over similar nonadvertised products. Children's advertising is effective in persuading children to like and request certain products.

During the past two decades, television, particularly cable, greatly expanded the ability of advertisers to reach children. Children are more vulnerable to commercials, which they view less critically than adults. Children's programs, especially on Saturday mornings, meant that advertisers could market directly to the age group of their choice. By the 1960s, advertisers had identified children as a separate market, and fast food chains joined junk food and soda companies in targeting children.

What makes this type of advertising even more powerful, as studies have demonstrated, is that 53 percent of all children aged two to eighteen years have a television in their bedroom. This means that children increasingly experience advertising without any parental supervision.

Many parents and pediatricians do not consider the occasional consumption of junk foods or fast foods to be harmful. It is harmful, however, when these foods are eaten regularly and supplant nutritional foods in the child's diet. The problem is that children are exposed to many more commercials for junk food and fast foods than for more healthy or nutritious food. In 2004, for instance, food, beverage, candy, and restaurant advertising expenditures hit $11.26 billion, while advertising for healthy foods was less than $10 million. It is believed that such advertising of foods high in calories, high in fat, high in salt, and low in nutrition has contributed to childhood obesity. As eating habits formed during childhood often persist throughout life, such advertising may well contribute to adult obesity as well.

In addition to television advertising, fast food chains also created child-oriented characters, such as Ronald McDonald, and began offering meals made especially for children, such as Happy Meals with toys and the creation of playgrounds for children. Chains then acquired endorsements from prominent sports, movie, and television figures.

Children pay attention to commercials because they like the messengers—usually cartoon characters. Companies create spokescharacters, such as Tony the

Tiger, who promotes Kellogg's Frosted Flakes. Spokescharacters create favorable attitudes toward specific brands more than any other form of information presented on a food package. Companies also license characters from children's movies or television programs to promote their product. For example, Sponge-Bob SquarePants and Dora the Explorer generate annual sales of branded goods of $2 billion. Some promotions are for healthy food: Sesame Street teamed with Apple & Eve in 1999 to promote a variety of character-themed fruit juices. Studies have found that the presence of an Elmo sticker on food packaging affected children's food selection behavior. Children prefer the taste of foods more often when a familiar character appears on the packaging. This is a particularly effective technique for young children who can recognize characters by the time they are two to three years old, but they do not have the ability to understand the persuasive intent behind advertisement.

Targeting Minority Children

One specific target of advertising has been minority children, according to a report issued by the Rudd Center on Food Policy & Obesity in 2010. African American children and adolescents saw 50 percent more fast food TV ads than did white youth. McDonald's was responsible for 25 percent of children's and adolescents' exposure to Spanish-language fast food advertising in 2009.

Deceptive Advertising

Some advertisements from junk food companies have been identified as deceptive by the Federal Trade Commission (FTC), the federal agency responsible for, among many other things, monitoring claims made in television advertising. The Kellogg Company launched a national campaign on television, in print, through the Internet, and on product packaging that its Frosted Mini Wheats was "clinically shown to improve kids' attentiveness by nearly 20%." The FTC believed that this claim was unfounded, and in 2009 the Kellogg Company settled with the FTC and withdrew its advertising. The FTC then admonished Kellogg for its marketing of Rice Krispies, which claimed that the cereal could boost children's immunity. In January 2010 FTC sent out warning letters to eleven different companies regarding claims promoting omega-3 fatty acids and the benefits to children's brains. With these actions, the FTC put food and beverage companies on notice that claims made in ads targeted at children would be reviewed with special scrutiny for the foreseeable future. The FTC will also more closely monitor product placement, video games, contests, character licensing, tie-ins with sports teams, and other children-centered advertising techniques.

Tie-Ins and Product Placement

Companies also place their products in the entertainment content of movies, television shows, music, and video games. For instance, overt and visual images of

Coca-Cola appear on the Fox television series *American Idol*, one of America's most popular shows. This includes a Coca-Cola banner and cups with the Coca-Cola logo on the judges' table.

Companies developed movie tie-ins and made special arrangements with theme parks such as Disneyland, which has had a long history of selling fast food and junk food. Frito-Lay sponsors park attractions, such as the steel roller-coaster ride California Screamin' at Disneyland. Mars has opened up M&M World stores in New York, Orlando, and Las Vegas to sell these products, just as Hershey has done in New York, Chicago, Niagara Falls, and Shanghai.

Licensing Agreements

Fast food, junk food, and soft drink companies advertise their products in a variety of other ways. Most fast food and many junk food companies have promoted their product by licensing their logos and trademarks for placement on clothing and other products. The Munchkin Bottling Company placed soft drink logos on baby bottles. There are spin-off products such as lunch boxes and clothing, and many companies sponsor kids' clubs.

Connectivity

During the past decade, children and adolescents have become increasingly connected through the Internet, cell phones, and handheld music/video players. Companies have developed extensive programs to reach youth directly through new technologies. These include marketing that encourages children and youth to visit corporate Web sites, view advertisements posted by fast food and junk food companies in other Web sites and blogs, and play "advergames"—online games for children and adolescents that contain images that help promote their products—that promote junk food and fast foods. One Web site, www.ronald.com, specifically targets preschoolers. Burger King and McDonald's had sixty to one hundred pages of advergames and virtual worlds that actively engage children on their Web sites in 2010.

Companies also advertise directly or indirectly on Facebook, Foursquare, MySpace, Twitter, and YouTube. In addition to advertising, some companies have begun to pay youth to advertise their products through social media, where they engage viral and buzz marketing.

As youth increasingly acquire cell phones, music players, and handheld video players, companies have developed programs to reach these new technologies. Advertisers have now developed programs to reach directly to youth via texting and other forms of messaging.

Marketing at Schools

Many students face a barrage of junk food advertising at schools. Company logos are on vending machines, school newspapers, yearbooks, posters, scoreboards, bulletin boards, rooftops and walls, in textbooks, on textbook covers, in magazines, and even in bathroom stalls. More than two hundred school districts nationwide signed exclusive contracts with soft drink companies. In addition, there are more than 4,500 Pizza Hut chains and 3,000 Taco Bell chains in school cafeterias around the country. School advertising also appears under the guise of educational TV: Channel One. Currently available in 12,000 schools, Channel One consists of ten minutes of current-events programming and two minutes of commercials.

Apps and Videos

Many companies have developed software games or applications to promote their brands, specific products, or in some cases nutrition. Kraft Foods, for instance, launched an iPad application with games and videos called Big Fork Little Fork, which offers parents recipes and advice on nutrition. McDonald's produced three computer videos in 2010 to promote fruit and vegetables: "Crave My Fave," "Fruit Is Fun," and "Yummivore," all of which are on the McDonald's YouTube Web site, and all of which star a cartoon character who loves healthy food.

Children's Food and Beverage Advertising Initiative

As children and adolescents have become increasingly overweight and obese, fast food and junk food companies have come under criticism for the nutritional qualities of their foods and their very effective marketing ploys. Several fast food and junk food manufacturers joined the Better Business Bureau's initiative to reduce advertising of nonnutritious food to children. The voluntary self-regulation program is called the Children's Food and Beverage Advertising Initiative (CFBAI). Members of the initiative pledged to reduce the use of third-party licensed characters in advertising primarily directed to children; to not seek food and beverage product placement in editorial or entertainment content that is primarily directed to children; to revise interactive games that are primarily directed to children that promote the company's food or beverages; and finally, to stop all advertisement of food or beverages in elementary schools.

A study examined food advertising on children's television between 2003 and 2007, and found that there was a 27 percent to 30 percent decrease in children's and teens' exposure to beverage ads; sugar-sweetened fruit drinks and nondiet soft drinks showed decreases of 60 percent to 75 percent. Likewise, there was a decline in ads for candy and chocolate—down 41 percent for children ages two to five; 29 percent for children ages six to eleven; and 12 percent for adolescents ages twelve to seventeen. The exposure to ads for fast food chains, however, increased for all age groups, up more than 20 percent for ages twelve to seventeen; more than 12 percent for ages six to eleven; and nearly 5 percent for ages two to five. By 2007, fast food ads were the most frequently viewed by children and teenagers. The greatest percentage increase in beverage ads was for bottled water, followed by diet soft drinks. As one observer noted, progress has been made, but there's still much to do.

Banning Junk Food Advertising to Children

The World Health Organization has called on member states to reduce the marketing of junk food and fast food to children. Its "Set of Recommendations on the Marketing of Foods and Non-Alcoholic Beverages to Children" called for the elimination of all advertising of such foods in nurseries, preschool centers, schools, school grounds, playgrounds, family and child clinics, and pediatric services. Several countries, including Sweden, have banned advertisements on television and radio programs targeted at children under the age of twelve. Belgium has prohibited commercials during children's programs and Australia has banned advertisements during television programming targeted at preschoolers. Calls for similar bans in the United States have been put forth regularly. The Center for Science in the Public Interest (CSPI) and Corporate Accountability International have protested marketing fast food to children, which they consider "predatory marketing," as especially young children are unable to evaluate advertising.

Those supporting the right of commercial companies to market their products to children claim that it is their right of free speech. They also state that parents should be the ones who decide what foods their children eat, not those opposed to fast food and junk food.

In 2009 Congress created an Interagency Working Group on Food Marketed to Children, consisting of representatives of the Federal Trade Commission, the Food and Drug Administration, the Centers for Disease Control, and the U.S. Department of Agriculture. It had the intent of making voluntary nutritional guidelines for the marketing of food to children and adolescents seventeen years old or younger. In July 2010 the Taskforce gave its recommendations that foods that did not reach a certain nutritional criteria, or foods that exceeded certain fat, sugar, and sodium levels, should not be marketed to children. Specifically, advertised food must contain at least 50 percent "by weight of one or more of the following: fruit; vegetable; whole grain; fat-free or low-fat milk or yogurt; fish; extra lean meat or poultry; eggs; nuts and seeds; or beans." As few fast foods and no junk foods meet these criteria, these recommendations, if implemented, would curtail the marketing of these products to children and adolescents.

Opponents of junk food and fast food advertising on children's television programs have urged eliminating the tax deduction that companies receive for such advertisements, which, according to a report issued in 2010 by the Rudd Center on Food Policy & Obesity, was close to $2 billion the industry deducts annually as a business expense. A longitudinal study of 13,000 children over a 30-year period concluded in 2008 that banning junk food advertising on American television would reduce the number of overweight children ages three to eleven in a fixed population by 18 percent, and would reduce the number of overweight adolescents ages twelve to eighteen by 14 percent. It also concluded that eliminating the tax deductability of such advertising would decrease overweight by only 5 to 6 percent.

See also Cartoon Characters; Center for Science in the Public Interest (CSPI); Children's Food and Beverage Advertising Initiative (CFBAI); Corporate Accountability International; Food and Drug Administration (FDA); Frito-Lay; General Mills; Happy Meals; Kraft Foods; U.S. Department of Agriculture; Vending Machines

For Further Information:

Barnett-Rhodes, Amanda. "Sugar Coated Ads and High Calorie Dreams: The Impact of Junk Food Ads on Brand Recognition of Preschool Children." Master's Thesis, University of Vermont, 2002.

Cairns, Georgina, Kathryn Angus and Gerard Hastings. *The Extent Nature and Effects of Food Promotion to Children: A Review of the Evidence to December 2008*. Geneva, Switzerland: World Health Organization, 2009, as at: whqlibdoc.who.int/publications/2009/9789241598835_eng.pdf

Campaign for a Commercial Free Childhood Web site: www.commercialexploitation.org

Chou, Shin-Yi, IAS Rashid, and Michael Grossman. "Fast-Food Advertising on Television and Its Influence on Childhood Obesity." *Journal of Law and Economics* 51, no. 4 (2008): 599–618.

Cornwell, T. Bettina, and Anna R. McAlister. "Alternative Thinking about Starting Points of Obesity. Development of Child Taste Preferences." *Appetite* (January 14, 2011), as at: www.ncbi.nlm.nih.gov/pubmed/21238522

Dibb, Sue. *A Spoonful of Sugar: Television Food Advertising Aimed at Children: An International Comparative Study*. London, UK: Consumers International 1996.

Fast Food Advertising Characters: Burger King Characters, McDonald's Characters, Colonel Sanders, McDonaldland, the Burger King, Brooke Burke. nl: General Books, 2010.

Food Advertising Characters: Beverage Advertising Characters, Burger King Characters, Cereal Advertising Characters. nl: General Books, 2010.

Food and Beverage Marketing to Children in the Digital Age Web site: www.nplanonline.org/childhood-obesity/products/digital-marketing

Harris, Jennifer L., et al. "Fast Food FACTS: Evaluating Fast Food Nutrition and Marketing to Youth." New Haven, CT: Rudd Center for Food Policy & Obesity, 2010, as at: www.fastfoodmarketing.org/media/FastFoodFACTS_Report.pdf

Haugen, David M. *How Does Advertising Impact Teen Behavior?* Detroit: Greenhaven Press, 2008.

Jain, Anjali. "Temptations in Cyberspace: New Battlefields in Childhood Obesity." *Health Affairs* 29 (March 2010): 425–29.

Kelly, Bridget, et al. "Television Food Advertising to Children: A Global Perspective." *American Journal of Public Health* 100 (September 2010): 1730–36.

Kunkel, Dale, and Walter Gantz. "Children's Television Advertising in the Multi-Channel Environment." *Journal of Communication* 42, no. 3 (1992): 134–52.

Macklin, M. Carole, and Les Carlson, eds. *Advertising to Children: Concepts and Controversies*. Thousand Oaks, CA: Sage, 1999.

Marketing Food to Children and Adolescents: A Review of Industry Expenditures, Activities and Self-Regulation. Washington, D.C.: Federal Trade Commission, 2008, as at: www.ftc.gov/os/2008/07/P064504foodmktingreport.pdf

Marketing of Food and Non-Alcoholic Beverages to Children: Report of a WHO Forum and Technical Meeting. Oslo, Norway: World Health Organization, May 2–5, 2006.

Mayo, Ed, and Agnes Nairn. *Consumer Kids: How Big Business Is Grooming Our Children for Profit.* London: Constable, 2009.

McDonald's YouTube Web site: www.youtube.com/user/mcdonaldscorp

McGinnis, J. Michael, Jennifer Appleton Gootman, and Vivica I. Kraak. *Food Marketing to Children and Youth: Threat or Opportunity?* Institute of Medicine's Committee on Food Marketing and the Diets of Children and Youth. Washington, D.C.: National Academies Press, 2006.

Montgomery, Kathryn C., and Jeff Chester. "Interactive Food and Beverage Marketing: Targeting Adolescents in the Digital Age." *Journal of Adolescent Health* 45, no. 3 Supplement (September 2009): S18–S29.

Morrison, Maureen. "Just How Happy Does the Happy Meal Make McDonald's?" *Advertising Age*, November 29, 2010, as at: www.adage.com/article?article_id=147271

Murray, John P. *Children and Television: Fifty Years of Research.* Mahwah, NJ: Lawrence Erlbaum, 2007.

Nestle, Marion. "Food Marketing and Childhood Obesity: A Matter of Policy." *New England Journal of Medicine* 354, n. 24 (2006): 2527–29.

Roden, Steve, and Dan Goodsell. *Krazy Kid's Food! Vintage Food Graphics.* Köln, Germany: Taschen, 2002.

Ronald McDonald Web site: www.ronald.com

Rudd Center for Food Policy & Obesity FACTS Web site: fastfoodmarketing.org

Turner, Lindsey, and Frank J. Chaloupka. "Wide Availability of High-Calorie Beverages in US Elementary Schools." *Archives of Pediatrics & Adolescent Medicine* 164, no. 11 (November 1, 2010, as at: http://archpedi.ama-assn.org/cgi/content/abstract/arch pediatrics.2010.215v1

Wilcox, Brian L., Dale Kunkel, Joanne Cantor, Peter Dowrick, Susan Linn, and Edward Palmer. *Report of the APA Task Force on Advertising and Children.* Washington, D.C.: American Psychological Association, 2004.

World Health Organization. "Set of Recommendations on the Marketing of Foods and Non-Alcoholic Beverages to Children." Geneva: World Health Organization, 2010, as at: www.who.int/dietphysicalactivity/publications/recsmarketing/en/index.html

Marriott Corporation

J. Willard Marriott opened an A&W Root Beer stand in 1927 in Washington, D.C. Two years later, he created the Marriott Corporation, which is better known for its hotel operations. The company also developed an extensive foodservice operation, serving institutions, schools, colleges, and universities. In 1967 it launched the Roy Rogers chain, makers of roast beef sandwiches. It purchased the Gino's chain in 1982 and converted 180 of its restaurants to the Roy Rogers brand. The company acquired the Howard Johnson lodging and restaurant chain in 1987, but it was more interested in the lodging part; the restaurant business rapidly declined, and as of 2010, only three Howard Johnson restaurants remain. Marriot bought Farrell's Ice Cream Parlours in 1971 but sold the chain in 1985. It has owned or held limited franchise rights to Big Boy, Popeyes, Dunkin' Donuts, Burger King, Dairy Queen, Denny's, and El Pollo Loco chains.

See also A&W; Big Boy; Burger King; Dairy Queen; Dunkin' Donuts; El Pollo Loco; Popeyes; Roy Rogers; Sandwiches

For Further Information:

Jakle, John A., and Keith A. Sculle. *Fast Food: Roadside Restaurants in the Automobile Age*. Baltimore: Johns Hopkins University Press, 1999.

Mars Bar

In 1932 Forrest Mars, the son of Frank Mars, the founder of Mars, Inc., launched Mars, Ltd., in England and opened a factory in Slough. The following year he reformulated the Milky Way bar, creating a sweeter product. He gave it a new name, the Mars Bar. It was the first successful combination candy bar sold in England and it was a tremendous success—in just one year he sold 2 million bars. Forrest Mars opened a factory in Brussels, Belgium, hoping to sell Mars Bars across Europe, but the outbreak of World War II ended this operation. Mars Bars were manufactured during the war and were mainly distributed to British armed forces. As soon as sugar was available after the war, Mars Bars again took their place on the British confectionary scene.

Mars Bars were imported into the United States from Canada and Europe. In addition, Mars, Inc., introduced a Mars Bar into the United States, but it was a very different confection than the European one. The American Mars Bar included almonds. It was not a great success and it was discontinued in 2002, but Mars introduced the Snickers bar with almonds as a substitute. In 2010, the Mars Bar was relaunched in the United States.

Mars Bars have been employed for a variety of unusual foods. Deep-Fried Mars Bars reportedly were invented in Glasgow or Stonehaven in 1995. Others claim the original source was the Bervie Chipper in nearby Inverbervie. Whatever the source, it was widely copied in Scotland's fish-and-chip shops, and some shops reportedly sold as many as two hundred a week. Frozen Mars Bars have also become popular at state and regional fairs, where they are served on sticks.

See also Fair Food; Mars, Forrest; Mars, Frank; Mars, Inc;

For Further Information:

Cadbury, Deborah. *Chocolate Wars: The 150-Year Rivalry Between the World's Greatest Chocolate Makers*. New York: PublicAffairs, 2010.

Mars Bar UK Web site: www.marsbar.co.uk

Mars, Forrest

Forrest Edward Mars (1904–1999) was the son of Frank Mars, the founder of Mars, Inc., and Frank's first wife, Ethel. Forrest's parents divorced and he did not see his father again until 1922, when he began working with Frank at Mars, Inc. Forrest later claimed that he invented the Milky Way bar, which was launched in 1923.

After a quarrel, Frank Mars removed Forrest from Mars, Inc., in 1932. Forrest was given $50,000 and the foreign rights to the Milky Way bar. Forrest traveled to Europe, where he claimed to have learned the chocolate business in Switzerland by working in various chocolate companies, including those of Tobler and Nestlé. Forrest settled in England, where he consulted with Rowntree's of York, assisting that company in producing what would become the Kit Kat Bar in 1935. Rowntree's also began manufacturing Smarties, a small, round chocolate enclosed in candy coating.

Forrest launched Mars, Ltd., in Slough, England, and began to manufacture a sweeter version of the Milky Way bar with a new name, the Mars Bar. By 1939, Mars, Ltd., was ranked as Britain's third-largest candy manufacturer. Mars opened a factory in Brussels, hoping to sell Mars Bars across Europe, but the outbreak of World War II ended these activities.

In the United States, Forrest Mars went into a limited partnership with Bruce Murrie, son of William Murrie, the president of the Hershey Company. Forrest Mars put up 80 percent of the capital and Murrie 20 percent, and Forrest was in charge of the company, which was named M&M, Inc., for the first initial of their respective last names. As a result of the partnership, Hershey supplied M&M, Inc., with all the chocolate they wanted. Hershey also supplied M&M, Inc., with equipment and technical advice. The new company introduced M&M's in 1940. Because sugar and chocolate were rationed during the war, Forrest bought a rice mill in 1942 and launched Uncle Ben's Rice. After the war, M&M launched print advertisements in national newspapers and magazines, radio spots, and billboards. In 1949 Forrest Mars bought out Bruce Murrie for $1 million. The company, M&M, Inc., was eventually renamed Food Manufacturers, Inc.

Now completely in charge of the company, Forrest Mars hired Ted Bates & Co., an advertising firm in Chicago, to help market the company's products. Bates came up with the slogan "Melts in your mouth, not in your hand," which was an instant success. The company added Peanut M&M's in 1954 and introduced the cartoon characters Mr. Plain and Mr. Peanut in the same year. Bates also developed a television commercial that showed M&M's jumping into pool of chocolate; the company's television advertisements ran on the *Howdy Doody Show* and the *Mickey Mouse Club*. By 1956, M&M's annual sales topped $40 million.

Forrest Mars had tried to gain control of Mars, Inc., after his father's death in 1934. For years he was unsuccessful in this quest, but when Ethel Mars (Frank Mars' second wife) died in 1945, she gave 50 percent of her stock to Forrest. This gave him a position on the board of directors and an office at Mars, Inc. In 1950 Forrest tried to oust the leadership of Mars, Inc., but he failed and was banned from the company. He was eventually given control of several seats on the company's board. In 1959 Forrest became chairman of Mars, Inc., and continued to acquire shares in the company. In 1964 Forrest Mars merged Food Manufacturers, Inc., into Mars, Inc., which became the new corporation's name.

In 1965 Mars, Inc., discontinued buying chocolate from Hershey and Forrest began to expand the company. To prevent trade secrets from leaking out, Forrest Mars required that all senior executives sign nondisclosure agreements. When Forrest Mars died in 1999, he left a fortune worth $4 billion, and he was ranked by *Forbes* magazine as among the wealthiest Americans, as were his children. Mars, Inc., is one of the largest companies in the world.

See also Advertising; Candy; Cartoon Characters; Chocolate; Hershey Company; Kit Kat; M&M's; Mars Bar; Mars, Frank; Mars, Inc.; Milky Way; Nestlé; Radio; Rowntree's of York; Television; United Kingdom

For Further Information:

Brenner, Joël Glenn. *The Emperors of Chocolate: Inside the Secret World of Hershey and Mars*. New York: Broadway Books, 2000.

Mars Web site: www.mms.com

Pottker, Janice. *Crisis in Candyland: Melting the Chocolate Shell of the Mars Family Empire*. Bethesda, MD: National Press Books, 1995.

Mars, Frank

The candy maker Frank Mars (1883–1934) was born in Minneapolis, Minnesota. His father was a gristmill operator in Philadelphia who had moved to St. Paul. Shortly after his birth, Frank Mars contracted polio; he remained in a wheelchair throughout his life. Frank Mars mastered his mother's candy recipes and experimented on his own, creating new confections. He started a business selling penny candies, which were usually manufactured on a small scale. By 1902, he was operating a wholesale candy firm in Minneapolis. That year, he married Ethel G. Kissack, and their only son, Forrest Mars, was born in 1904.

Frank Mars and his wife barely survived financially. When their money ran out in 1910, his wife divorced him. Mars married another woman, also named Ethel, and moved to Tacoma, Washington, where he began making nougat. He was bankrupt within a year. He kept trying but his efforts failed, so in 1920 he skipped town (owing money) and returned to Minnesota.

Back in Minneapolis, Frank Mars founded a candy company, later named Mars, Inc., which turned out to be a success. It was during this time that Frank Mars was reintroduced to his son, Forrest, whom he had not seen since his divorce from his first wife. In 1923 the company introduced the Milky Way bar, which received local distribution. In 1930 Mars introduced the Snickers bar, which quickly became the most popular candy bar in America, a position it has held ever since. Snickers was followed by 3 Musketeers in 1932. Frank and Forrest Mars quarreled and Forrest was forced out of the company. Fifteen months later, Frank Mars died at the age of fifty-one. He left Mars, Inc., to his second wife.

See also Candy; Chocolate; Mars, Forrest; Mars, Inc.; Milky Way; Nougat; Snickers; 3 Musketeers

For Further Information:

Brenner, Joël Glenn. *The Emperors of Chocolate: Inside the Secret World of Hershey and Mars*. New York: Broadway Books, 2000.

Mars Web site: www.mms.com

Pottker, Janice. *Crisis in Candyland: Melting the Chocolate Shell of the Mars Family Empire*. Bethesda, MD: National Press Books, 1995.

Mars, Inc.

In 1922, after almost twenty years of business failure, Frank Mars founded the Mar-O-Bar Company in Minneapolis. The company was named after one of its confections, a gooey combination of caramel, nuts, and chocolate. His estranged son, Forrest Mars, joined him and they changed the name of the company to Mars, Inc. Within a year, the company was successfully selling butter creams. Frank Mars borrowed a technique developed at Minneapolis' Pendergast Candy Company to create a fluffy, chewy nougat center for its Fat Emma bar. In 1923 Mars, Inc. introduced the Milky Way bar, which was different from its competitors in that the malt-flavored nougat—a whipped filling made of egg whites and corn syrup—was encased in a solid chocolate covering to keep it fresh. In its first year on the market, the Milky Way brand had grossed $800,000. The company moved to Chicago in 1928.

In 1930 Mars introduced the Snickers bar, a peanut-flavored nougat bar topped with nuts and caramel and coated with chocolate. It quickly became the most popular candy bar in America, a position it has held ever since. In 1932 Mars released the 3 Musketeers bar. The company used so much chocolate that the Hershey Company ended up supplying it to Mars, a relationship the two companies maintained until 1965.

In 1932 Frank and Forrest Mars had a falling out. Forrest was given $50,000 and the foreign rights to Mars' products. Forrest visited Switzerland, where he claimed to have learned chocolate manufacturing as a worker at the Jean Tobler factory, which produced the Toblerone chocolate bar, and at Nestlé's factories. Mars then moved to England. At the time, England was saturated with sweets from Rowntree's of York and Cadbury Brothers. Despite stiff competition, Mars set up a factory in Slough, England. Because he had no chocolate, he purchased it from Cadbury, a practice that was continued until the 1950s. Among that factory's first products was the Mars Bar, which was a slightly sweeter version of the American Milky Way. It was released in 1933 and became an immediate success. Mars battled Cadbury and Rowntree's for retail shelf space and it was only after the Mars Bar became England's best-selling bar that this problem was resolved. By 1939, Mars, Ltd., was ranked as Britain's third-largest candy manufacturer.

In addition to his business in England, Forrest Mars also created a candy business in the United States, where he teamed up with Bruce Murrie, son of William Murrie, the president of the Hershey Company. They named their company M&M for the first letter of each founder's last name. Owing to Murrie's influence, M&M obtained as much chocolate as it needed from Hershey. The company also received technical assistance and the latest production equipment. The company's first product was a small chocolate confection that was covered by a hard sugar shell, which they named M&M's Chocolate Candies. In 1942 Forrest bought a rice mill and launched Uncle Ben's Rice. (Uncle Ben was evidently a real person, but the caricature on the box was of a Chicago waiter.) After the war, the relationship between Mars and Murrie became strained, and in 1949 Mars bought out Murrie for $1 million and changed the name of his company to Food Manufacturers, Inc. Forrest launched a major advertising campaign in national newspapers and magazines, radio spots, and billboards. By 1949, annual sales had increased to $3 million.

Merger

When Frank Mars died in 1934, Forrest tried to gain control of Mars, Inc. Unfortunately for Forrest, Frank Mars had left the company to his second wife, Ethel. Ethel left management of the company in the hands of her brother, William Kruppenbacher. In 1945 Ethel died and half of her stock passed to Forrest Mars, who was given a seat on the board of directors and an office at Mars, Inc.'s headquarters. When Forrest Mars tried, but failed, to oust Kruppenbacher, Forrest was banned from the company's grounds. In 1950 Kruppenbacher offered Forrest one-third of the seats on the board, which Forrest accepted. He pushed Mars to update its equipment. At that time, Mars still hand-wrapped its candy. New equipment was purchased from Germany and in 1953 Mars mechanized its process for making candy bars. This allowed for continuous-flow production, which reduced manufacturing time. Forrest Mars also pushed Mars, Inc., to expand abroad and globalize its operations. He introduced Snickers, Milky Way, and other products into other countries, and he introduced successful European candies, such as Starburst Fruit Chews and the Twix bar, into the United States.

Mars was the first candy company to date its products and remove them from distributors if they were not sold in time. Forrest pioneered the use of computers on the production line to measure the consistency of output; if a candy bar was defective it was scrapped, and the scrap would be ground up for use in another candy bar. In 1959 Forrest became chairman of Mars, Inc., and in 1964 he merged the company with his Food Manufacturers, Inc. By agreement, the name of the merged company was Mars, Inc.

Mars, Inc. has continued to expand, both through acquisitions (such as its purchase of the Dove Bar brand in 1986) and by creating new products, not all of which were successful. Mars tried to launch a version of M&M's Peanuts that copied the coloring and styling of Hershey's Reese's Pieces. But Hershey sued Mars, maintaining that Mars was capitalizing on Hershey's goodwill and investment in Reese's Pieces. The Hershey Company won.

As of 2011, Mars, Inc., was a $30 billion operation with interests from Helsinki to Hong Kong. Mars controls 15 percent of the global candy market. Mars is four times larger than Hershey on a global basis. As a chocolate maker, Mars leads the market in the United Kingdom, but not in the United States.

See also Advertising; Cadbury; Candy; Caramels; Chocolate; Dove Bar; Hershey Company; M&M's; Mars Bar; Mars, Forrest; Mars, Frank; Milky Way; Nestlé; Nougat; Peanuts; Radio; Snickers; Television; 3 Musketeers; Toblerone; United Kingdom

For Further Information:

Brenner, Joël Glenn. *The Emperors of Chocolate: Inside the Secret World of Hershey and Mars.* New York: Broadway Books, 2000.

Mars Web site: www.mms.com

Pottker, Janice. *Crisis in Candyland: Melting the Chocolate Shell of the Mars Family Empire.* Bethesda, MD: National Press Books, 1995.

Marshmallow Fluff

In 1917 Archibald Query of Somerville, Massachusetts, invented Marshmallow Fluff, a semi-liquid product that could be spread on confections, sandwiches, or eaten directly out of the jar. Query made the fluff in his kitchen and sold it door to door. When the United States entered World War I in 1917, sugar, the main ingredient in Marshmallow Fluff, was rationed, and Query stopped making his product. When the war ended and sugar was once again available, Query again started selling Marshmallow Fluff, and recipes for making it appeared in cookbooks. In 1920 Query sold the formula to H. Allen Durkee and Fred L. Mower, who created the firm of Durkee-Mower, Inc., to manufacture Marshmallow Fluff. They, too, sold their products door to door, but they finally convinced some grocery stores to distribute it. In 1927 the company began advertising extensively in Boston. By 1930, Marshmallow Fluff was distributed throughout New England. They also began publishing a cookbook that used Fluff as an ingredient in every recipe. The company advertised the product on the radio and sales continued to expand during the 1930s.

Circus Peanuts

Circus Peanuts are chewy, marshmallow-based candies shaped like a peanut. They have been sold in the United States since the nineteenth century. Recently, heart-shaped Peanuts have been manufactured for Valentine's Day, and chick- and bunny-shaped Peanuts have been created for Easter. In 1963 General Mills added Circus Peanuts bits to its Lucky Charms cereal. Major producers of Circus Peanuts today include Spangler Candy Company and Brach's.

When the United States entered World War II in December 1941, sugar was again rationed, and Durkee-Mower had to greatly reduce their production. When the war ended, however, sales again continued to increase. In 1956 the company teamed up with Nestlé to promote a fudge recipe that used both Nestlé chocolate and Marshmallow Fluff, a recipe that is still favored by many fudge lovers. Ten years later, the company teamed up with the Kellogg Company to produce a "marshmallow treat" using Rice Krispies.

Today, Marshmallow Fluff is widely available throughout the United States and several other countries. Marshmallow Fluff is a junk food; it is high in calories and low in nutrition. In 2008 a Massachusetts state legislature proposed that Marshmallow Fluff be banned from public schools to help reduce obesity.

See also Brach's Confections; Fudge; General Mills; Kellogg Company; Marshmallows; Spangler Candy Company

For Further Information:

Marshmallow Fluff Web site: www.marshmallowfluff.com

McMullen, Gretchen. *The "Yummy" Book: Marshmallow Fluff Recipes*. Lynn, MA: Durkee-Mower, circa 1930s.

Schwartz, Justin. *The Marshmallow Fluff Cookbook*. Philadelphia: Running Press, 2004.

Marshmallows

Marshmallows are a spongy confection historically made from a plant called *Althaea officinalis*, an herb that grows in marshes and on the banks of rivers. It is native to Asia and Europe and it is naturalized in eastern America. Traditionally, the sap was extracted from the plant's roots. Europeans, probably the French, began to sweeten the sap, add egg whites, and fluffed up the mixture, thus creating a fluffy, aerated confection. Today, marshmallows are typically made from sugar

Marshmallows on sticks. (Dreamstime.com)

or cornstarch, gelatin, and flavorings. They are molded into a variety of shapes and come in various flavors and colors.

In 1948 Alex Doumakes patented an extrusion process that improved the efficiency and speed of making marshmallows. His company, Doūmak, Inc., purchased Campfire Marshmallows in 2003. It co-produces with Kraft Foods most of the marshmallow brands available in the United States. The Just Born Company in Bethlehem, Pennsylvania, produces Peeps, and it is the largest marshmallow candy producer in the world.

A number of confections contain marshmallows, including a treat popularized by the Girl Scouts, S'Mores, as well as Rocky Road ice cream, Marshmallow Fluff, and Mallomars.

Marshmallows have even made it into movies. Perhaps their most famous role was in *Ghost Busters*, when the Stay Puft Marshmallow Man, inspired by the Pillsbury Doughboy, explodes, spreading marshmallow pieces all over part of New York.

See also Girl Scout Cookies; Ice Cream; Just Born; Kraft Foods; Mallomars; Marshmallow Fluff; Peeps; Pillsbury

For Further Information:

Campfire Marshmallows Web site: www.campfiremarshmallows.com

Mary Jane Candies

In 1884 Charles N. Miller of Boston formed a small business making and selling homemade candy. In 1914 the company began manufacturing Mary Janes, a bite-sized, chewy molasses-and-peanut-butter candy. Miller named it for a favorite aunt, and on the candy wrappers appeared the likeness of a little girl. In 1989 the Charles N. Miller Company was sold to Stark Candy Company, which was itself acquired a year later by the New England Confectionery Company (NECCO). NECCO markets a wide range of Mary Jane products, including Mary Jane Tubs and Mary Jane Peanut Butter Kisses. Although still marketed, Mary Jane candies are nostalgia candies today.

See also Candy; New England Confectionery Company (NECCO); Peanut Butter

For Further Information:

New England Confectionery Company Web site: www.necco.com

Mascots, Logos, and Icons

Most fast food chains and many junk food manufacturers have adopted mascots. Among the first food mascots was the Big Boy, a plump boy wearing red-and-white-checked overalls with the words "Big Boy" written across his chest. He carries a large, triple-decker hamburger, and twelve-foot statues of the Big Boy are erected in front of each restaurant in the Big Boy chain.

Burger King developed a little "Burger King," attired in a royal robe and crown. It stopped using that mascot for a while but revived it later. The chain regularly gives out paper crowns to children so that they, too, can be kings. Little Caesars Pizza created a Little Caesar mascot. McDonald's first mascot was Speedee, a little chef with a hamburger head. This had to be changed because Alka Seltzer had already adopted a mascot named Speedy. McDonald's settled on Ronald McDonald, and today about 96 percent of American children recognize him.

Not all mascots and icons have been successful, however. Taco Bell initially created a sleepy Mexican wearing a sombrero. When PepsiCo acquired Taco Bell, it jettisoned the existing icon and replaced it with a mission bell. Pizza Hut had and Italian chef tossing dough, but it was considered "too Italian" by PepsiCo, which had acquired the chain, and the company shifted to the red roof that symbolized the "hut" in Pizza Hut. Frito-Lay, Inc., launched the Frito Bandito, only to be charged with ethnic stereotyping; the symbol was soon shelved.

Unusual mascots have been developed by Taco Bell and KFC. In the case of Taco Bell, a massive television advertising campaign starred a talking Chihuahua, who squealed "Yo Quiero Taco Bell!" In the case of KFC, the mascot was based on a real person, the founder of the chain, Harland Sanders. When he started franchising his chicken, he had no money to advertise, so he dressed in a white suit and black string tie and called himself a colonel (he was, in fact, an honorary colonel). His image graces KFC paperware, posters, advertisements, and commercials.

In the snack food world, in 1969 Keebler came up with Ernie Keebler and the Elves who bake snacks in the Hollow Tree in the fictional community of Sylvan Glen.

For M&M's, Mars, Inc., developed the cartoon characters Mr. Peanut and Mr. Plain, while individual characters were named for their colors. Planters Peanuts developed its own Mr. Peanut, and McKee Foods created Little Debbie.

See also Big Boy; Burger King; Frito Bandito; Frito-Lay; Hamburger; Keebler; KFC; Little Caesars Pizza; Little Debbie; M&M's; Mars, Inc.; McDonald's; Mr. Peanut; Peanuts; PepsiCo; Pizza Hut; Ronald McDonald; Sanders, Harland; Taco Bell

For Further Information:

Hine, Thomas. *The Total Package: The Evolution and Secret Meanings of Boxes, Bottles, Cans, and Tubes*. New York: Little, Brown and Company, 1995.

McCafé

In 1993 McDonald's Australia launched a new concept—the McCafé. It was a separate area within McDonald's restaurants that sold pastries, premium coffee, mocha frappes, and cappuccinos. Its intent was to compete with the wildly successful Starbucks franchises, but the McCafé was less expensive. McDonald's slowly introduced McCafés into its restaurants in Canada, Europe, and the United States. Store revenues are reported to have jumped an estimated 20 percent to 25 percent with the addition of a McCafé. As of 2011, there were about 1,200 McCafés and more are in the planning stage. Many McCafés now offer free WiFi for their customers.

In 2006, however, McDonald's upgraded its coffee to compete with Dunkin' Donuts and Starbucks. American McDonald's restaurants sell the premium coffee, which now accounts for an estimated 6 percent of the company's sales. In March 2007, *Consumer Reports* proclaimed McDonald's Premium Roast coffee to be "cheapest and best," beating Starbucks, Burger King, and Dunkin' Donuts coffee.

See also Burger King; Coffee; Dunkin' Donuts; McDonald's; Starbucks

For Further Information:

"Starbucks War." *Consumer Reports* Web site: www.consumerreports.org/cro/food/beverages/coffee-tea/coffee-taste-test-3-07/overview/0307_coffee_ov_1.htm

McCain Foods

McCain Foods is a large Canadian firm that manufactures frozen food products, such as french fries, pizzas, frozen onion rings, and desserts. In the late 1970s McCain Foods established a subsidiary in the United States, which is headquartered in Lisle, Illinois. McCain Foods USA supplies frozen french fries marketed under the McCain and Ore-Ida brand names. Its frozen pizzas are sold under the Ellio's brand name, and its frozen onion rings are sold under the Moore's brand name.

See also Canada; French Fries; Onion Rings

For Further Information:

McCain Foods USA Web site: www.mccainusa.com

McDonaldization

The term "McDonaldization" was coined by Jim Hightower in his book *Eat Your Heart Out* (1975). Hightower was a farm activist who warned that fast food threatened independent businesses and family-owned farms. He believed that the practices of large fast food corporations, such as McDonald's, were creating a food economy dominated by giant corporations.

The term was picked up and popularized in academic circles by George Ritzer, whose book *The McDonaldization of Society* (1993) examined the social effects of McDonald's in the United States. McDonald's rigorously controlled the appearance of each of its outlets, as well as their menus, equipment, procedures, advertising, suppliers, and policies. McDonald's success had launched many imitators, not only in the fast food industry but also throughout America's retail economy. Ritzer defined McDonaldization as "the principles by which the fast-food restaurant[s] are coming to dominate more and more sectors of American society and of the world." The principles included efficiency, predictability, and control. According to Ritzer, McDonald's is "the irrationality of rationality." Like Hightower, Ritzer attacked the fast food industry for its homogenizing influence.

McDonald's and other fast food chains have been exported to the rest of the world, and the phenomenon has been studied by numerous individuals, including James L. Watson, whose *Golden Arches East: McDonald's in East Asia* (1997) examined the effects of McDonald's in East Asia. Subsequently, many other academic articles and books have been written on McDonaldization, such as *McDonaldization Revisited: Critical Essays on Consumer Culture* (1998), edited by Mark Alfino, John S. Caputo, and Robin Wynyard.

The term "McDonaldization" has spawned similar terms, such as "Snickerize," used to described the influence of Mars, Inc., in Russia after the fall of the Berlin

Wall in 1989; "Coca-Colonisation," which refers to American influence in other parts of the world, such as Europe and China; and "Walmartization," reflecting the major influence that Walmart has had upon the United States and the world.

See also Advertising; Efficiency; Mars, Inc.; McDonald's; Suppliers; Walmart

For Further Information:

Alfino, Mark, John S. Caputo, and Robin Wynyard, eds. *McDonaldization Revisited: Critical Essays on Consumer Culture*. Westport, CT: Greenwood Press, 1998.

Hightower, Jim. *Eat Your Heart Out: Food Profiteering in America*. New York: Crown Publishers, 1975.

Ritzer, George. *The McDonaldization of Society*. Editions 1–6. Thousand Oaks, CA: Pine Forge Press, 1996–2010.

Ritzer, George. *The McDonaldization Thesis: Explorations and Extensions*. Thousand Oaks CA: Sage Publications, 1998.

Ritzer, George, ed. *McDonaldization: The Reader.* 2nd ed. Thousand Oaks, CA: Pine Forge Press, 2006.

Smart, Barry, ed. *Resisting McDonaldization*. Thousand Oaks, CA: Sage Publications, 1999.

McDonald's

In 1930 two New Hampshire brothers, Richard and Maurice McDonald, moved to Los Angeles, attracted by potential employment in the movie industry. They bought a small movie theater, but it was not successful. To make ends meet, in 1937 they opened an orange juice and hot dog stand near the Santa Anita racetrack in Arcadia, a suburb of Los Angeles. Their stand grew and they shifted from hot dogs to barbecue and hamburgers. In 1940 they opened the McDonald Brothers Burger Bar Drive-In on E Street in San Bernardino, California. It featured twenty female carhops picking up and delivering food. The brothers noted that 80 percent of their sales were hamburgers, so they dropped the barbecue (which also took too long to make). After World War II, they had to deal with a labor shortage; the economy was booming and many young men who had been in the service were now at college on the GI Bill. As a result, the McDonald brothers often ended up with unreliable fry cooks and dishwashers.

The brothers decided upon radical shifts that would reduce expenses and increase profits by increasing efficiency. A central feature of their operation was an industrial assembly line model popularized by Henry Ford, whose techniques had previously been adapted for use in food service by cafeterias, automats, railway dining cars, and at the Howard Johnson restaurant chain. The model included division of labor into simple tasks that could be performed with a minimum of training. This meant that their employees were essentially interchangeable and could easily be shifted from one task to another. The brothers redesigned the kitchen, making room for larger grills and labor-saving equipment. They created an efficient assembly line to make hamburgers and french fries. This assembly line model provided customers with fast, reliable, and inexpensive food; in return, customers were expected to stand in line and pick up their own food, eat quickly, clean up their own waste, and leave without delay, thereby making room for more customers.

The McDonald brothers were convinced that their target audience was families, so they tried to create an environment that would discourage loitering teenagers, who littered and broke or stole cups, glasses, plates, silverware, and trays. Therefore, they did away with the attractive female carhops, whom the brothers believed were more interested in socializing than in selling burgers. They also did away with the plates, glasses, and tableware, replacing them with disposable paper and plastic utensils.

To implement these ideas, the brothers closed their restaurant, installed larger grills and purchased Multimixers (which made several milkshakes at a time in metal containers; the contents could then be poured into paper cups). To speed this up, the brothers reduced the length of the machine's arm so that milkshakes could be made directly in 12-ounce paper cups, thus eliminating a step. Eighty or more shakes were prepared in advance and placed in a refrigerated holding case, thus speeding up the process of fulfilling orders.

This model created a militarized production system that was geared toward teen-aged male employees, who were responsible for simple tasks—some heated the hamburgers, others packaged the food or poured the soft drinks and shakes, and still others placed orders in paper bags.

This new model did away with indoor seating and greatly reduced the menu to a few low-cost items, including 15-cent hamburgers, 19-cent cheeseburgers, 10-cent fries, 20-cent shakes, and large and small sodas. The hamburger patties weighed only 1.5 ounces and all burgers came with the same condiments: ketchup, chopped onion, and two pickle slices. In this new self-service restaurant, customers placed their orders at a window and ate the food in their cars. All food was packaged in disposable paper wrappers and paper cups, so there was no breakage or loss owing to theft.

The McDonald brothers' restaurant was octagon-shaped, which was not unusual for Los Angeles at that time. The "McDonald's New Self-Service System" got off to a rocky start when it was launched in 1948: customers honked their horns and expected carhops to come out and pick up their orders. Eventually, they understood the new system and they were attracted by the low prices, fast service, and good hamburgers. The service was speedy: the McDonald brothers claimed that their employees could serve a customer who ordered everything that they had—hamburger, fries, and a beverage—in twenty seconds. Increased volume led to higher profits. By 1951, the brothers grossed $275,000, of which $100,000 was profit.

Reports of their phenomenal success spread around the nation and *American Restaurant* ran a cover story on the "McDonald's New Self-Service System" in July 1952. The brothers believed that they were ready to franchise their operation, so they began advertising for franchisees.

As good as their new design was, the McDonalds believed that they could make an even more efficient operation by changing the layout. They also wanted a more distinctive architectural design to make it easier to spot from the road and to make their drive-in stand out from the hundreds of other similar fast food establishments. Their new-model restaurant was constructed with a forward-sloping front; its walls were painted with red-and-white stripes. Richard McDonald came up with the idea for the "golden arches," which poked through the roof. Under the arches was white tile that implied cleanliness, and lots of glass that made food preparation visible to all.

Before their new restaurant was completed in San Bernardino, the McDonald brothers sold their first franchises based on their new design. Franchisees paid the McDonald brothers a relatively small fee plus a percentage of their sales. Unlike previous foodservice franchises, the brothers demanded that every franchise be constructed in the same way as their model, and that each outlet sell exactly the same food prepared in exactly the same way. Their new model had no indoor dining; customers were expected to eat in their cars. A couple of plastic chairs and cheap tables were provided outside for walk-up customers or for those who preferred to eat outside. This model gave McDonald's a significant advantage over other emerging fast food chains, for it promised consistency, predictability, and safety. However, it was not considered an advantage by potential franchisees at the time because it meant they could not use existing facilities—a criterion not required by other franchisers. By the end of 1953, the brothers had sold only twenty-one franchises, of which only ten became operating units (two in Phoenix, Arizona, and the rest in the Los Angeles area). Compared with other fast food chains, such as Dairy Queen, this was not a great success.

The McDonald's restaurant in San Bernardino attracted large crowds. Many subsequent fast food entrepreneurs visited the San Bernardino site. For instance, in 1952 Matthew Burns of Long Beach, California, invited his stepson, Keith G. Cramer (who owned a carhop restaurant in Daytona Beach, Florida), to fly out to California and visit McDonald's. The following year, Cramer opened his Insta-Burger King in Jacksonville, Florida, which evolved into Burger King. After a visit to McDonald's, restaurant owner Carl Karcher of Anaheim, California, decided to develop a fast food chain of his own; he named it Carl's Jr. Glen Bell of San Bernardino also studied the McDonald's operation and tried to develop something similar using Mexican-themed food instead of hamburgers. He eventually launched Taco Bell. James Collins, chairman of Collins Foods International, visited San Bernardino, took notes on the operation, and opened up a KFC franchise based on the brothers' design. Numerous others opened up McDonald imitations, so that by 1954 many other fast food operations were under way in Southern California.

Another visitor to San Bernardino was Ray Kroc, an owner of the Chicago company that sold Multimixers. Kroc had sold Multimixers to many fast food franchisees, including Dairy Queen and Tastee-Freez. This experience gave Kroc a deeper understanding of the fast food business and some knowledge of problems related to franchising. In the early 1950s increased competition reduced the sales of Multimixers and Kroc needed new outlets. He saw advertisements for McDonald's and was surprised to find that the McDonald brothers had purchased eight of his company's Multimixers. In 1954 he visited the McDonald brothers and was astounded by the crowds ordering food.

Kroc saw the potential of the McDonald's operation. He met with the brothers and signed an agreement allowing him to sell McDonald's franchises nationwide. In the mid-1950s, franchising consisted mainly of assigning territories to franchisees for huge up-front fees. However, Kroc wanted to control the McDonald's operations. He avoided territorial franchises by selling one store franchise at a time, thereby controlling the number of stores a licensee could operate. He also required strict conformity to operating standards, equipment, menus, recipes, prices, trademarks, and architectural designs. In 1955 Kroc created McDonald's System, Inc., and sold himself the first franchise in Des Plaines, Illinois, which he opened in 1955. He intended it to be a model operation that would attract potential franchisees.

Meanwhile, Kroc hired Harry Sonneborn, who had worked for Tastee-Freez and had established its franchising operation. Sonneborn designed McDonald's Franchise Realty Corporation, which purchased land for McDonald's franchises and then rented the land to franchisees. In this way, McDonald's became one of America largest landowners. The corporation made money off the rental agreements and, if a franchisee violated the agreement, McDonald's could evict them. Franchisees therefore did basically whatever the parent company wanted. In this way, Kroc controlled the franchise operations, ensuring uniformity, maintaining standards, and generating profits. McDonald's became one of the largest owners of retail estate in the world, and at one time the company earned the majority of its profits from collecting rent, not from selling food.

By the end of 1959, there were more than one hundred McDonald's operations. The early success of McDonald's rested, in part, on the managers selected to oversee operations. Kroc's mantra was "Quality, Service, Cleanliness, and Value," which he tried to instill in every franchisee. Kroc also believed in training managers. The company established Hamburger University, which offered a degree in Hamburgerology. The first class of 15 students graduated in February 1961. Since then, 65,000 managers have graduated from that institution.

Kroc had numerous disagreements with the McDonald brothers. The brothers required that Kroc follow their architectural and operational design exactly, but Kroc wanted to innovate. Kroc finally bought them out for $2.7 million. The buyout included a provision that permitted the McDonald brothers to continue operating the original McDonald's outlet in San Bernardino. That building burned down and Kroc then proclaimed that his operation in Des Plaines was the first real McDonald's hamburger outlet. Today, it is a McDonald's museum.

A significant component of McDonald's success was the changing demographics in America. Previous fast food chains (e.g., White Tower, White Castle, and the automats) were in inner cities. McDonald's targeted suburban America, which had begun to rapidly grow after World War II. The suburbs were home to families with plenty of baby-boom children, and residents were dependent upon the automobile. McDonald's tied franchising to fast food, cars, and families. McDonald's did everything it could to prevent its outlets from becoming teen hangouts. Kroc expanded upon the policies established by the McDonald brothers by banning jukeboxes, vending machines, and telephones. He refused to hire female employees until he was required to do so by law. Kroc encouraged franchisees to support local, family-oriented community activities.

Within a decade of his first encounter with the McDonald brothers, Ray Kroc revolutionized fast food service. By 1963, McDonald's was selling one million burgers a day, and this was only the beginning. The company began advertising nationally in 1966, the same year that McDonald's was first listed on the New York Stock Exchange. Kroc's model for success was emulated by virtually every new local, regional, and national fast food operation in America. McDonald's symbolized success and it generated huge profits. Kroc had originally envisioned 1,000 McDonald's operations in the United States; when he died in 1984 at the age of 81, there were 7,500 McDonald's outlets worldwide.

Targeting Children

McDonald's national promotional campaigns have been a significant reason for its success. Its slogans, such as "You Deserve a Break Today" (which *Advertising Age* rated as the top advertising campaign in the twentieth century) and "Two All-Beef Patties, Special Sauce, Lettuce, Cheese, Pickles, Onions on a Sesame Seed Bun," became national hits. According to Eric Schlosser, author of *Fast Food Nation* (2001), McDonald's expends more on advertising and promotion than does any other food brand.

In the 1950s few major companies in America targeted their advertising toward children. The conventional wisdom was that children did not have money (which was true); hence, they targeted adults who brought the children into stores. Kroc had targeted the middle-class families with children in the suburbs, but he learned that children had "pester" power; studies indicated that children determined where many families ate. To encourage children to prefer McDonald's, Kroc set out to make their visits to its outlets "fun." Ronald McDonald was selected as the company's national spokesperson in 1966.

The McDonald's outlet in Chula Vista, California (near San Diego), opened the first McDonaldland Park in 1972. In its two-day grand opening, ten thousand people came to visit. This proved to be such a success that McDonald's began opening bright-colored PlayPlaces for children, complete with playgrounds and mythical characters. Today, McDonald's restaurants have eight thousand Playlands, and the company is the largest private operator of playgrounds in the world.

The company has also tied in much of its marketing with major children's motion pictures. McDonald's Happy Meals, inaugurated in 1979, packaged the food with toys; as a result, McDonald's became the world's largest toy distributor. By 1980, the millions of dollars spent on child-oriented television advertising and local promotions had succeeded: 96 percent of American children recognized Ronald McDonald, second only to Santa Claus. As advertisers later pointed out, brand loyalty begins with children, and advertising targeted at children today is intended to create such loyalty for future payoffs. In 2010 Harris Interactive's Youth EquiTrend study, which asked 8- to 12-year-olds to rate major brands on several criteria, such as brand recognition, named McDonald's the highest-ranking fast food chain.

Not everyone was happy about McDonald's Happy Meals. Concerned about the growing childhood obesity crisis, the Santa Clara County Board of Supervisors in California banned the inclusion of giveaway toys in many fast food meals. In November 2010 San Francisco's city supervisors voted to ban the inclusion of toys in fast food meals unless the meals contained fewer than six hundred calories, included vegetables and fruit, and met other nutritional standards. The following month, the Center for Science in the Public Interest (CSPI) filed a class-action suit against McDonald's, claiming that the toys in its Happy Meals were "bait" used to lure children into gorging on "unhealthy junk food."

Recently, perhaps as a result of lawsuits and negative publicity, McDonald's has shifted its advertising in the United States from children to adults. It has specifically stressed its new coffee products.

Influence on Other Fast Food Chains

Kroc's success encouraged the growth of other fast food chains, which readily adopted McDonald's methods. The competition also innovated, and McDonald's needed to keep up with them. In 1967 Burger King launched a newly designed restaurant with indoor seating. This challenged one of the basic tenets of McDonald's model, which stressed eating in the car. But by the 1960s, the novelty of eating in the car had worn off. It was also uncomfortable on hot and humid days, as well as on extremely cold days during the winter. Indoor eating areas permitted year-round climate control, and customers greatly appreciated Burger King's new model. McDonald's reciprocated by developing a new model with indoor seating, which it inaugurated in 1968.

Initially, McDonald's had intentionally not constructed outlets in major cities. With the newly designed stores, it was possible for McDonald's to do so, which they did beginning in 1972. Several chains developed drive-thru windows, including Wendy's, Jack in the Box, and Burger King; McDonald's began installing drive-thru windows in 1975. Today, drive-thru windows generate about 50 percent of McDonald's sales.

New Product Development

To keep ahead of the competition, McDonald's also regularly developed new products. It diversified its menu beginning in the 1960s. The Big Mac with its two patties originated with a Pittsburgh franchisee, who was trying to create a competitive product to Burger King's Big Whopper. The Big Mac was released nationally in 1968.

Other innovations include the Quarter Pounder and the McBLT. In 1983 McDonald's introduced Chicken McNuggets, consisting of reconstituted chicken delivered frozen and then reheated before serving. McDonald's listened to its customers, and many said they wanted a hamburger with much less fat. So in 1991 the company introduced the McLean Deluxe, a 90 percent fat-free hamburger, which failed and was removed from menus in 1994.

Breakfast

The Egg McMuffin debuted in 1973. By 1977, McDonald's was serving a complete line of breakfast sandwiches and biscuits for eating on the run. These included Egg McMuffins, Sausage McMuffins, and the Big Breakfast (eggs, hash browns, and pancakes). The company has continued to add to and change its breakfast offerings. In 2010 McDonald's introduced maple-flavored oatmeal with diced apples, raisins, cranberries, and cream on its breakfast menu, which the company has promoted as a good healthy option. However, as the *New York Times* food columnist and cookbook writer Mark Bittman pointed out: "The McDonald's product contains more sugar than a Snickers bar and only 10 fewer calories than a McDonald's cheeseburger or Egg McMuffin. (Even without the brown sugar it has more calories than a McDonald's hamburger.)" Whatever the nutrition, McDonald's has been very successful in its breakfast sales: the company generates one-fourth of its U.S. revenue from breakfast.

Problems and Issues

Despite this success, McDonald's and other large fast food chains have faced numerous problems. The most serious problems identified by managers at McDonald's were rising labor costs, the high employee turnover rate, and the lack of reliable workers. Fast food is based on low salaries for employees. To keep salaries low, McDonald's and other fast food chains have intentionally engaged in anti-union activities. In addition, companies have consistently lobbied government and legislative agencies against increased minimum wages and worker benefits. A related problem is the high turnover rate for workers experienced at many McDonald's and other fast food chains. Some McDonald's outlets' turnover rates approach 300 percent per year. In part, this is caused by the low pay workers receive and the view (instilled by the company) that employment at McDonald's is mainly part-time, so the company does not have to pay employee benefits, overtime, or increase wages for longevity of service. When McDonald's was growing quickly during the 1950s and 1960s, it had an almost inexhaustible supply of young workers owing to lack of other opportunities for employment and the baby-boom teens who came of age at that time. Teenagers were more impressionable and more manageable than older workers. When the baby-boom bulge began to decline, McDonald's was obliged to seek nontraditional workers. The company shifted from its all-male workforce and began hiring women and teenaged girls as a result of federal antidiscrimination laws and its need for good employees. Then it began hiring recent immigrants, the elderly, and those with disabilities. This has meant that more training and supervision are required. Another solution was to adopt more automation and touchscreen cash registers that made counter duty easier.

In part because of McDonald's success, the company has been criticized for a variety of issues, and it has frequently responded positively to such criticism. When the company was criticized in the 1960s for the lack of African American managers in its restaurants, McDonald's made an effort to recruit more African American franchisees. When it was charged with promoting junk food, the company began selling salads, reduced the fat content of its hamburgers, and changed the way it made its french fries.

McDonald's has been accused of causing harm to the environment, specifically for its use of polystyrene foam for its coffee cups and food containers for Big Macs and Quarter Pounders. Polystyrene is a plastic that is not easily biodegradable, and McDonald's was the world's largest purchaser of it. McDonald's responded by creating an alliance with the Environmental Defense Fund (EDF) to make McDonald's more environmentally friendly. The company switched from polystyrene to paper products and it encouraged recycling. Since 1989 McDonald's has eliminated more than 300 million pounds of packaging, recycled 1 million tons of corrugated boxes, and reduced waste by 30 percent. The collaboration between McDonald's and the EDF has continued, and it has spawned additional programs and partnerships. For instance, McDonald's requires its animal handling suppliers to pass annual animal welfare audits conducted by the EDF. McDonald's developed a scorecard with Conservation International to measure and reduce water, energy, air, and waste impacts in its bakery, beef, poultry, pork, and potato suppliers. In addition, McDonald's has purchased more than $4 billion of recycled materials for its own operations. As a result of its environmentally friendly programs, McDonald's has received a good deal of positive press coverage.

McDonald's has also been criticized for its influence on suppliers. The logic for this is simple: McDonald's is the largest purchaser of beef in the world and it has some responsibility for the practices of its suppliers. In the 1980s, for example, McDonald's was specifically charged with destroying the rainforests in Brazil because the company's suppliers in that country were reportedly burning down rainforests to create grazing land for cattle supplied to McDonald's. The company changed its suppliers (specifically refusing to purchase beef from Brazil) and has made substantial contributions to environmental groups to help save the environment. McDonald's has also been attacked for the inhumane conditions at the feedlots and slaughterhouses of some of the company's meat suppliers. For example, Eric Schlosser's *Fast Food Nation: The Dark Side of the All-American Meal* (2001) maintains that, as a result of practices followed at McDonald's and other fast food chains, meatpacking is the most dangerous job in the United States, and that practices followed by meatpackers "facilitated the introduction of deadly pathogens, such as *E. coli* 0157:H7, into America's hamburger meat." When McDonald's finally required that its ground beef be certified as safe, the company's suppliers acquired the equipment necessary for better testing.

McDonald's has also been criticized for its influence on potato growers; the company's annual orders for french fries constitute 7.5 percent of America's entire potato crop. Potential concern for genetically modified organisms (GMOs) encouraged McDonald's to state that it would no longer purchase genetically altered potatoes in the United States. Because McDonald's largely buys from local farmers, it does not use genetically modified foods in European markets owing to restrictions imposed by the European Union and national laws.

In 2010 the Physicians Committee for Responsible Medicine released an anti-McDonald's television advertisement featuring a corpse in a morgue holding a partially eaten hamburger. A McDonald's golden arch logo appears on the corpse's feet, along with the words, "I was lovin' it." A voice over says, "High cholesterol, high blood pressure, heart attacks. Tonight, make it vegetarian." Few television stations permitted the commercial to air, but the advertisement received extensive visibility in television news programs, newspapers, and the Internet. Thousands have watched it on YouTube. McDonald's, the National Restaurant Association, and others condemned the advertisement, calling it "irresponsible."

Globally, McDonald's has also been charged with causing adverse effects on local cultures and businesses. McDonald's success abroad has caused deep resentment among some people who see the company as a symbol for the United States and who believe that McDonald's expansion threatens local culinary traditions. In France, radical farmer José Bové demolished a McDonald's restaurant nearing completion, and similar actions have occurred in other European countries. McDonald's has pointed out that many of its foreign operations are locally owned and most products used in McDonald's are produced in the country where the restaurant is located.

McDonaldization

Studying McDonald's has also become a hot academic topic, and many popular works have tried to dissect its success and examine the company's influence. Among the more famous studies are George Ritzer's *The McDonaldization of Society* (1993), which examined the social effects of McDonald's in the United

States, and Benjamin Barber's *Jihad vs. McWorld* (1995), which used McDonald's as a global symbol for modernization. Dozens of other works have examined the company's worldwide impact.

In other countries, McDonald's is often viewed as an American symbol, and it has both gained and suffered as a consequence. McDonald's outlets have been trashed, bombed, and boycotted owing to policies of the U. S. government. On the other hand, at other times and in other places, McDonald's has been considered a modernizing force that has improved the local culinary conditions.

Globalization

McDonald's opened its first Canadian outlet in 1967. Its success convinced Kroc that McDonald's should aggressively expand to other countries. It has continued to expand abroad ever since. McDonald's opened its first Tokyo outlet in 1971, followed by Australia and European countries. By 1988, McDonald's had established itself as one of France's most popular fast food operations. By 1994, McDonald's maintained more than 4,500 restaurants in 73 foreign countries. Today, McDonald's has more than 30,000 restaurants in 121 countries. McDonald's operates more than 1,000 restaurants in Japan alone. The most popular restaurant in Japan, measured by volume of customers, is McDonald's. The world's largest McDonald's is operated near Red Square in Moscow, which has 900 seats and serves 40,000 people every day. As of 2010, McDonald's boasted more than 1,100 restaurants in China, half of which have drive-thru options. McDonald's plans to double this number by 2013.

McDonald's faced numerous problems when it expanded its American model abroad. The most serious was what food to serve. Selling the products in other countries that it sold in the United States just didn't work. For instance, they could not sell hamburgers in India, where the cow is considered sacred by many Hindus. So they tried a mutton burger, which was just too dry. But then they hit on a vegetarian potato-based burger, called the McAloo Tikki, and that worked. The company has been modifying its menu in other countries to meet local food preferences.

Another problem that McDonald's faced in other countries was the way customers needed to behave. In America, it is understood that customers stand in line to place their order, but this idea was not necessarily a tradition that existed in other countries. McDonald's model was based on customers paying before they received their food, which, of course, is quite the reverse in restaurants, even in the United States. Customers were also expected to eat quickly and leave so that other customers would have room to sit and eat. In other countries, eating is not necessarily a "fast" activity. Hence, McDonald's had to educate customers and it had to localize its operations.

When McDonald's opened outlets in new countries, most customers were unprepared for the experience. James L. Watson in his *Golden Arches East: McDonald's in East Asia* (1997) pointed out problems confronting McDonald's. McDonald's

---

The McDonald's Hamburger That Won't Decay

The Internet contains numerous stories about McDonald's hamburgers that were acquired months or years ago that purportedly look exactly like they did when they were bought. Many people claim that this is the case because the hamburgers are filled with preservatives and are therefore bad to eat. According to a spokesman from McDonald's, their hamburger patties are made with 100 percent beef inspected by the U.S. Department of Agriculture. Their burgers contain salt, pepper, and no preservatives or fillers. This doesn't necessarily mean that those making the claims for the non-decaying McDonald's hamburgers are wrong, because bacteria and mold only grow under certain conditions. If there is not sufficient moisture in the food itself or in the environment, hamburger will not decompose, regardless of whether it is from McDonald's, other burger chains, or the supermarket.

---

employees were trained to smile at customers, which was standard practice in the United States, but this raised suspicions in Moscow and China where it was not the custom for foodservice employees to smile. Most first-time customers had no idea of what a hamburger was or how it should be consumed. McDonald's had to expend resources to educate customers. In most countries customers easily adapted to the McDonald's experience, but in other countries McDonald's changed its procedures to fit in with local customs. In Rio de Janeiro, Brazil, McDonald's hires waiters and serves champagne along with its hamburgers. In Caracas, Venezuela, hostesses seat customers, take orders, and deliver meals. In Taiwan, Hong Kong, and Beijing customers are attracted to McDonald's because of its uniformity and egalitarian atmosphere. In Korea, employees seat customers at tables occupied by others when the restaurant is busy. However, some of McDonald's traditional practices have been rejected in some countries. For instance, the assumption that customers will eat and leave quickly has been reversed in East Asia, where many consumers have concluded that the "fast" in fast food refers to its delivery, not its lconsumption.

In addition to efficiency and reliability, McDonald's is also appreciated for its hygienic procedures and cleanliness. People in Asia with disposable income who can eat at McDonald's have now rejected street cuisine owing to the fear of food poisoning, adulteration, and unsanitary conditions. In China, Chicken McNuggets come with the traditional sauces, as well as a chili-garlic sauce. Crispy chicken wings are also a menu item. A Beijing franchise sells purple-hued taro pies, red bean sundaes, and deep-fried chicken wings. In Rome, the McDonald's sells shrimp salad, fresh-squeezed blood-orange juice, and espresso. In Morocco, the company offers the McArabia (two grilled Kofta patties, tahini sauce, lettuce, tomatoes, and onions in Arabic bread). In Canada (and in Maine), the company offers the McLobster Roll, consisting of lobster salad on a roll. In Poland, it offers a Cordon Bleu Burger (a hamburger topped with a ham-stuffed fried chicken patty and bacon). In Germany, it's the Das Nurnburger (a triple bratwurst sandwich). In Japan, it offers the Mega Tamago (a double Big Mac with an egg patty and bacon). In 2009 McDonald's in Japan created the Big American series of hamburgers, which are named for American place names, such as the Texas Burger with chili beans, bacon and a beef patty; and the Manhattan Burger, with mozzarella cheese, pastrami, and a beef patty.

Not all of its products have been successful. In Asia, outlets offered a rice burger—a meat patty sandwiched by sticky rice molded into a bun. Customers initially responded favorably to the product but later lost interest. Despite such setbacks, McDonald's is rapidly expanding abroad: 70 percent of its new restaurant openings are in other countries.

Influence

By the beginning of the twenty-first century, one out of every eight American workers had at some time been employed by McDonald's. Studies proclaim that 96 percent of Americans have visited McDonald's at least once. McDonald's serves an estimated 22 million Americans every day and has expanded even more rapidly abroad. In 1994 McDonald's operating revenues from non-U.S. sales passed the 50 percent mark. Two years later, McDonald's overtook Coca-Cola as the best-known brand in the world, and the company's golden arches symbol is recognized by more people worldwide than the Christian cross.

McDonald's has become an icon for efficient and successful business that is ingrained in popular culture throughout the world. McDonald's is the largest purchaser of beef, pork, and potatoes and the second-largest purchaser of chicken. As of 2011, McDonald's had more than 32,700 restaurants in 117 nations and territories; it is headquartered in Oak Brook, Illinois.

See also Advertising; Anti-Unionization; Architecture/Design; Automobiles; Beef; Breakfast Fast Foods; Burger King; Calories; Carhops; Carl's Jr.; Center for Science in the Public Interest (CSPI); Chains; Chicken; Chicken McNuggets; China; Coffee; Condiments; Corporate Accountability International; Corporate Charities; Drive-Ins; Drive-Thru; Efficiency; Entrepreneurs; Environment; Fat, Dietary; *Fast Food Nation*; Franchising; French Fries; Genetically Modified Food; Hamburger University; Happy Meals; Internet; Jack in the Box; Japan; Karcher, Carl N.; Ketchup; KFC; Kroc, Ray; Lawsuits; Lobbying; Marketing to Children; "McLibel"; Meatpacking Industry; Milkshakes, Malts, and Ice Cream Sodas; Movie Tie-Ins; National Restaurant Association; Nutrition; Obesity; Packaging; Physicians Committee for Responsible Medicine (PCRM); Pork; Potatoes; Ronald McDonald; Salads; Slogans/Jingles; Soda/Soft Drinks; Sodium/Salt; *Super Size Me*; Supersizing; Suppliers; Taco Bell; Teen Hangouts; Television; Toys; Transfats; Uniforms; United Kingdom; Vegetarian/Vegan

For Further Information:

Armstrong, Franny. *McLibel: Two People Who Wouldn't Say Sorry*. Oley, PA: Bullfrog Films, 2005.

Barber, Benjamin R. *Jihad vs. McWorld*. New York: Times Books, 1995.

Big Mac: Inside the McDonald's Empire. Princeton, NJ: Films for the Humanities and Sciences, 2007.

Bittman, Mark. "How to Make Oatmeal . . . Wrong." *New York Times*, February 22, 2011, as at: http://opinionator.blogs.nytimes.com/2011/02/22/how-to-make-oatmeal-wrong/?partner=rss&emc=rss

Boas, Max, and Steve Chain. *Big Mac: The Unauthorized Story of McDonald's*. New York: Mentor Books, The New American Library, 1977.

Cartensen, Laurence W. "The Burger Kingdom: Growth and Diffusion of McDonald's Restaurants in the United States, 1955–1978." In George O. Carney, ed. *Fast Food, Stock Cars, & Rock 'n' Roll: Place and Space in American Pop Culture*. Lanham, MD: Rowman & Littlefield Publishers, 1995.

Facella, Paul, and Adina M. Genn. *Everything I Know about Business I Learned at McDonald's: The 7 Leadership Principles That Drive Break -Out Success*. New York: McGraw-Hill, 2009.

Fishwick, Marshall, ed. *Ronald Revisited: The World of Ronald McDonald*. Bowling Green, OH: Bowling Green University Popular Press, 1983.

Funderburg, Anne Cooper. *Sundae Best: A History of Soda Fountains*. Bowling Green, OH: Bowling Green State University Popular Press, 2002.

Gould, William. *Business Portraits: McDonald's*. Lincoln-Wood, IL: VGM Career Horizons, 1996.

Henriques, Gary, and Audre DuVall. *McDonald's Collectibles: Identification and Value Guide*. Paducah, KY: Collector Books, nd.

Jakle, John A., and Keith A. Sculle. *Fast Food: Roadside Restaurants in the Automobile Age*. Baltimore: Johns Hopkins University Press, 1999.

Kroc, Ray, with Robert Anderson. *Grinding It Out: The Making of McDonald's*. Chicago: Henry Regnery Company, 1977.

Losonsky, Joyce, and Terry Losonsky. *McDonald's Pre-Happy Meal Toys from the Fifties, Sixties, and Seventies*. Atglen, PA: Schiffer Publishing Ltd., 1998.

Love, John F. *McDonald's: Behind the Arches*. Rev. ed. New York: Bantam Books, 1995.

McDonald's Web site: www.mcdonalds.com

Newman, Jerry M. *My Secret Life on the McJob: Lessons from Behind the Counter Guaranteed to Supersize Any Management Style*. New York: McGraw-Hill, 2007.

Ozersky, Josh. *Hamburgers: A Cultural History*. New Haven, CT: Yale University Press, 2008.

Prince, Jackie. *Launching a New Business Ethic: The Environment as a Standard Operating Procedure at McDonald's and at Other Companies*. Washington, D.C.: Environmental Defense Fund, 1991.

Ritzer, George. *The McDonaldization of Society*. Newbury Park, CA: Pine Forge Press, 1993.

Ritzer, George, ed. *McDonaldization: The Reader*. 2nd ed. Thousand Oaks, CA: Pine Forge Press, 2006.

Royle, Tony. *Working for McDonald's in Europe: The Unequal Struggle?* New York: Routledge, 2001.

Schlosser, Eric. *Fast Food Nation: The Dark Side of the All-American Meal*. New York: Houghton Mifflin Company, 2001.

Smith, Andrew F. *Hamburger: A Global History*. London: Reaktion Books, 2008.

Smith, Andrew F. *Eating History: Thirty Turning Points in the Making of American Cuisine*. New York: Columbia University Press, 2009.

Watson, James L., ed. *Golden Arches East: McDonald's in East Asia*. Stanford, CA: Stanford University Press, 1997.

Williams, Meredith. *Tomart's Price Guide to McDonald's Happy Meal Collectibles*. Rev. Dayton, OH: Tomart Publications, 1995.

"McLibel"

In 1986 the London chapter of Greenpeace, a small but active group of pacifists, anarchists, and vegetarians, targeted what it believed were the evils of McDonald's. It distributed a six-page leaflet titled "What's wrong with McDonald's? Everything you don't want to know," which accused the company of promoting poverty, selling unhealthy food, exploiting workers and children, torturing animals, and destroying the Amazon rainforests. It included such statements as "[McDonald's used] lethal poisons to destroy vast areas of Central American rainforests." Members of London's Greenpeace distributed the flyer for four years, often in front of McDonald's outlets. In 1989 McDonald's infiltrated Greenpeace by hiring detectives to determine who was responsible for the leaflet and its distribution. Based on this information, McDonald's issued writs against five members for distributing the leaflet, which the company claimed was libelous.

Libel laws in the United Kingdom require defendants to prove in court the truth of their statements. McDonald's had previously used British libel laws to silence its critics. During the 1980s, for example, it threatened to sue British publications and organizations, which prompted retractions and apologies from the press. The cost of losing a libel case (legal fees and damages) can be huge. Three of the accused Greenpeace activists appeared in court and apologized to McDonald's. The other two, Helen Steel and Dave Morris, decided to defend themselves. They were not given any legal help from the court, but they were assisted by the Haldane Society of Socialist Lawyers on a pro bono basis. This David-and-Goliath fight was dubbed "McLibel." As news of it spread, the British media seized upon it and often the trial ended up as frontpage news. Steel and Morris received help from a large numbers of volunteers, some of whom formed the McLibel

Support Campaign to assist the defendants with research. The trial began in March 1994 and continued for three years, becoming the longest-running trial in British history.

It also was a public relations disaster for McDonald's, which was required to defend itself regarding its labor, marketing, environmental, nutrition, food safety, and animal welfare practices. Steel and Morris forced the company's top executives to testify for days. In the midst of the testimony, it came out that McDonald's had spied on the defendants before and after the company had sued them and that Scotland Yard had supplied information to McDonald's. The McSpotlight Web site covered the trial and McDonald's alleged worldwide abuses. E-mail and press releases were sent out and "Days of Action" were held around the world protesting McDonald's. The original leaflet was translated into twenty-seven different languages and, since 1990, an estimated 3 million copies have been handed out.

In the final judgment, Morris and Steel were found to have libeled McDonald's and were fined £60,000. The judge stated that most of the Greenpeace charges were unproven, but he did find that McDonald's had exploited children, endangered the health of its customers, paid workers extremely low wages, and opposed union activity. He also found that the company did bear responsibility for the cruelty inflicted upon animals by many of its suppliers.

Morris and Steel appealed the decision and sued Scotland Yard. On March 31, 1999, the Court of Appeals overruled parts of the original "McLibel" verdict, supporting the leaflet's assertion that eating McDonald's food can cause heart disease and that McDonald's employees were treated badly. The Court of Appeals reduced the damages to £40,000. Steel and Morris refused to pay and appealed the case to the British House of Lords, which refused to hear it. In 2000 Morris and Steel filed an appeal with the European Court of Human Rights, challenging the verdict and stating that the trial breached their right to a fair trial and their right to freedom of expression. In June 2004 the European Court of Human Rights declared their claim to be admissible, and in February 2005 the court held that Steel's and Morris's rights of free expression had been violated because they had not been given legal aid and, therefore, had been denied a fair trial. The decision was nonbinding. A documentary film titled *McLibel* was released in 2005 based on the story.

See also Environment; Exploitation; Lawsuits; McDonalds; Nutrition; Vegetarian/Vegan

For Further Information:

McLibel. DVD, 2005.

McSpotlight Web site: www.mcspotlight.org

Schlosser, Eric. *Fast Food Nation: The Dark Side of the All-American Meal.* New York: Houghton Mifflin Company, 2001.

Vidal, John. *McLibel: Burger Culture on Trial.* New York: The New Press, 1997.

Meatpacking Industry

The first major exposé of the meatpacking industry was in the novel titled *The Jungle*, written by Upton Sinclair. It was released in 1906, a few months before Congress voted on the passage of the Pure Food and Drug Act. Many observers at the time believed that its publication helped ensure passage of the act. The act created what would become the Food and Drug Administration (FDA), which has been charged with the task of ensuring that the nation's food supply is safe. Simultaneous with the passage of this act was the passage of the Meat Inspection Act, which empowered federal inspectors in the U.S. Department of Agriculture to examine animals before and after slaughter, to be present when diseased animals are destroyed, and to inspect processed products for dangerous chemicals, preservatives, or dyes. In addition, no meat that had not been inspected could be shipped across state lines. Rules and regulations were established for meatpacking; inspectors examined meatpacking plants to ensure compliance. During the following seventy years, the meatpacking industry gradually improved, and by the 1960s meatpackers were among the highest-paid industrial workers in the United States.

Beginning in the 1960s, however, the industry began to feel the brunt of the fast food revolution. Fast food operators mainly developed menus based on beef and chicken. Large chains pressured meatpackers for uniform products that tasted the same regardless of where they were produced. This fundamentally affected how cattle and chickens were raised, slaughtered, and processed. It also encouraged consolidation in the meatpacking industry, such that there are now only thirteen major meatpackers in America.

The fast food chains were so large that they used their purchasing power to negotiate among meatpackers for the lowest possible price. To compete, meatpackers lowered wages, decreased training, and reduced safety requirements. They also had to increase the volume of meat processed. Therefore, lines that once processed two hundred head of cattle per hour were sped up to handle three or four hundred per hour. Increased volume, even with decreased price, meant increased profits for meatpacking companies. It also meant installing new equipment that scraped bones for the maximum output of meat. In scraping bones, small fragments of bone came off, as well as pieces of spinal columns, with their potential for spreading Mad Cow disease. Hygiene declined and injuries to workers increased. As a consequence, the meatpacking occupation became one of the most dangerous jobs in the United States. In addition, vast shifts in the amount of meat processed have meant that the industry has become more prone to the introduction of pathogens, such as *Salmonella* and *Escherichia coli* 0157:H7, than in the past.

In 1982 the entire industry was deregulated by President Reagan. The unions that represented workers at meatpackers were busted and strikebreakers (mainly migrant workers from Mexico) were brought in to operate the slaughterhouses and meat-processing facilities. Pressure from fast food chains for lower prices resulted in sharply lower costs for raising animals and a vast increase in the speed of the slaughtering and butchering. Today, the meatpacking industry has some of the lowest-paid jobs in America.

The meat industry has continually lobbied against regulations for food safety. The FDA cannot order meatpacking companies to remove contaminated meat from fast food kitchens or supermarket shelves. In addition, the meatpacking industry has supported so-called veggie laws, which forbid defaming agricultural products. For comments about beef that Oprah Winfrey made on her television show, she was sued by cattle ranchers in a Texas court. She won the case but the meatpacking industry proved that it has the ability to threaten critics with expensive lawsuits. The Occupational Safety and Health Administration (OSHA) is authorized to levy fines on noncompliant meatpackers, but the maximum fine for a human death is $70,000, which is not a great burden for meatpackers who are making millions of dollars a year. However, McDonald's is the largest purchaser of beef and the company has the ability to influence meatpackers' practices. For example, when McDonald's demanded that its ground beef be certified to be free of lethal pathogens, meatpacker suppliers had to purchase microbial testing equipment.

See also Escherichia coli; *Fast Food Nation*; Food and Drug Administration (FDA); Foodborne Illnesses; Mad Cow Disease; McDonald's; Occupational Safety and Health Administration (OSHA); *Salmonella*; U.S. Department of Agriculture

For Further Information:

Lee, Paula Young, ed. *Meat, Modernity, and the Rise of the Slaughterhouse*. Durham, NH: University of New Hampshire Press; Hanover: published by University Press of New England, 2008.

Nierenberg, Danielle. *Happier Meals: Rethinking the Global Meat Industry*. Washington, D.C.: Worldwatch Institute, 2005.

Schlosser, Eric. *Fast Food Nation: The Dark Side of the All-American Meal*. New York: Houghton Mifflin Company, 2001.

Memoirs

Memoirs have been written by many fast food innovators. The first to do so was Billy Ingram, the promoter of White Castle, America's first fast food chain. His purpose in writing *All This from a 5-Cent Hamburger! The Story of the White Castle System* (1964) was to set the historical record straight. By 1964, when the book was published, Billy Ingram was in the twilight of his life and his famed White Castle chain was only a bit player in the rapidly growing drama of the fast food business. Ingram tried to make the case that he had established the model for the industry, and indeed he had.

Many others in the fast food industry followed in Ingram's footsteps, not only as inheritors of his system for making hamburgers but also as writers (usually with collaborators) of their own memoirs. Harland Sanders had sold his Kentucky Fried Chicken business ten years prior to the release of his memoirs, *Life as I Have Known It Has Been Finger Lickin' Good* (1974). It was part inspirational—how someone without an education (he only finished sixth grade) could make it to the pinnacle of business success in America, and his greatest success, the founding of KFC, was not achieved until after his sixty-fifth birthday. Sanders told his story in a humorous and engaging way.

Three years later, Ray Kroc published his memoirs, *Grinding It Out: The Making of McDonald's* (1977). It told of his early life and his relationship with Richard and Maurice McDonald. Kroc brags about the fact that when the brothers finally agreed to sell McDonald's to Kroc, they had insisted in keeping their original restaurant in San Bernardino, California, but when he launched a McDonald's hamburger outlet across the street from the brothers' restaurant, he ran them out of business. The book was collaboratively written by Robert Anderson, who would also collaborate on an autobiography with Tom Monaghan (the founder of Pizza Hut) titled *Pizza Tiger* (1986).

In most cases, autobiographies were promotion pieces written by others to advertise their businesses and settle old scores. Wally Amos, in collaboration with Leroy Robinson, published his *Famous Amos Story: The Face That Launched a Thousand Chips* (1983) while his business was floundering. In 1984 Famous Amos was taken over by investors and Wally Amos became an employee of the company. This did not work out, so he engaged in other businesses. To tell of these terrible experiences, he wrote another memoir, in collaboration with Camilla Denton, *The Man with No Name* (1994).

Chocolate chip mogul Debbi Fields (founder of Mrs. Fields) and the editors of Time-Life Books promoted business by writing two partly autobiographical books that were also sold as a cookbook: *Mrs. Fields Cookie Book: 100 Recipes from the Kitchen of Mrs. Fields.* This was so successful that she published a second cookbook after she had sold her business.

Dave Thomas, founder of Wendy's, published three books. His first two, *Dave's Way: A New Approach to Old-Fashioned Success* (1991) and *Dave Says—Well Done! The Common Guy's Guide to Everyday Success* (1994), were partly autobiographical, partly instructive, and partly promotional for Wendy's. His third book, written in collaboration with Michael Seid, was *Franchising for Dummies* (2000) and was intended to offer advice for prospective franchisees. Likewise, Carl Karcher, founder of Carl's Jr., published *Never Stop Dreaming: The Story of Carl Karcher Enterprises* (1991), which was mainly a promotional book for his business enterprise. It was written in collaboration with B. Carolyn Knight, who wrote another promotional book, *Making It Happen: The Story of Carl Karcher Enterprises*, that was published by the firm.

Three unusual books were penned by "Ronald L. McDonald," the fictitious mascot for McDonald's. The first book, *The Complete Hamburger: The History of America's Favorite Sandwich* (1997), includes a history of the company along with a myth-filled history of the hamburger. The second book, *Ronald McDonald's Franchise Buyers Guide: How to Buy a Fast Food Franchise* (2003), was targeted at those interested in buying McDonald's franchises. The third book, *Ronald McDonald's International Burger Book* (2004), adopted an international slant for a company that generated more revenue from its outlets in other countries than it did in the United States.

Many more have been published: George Cohon's *To Russia with Fries* (1997) describes how he set up McDonald's in Russia after the Berlin Wall fell in 1989; James W. McLamore's *The Burger King: Jim McLamore and the Building of an Empire* (1998) was published posthumously, more than thirty years after he sold the company to the Pillsbury Company; and Tony Conza's *Success: It's a Beautiful Thing. Lessons on Life and Business from the Founder of Blimpie International* (2000) offers sage advice and lots of personal anecdotes.

Compared to the fast food world, few memoirs have been written by those who helped make the junk food world. An exception was Orville Redenbacher, who published his *Orville Redenbacher's Popcorn Book* (1984) ten years after he sold his business to Hunt-Wesson. Other founders of the snack food industry, such as Frank Mars, Forrest Mars, and Milton S. Hershey, preferred anonymity.

See also Advertising; Blimpie International; Burger King; Carl's, Jr.; Chicken; Famous Amos; Hamburger; Hershey, Milton S.; Karcher, Carl N.; KFC; Kroc, Ray; Mars, Forrest; Mars, Frank; Mascot; McDonald's; Monaghan, Tom; Mrs. Fields Famous Brands; Pillsbury; Pizza Hut; Redenbacher, Orville; Ronald McDonald; Thomas, Dave; Wendy's; White Castle

For Further Information:

Amos, Wally, with Leroy Robinson. *The Famous Amos Story: The Face That Launched a Thousand Chips*. Garden City, NY: Doubleday, 1983.

Amos, Wally, with Camilla Denton. *The Man with No Name: Turn Lemons into Lemonade*. Lower Lake, CA: Aslan Publishers, 1994.

Conza, Tony. *Success: It's a Beautiful Thing: Lessons on Life and Business from the Founder of Blimpie International*. New York: Wiley, 2000.

Ingram, Billy. *All This from a 5-Cent Hamburger! The Story of the White Castle System*. New York: Newcomen Society in North America, 1964.

Karcher, Carl, and B. Carolyn Knight, *Never Stop Dreaming: The Story of Carl Karcher Enterprises*. San Marcos, CA: Robert Erdmann Publishing, 1991.

Kroc, Ray, with Robert Anderson, *Grinding It Out: The Making of McDonald's*. Chicago: Henry Regnery Company, 1977.

McDonald, Ronald L. *The Complete Hamburger: The History of America's Favorite Sandwich*. Secaucus, NJ: Carol Publishing Group, 1997.

McDonald, Ronald L. *Ronald McDonald's International Burger Book*. Tucson, AZ: Hats Off Books, 2004.

McLamore, James W. *The Burger King: Jim McLamore and the Building of an Empire*. New York: McGraw-Hill, 1998.

Monaghan, Tom, with Robert Anderson. *Pizza Tiger*. New York: Random House, 1986.

Redenbacher, Orville. *Orville Redenbacher's Popcorn Book*. New York: St. Martin's Press, 1984.

Sanders, Harland. *Life as I Have Known It Has Been Finger Lickin' Good*. Carol Stream, IL: Creation House, 1974.

Thomas, R. David. *Dave's Way: A New Approach to Old-Fashioned Success*. New York: G. P. Putnam's Sons, 1991.

Thomas, R. David. *Dave Says—Well Done! The Common Guy's Guide to Everyday Success*. Grand Rapids, MI: Zondervan, 1994.

Menu Labeling

The Nutrition Labeling and Education Act of 1990 required that nutrition labels be placed on food products, but it exempted restaurants from the requirement of placing nutritional labels on their menus. In 2004 the Food and Drug Administration's (FDA) Obesity Working Group report, "Calories Count," recommended providing nutritional information, such as calorie counts, in restaurants. The FDA funded the Keystone Center in Washington, D.C., a not-for-profit research organization, to review the status of nutritional information in chain restaurants. In 2006 the Keystone Center gave their report, "Calories Count," which concluded that while about one-half of chain restaurants did have such information, it was presented in such a way in most restaurants that it was unlikely to be seen. Preliminary studies indicated that menu labeling did lead to small reductions in the number of calories people consumed, especially when the labeling included a statement referring to a recommended intake of two thousand calories per day.

New York City required menu labeling in chains with more than fifteen stores in 2006, although owing to opposition by the New York Restaurant Association, the requirement did not go into effect until 2008. California, Maine, and Oregon passed similar legislation, as did many other cities and communities. Some required restaurant chains to publically list the fat content and number of calories contained in each food item. Some evidence from these communities indicated that restaurants reduced the number of calories in some items, and at least some customers used this information to reduce the number of calories they consumed while eating in these restaurants.

In 2010 the U.S. Congress passed the Patient Protection and Affordable Care Act, signed into law March 23, 2010; it includes a provision that created a national, uniform nutrition-disclosure standard for restaurants. It requires chain restaurants, drive-thrus, convenience stores such as 7-Eleven, and vending machines and retail stores—with twenty or more locations—to post nutrition information in plain sight. Stores must also display "a succinct statement concerning suggested daily caloric intake." The FDA is preparing the standards and they go into effect in 2011. These federal standards replace the differing regulations and laws that a growing number of cities, counties, and states have passed over the past few years.

The effectiveness of menu labeling in reducing the consumption of junk food at fast food restaurants has been questioned. A University of Washington study published in 2010 found that when parents were provided with calorie information they chose about one hundred calories fewer per meal for their 3- to 6-year-old children, compared with parents who didn't have that information. Yet several other studies suggest no impact on calorie consumption from menu labeling. TacoTime, a Mexican American–themed fast food restaurant chain, placed nutritional information (calories, fat, and sodium) at all of its 350 outlets. A study published in the *American Journal for Preventive Medicine* found that menu labeling at TacoTime did not promote healthier food-purchasing behavior in one restaurant before and after the menu labeling went into effect. Another study published in *Health Affairs* found that menus with calorie counts made little difference in the choices low-income people made in KFC, McDonald's, Burger King, and Wendy's restaurants in New York and New Jersey. The lead researcher in the study, Brian Elbel, concluded "that labeling is not likely to be enough to influence obesity in a large scale way. Other public policy approaches, as well as the efforts of food companies and other actors, will be needed."

See also Convenience Stores; Drive-Thrus; Food and Drug Administration (FDA); Food Labeling; Obesity; 7-Eleven; Vending Machines

For Further Information:

Anyone's Guess: The Need for Nutrition Labeling at Fast-Food and Other Chain Restaurants. Washington, D.C.: Center for Science in the Public Interest, November 2003.

Calories Count: Report of the Working Group on Obesity. Washington, D.C.: Food and Drug Administration, 2004.

Elbel, Brian, Rogan Kersh, Victoria L. Brescoll, and L. Beth Dixon. "Calorie Labeling and Food Choices: A First Look at the Effects on Low-Income People in New York City." *Health Affairs* 28, no. 6 (2009): w1110–w1121.

Farley, Thomas A., Anna Caffarelli, Mary T. Bassett, Lynn Silver, and Thomas R. Frieden. "New York City's Fight over Calorie Labeling." *Health Affairs* 28, no. 6 (2009): w1098–w1109.

Finkelstein, Eric A., et al. "Mandatory Menu Labeling in One Fast-Food Chain in King County, Washington." *American Journal for Preventive Medicine* 40 (February 2011): 122–27.

Keystone Forum on Away-From-Home Foods: Opportunities for Preventing Weight Gain and Obesity Final Report. Washington, D.C.: Keystone Center, 2006, as at: keystone. org/files/file/about/publications/Forum_Report_FINAL_5-30-06.pdf

Larson, Nicole, and Mary Story. *Menu Labeling: Does Providing Nutrition Information at the Point of Purchase Affect Consumer Behavior?* Princeton, NJ: Robert Wood Johnson Foundation, June 2009.

Menus

Fast food chains initially offered no-frills menus. During the 1920s, White Castle and its imitators served only hamburgers, coffee, soda, and pie. Hamburgers composed of fried ground beef in a bun were easy and fast to prepare, and required little space to store. A limited menu was easier to prepare, required limited skills, and meant that preparation and service could be sped up. In addition, simple menus made it easy for fast food chains to order food from suppliers. Large orders for beef, buns, and potatoes gave the fast food chain corporations the power to set quality standards and seek the lowest possible prices from suppliers.

During the 1930s, a few new items were tried but menus generally remained limited. This changed during World War II, owing to wartime restrictions, such as rationing of beef and sugar. Because there were no restrictions on eggs, White Castle tried to replace hamburgers with egg sandwiches, but they were not successful. There was also no restriction on potatoes, so french fries became an important part of fast food menus, only to be discontinued after the war owing to hazards associated with the deep-frying equipment at the time. When the equipment improved during the 1950s, french fries were again added to the menus.

During the 1950s, the McDonald's menu was also highly restricted: hamburgers, cheeseburgers, sodas, shakes, and french fries. Other fast food chains, such as pizza parlors, fried chicken establishments, and hot dog purveyors, had similarly limited their menus. Burger King broke out of the mold when it introduced the Whopper in 1956. Its success encouraged McDonald's to introduce Big Macs and Quarter Pounders.

During the 1960s, Burger King and McDonald's added large dining areas, and fast food chains began to expand their menus. Another innovation, drive-thru windows, required the addition of items that could be consumed easily in the car, such as Chicken McNuggets, Chicken Tenders, and Chicken Fingers. During the 1970s, fast food chains added breakfast items to their menus, such as McDonald's Egg McMuffin and Burger King's Croissant Breakfast Sandwiches, French Toast Sticks, and Cini-Minis.

In 1973 Burger Chef added children's food to its menu. The chain was not successful, but McDonald's introduced child-oriented Happy Meals in 1978; other fast food chains did likewise. Studies of children's menus at Burger King, KFC, Wendy's, Taco Bell, and Pizza Hut demonstrated that children's menus exceeded dietary recommendations in fat and calories.

Other menu innovations included so-called value meals, consisting of a preselected combination of foods such as hamburgers, french fries, and sodas. Customers order by the value meal number; this encourages customers to purchase more than they might if they just selected individual items. It also makes it easier and less time consuming for the order taker and the person assembling the orders. Value meals led to another menu innovation, supersizing, which included extremely large portions of specific items such as french fries and sodas, and their inclusion in meal combinations.

Beginning in the 1980s, some restaurant chains added ethnic touches to their menus (e.g., McDonald's added its Breakfast Burrito). When fast food came under attack for being a junk food, salads, salad bars, carrot sticks, fat-free bran muffins, and low-fat milkshakes were added to many menus.

An unusual menu variation has been developed by In-N-Out Burger. It has a very simple public menu consisting of hamburgers, fries, sodas, and milkshakes. It also offers what it calls "secret menu" options, which are listed on its Web site, with all sorts of special variations on the basic menu. For instance, a "2x4" hamburger consists of two meat patties and four slices of cheese; "Animal Fries" include cheese and grilled onions with french fries; and a "Neapolitan Shake" is a combination of chocolate, vanilla, and strawberry.

The launching of fast food restaurants in other countries necessitated changing menus to exclude items that might offend local sensibilities (such as beef hamburgers in India), and adding items intended to attract locals. Thus, beer and frankfurters are served at McDonald's in Germany; wine is served in France; chilled yogurt drinks are offered in Turkey; and espresso coffee, pasta, and Mediterranean Salad are on the menu in Italy. In India, Veggie Burgers, Chicken Maharaja, Pizza McPuff, and cold coffee are offered. Teriyaki McBurgers are on the menu in Japan, Taiwan, and Hong Kong; and Samurai Pork Burgers are served in Thailand. A burger with a fried egg and beetroot, called the Kiwi Burger, is a big item in New Zealand, and grilled salmon sandwiches, called McLaks, are served in Norway. The McNifica, a hamburger sandwich with cheese, is on the menu in Argentina, and the McPepper is sold in Singapore. Customers in Athens can order a Greek Mac made with pita bread, beef patties, and a yogurt sauce.

Not all menu innovations have proven successful. In 2002 the McDonald's outlets in Norway released the McAfrika Burger, which supposedly had a "taste of Africa." At the time, South Africa was in the midst of disasters—heavy floods, drought, and finally starvation. Protesters complained that McDonald's should not have been profiting from a name when there were millions of people starving.

During the past fifty years, fast food menus have shifted from being simple and inexpensive (catering mainly to families and the working class) to being highly complex and occasionally costly, depending on location.

See also Breakfast Fast Foods; Burger King; Chicken; Chicken McNuggets; Chocolate; Croissants; French Fries; Hamburger; Happy Meals; Hot Dog; In-N-Out Burger; KFC; McDonald's; Milkshakes, Malts, and Ice Cream Sodas; Pizza Hut; Sandwiches; Soda/Soft Drinks; Sugars/Sweeteners; Supersizing; Suppliers; White Castle

For Further Information:

Schlosser, Eric. *Fast Food Nation The Dark Side of the All-American Meal.* New York: Houghton Mifflin Company, 2001.

Schlosser, Eric, and Charles Wilson. *Chew On This: Everything You Don't Want to Know about Fast Food.* Boston: Houghton Mifflin, 2006.

Mexican American Food

Mexican food has been consumed in the United States ever since the American annexation of Texas in 1845 and the American conquest of California and the Southwest in 1848. Mexican food, such as tamales, enchiladas, beans, and later tacos, was frequently served by street vendors in cities of the Southwest. To make them more appealing to Anglo tastes, Mexican foods were adapted in America. The taco was the staple of Cal-Mex food. Mexican tacos are basically any food rolled, folded, or fried into tortillas that are consumed by hand. The various fillings for tacos include chili sauce, beef (shredded or ground), chicken, pork, chorizo or sausage, egg, tomato, cheese, lettuce, guacamole, onions, and refried beans. Mexican tacos are usually soft shelled, unlike the U-shaped, crisp fried tortillas served in many American Mexican restaurants and fast food outlets.

Although avocados were grown in Florida during the early twentieth century, it was in California that their use took off. After World War II, corn chips and potato chips were recommended as guacamole dippers, but the potato chips were soon replaced solely by corn chips.

The burrito became irreversibly linked to the tortilla-rolled packages. Burritos entered Mexican American cuisine in the Southwest around the 1950s and went nationwide a decade later. Many so-called Mexican dishes were concocted to please the American palate. Leftover tortillas could easily be cut up and used to scoop up sauces, beans, and other foods. Nachos, for instance, originated in a Mexican border restaurant catering to Americans. They quickly spread throughout Texas, where they were served at a concession stand at the Texas State Fair in Dallas in 1964. Within two decades, nachos were served nationwide in stadiums, airports, and fast food establishments.

The success of corn chips can be attributed in part to the related popularity of salsas, which are generally composed of various combinations of chili peppers, tomatoes, herbs, and spices. Salsa has been around since the time of the Aztecs. The first known manufacturer of salsa was Pace Foods of San Antonio, Texas. Dave Pace experimented with bottling salsa in 1947 and finally succeeded in getting the formula right the following year. Pace's initial market was regional. Other salsa products were produced by Old El Paso and Ortega. During the 1970s, salsa sales skyrocketed and Pace became the largest producer of Mexican sauces. The fresh salsa market exploded during the 1980s and continued to increase during the following decade. By the 1990s, salsa outsold ketchup in the United States. Consumption of these quasi-Mexican products was abetted by the American mania for salty snack food. Fritos, potato chips, Doritos, and tortilla chips spurred supermarket sales of salsa and spicy dips, which in turn created a core of consumers willing to try more authentic Mexican food.

Thus, another significant type of commercialization was the establishment of Mexican fast food. Several small fast food operators established multiunit, drive-in outlets near Los Angeles. Small Mexican American roadside restaurants were often called taco stands. The first Mexican fast food franchise was launched in Downey, California, in 1962 by Glen Bell. Taco Bell quickly expanded around Los Angeles, and in 1978 Taco Bell sold out to PepsiCo. Taco Bell had numerous imitators, but it did not stray too far from the traditional American palate. The historian Harvey Levenstein attributes its success to being "no more spicy or un-American tasting than hamburgers." Still, Taco Bell had to overcome vast distrust and prejudice from consumers against Mexican restaurants, and it had to emphasize that these were *American* restaurants that happened to serve somewhat-Mexican ethnic food; Taco Bell changed its symbol from a sleeping Mexican in a sombrero to an innocuous pastel-colored mission bell. In terms of profit and popularity, tacos and other Mexican foods pale in comparison to pizza and other Italian foods. Other regional chains include Del Taco (Barstow, California), Taco Bueno (Abilene, Texas), Taco Time (Eugene, Oregon), Taco John's (Wyoming), Taco Maker (Ogden, Utah), Taco Casa (Topeka, Kansas), Pepe's (Chicago), and Pedro's Fine Mexican Foods (Mississippi).

Many new Mexican-style fast-casual restaurants have also opened. These include Chipotle Mexican Grill, Rubio's Fresh Mexican Grill, and Qdoba Mexican Grill.

See also Burrito; Chicken; Chipotle Mexican Grill; Condiments; Del Taco; Pork; Qdoba Mexican Grill; Quesadillas; Rubio's Fresh Mexican Grill; Taco Bell; Taco Bueno; Tacos

For Further Information:

Gabaccia, Donna R. *We Are What We Eat: Ethnic Food and the Making of Americans*. Cambridge, MA: Harvard University Press, 1998.

Guenther, Keith J. "The Development of the Mexican-American Cuisine." In Alan Davidson, ed. *Oxford Symposium 1981: National & Regional Styles of Cookery. Proceedings*. London: Prospect Books, 1981.

Levenstein, Harvey. *Paradox of Plenty: A Social History of Eating in Modern America*. New York: Oxford University Press, 1993.

Pillsbury, Richard. *No Foreign Food: The American Diet in Time and Place*. Boulder, CO: Westview Press, 1998.

Smith, Andrew F. "Tacos, Enchiladas and Refried Beans: The Invention of Mexican-American Cookery." In Mary Wallace Kelsey and ZoeAnn Holmes, eds., *Cultural and Historical Aspects of Foods*. Corvallis: Oregon State University, 1999, 183–203; also at: http://food.oregonstate.edu/ref/culture/latinamerica/la_smith.html

Mexico

American junk food began to appear in Mexico in the early twentieth century. Kellogg began selling Corn Flakes in Mexico in 1922. In 1950 the company opened a production facility there and expanded their range of products, including Coco

---

El Pollo Loco

While there are many Mexican-style restaurant chains in the United States, only one originated in Mexico. El Pollo Loco began as a roadside chicken stand in Guasave on Mexico's Pacific Coast. In 1980, it opened its first outlet in the United States in Los Angeles.

Puffs, Eggos, and Froot Loops. Coca-Cola opened up bottle plants in Mexico during the 1920s, but it wasn't until the 1960s that other junk food companies began to operate there. Tootsie Roll Industries, for instance, opened a subsidiary in Mexico, where their candy became known as "Tutsi." It was advertised on Televisa, Mexico's largest TV network, beginning in 1968.

Fast Food

American fast food operations in Mexico had many problems to overcome. Church's Chicken opened its first restaurant in 1979, followed by McDonald's in 1985. McDonald's, with its corporate emphasis on maintaining quality and consistency among its restaurants, faced serious supply chain problems. Owing to the large number of outlets in the United States, most supply centers for outlets are within one hundred miles. In Mexico, the distance was closer to one thousand miles, even with considerable local sourcing. Mexico, however, does not grow the type of potatoes that McDonald's needed; these had to be imported from the United States if McDonald's were to sell its flagship french fries. These problems were resolved and currently McDonald's has more than two hundred outlets in Mexico.

McDonald's has had to change its menu in its Mexican outlets, as well. Items include: Cuernito con Jamon y Queso (Ham and Cheese Crossaint); Ensalada Pechuga Empanizada (Breaded Chicken Breast Salad); Hamburguesa Pechuga Grill (Grilled Chicken Breast Hamburger); McNifica (beef patty with cheese, pickle, onion, tomato, lettuce, mayonnaise, ketchup, and mustard on a regular bun); and Yogur con Frutas (Yogurt and Fruit).

When Taco Bell opened its first outlets in Mexico in 1992, a company spokesperson announced, "We don't think of ourselves as making Mexican food. We think of ourselves as making Taco Bell food." It comes as no surprise that Taco Bell restaurants failed and were closed in 1994. The company tried again in 2007, but only after changing many of their products. The Taco Bell hard-shell taco served in the United States, for instance, was not competitive with the tacos served in Mexico's taquerias (taco stands/shops). When Taco Bell opened its outlet in 2007, it changed the name of this product from "taco" to "tacostada," a made-up word that combined "taco" with "tostada." The company also offered new items on their menus—eggs "à la Mexicana"—and even handed out packets of jalapeno sauce with its hamburgers. They failed and the outlets were closed in 2010.

It wasn't until after the passage of the North American Free Trade Association (NAFTA) in 1994 that American fast food had much of an influence on Mexico. Since NAFTA was signed, American fast food chains have expanded, including McDonald's, Burger King, KFC, Subway, and Pizza Hut. One of the more successful American chains has been Starbucks, which has more than 150 stores in Mexico.

Junk Food

Likewise, American junk foods are now sold in Mexico. Hershey, which traditionally was not successful in selling its products outside of the United States, now has operations in Mexico owing to NAFTA. Frito-Lay's Cheetos and other junk foods have also been successful in Mexico.

NAFTA also made it possible for American junk foods to be economically manufactured in Mexico and shipped to the United States. Besides lower labor costs in Mexico, sugar (a major ingredient in junk foods) is also less expensive because the United States has high federal price supports to protect domestic sugar beet growers. Mexico has no such price supports, and the cost of sugar in Mexico is about half that of the United States. In addition, many fast food facilities have been established in Mexico. Guacamole, for instance, is made in Mexico and shipped to the United States for sale in fast food chains.

In 1998 Starbucks began partnering with Conservation International, a nonprofit organization, to develop a plan to responsibly source coffee from the Chiapas region of Mexico. The result was fair trade coffee, which Starbucks offered as one of its options in 2003.

Obesity

Obesity rates in Mexico have soared during the past thirty years. This is especially true among Mexican youth. Mexico now ranks behind the United States as the world's second-largest obese nation. Mexican authorities have blamed junk food and they have begun a major effort to ban it from their schools. Some observers have blamed American fast food and junk food for the rise in obesity. They point out that McDonald's fries more than eight thousand tons of potatoes every year in Mexico. The main cause, though, claimed Antonio Villa Romero of the medical faculty at the National Autonomous University of Mexico, is the consumption of sugar-added soft drinks.

Bimbo Bakeries

Bimbo Bakeries USA, a subsidiary of Mexico's Grupo Bimbo, has acquired a number of American brands, such as Entenmann's and Thomas's English Muffins. In 2010 the company acquired Sara Lee's North American bakery brand.

See also Burger King; Church's Chicken; Coca-Cola Company; Coffee; Entenmann's; Frito-Lay; McDonald's; North American Free Trade Association (NAFTA); PepsiCo; Pizza Hut; El Pollo Loco; Sara Lee; Soda/Soft Drinks; Starbucks; Subway; Taco Bell; Tacos

For Further Information:

Dairy Queen (Mexico) Web site: www.dairyqueen.com.mx

Kellogg Company (Mexico) Web site: www.kelloggs.com.mx

El Pollo Web site (Mexico): elpolloloco.com.mx

Middle East

American junk food and fast food have made inroads into Islamic countries and other nations with large Muslim populations. In the Middle East, both McDonald's and Burger King have opened franchises in many countries. Hamburger chains follow halal dietary laws. McDonald's offers the McArabia, consisting of two grilled Kofta patties, tahini sauce, lettuce, tomatoes, and onions in Arabic bread.

American hamburger franchises in the Middle East have had their ups and downs, depending upon political events. Shortly after the Iraq war in 1992, in which American-led military forces liberated Kuwait, McDonald's opened a restaurant in Kuwait and the line of cars waiting to get in was seven miles long. In other Middle Eastern countries, American-associated hamburger outlets have been vandalized and firebombed. Fast food represents a lifestyle very different from that desired by many Muslims in the Middle East.

Other fast food chains that have outlets in the Middle East include Baskin-Robbins, Cinnabon, Dunkin' Donuts, Johnny Rockets, Quiznos, and many more.

See also Baskin-Robbins, Burger King; Cinnabon; Dunkin' Donuts; Halal; Hamburger; Israel; Johnny Rockets; McDonald's; Quiznos

For Further Information:

Barber, Benjamin R. *Jihad vs. McWorld*. New York: Ballantine Books, 1996.

Mike and Ike

Mike and Ike candies were first manufactured in 1940 by Just Born of Bethlehem, Pennsylvania. The original Mike and Ike was a chewy, fruit-flavored candy. Early flavors included Root-T-Toot (root beer) and Jack and Jill (licorice). In 1953 Just Born acquired the Rodda Candy Company, one of whose specialties was making jelly beans. With this technology, Just Born was able to create additional types of fruit-flavored Mike and Ike candies. During the late twentieth century, the company

Mike and Ike candy. (AP/Wide World Photos)

began manufacturing stronger flavors, such as their Tropical Fruits and Berry Fruits. These were followed by Tropical Typhoon, Berry Blast, and Tangy Twister. Unlike most other large candy companies, Just Born remains family owned.

See also Candy; Jelly Beans; Just Born; Licorice

For Further Information:

Just Born Web site: www.justborn.com

Richardson, Tim. *Sweets: A History of Candy*. New York: Bloomsbury, 2002.

Milk Duds

Introduced in 1926 by the Halloway Company of Chicago, Milk Duds are small pieces of caramel candy covered with chocolate, packaged in a small cardboard box. They were supposed to be round, but they ended up oval shaped, hence their name—duds. Milk Duds are commonly sold in movie theaters and in grocery stores. The company was sold to Beatrice Foods Company in 1960, which was then merged with the D. L. Clark Company, makers of the Clark Bar. Today, Milk Duds are manufactured by the New England Confectionery Company (NECCO).

See also Candy; Caramels; Chocolate; Movie Theaters; New England Confectionery Company (NECCO)

For Further Information:

Broekel, Ray. *The Great America Candy Bar Book*. Boston: Houghton Mifflin Company, 1982.

Richardson, Tim. *Sweets: A History of Candy*. New York: Bloomsbury, 2002.

Milkshakes, Malts, and Ice Cream Sodas

Before the advent of high-speed blenders, thick milkshakes remained a novelty sold largely at soda fountains. The term "malted milk" was trademarked by William Horlick of Racine, Wisconsin. His product consisted of malted barley and wheat flour mixed with powdered milk.

With the invention of practical electric blenders by Hamilton Beach in 1911, milkshakes and similar drinks, such as malts, became popular, particularly during Prohibition. Fast food restaurants began selling milkshakes by the 1930s, but White Castle discontinued them when they concluded that they took too long to make and they ruined customers' appetites for hamburgers.

In the late 1930s the invention of the Multimixer allowed for several milkshakes to be made simultaneously. Salesman Ray Kroc was so impressed with the invention that he purchased the rights for the Multimixer in 1939. After World War II, Multimixers were sold to ice cream fast food chains such as Tastee-Freez and Dairy Queen. Owing to stiff competition, sales declined in the early 1950s. At that time, Kroc noted that Richard and Maurice McDonald had purchased eight Multimixers. He decided to visit their new fast food restaurant in San Bernardino, California. Employees made eighty milkshakes before the fast food operation opened, and stored them in the freezer. When those sold out, a new batch was made. The result was that the brothers were selling 20,000 shakes a month. Just as important, Kroc saw hundreds of customers waiting in line to buy hamburgers, french fries, and beverages, and he was impressed. The visit ended with Kroc acquiring the rights to franchise McDonald's nationwide.

In the early 1950s George Read invented Miracle Insta Machines, which was an improved version of the Multimixer. Keith Cramer, a drive-in restaurateur from Daytona Beach, Florida, acquired the rights to this and another machine. Cramer launched Insta-Burger King in 1952 in Jacksonville, Florida. The name of the company was subsequently shortened to Burger King.

Chocolate milkshake. (Dreamstime.com)

First Ice Cream Soda

Milk, flavorings, and ice cream were combined by the mid-nineteenth century. The first ice cream soda is credited to Robert Green, of the Franklin Institute of Philadelphia; he reportedly added ice cream to soda water in 1874.

Since the 1950s, shakes have been an integral part of most fast food operations, although some chains have created similar products, such as Wendy's Frosty, a combination of milk, sugar, cream, and flavorings.

Most shakes and other frozen beverages have come under considerable criticism owing to their high caloric content. Krispy Kreme's Lemon Sherbet Chiller weighs in at 980 calories, while McDonald's large Triple Thick Chocolate Shake hits 1,160 calories.

See also Beverages; Burger King; Dairy Queen; Ice Cream; Krispy Kreme; Kroc, Ray; McDonald's; Soda/Soft Drinks; Soda Fountains; Tastee-Freez; Wendy's; White Castle

For Further Information:

Funderburg, Anne Cooper. *Sundae Best: A History of Soda Fountains*. Bowling Green, OH: Bowling Green State University Popular Press, 2002.

Jakle, John A., and Keith A. Sculle. *Fast Food: Roadside Restaurants in the Automobile Age*. Baltimore: Johns Hopkins University Press, 1999.

Milky Way

In 1923 Frank Mars of Minneapolis introduced the Milky Way bar, which received local distribution. It consisted of a center of malt-flavored nougat (made with egg whites, corn syrup, and air) and a chocolate coating that kept the candy bar fresh. It was bigger than the other candy bars, such as Hershey's Milk Chocolate Bar, then on the market. It was also less costly to make than Hershey's bar because it used half as much chocolate, which was the most expensive ingredient. In 1924 Milky Way was marketed nationally and its sales topped $800,000 in its first year. Because Mars, Inc., did not have the technology to make chocolate, its chocolate was supplied by Hershey's. In 1935 Milky Way was advertised as "the sweet you can eat between meals." Forrest Mars, Frank Mars' son who later became the head of Mars, Inc., claimed that he gave the idea for the candy bar to his father. Today, Milky Way remains one of America's best-selling candy bars.

See also Candy; Chocolate; Hershey's Milk Chocolate Bar; Mars, Forrest; Mars, Frank; Mars, Inc.; Nougat

For Further Information:

Brenner, Joël Glenn. *The Emperors of Chocolate: Inside the Secret World of Hershey and Mars*. New York: Broadway Books, 2000.

Broekel, Ray. *The Great America Candy Bar Book*. Boston: Houghton Mifflin Company, 1982.

Richardson, Tim. *Sweets: A History of Candy*. New York: Bloomsbury, 2002.

Minimum Wage

Historically, fast food chains have thrived because of their low costs, which are directly connected to low employee wages. While most chains give outlet managers the responsibility of setting wages depending upon local conditions, by and large most employees receive minimum wage. In the United States, minimum wages are set by the federal and state governments. In 2011 the federal minimum wage was $7.25 per hour. States may have higher minimum wages; Connecticut's minimum wage, for instance, is $8.25 per hour, and Washington's is $8.67.

Minimum wage does not encourage workers to remain long, and most employees leave such jobs after a few months. The incredibly high turnover rate for most fast food chains is one of the reasons why James C. Doherty, the publisher of *Nation's Restaurant News*, has encouraged fast food chains to increase employee wages to attract better and more loyal workers. Minimum wages do not provide enough income for a worker to make an independent living. There is minimal opportunity for upward mobility, and fast food employment is not respected socially. Nevertheless, the National Restaurant Association and the fast food chains have all opposed increases in minimum wage. Some corporations have lobbied for even lower youth minimum wages, which would exempt them from paying minimum wages for 16- and 17-year-olds. They have also lobbied for exemptions from minimum wages for immigrant workers. As it is, fast food chains pay minimum wage to a higher percentage of workers than does any other industry in America.

See also Anti-Unionization; Corporate Response to Criticism; Lobbying; National Restaurant Association

For Further Information:

Hogan, David Gerald. *Selling 'em by the Sack: White Castle and the Creation of American Food*. New York: New York University Press, 1997.

Schlosser, Eric. *Fast Food Nation: The Dark Side of the All-American Meal*. New York: Houghton Mifflin Company, 2001.

Talwar, Jennifer Parker. *Fast Food, Fast Track: Immigrants, Big Business, and the American Dream*. Cambridge, MA: Westview Press, 2002.

Mints

Mints are characterized by peppermint flavoring, either artificial or from oil from the herb peppermint (*Mentha x. Piperita*). The active ingredient is menthol. Historically, mints, such as Altoids, which were invented in 1780, were used for medicinal purposes, particularly dealing with problems related to indigestion. Mints are often given at the end of meals to improve digestion.

In the twentieth century, peppermint began to be used for making a wide variety of junk foods. Hard candies were often peppermint flavored, and so were candy canes. Peppermint was also frequently used to flavor gum.

Pep-O-Mint LifeSavers were first marketed in 1912. Peppermint-flavored PEZ, and its unique plastic dispensers, were introduced from Austria into the United States in 1948. Likewise, Certs has a peppermint-flavored variety, which made its debut in 1956. Chocolate-covered mints, such as York Peppermint Patties, were first marketed in 1940. Junior Mints were launched in 1949.

Mint has also been a common flavor added to ice cream, such as Ben & Jerry's Mint Chocolate Chip and Dreyer's Peppermint Light Ice Cream, and mint has been used in herbal teas. Breath mints, such as Altoids, Tic Tacs, Eclipse Sugarfree Mints, or Velamints, were marketed beginning in the 1960s.

See also Ben & Jerry's; Cadbury; Candy; Candy Canes; Junior Mints; LifeSavers; PEZ; Tic Tacs; York Peppermint Patties

Peppermints. (Dreamstime.com)

For Further Information:

American Mint: A Documentary. Fresno, CA: Ephraim K. Smith, 2002.

Landing, James E. *American Essence: A History of the Peppermint and Spearmint Industry in the United States*. Kalamazoo, MI: 1969.

Miracle Juices

During the 1920s and 1930s, orange growers in California and Florida began promoting the healthful qualities of orange juice. The result was that many Americans began drinking orange juice for breakfast; and fruit juices in particular became associated with their healthful qualities.

Beginning in the 1930s, fruit juices were employed for their purported qualities to help dieters lose weight. The 1930s saw the advent of a variety of fad diets, some fairly sensible and others quite strange. "Dr. Stoll's Diet-Aid, the Natural Reducing Food" was a liquid diet, consisting of one teaspoon each of milk chocolate, starch, whole wheat, and bran, mixed with one cup of water, to be consumed for breakfast and lunch. The diet was promoted through beauty parlors. The "grapefruit diet" appeared in the early 1930s. The grapefruit diet, renamed the Hollywood Diet, reemerged in the 1970s, with the rationale that the fruit's low glycemic index helped speed up the body's metabolism to burn fat. Medical professionals opposed the diet for the simple reasons that it did not help dieters lose weight and there was considerable evidence that it caused some dieters medical problems.

During the early twenty-first century, commercial producers began manufacturing "miracle juices," which were promoted for their purported healthful qualities. The self-proclaimed miracle juices include a wide variety of ingredients. In addition to one or more fruit juices, such as apples, oranges, pineapples, lemons, prunes, mangosteens, and grapes, they also include a wide variety of other ingredients, such as water, fructose, ginkgo biloba, preservatives, and extracts of bilberry, green tea, and grape seed. Virtually none of the miracle juices have any scientific evidence of their healthful qualities. The few healthful qualities that are in the ingredients of some of these juices are often lost in the manufacturing process, and many miracle juices are extremely high in calories from added sugar.

See also Beverages; Dieting; Sugars/Sweeteners

For Further Information:

Yabsley, Charmaine, and Amanda Cross. *Miracle Juices: Over 50 Juices for a Healthy Life*. London: Hamlyn, 2009.

Modern Marvels

Modern Marvels is the longest-running documentary television series. It was developed for the History Channel and was launched in 1995. The more than five hundred episodes stress the science and technology of particular topics. Many of the episodes deal with fast food and junk food. These include "Snack Food Tech" (2004), "More Snack Food Tech" (2005), "Sugar" (2005), "Cereal, History in a Bowl" (2005), "Corn" (2007), "Chocolate" (2007), "Fast Food Tech" (2007), "Ice Cream," (2008), "Soft Drinks" (2008), "Salt" (2008), "Soft Drinks" (2010), and "Supersized Food" (2011).

See also Cereals; Chocolate; Corn; Junk Foods; Snack Foods; Soda/Soft Drinks; Sodium/ Salt; Sugars/Sweeteners; Supersizing; Television

For Further Information:

Modern Marvels Web site at the History Channel: www.history.com/shows/modern-marvels

Moe's Southwest Grill

Moe's Southwest Grill is a fast food chain that was launched in 2000 in Atlanta, Georgia. It features Tex-Mex foods, such as burritos, tacos, quesadillas, nachos, salads, and fajitas.

In 2007 Moe's Southwest Grill was acquired by the Atlanta-based FOCUS Brands Inc. Moe's has about four hundred locations in thirty-five states.

See also Burrito; FOCUS Brands; Mexican American Food; Nachos; Quesadillas; Salads; Tacos

For Further Information:

Moe's Web site: www.moes.com

Monaghan, Tom

Pizza king Thomas S. Monaghan (1937–) was born in Ann Arbor, Michigan, and spent much of his early life in a Catholic orphanage and foster homes. He worked as a soda jerk and barely graduated from high school. He joined the Marine Corps in 1956. When he left four years later, he enrolled in the University of Michigan. While still a student, he and his brother James bought a pizzeria called Dominick's Pizza in Ypsilanti, Michigan. His brother quit the partnership eight months later, and Tom Monaghan changed the name of the restaurant to Domino's Pizza.

Monaghan visited New York pizzerias and spent twelve years blending sauces before he ended up with one combination that he liked. Domino's developed a fast food delivery system and the company rapidly expanded. Under Monagham's leadership, Domino's prospered and he became a wealthy man.

In 1983 Monaghan bought the Detroit Tigers, who won the World Series a year later. Monaghan ultimately sold the Tigers to his pizza competitor, Mike Ilitch of Little Caesars Pizza. In 1992 Monaghan, a conservative Catholic, supported efforts to ban abortion. Domino's Pizza was adversely affected by the position he took, and in 1998 Monaghan sold most of his interest in the company to a private investment group. He subsequently became chancellor of Ave Maria University.

See also Domino's Pizza; Entrepreneurs; Little Caesars Pizza; Pizza; Soda/Soft Drinks

For Further Information:

Monaghan, Tom, with Robert Anderson. *Pizza Tiger*. New York: Random House, 1986.

Moon Pie

In 1917 the Chattanooga Bakery released the Moon Pie, a small, round confection consisting of two chocolate-covered, wheat-based cakes with a marshmallow filling. Earl Mitchell Sr. claimed to have invented it based on what coal miners said they wanted in a snack. The Moon Pie was so successful that by the late 1950s the Chattanooga Bakery was producing them exclusively. The company has extended the product line with Mini Moon Pies, Double and Single Deckers, and Fruit-Filled Moon Pies. Moon Pies are mainly consumed in the South but have become an American icon.

See also Bakery Goods; Chocolate; Pie

For Further Information:

Dickson, Ron, with William M. Clark and others. *The Great American Moon Pie Handbook*. Atlanta: Peachtree Publishers, 1985.

Magee, David. *Moon Pie: Biography of an Out-of-This-World Snack*. Lookout Mountain, TN: Jefferson Press, 2007.

Moon Pie Web site: www.moonpie.com

Mounds Bar

In 1922 the Peter Paul Candy Company of New Haven, Connecticut, introduced the Mounds bar, consisting of chocolate-covered sweetened coconut. Each package included two bars. The company released the Almond Joy candy bar in 1946. It was similar to the Mounds bar, except that each bar included two almonds.

The company's advertising campaign for Mounds and Almond Joy remains a classic. Its jingle, "Sometimes you feel like a nut, sometimes you don't," was inducted into the Advertising Slogan Hall of Fame in 2002.

Cadbury USA acquired the Peter Paul Candy Company in 1978. Ten years later, the Hershey Company acquired the brand and extended its product line to include new flavors, such as Pina Colada, Key Lime, Milk Chocolate, and Passion Fruit.

See also Advertising; Cadbury; Candy; Chocolate; Hershey Company; Peter Paul Candy Company; Slogans/Jingles

For Further Information:

Brenner, Joël Glenn. *The Emperors of Chocolate: Inside the Secret World of Hershey and Mars*. New York: Broadway Books, 2000.

Hershey's Web site: www.hersheys.com

Richardson, Tim. *Sweets: A History of Candy*. New York: Bloomsbury, 2002.

Mountain Dew

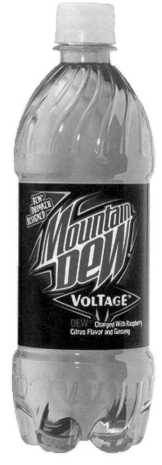

This soft drink was developed over a period of years, beginning in the 1940s. Bill Bridgforth of Tri-City Beverage in Johnson City, Tennessee, was instrumental in creating its final formula in 1958. Mountain Dew was acquired by the Pepsi-Cola Company (now PepsiCo) in 1964. PepsiCo aggressively promoted Mountain Dew nationally during the late 1980s, and expanded the product line. Diet Mountain Dew made its debut in 1988 and in 2001, PepsiCo introduced Mountain Dew Code Red and Amp Energy Drink. A 1993 Mountain Dew commercial popularized the phrase, "Been there, done that." The Coca-Cola Company introduced Mello Yello to compete with Mountain Dew in 1979.

See also Coca-Cola Company; PepsiCo; Soda/Soft Drinks

For Further Information:

Mountain Dew Web site: www.mountaindew.com

Mountain Dew Voltage.
(AP/Wide World Photos)

Movie Theaters

When motion pictures arrived in the early twentieth century, they drew huge audiences, which were prime targets for snack food sales, but theater owners refused to sell them. To some owners, vending concessions was an unnecessary nuisance or "beneath their dignity." In the rowdy burlesque days, hawkers went through the aisles with baskets, selling snack foods such as Cracker Jack and popcorn, which were tossed in the air or strewn on the floors. In addition, vendors were often slovenly and did not always follow the hygienic practices preferred by the middle classes who frequented movie theaters. These were not the images most theater owners wanted to cultivate for their upscale venues. Other owners considered the profits on concession sales to be negligible compared with the trouble and expense of cleaning up spilled popcorn and scattered boxes and sacks. Many movie theaters had carpeted their lobbies with valuable rugs to emulate the grand theater lobbies. Operators were not interested in having their expensive carpets destroyed by spilled sodas and other confections. Until the 1930s, most theater owners considered snacks to be a liability rather than an asset.

Theater owners shifted their perspectives dramatically during the Depression. Snacks, which cost 5 or 10 cents, were an affordable luxury for most Americans, and movie theaters needed the profits to survive. At first, independent concessionaires leased lobby privileges in theaters. Vendors paid about a dollar a day for the right to sell snacks. Because many theaters did not have lobby space, operators leased space outside the theaters. This suited the vendors because they were able to sell both to movie patrons and passersby on the street.

However, when theater owners saw their customers entering the theater with snacks, they quickly saw the light. Independent movie theaters were the first to capitulate to the financial lure of snack food. By the mid-1930s, movie chains started to crumble, too. Popcorn was the main snack attraction. It sold so well because of its aroma—the same smell that some theater owners had reportedly despised earlier. The aroma was maximized during the popping process. As soon as popping machines were placed in the lobbies, business picked up. Popcorn and other confections were progressively introduced into more theaters as tales of snack bar–generated wealth circulated. These experiences and stories, whether accurate or not, convinced even more theater operators to examine the reality of snack food profits. To control expenses, the managers required concession stand operators to account for the boxes and sacks. The net weekly profit on some confections was about 70 percent.

In some small, independent theaters, concession stands paid the entire overhead. In other places, it grossed more than admissions. Snack bar sales dramatically increased with movies aimed at children. The highest sales were counted during Abbott and Costello comedies, while the lowest were generated with horror films. As baby boomers grew up, so did their worship of movie stars. During the 1950s,

Elvis Presley was the movie star who generated the highest snack bar sales. Bob Hope, a close second in 1958, triumphed the following year.

Movie theaters not only sold snacks in the lobbies, they also advertised them. At drive-in theaters, snack foods were even more important. In 1946 only about three hundred drive-in movie theaters existed in America. By 1958, this number had dramatically expanded to more than six thousand. Because these theaters were designed from scratch, large cafeteria interiors were originally constructed to accommodate thousands of people during the eighteen-minute intermissions. Advertisements for snack foods appeared on the screen before the show began, and the speakers blared out, "At the snack bar now!" As sales increased through advertising, indoor theaters also advertised snack foods before the main feature.

Likewise, when snacks appeared on-screen in films, sales at snack bars also increased. This gave product manufacturers and filmmakers the idea for product placements in movies. Product manufacturers paid filmmakers for the placement of their product in the film. The best example of product placement for a snack food was Reese's Pieces, which consequently received huge national visibility in the blockbuster film *E.T.: The Extra-Terrestrial* (1982).

Virtually all foods sold at movie theaters are high in calories, fat, and sodium. The large tubs of popcorn, for instance, contain 1,500 calories (about the same as three Big Macs) and large quantities of salt. A federal law passed in 2010 requires chain restaurants to post the nutritional content of the foods and beverages they serve. Theater owners claim that they are exempt from these regulations because they're not restaurants. Others have argued that the intent of the law is to inform potential customers of nutritional content of food served at chains, and that movie theaters should therefore post nutritional information.

See also Advertising; Candy; Cracker Jack; Drive-Ins; Movie Tie-Ins; Movies; Popcorn; Soda/Soft Drinks

For Further Information:

Smith, Andrew F. *Popped Culture: A Social History of Popcorn in America.* Columbia: University of South Carolina Press, 1999.

Smith, Andrew F. *Peanuts: The Illustrious History of the Goober Pea.* Urbana: University of Illinois Press, 2006.

Movie Tie-Ins

Tie-ins are broadly defined as promotional campaigns that link two different media. Movie tie-ins began in the 1920s, particularly between movies and print media. Movie companies wanted free publicity for their films, hence they encouraged magazines and newspapers to print stories about the actors and actresses, or about how their films were made.

Junk food companies have been heavily engaged in movie tie-ins for decades. In 1971 a candy company, Breaker Confections in Chicago, bought the rights to the Willy Wonka name from the 1971 musical film *Willy Wonka & the Chocolate Factory*, based on Roald Dahl's book *Charlie and the Chocolate Factory*. It produced a series of candies, including Everlasting Gobstoppers, that were mentioned in the movie. The company was eventually acquired by Nestlé, who began producing Wonka Bars in 1998. Sales were not great, and in 2000 Nestlé had decided to discontinue the line, when director Tim Burton acquired the movie rights to *Charlie and the Chocolate Factory* and announced his plans to remake the 1971 film. Nestlé jumped at the chance for product placement in the movie. It provided hundreds of candy bars and thousands of props, and engaged in a massive promotional campaign for the movie and its own candy. It supplied 30,000 retailers, including Walmart, Target, Barnes & Noble, grocery stores, and Warner Bros. movie theaters, with special in-store promotions, and manufactured 60 million candy bars. The placement of Nestlé chocolates in the movie and the massive advertising campaign relaunched the brand. The new movie was a tremendous success, as was the sale of Nestlé candies featuring a cartoon likeness of Willy Wonka.

In 2001 Coca-Cola paid Warner Bros. an estimated $150 million for global marketing rights to the first Harry Potter movie. As a result, the Center for Science in the Public Interest, along with other organizations around the world, launched the "Save Harry" campaign to protest the use of a children's film to promote junk food.

Burger King was the first fast food chain to use product tie-ins with films. In 1977 the company partnered with George Lucas's Lucasfilm to promote the film *Star Wars*. Burger King issued a set of glasses featuring the main characters from the film, which promoted the movie and Burger King. Burger King's success was overshadowed by a deal between McDonald's and the Walt Disney Company to promote Disney's animated films beginning in the mid-1980s. In 1994 Disney switched from McDonald's to Burger King, signing a ten-film promotional contract that would include such top-ten films as *Beauty and the Beast* (1991), *Aladdin* (1992), *The Lion King* (1994), and *Toy Story* (1995).

Burger King has recently partnered with Marvel Enterprises, Inc., a subsidiary of the Walt Disney Company, to distribute Marvel-related merchandise, such as toys based on Marvel's Super Hero Squad in Marvel movies like *Thor* and *Captain America—The First Avenger*.

When Steven Spielberg's Amblin Entertainment was preparing to film *E.T.: The Extra-Terrestrial*, the producers approached Mars, Inc., hoping to use M&M's in a scene that drew ET into the open. Mars turned them down. The producers then approached Hershey, which manufactured a new product called Reese's Pieces. Universal and Hershey came to an informal agreement. Reese's Pieces were used in the movie, and Hershey promoted the movie with $1 million worth of advertising. Hershey came out a winner. When *E.T.: The Extra-Terrestrial* was released, sales of Reese's Pieces skyrocketed.

During the 1990s, the fast food industry began to take advantage of movie tie-ins. Tie-in campaigns typically include posters; advertisements on cups, bags, and containers; toys representing figures from the movie; and contests giving customers the ability to acquire tickets to special events or special showings of the film. The toys are given away or sometimes sold at low cost. Fast food chains still make a substantial profit on the sale of these toys, in addition to the sale of food items in the outlets. In 1997 McDonald's, for instance, made a deal for a tie-in with Disney's movie *Flubber*. The movie was not a great hit but the tie-in was considered a success. Fast food chains have been particularly interested in films targeted at children. In 2005 alone, Burger King bought into Lucas Films and 20th Century Fox's *Star Wars: Episode III—Revenge of the Sith* and 20th Century Fox's *Fantastic Four*; McDonald's tied-in with Disney's *Herbie: Fully Loaded* and Miramax's *The Adventures of Shark Boy and Lava Girl*; and Wendy's went in with Warner Bros.' *Charlie & the Chocolate Factory*.

McDonald's has developed a wide range of tie-ins with other movies, including *AVATAR*, *Night at the Museum: Battle of the Smithsonian*, and *Ice Age: Dawn of the Dinosaurs*. They developed interactive Web-based games, toys, and commercials. Tie-ins have also connected with other media. For instance, in 2004 McDonald's announced a huge global promotion arrangement with Sony Music, in which McDonald's gave away free music when customers bought their products.

Tie-ins have generated millions of dollars from box office attendance, as well as sales of soft drinks, fast food, junk food, toys, and other merchandise.

See also Burger King; Center for Science in the Public Interest (CSPI); Coca-Cola Company; M&M's; Mars, Inc.; McDonald's; Movie Theaters; Movies; Nestlé; Product Placements; Toys

For Further Information:

Schlosser, Eric. *Fast Food Nation: The Dark Side of the All-American Meal*. New York: Houghton Mifflin Company, 2001.

Movies

Films have greatly influenced snack food and fast food in America. Because food is an important part of life, it is often a central theme in films. In addition, the movie industry has had a lengthy and financially lucrative relationship with junk food and fast food chains. The earliest relationship was the selling of junk food in theaters. Early movie theaters did not sell food of any kind because theater operators were not interested in having their expensive carpets soiled by spilled popped kernels, soda, and other confections. The cost of cleaning up popcorn, gum, candy wrappers, and soda containers was not worth the income generated by the sale of junk food.

Theater owners shifted their perspectives dramatically during the Depression, however, when they were required to lower their ticket prices to attract customers. Once theater owners discovered that they could make a substantial profit selling junk foods and beverages, they began promoting and advertising their concession stands and the foods they sold. Today, many theaters make more profit from their concession stand sales than they do from their ticket fees.

Beginning in 1949, snack foods began appearing onscreen in films. For example, in *White Heat*, a 1949 thriller, Buddy Gorman plays a popcorn vendor. *Good Humor Man*, starring Jack Carson, featured a man selling Good Humor ice cream. A McDonald's restaurant appeared in Woody Allen's 1973 movie, *Sleeper*. When these movies were released, Good Humor ice cream, McDonald's hamburgers, and popcorn received extensive visibility. This led to a different arrangement between movies and junk food and fast food companies.

The George Lucas film *American Graffiti* centered around Mels drive-in, which was a restaurant chain founded in 1947 by Mel Weiss and Harold Dobbs in San Francisco. When Lucas was looking for a location to shoot part of the film, they used an old Mel's Drive-In that was scheduled for destruction. The movie portrayed America in the early 1960s, and the drive-in was complete with carhops on roller skates.

In addition to reflecting American life, films have been used to sell junk food and fast food through placements of products in the films, such as Reese's Pieces and PEZ in *E.T.: The Extra-Terrestrial*. In 1990 Domino's pizza appeared as a product placement in the blockbuster movie *Teenage Mutant Ninja Turtles*.

In addition, movie producers have developed tie-ins with fast food, soft drink, and junk food companies, including McDonald's, Burger King, Coca-Cola Company, and the Hershey Company. Until recently, for instance, Disney had a close connection with McDonald's. Figures related to Disney films were sold at McDonald's or included as promotional items in Happy Meals.

In 2004, yet another relationship between film and fast food came to fore: the use of a documentary film to attack the fast food industry. Morgan Spurlock's film *Super Size Me* (2004) generated bad publicity for McDonald's throughout the world. Spurlock converted the movie into a book in 2005. The reverse happened with Eric Schlosser's book *Fast Food Nation* (2001), which was made into a movie in 2006. In 2005 *The Future of Food*, a polemic against genetically modified foods, demonstrated yet another dimension of film's relationship with food.

See also Burger King; Candy; Chocolate; Coca-Cola Company; Domino's Pizza; Drive-Ins; *Fast Food Nation*; Good Humor; Hamburger; Happy Meals; Hershey Company; Hot Dog; McDonald's; Movie Theaters; Movie Tie-Ins; PEZ; Pizza; Popcorn; Product Placements; Spurlock, Morgan; *Super Size Me*

For Further Information:

Schlosser, Eric. *Fast Food Nation: The Dark Side of the All-American Meal*. New York: Houghton Mifflin Company, 2001.

Spurlock, Morgan. *Don't Eat this Book: Fast Food and the Supersizing of America*. New York: G. P. Putnam's Sons, 2005.

Super Size Me. Dir. Morgan Spurlock. Goldwyn Films, 2004.

Moxie

In 1876 Augustin Thompson, an itinerant pharmacist, concocted Moxie Nerve Food in Lowell, Massachusetts. He began distributing the dark syrup and other patent medicines throughout New England. Thompson promoted Moxie as a cure for such ailments as "dullness of the brain" and baldness. He was so successful in his promotional efforts that by 1890 the word "moxie" entered the American language as a synonym for nerve, courage, and vigor.

As many aficionados admit, the taste for Moxie is acquired. Its main ingredient is gentian root, which gives the beverage its distinctive medicinal smell and taste. When soda was first added to Moxie is unclear.

Frank M. Archer started his career as a clerk at Moxie and worked his way up to its advertising executive. He was an innovator in the use of creative advertising. In 1904 he released a Moxie song at the St. Louis World's Fair, one of the first food companies to do so. He reinvented Moxie's image after the passage of the Pure Food and Drug Act in 1906. The drink became "the distinctive beverage for those of discerning taste." The Moxie logo was printed on everything from cardboard fans to Tiffany lamps, and eight-foot-tall Moxie bottles were pulled by horse-drawn wagons to promote the beverage at seaside amusement parks and in small towns across New England.

By 1920, Moxie's sales of 25 million cases a year was greater than Coca-Cola. In 1925 high sugar prices forced the company to cut back on its promotional efforts. Moxie sales declined while those of Coca-Cola increased. Baseball player Ted Williams promoted the beverage in the 1940s and 1950s, but sales continued to decline and the Moxie Company was eventually acquired by the Monarch Company of Atlanta.

Several books and numerous articles have told and retold the Moxie story. Moxie has a loyal following in New England, especially in Maine, where a Moxie festival draws 25,000 people annually.

See also Advertising; Beverages; Coca-Cola Company; Soda/Soft Drinks; Sugars/ Sweeteners

For Further Information:

Bowers, Q. David. *The Moxie Encyclopedia*, Vol. 1. Vestal, NY: Vestal Press, 1985.

Funderburg, Anne Cooper. *Sundae Best: A History of Soda Fountains*. Bowling Green, OH: Bowling Green State University Popular Press, 2002.

Potter, Frank N. *The Moxie Mystique*. Virginia Beach, VA: Donning Company, 1981.

Potter, Frank N. *The Book of Moxie*. Paducah, KY: Collector Books 1987.

Veilleux, Joseph A. *Moxie: Since 1884, An Acquired Taste*. Bloomington, IN: 1st Books, 2003.

Mr. Peanut

Two Italian immigrants, Amedeo Obici and Mario Peruzzi, launched Planters Peanuts in 1906. Ten years later, their firm was thriving and the partners believed that they needed to promote their company nationally. As the story goes, Planters conducted a contest to help select a logo for the company, which offered $5 for the best design. The winner was a fourteen-year-old boy named Anthony Gentile, who submitted a drawing of "a little peanut person." With this image as a starting point, Planters hired a Chicago art firm that commissioned a commercial artist named Andrew Wallach to draw several different caricatures. Planters selected the image of a peanut person with a top hat, monocle, cane, and the look of a rakish gentleman, which was subsequently dubbed Mr. Peanut. Despite the preceding story perpetuated by the company, similar peanut figures, complete with top hat, monocle, cane, and gloves, had appeared in print years before, in an illustrated article in *Good Housekeeping* magazine.

Whatever the origin, Mr. Peanut was a solid advertising success aimed at America's youth. Planters applied for a trademark on it on March 12, 1917. Mr. Peanut made his debut in New England newspapers and on advertising posters in New York City subways. This was followed by a national advertising campaign in which Mr. Peanut appeared in the *Saturday Evening Post*. These were so successful that Planters increased its advertising budget for each succeeding year, spending hundreds of thousands of dollars on ads in the best newspapers and magazines in the country. In advertisements, Mr. Peanut proclaimed that peanuts were a perfect food for picnics and baseball games, and that they were an ideal ingredient in main dishes served at lunch and dinner.

The company used other media as well; they published *Mr. Peanut's Paint Book*, and the company's print promotions moved from commonplace advertising to novel schemes that drew in readers. Such advertising paid off, and annual sales rose from $1 million in 1917 to $7 million five years later.

Since its origin, Mr. Peanut has been on virtually every Planters package, container, premium, and advertisement. As a result, the Mr. Peanut caricature has become one of the most familiar icons in advertising history. His likeness graces mugs, pencils, pens, and tote bags that are available by redeeming product wrappers. Planters has offered a variety of premium items with its products: glass jars, charm bracelets, clocks, metal tins, wristwatches, ashtrays, plastic whistles, and display figures with monocles that light up. At the beginning of the twenty-first century, Mr. Peanut is an American culinary icon known the world over.

See also Advertising; Cartoon Characters; Marketing to Children; Peanuts; Toys

For Further Information:

Lindenberger, Jan, with Joyce Spontak. *Planters Peanut Collectibles since 1961*. Atglen, PA: Schiffer Publishing, 1995.

Lindenberger, Jan, with Joyce Spontak. *Planters Peanut Collectibles 1906–1961*. 2nd ed. Atglen, PA: Schiffer Publishing, 1999.

Smith, Andrew F. *Peanuts: The Illustrious History of the Goober Pea*. Urbana: University of Illinois Press, 2002.

Mrs. Fields Famous Brands

In 1977 Debra "Debbi" Fields, a twenty-year-old mother with no business experience, and her husband opened their first cookie store near Stanford University in Palo Alto, California. Mrs. Fields began franchising in 1990. In 1992 she teamed up with Time-Life Books to publish a cookie cookbook. The following year, she sold Mrs. Fields Cookies to private investors in Utah, who created Mrs. Fields' Original Cookies, Inc.

In the 1990s the company acquired Great American Cookies, Pretzel Time, and Pretzelmaker. In 2000 the company acquired TCBY, the largest seller of frozen yogurt in the United States. In 2003 it created a subsidiary, named Mrs. Fields Famous Brands, as the franchiser of its brands and its four thousand outlets. Mrs. Fields ran into financial difficulties and sold its pretzel brands in 2007 and Great American Cookies the following year. It filed for Chapter 11 bankruptcy protection in August 2008 and emerged from bankruptcy in October 2008, with less than one-third the outlets that it had before the bankruptcy.

In 2009 the company began co-branding with Java Detour, Inc., a gourmet coffee roasting company and operator and franchiser of twenty-two retail coffee stores. As of 2011, Mrs. Fields Famous Brands had about 1,200 outlets—380 Mrs. Fields and 800 TCBY outlets. They sell cookies, cakes, smoothies, muffins, bagels, and croissants. Mrs. Field Famous Brands is headquartered in Salt Lake City; Mrs. Fields' Original Cookies is headquartered in Cottonwood Heights, Utah.

See also Cakes; Chocolate; Chocolate Chip Cookies; Coffee; Cookies; Pretzels; Smoothies; Yogurt

For Further Information:

Fields, Debbi, and the editors of Time-Life Books. *Mrs. Fields Cookie Book: 100 Recipes from the Kitchen of Mrs. Fields*. Alexandria, VA: Time-Life Books, 1992.

Fields, Debbi, and the editors of Time-Life Books. *Mrs. Fields Best Cookie Book Ever!* Alexandria, VA: Time-Life Books, 1996.

Mrs. Fields Web site: www.mrsfields.com

Muffins

Historically, muffins, a small, circular, flat bread, were part of English culinary traditions brought to America by English immigrants. One of these immigrants was Samuel Bath Thomas, who in 1880 opened a bakery called the Muffin House in New York. Other immigrants brought recipes for similar products to the United States. English muffins were sold at the Chicago World's Fair in 1893, and this created some interest in the product. To capitalize on this interest, Thomas formed the S. B. Thomas Company, which began manufacturing English Muffins. Thomas' English Muffins and similar products are commonly sold in grocery stores and delicatessens. They are typically breakfast foods that are split in two, toasted, and buttered. Jams and jellies are frequently added.

This type of muffin received some attention during the 1970s, in part because they were considered healthier than traditional bakery foods. When fast food came under attack for being a junk food, muffins and other low-calorie foods were added to many menus. They were nationally popularized when McDonald's launched the Egg McMuffin in 1973. Other fast food chains were soon to add their own muffin products. Subway added the Western Egg White & Cheese Muffin Melt to their menu. Burger King offered a Muffin Sandwich.

During the 1960s, another type of muffin was popularized. These were cupcake-shaped muffins that were usually filled with sugar, although, unlike cupcakes, they were not topped with frosting. They contained many different ingredients, such as blueberries, chocolate, bananas, nuts, and carrots. These are available in many supermarkets as well as fast food chains, such as Mrs. Fields, TCBY, and Winchell's. In London and in Spain, Burger King has developed the Dessert Bar, which also serves muffins.

In 2011 Hostess Brands released a new line of whole-grain muffins available in blueberry, banana-nut, and chocolate chip varieties. These are high in fiber and relatively low in calories (150 per muffin), and they are targeted at children as a healthier alternative to other fast breakfast foods.

See also Burger King; Hostess Brands; McDonald's; Mrs. Fields Famous Brands; Subway; TCBY; Winchell's Donut House

For Further Information:

Hostess Brands Web site: www.hostessbrands.com

Thomas's English Muffin Web site: thomas.bimbobakeriesusa.com

Music

Music has been used to promote food products since at least the early twentieth century. In 1904 the soft drink Moxie released a song at the 1904 St. Louis World's

Fair, one of the first food companies to do so. As radio became an important vehicle for snack food promotion, songs and jingles were used by various manufacturers such as the Cracker Jack Company.

Songs have also affected the adoption of foods. In 1953 a popular song, "That's Amore," sung by Dean Martin included the lyric: "When the moon hits your eye like a big pizza pie," and it is believed to have helped popularize pizza in the United States. So important was snack food in America that the song "Junk Food Junkie" climbed to the top of the charts in 1976.

Fast food chains have historically piped music into their outlets to attract a particular audience. Currently, most fast food chains are interested in attracting parents, so the music usually comes in the form of the soft-rock tunes of the 1960s through the 1980s.

Most fast food chains and junk food manufacturers have advertised extensively on radio and television, and many have developed jingles. Some of the most popular include: Pizza Hut's 1965 musical jingle, "Putt-Putt to Pizza Hut"; Peter Paul's jingle for Mound's/Almond Joy candy bars, "Sometimes you feel like a nut, sometimes you don't"; or McDonald's jingle for Big Macs, "Two all-beef patties, special sauce, lettuce, cheese, pickles, onions on a sesame seed bun." This last jingle originally aired in 1982 and was revived in 2003.

Fast food chains have begun to produce and sell music videos. McDonald's, for instance, has its own line of music videos featuring McDonaldland characters; they sell for $3.49. In 2005 McDonald's tested digital-media kiosks that allow customers to burn custom CDs from a catalog of 70,000 hit songs.

In 2010 Japanese Burger King franchises introduced the "Musical Shower," which permits diners to listen to their own music at their table with an extremely directional speaker that does not disturb nearby diners.

See also Cracker Jack; Japan; McDonald's; Moxie; Peter Paul Candy Company; Pizza; Pizza Hut; Radio; Slogans/Jingles; Television

For Further Information:

Jakle, John A., and Keith A. Sculle. *Fast Food: Roadside Restaurants in the Automobile Age*. Baltimore: Johns Hopkins University Press, 1999.

Schlosser, Eric. *Fast Food Nation: The Dark Side of the All-American Meal*. New York: Houghton Mifflin Company, 2001.

N

Nabisco

In 1889 William Moore united six eastern bakeries into the New York Biscuit Company. In 1890 Adolphus Green united forty midwestern bakeries under the name the American Biscuit & Manufacturing Company. In 1898 Moore and Green merged their two companies, along with the United States Baking Company, to form the National Biscuit Company (its corporate name did not change to Nabisco until 1971).

In 1898 Adolphus Green, the first president of the National Biscuit Company, launched a cracker with a new shape that was lighter and flakier than other crackers at the time. Green named it Uneeda Biscuit and packaged it with an inner-seal package that kept the crackers fresh. The company then launched one of the first national advertising campaigns for a food product.

The National Biscuit Company acquired other companies, including the Shredded Wheat Company, maker of Triscuits and Shredded Wheat cereal. During this time, the company was also busy developing new cookies and crackers, including Barnum's Animal Crackers, Oreos, Ritz Crackers, and Honey Maid Graham Crackers. During the 1920s, the company expanded rapidly, acquiring companies such as Jell-O (1925), and opening offices abroad, including in Canada, Puerto Rico, France, and the United Kingdom.

In 1981 Nabisco merged with Standard Brands, maker of Planters Nuts, Life-Saver candies, and other successful businesses. Philip Morris Companies, Inc., acquired Nabisco in December 2000 and merged it with Kraft Foods.

In 2010 Kraft Foods announced that it was making its Nabisco line of crackers healthier by adding more whole wheat. By 2013, the company will increase the whole grain content in more than one hundred products, including Wheat Thins and Ritz Crackers.

See also Advertising; Cookies; Graham Crackers; Jell-O; Kraft Foods; LifeSavers; Mr. Peanut; Oreos; Peanuts; Ritz Crackers

For Further Information:

Burrough, Bryan, and John Helyar. *Barbarians at the Gate: The Fall of RJR Nabisco*. New York: Harper Business Essentials, 2003.

Cahn, William. *Out of the Cracker Barrel: The Nabisco Story, from Animal Crackers to Zuzus*. New York: Simon and Schuster, 1969.

Nachos

Nachos are tortilla chips covered with melted cheese and jalapeño peppers. They are credited to Ignacio Anaya, a chef at the old Victory Club in Piedras Negras, Mexico, across the border from Eagle Pass, Texas. Anaya assembled nachos for some Eagle Pass ladies who stopped in during a shopping trip in the 1940s. Nachos were popularized at the 1964 Texas State Fair and were disseminated throughout the United States during the late 1960s and 1970s. Nacho-flavored corn chips and potato chips were soon on the market. Nachos were also the spearhead of a national interest in ethnic flavors that were soon applied to corn chips, including jalapeño, cheese, nacho cheese flavor, and other spicy seasonings. Ballpark nachos were first introduced at the Texas Rangers' Arlington Stadium in 1975. The Frito-Lay company introduced Nacho Cheese Flavored Doritos in 1972. Today, nachos are sold in a variety of different outlets, including fast food restaurants, airports, fairs, and movie theaters.

See also Corn Chips; Doritos; Fair Food; Frito-Lay; Movie Theaters; Potato Chips

Nachos. (Dreamstime.com)

For Further Information:

Smith, Andrew F. "Tacos, Enchiladas and Refried Beans: The Invention of Mexican-American Cookery." In Mary Wallace Kelsey and ZoeAnn Holmes, eds., *Cultural and Historical Aspects of Foods*. Corvallis: Oregon State University, 1999, 183–203; also at: http://food.oregonstate.edu/ref/culture/latinamerica/la_smith.html

Nathan's Famous

In 1915 Nathan Handwerker, a Polish immigrant, answered a help wanted advertisement for Charles Feltman's restaurant in Coney Island, New York. Feltman originated the sausage in a bun concept, which he sold for a dime apiece. Handwerker worked at Feltman's for a year, and with $300 in savings he opened a hot dog stand of his own a few blocks from Feltman's.

Using a twelve-foot grill, Handwerker cooked and sold his take-out hot dogs for a nickle, thus undercutting Feltman. Handwerker installed signs with horns that sounded like fire engine sirens. Tradition has it that he hired students to wear white coats (imitating doctors) and sit and eat at his stand, giving the impression that his low-cost hot dogs were healthy.

When the New York subway opened in the 1920s, Nathan's became extremely popular, but Coney Island faded after World War II. Feltman's closed in 1954. Nathan's survived by expanding its operation and opening outlets in other cities. Nathan's expanded rapidly during the 1980s, when investors encouraged the growth of larger restaurants. They proved unsuccessful, and the company downsized.

Nathan's Famous, Inc., has attempted to promote its operation in a variety of ways. In the 1980s it published a series of hot dog cookbooks. More spectacular has been its sponsorship of a hot dog eating contest, which is conducted at its outlet on Coney Island every Fourth of July. In 2011 the winner, Joey Chestnut of San Jose, California, ate sixty-two Nathan's Famous hot dogs and buns in twelve minutes.

As of 2011, Nathan's consisted of 6 company-owned units and 234 franchised or licensed outlets. Nathan's branded products are also sold by more than 18,000 independent foodservice operators, which have outlets at airports, hotels, sports arenas, convention centers, colleges, and convenience stores. Nathan's co-branded with Arthur Treacher's Fish & Chips, and it has acquired Kenny Rogers Roasters and Miami Subs.

See also Arthur Treacher's; Hot Dog

For Further Information:

Handwerker, Murray. *Nathan's Famous Hot Dog Cookbook*. New York: Gramercy Publishing, 1983.

Nathan's Web site: www.nathansfamous.com

National Confectioners Association

In 1884 sixty-nine confectionery manufacturing companies met in Chicago and formed the National Confectioners Association (NCA). At the time, some confectioners adulterated their products with varnish, brick dust, lead, and insect parts to improve coloring. The NCA's goal was to foster industry self-regulation and lobby against adulterants. The NCA also encouraged its members to connect candy promotions to holidays, such as Valentine's Day, Christmas, Mother's Day, and Halloween. It has held annual meetings to address problems confronting the industry. Its 2005 All Candy Expo, held in Chicago, drew more than 17,000 participants. Today, the NCA has a membership of seven hundred candy manufacturers and suppliers. The NCA is affiliated with the Chocolate Manufacturers Association and the World Cocoa Foundation. According to its Web site, the NCA "sponsors education programs, technical research, public relations, retailing practices, and statistical analyses." NCA is headquartered in Vienna, Virginia.

The NCA has also promoted the interests of its members by lobbying at all levels of government. It has been responsible for federal and state legislation prohibiting adulteration of confections. During World War II, the NCA successfully opposed government efforts to declare candy manufacturing a nonessential industry. In 1944 the NCA spent $21 million on magazine and other advertising proclaiming that candy gave the American military its energy. The NCA spent money on promotions that presented confections as healthful foods, using the slogan "Eat Candy, the Energy Food."

Today, the NCA lobbies on matters of concern to the industry, favoring price supports for sugar and peanuts and the repeal of state taxation of candy, and opposing nutrition labeling. It has also weighed in on matters connected with international trade affecting the industry. Since 1968, the NCA and the Chocolate Manufacturers Association have stocked the U.S. Senate's "Candy Desk" so that candy is always available to senators. In addition, the NCA has joined with other junk food purveyors to create the American Council on Fitness and Nutrition, which encourages exercise and opposes the reduction of high-fat, high-sugar, low-nutrition junk foods.

See also Candy; Easter Candies; Halloween Candies; Lobbying; Peanuts; School Food; Sugars/Sweeteners; Valentine's Day Candies

For Further Information:

Brenner, Joël Glenn. *The Emperors of Chocolate: Inside the Secret World of Hershey and Mars*. New York: Broadway Books, 2000.

National Confectioners Association Web site: www.ecandy.com

National Restaurant Association

In 1919 representatives of restaurants met in Kansas and formed what would become the National Restaurant Association. At the time, there were an estimated 43,000 restaurants in the United States. The National Restaurant Association meets annually to discuss matters affecting restaurants.

The National Restaurant Association researches the hospitality industry in America. As of 2010, the restaurant industry generates $580 billion in annual sales and serves more than 130 million guests each day, reports the association. The industry employs 12.7 million people, and provides more than 9 percent of the nation's jobs. The association also examines legislation pending before Congress and lobbies on behalf of association positions. For instance, the association has opposed increases in minimum wage. It opposed those Occupational Safety and Health Administration (OSHA) guidelines on retail violence. In 2004 it led the effort to pass the Personal Responsibility in Food Consumption Act in Congress that would exempt fast food chains from lawsuits related to obesity. It has also supported "cheeseburger laws" to prevent people from suing fast food restaurants or food manufacturers on grounds that their food is to blame for causing obesity or related illnesses.

The association also develops educational materials for improving food safety, and it lobbies the U.S. Congress on behalf of the industry. Today, the National Restaurant Association is headquartered in Washington, D.C.

See also Cheeseburger Laws; Corporate Response to Criticism; Occupational Safety and Health Administration (OSHA)

For Further Information:

National Restaurant association Web site: www.restaurant.org

Neighborhoods

Fast food chains have always selected specific neighborhoods for opening their outlets. For example, prior to World War II, White Castle intentionally selected inner-city sites, but after World War II crime increased in inner cities and the traditional customers of fast food establishments left those areas. Fast food outlets closed or deteriorated along with the neighborhoods they were in, and many critics blame fast food establishments for contributing to urban blight.

After World War II, fast food chains initially targeted suburbs as the best location for their outlets. At the time, fast food chains were mainly drive-ins, they needed space for parking lots, and space was readily available in fast-growing suburbs.

Fast food drive-ins, such as McDonald's and Burger King, in the 1950s did not have indoor dining space, making it more difficult for them to operate in inner cities. This changed in the 1960s when Burger King, and then McDonald's, began developing outlets with indoor dining areas, and moved full-speed into cities. Concern has been expressed that fast food chains run local restaurants out of businesses, thus homogenizing neighborhoods.

See also Burger King; Crime; Drive-Ins; McDonald's; Urban Blight; White Castle

For Further Information:

Jakle, John A., and Keith A. Sculle. *Fast Food: Roadside Restaurants in the Automobile Age*. Baltimore: Johns Hopkins University Press, 1999.

Nestlé

Henri Nestlé, a pharmacist, developed an infant formula and launched a company to promote and sell his product. He was bought out in 1874, although the company retained his name. Henri Nestlé worked with his friend Daniel Peter to help develop and market a milk chocolate bar. Peter's chocolates used Nestlé condensed milk, and they quickly became one of the most important brands of chocolate in Europe.

World War I depressed Nestlé sales, but after the war the company again began an expansion phase. By the late 1920s the second-best-selling product that the company made was chocolate. In 1929 Nestlé acquired the company that Daniel Peter had launched, and Nestlé began manufacturing powdered chocolate for making chocolate milk, premium chocolates, and solid chocolate bars. It was one of Nestlé's semisweet chocolate bars that Ruth Wakefield used to make her famous Toll House chocolate chip cookies in the 1930s. She simply broke the bar into small pieces and folded them into the cookie dough. As a result of their great popularity, Nestlé made a deal with Wakefield: Nestlé could use her recipe on their semisweet chocolate bars, and Wakefield would be supplied with the product for the rest of her life. In 1939 the company began manufacturing Nestlé's Toll House Morsels, which became an immediate success in the United States. Nestlé also began making new candy bars, such as Nestlé's Crunch in 1938.

After World War II, Nestlé began to grow rapidly, in part by acquiring other companies, but it did not expand its interest in candy manufacturing until the 1980s. In 1984 it gobbled up six American brands—Chunky, Bit-O-Honey, Raisinettes, Oh Henry!, Goobers, and Sno Caps—when it acquired Ward-Johnston, a division of Terson Co. The following year, Nestlé introduced new variations of Chunky, Raisinettes, and Oh Henry!

In 1988 Nestlé acquired the Italian chocolate maker Perugina, and the English chocolate maker Rowntree's, which had a subsidiary in the United States called

Sunmark Companies. Sunmark manufactured a number of confections, such as Everlasting Gobstoppers, Bottle Caps, and Pixy Stix. In 1990 Nestlé acquired Standard Brands, which manufactured Butterfinger and Baby Ruth. Sunmark also controlled the rights to using the name Willy Wonka on its products. Five years later, Nestlé released Wonka Bars, the only candy other than Gobstoppers that was specifically mentioned in *Charlie & the Chocolate Factory*. Nestlé combined several candies acquired by the company under the Wonka brand name, including Bottle Caps, Pixy Stix, Nerds, Fun Dip, and Laffy Taffy.

In 1989 Nestlé formed a joint venture, called Cereal Partners Worldwide, with General Mills to distribute cereals and other products outside of North America. It manufactures and distributes more than fifty brands, including Cheerios and Nesquik. It operates in more than 130 countries worldwide.

Nestlé also acquired ice cream companies, such as Dryer's in 2002 and Eskimo Pie in 2007. Today, Nestlé's subsidiary, Dreyer's Grand Ice Cream Holdings, includes the following brands: Drumstick, Push-Ups, Häagen-Dazs, Dreyer's/Edy's, Eskimo Pie, and many others.

In addition to buying junk foods, Nestlé has also developed diet products, such as Nestlé's Sweet Success, released in 1993. It is a low-calorie, nutritionally balanced shake made from skim milk. Nestlé sold it off in 2000 so that it could focus on PowerBar, which it acquired in the same year, and its Carnation Instant Breakfast drinks. Nestlé also acquired the weight-loss company Jenny Craig in 2006.

Nestlé is headquartered in Vevey, Switzerland, and it is the largest food company in the world.

See also Baby Ruth; Bit-O-Honey; Bottle Caps; Butterfinger; Chocolate; Dreyer's/Edy's Ice Cream; Eskimo Pie; General Mills; Häagen-Dazs; Ice Cream; Oh Henry!; Perugina; Pizza, Frozen; Pixy Stix; Push-Ups; Rowntree's of York; Taffy; Wonka Brand

For Further Information:

Nestlé Web site: www.nestle.com

Schwarz, Friedhelm [Maya Anyas, trans.]. *Nestlé: The Secrets of Food, Trust, and Globalization*. Toronto: Key Porter Books, 2002.

New England Confectionery Company (NECCO)

Begun in 1847, the New England Confectionery Company (NECCO) is the oldest continuously operating candy company in America. One of its earliest products was Conversation Hearts. NECCO renamed them Sweethearts in 1902, when they became associated with Valentine's Day. The company introduced a profit-sharing system for its workers in 1906 and a life insurance program in 1920. The famous NECCO wafers—hard disks of various-flavored and -colored candy—first appeared in 1912; previously they had been called Peerless Wafers. The Bolster Bar—peanut crunch covered with milk chocolate—was also manufactured by NECCO. The company introduced its Sky Bar in 1937 with a dramatic airplane skywriting campaign. NECCO has made a number of acquisitions: In 1990 it purchased the Stark Candy Company, which brought to NECCO the Peanut Butter Kiss, Salt Water Taffy, and Mary Jane Candies. It acquired the Clark Bar in 1999. Today, Sweethearts are the best-selling Valentine's Day candy in the United States.

See also Candy; Chocolate; Clark Bar; Mary Jane Candies; Peanut Butter; Taffy; Valentine's Day Candies

For Further Information:

Broekel, Ray. *The Great America Candy Bar Book*. Boston: Houghton Mifflin Company, 1982.

Richardson, Tim. *Sweets: A History of Candy*. New York: Bloomsbury, 2002.

Smith, Andrew F. *Peanuts: The Illustrious History of the Goober Pea*. Urbana: University of Illinois Press, 2002.

Untermeyer, Louis. *A Century of Candymaking 1847–1947: The Story of the Origin and Growth of the New England Confectionery Company*. Boston: The Barta Press, 1947.

New Zealand

American cereal companies, such as Kellogg, began operations in New Zealand in 1929. It sells some traditional American products, such as Corn Flakes and Special K, but it has a number of other products, such as Rice Bubbles.

American fast food, such as hamburgers and pizza, entered into Australia, New Zealand, and the Pacific Islands as a result of World War II, when U.S. Army and Navy personnel were stationed there. Hamburgers continued to be served in indigenous restaurants in these countries and islands after American forces left.

McDonald's opened its first outlet in New Zealand in 1976, and it now has 144 outlets. It offers a large number of menu items traditionally found in American outlets, and many unusual items, such as tandoori chicken wraps and a Bakehouse Brekkie Roll (bacon, egg, cheese, and potatoes on a sourdough roll). Burger King got off to a slow start in New Zealand; as of 2011, it had eleven outlets. Domino's opened its first franchise in New Zealand in 2003. Within two years, Domino's was New Zealand's second-largest pizza chain.

See also Burger King; Domino's Pizza; McDonald's

For Further Information:

Burger King (New Zealand) Web site: www.burgerking.co.nz

Domino's (New Zealand) Web site: www.dominospizza.co.nz

Kellogg's Australia/New Zealand Web site: www.kelloggs.com.au

McDonald's New Zealand Web site: www.mcdonalds.co.nz

Newspapers

Since the advent of commercial snack food in the late nineteenth century, manufacturers and retailers have used newspapers to advertise their products. Because most newspapers are generally distributed within a limited geographic region, advertisers are usually local retailers of products. Likewise, fast food outlets began advertising in newspapers beginning in the 1920s. Successful types of newspaper advertising include coupons that offer reduced prices for products.

Junk food and fast food companies have also worked hard to acquire space in the news sections of newspapers, through press releases and by conducting unusual promotional activities.

See also Advertising; Fast Food; Junk Foods; Snack Food

For Further Information:

Jakle, John A., and Keith A. Sculle. *Fast Food: Roadside Restaurants in the Automobile Age*. Baltimore: Johns Hopkins University Press, 1999.

North American Free Trade Association (NAFTA)

The North American Free Trade Association is an agreement between the United States, Mexico, and Canada signed in 1994 that pledged to eliminate barriers of trade and investment over time.

Since NAFTA was signed, Mexico has been inundated with fast food chains such as McDonald's, Burger King, KFC, Taco Bell, and Pizza Hut. In addition, it has been inundated with cheap American corn, while Mexican produce, such as tomatoes, have flooded into the United States.

See also Burger King; Canada; KFC; McDonald's; Mexico; Pizza Hut; Taco Bell; Tomatoes

For Further Information:

Brandt, Deborah, ed. *Women Working the NAFTA Food Chain: Women, Food & Globalization*. Toronto: Second Story Press, 1999.

Folsom, Ralph Haughwout. *NAFTA and Free Trade in the Americas in a Nutshell*. 3rd ed. St. Paul, MN: Thomson/West, 2008.

Nougat

Originally made from roasted nuts, candied fruit, and honey, nougat is a traditional type of European candy. Torrone, for instance, is a popular Italian nougat candy made from sugar, honey, nuts, and egg whites. Toblerone, a chocolate bar with almond and honey nougat, is a popular Swiss candy that is now sold throughout the world. Nougat fillings are very common in some of America's most popular candy bars, such as Milky Way, Snicker's, and 3 Musketeers.

See also Candy; Milky Way; Snicker's; 3 Musketeers; Toblerone

For Further Information:
Kimmerle, Beth. *Candy: The Sweet History*. Portland, OR: Collectors Press, Inc., 2003.

Nutrition

For millennia, humans have been aware of the relationship between food and health. By 1840, chemists had classified food into three categories: carbohydrates, fats, and proteins. Carbohydrates, mainly sugars and starches, make up the bulk of our diet and constitute our chief source of energy. Dietary fats, now generally called lipids, include vegetable oil and animal fat. Lipids are highly concentrated sources of energy, furnishing more calories than either carbohydrates or proteins. Proteins are the major source of building material for the body; they repair and replace worn tissue.

During the twentieth century, vitamins were discovered, isolated, and identified. Today, seventeen vitamins have been identified as essential, which means that the human body cannot synthesize them and they must be ingested for the body to function properly.

Minerals were also found to be essential for the proper functioning of the human body. Minerals act as catalysts in many biochemical reactions of the body and are also vital to the growth of bones, muscular contractions, digestion, and many other functions. Calcium, for instance, is essential for proper heart rhythm, iron for blood formation, and phosphorus for healthy bones and teeth. Some minerals, such as calcium, iron, and sulfur, are required in relatively large amounts, whereas others, such as zinc, copper, iodine, and fluoride, are required in smaller (trace) amounts. Today, twenty-four minerals, called micronutrients, have been identified as essential.

During the late twentieth and early twenty-first centuries, the major focus of nutrition has shifted from concern about which foods are required to avoid deficiencies and illness, to which foods and supplements may be consumed to promote health. Nutrition studies today are spread over the fields of medicine, biochemistry, physiology, behavioral and social sciences, as well as public health sciences.

Beginning in the 1970s, nutritionists began to attack junk food and fast food, which were linked with diabetes, heart disease, and obesity. Junk foods were vilified as containing empty calories. John Yudkin, a professor of nutrition at London University, attacked sugar in his *Pure, White and Deadly* (1972). The British Heart Foundation's attacks included: "[S]aturated fat from red meat, biscuits, cakes, chips and dairy products can clog up your arteries and put strain on your heart." Many people prefer high-sugar and high-fat diets to healthier foods.

The Center for Science in the Public Interest (CSPI) has attacked soft drinks because of their calories and because consumers prefer soda instead of healthy, low-fat milk, fruit juice, or fruit—foods that contribute to reduction "of osteoporosis, cancer, or heart disease."

See also Calories; Cancer; Carbohydrates; Center for Science in the Public Interest (CSPI); Diabetes; Fat, Dietary; Hypertension; Nutritional Guidelines; Obesity; Soda/Soft Drinks; Sodium/Salt; Strokes; Sugars/Sweeteners

For Further Information:

Berdanier, Carolyn D., et al. *Handbook of Nutrition and Food*. Boca Raton, FL: CRC Press, 2002.

Desai, Babasaheb B. *Handbook of Nutrition and Diet*. New York: Marcel Dekker, 2000.

Goldstein, Myrna Chandler, and Mark A. Goldstein. *Controversies in Food and Nutrition: A Reference Guide*. 2nd ed. Westport, CT: Greenwood Press, 2009.

Gratzer, Walter. *Terrors of the Table: The Curious History of Nutrition*. New York: Oxford University Press, 2005.

"Junk Pack." *Nutrition Action HealthLetter* 32 (March 2005): 16.

Libal, Autumn. *Fats, Sugars, and Empty Calories: The Fast Food Habit*. Philadelphia: Mason Crest Publishers, 2006.

Nestle, Marion. *Food Politics: How the Food Industry Influences Nutrition and Health*. Berkeley, CA: University of California Press, 2002.

Yallop, Jacqueline, and Bill Campbell. "Junk Food." *Times Educational Supplement* (June 10, 2005): F11–F14.

Nutritional Guidelines

Various groups around the world have issued nutritional guidelines. Special guidelines have been issued for sports, the elderly, children, diabetics, babies, school meals, and so forth. For example, the Sloan-Kettering Cancer Center recommends a diet "low in fat (20 percent of daily calories from fat), high in fiber, and rich in fruits and vegetables (five to nine servings per day), which can encourage weight loss and may reduce the risk of some cancers, as well as other chronic diseases such as heart disease, diabetes, and hypertension."

In 1940 the National Academy of Sciences established a committee to advise the government on nutrition. The following year it established standards for the armed forces and for the general population and offered recommended dietary allowances (RDA) for energy, along with eight essential vitamins and minerals. During the war, the U.S. Department of Agriculture (USDA) developed food guides based on the availability of food during wartime food shortages. Its *National Wartime Nutrition Guide* promoted the Basic Seven, which were food categories to be consumed every day. This was modified after the war to the Basic Four, which stressed protein from meat, eggs, poultry, and fish in one category; dairy; vegetables, and fruits; and grain products. As new research demonstrated additional requirements, new guidelines were developed.

In the 1980s the Department of Health and Human Services and the USDA developed the *Dietary Guidelines for Americans*, and it is updated and rereleased every five years. Based on the 1990 guidelines, the USDA developed the Food Pyramid, which is a visual representation of the recommendations in *Dietary Guidelines for Americans* in 2005.

Food Pyramid

In 1992 the USDA developed the Food Guide Pyramid, which recommended a hierarchal—and therefore controversial—dietary pattern based on breads, cereals, rice, pasta, dairy products, and fruits and vegetables. It also recommended that high-fat processed meats be limited and that only two to three servings of meat, poultry, fish, beans, eggs, or nuts be consumed daily. These recommendations were based on four major studies conducted during the 1980s that identified the need to restrict fat, particularly saturated fat. Because the pyramid was hierarchal, many food companies felt threatened and applied pressure to change the recommendation. A revised Food Pyramid was eventually released.

In 1994 the Center for Nutrition Policy and Promotion, a part of the USDA, was established to improve American nutrition. It began working on a replacement for the controversial Food Pyramid. In 2005 the center unveiled its new Food Pyramid, now called MyPyramid, which was based on the *Dietary Guidelines for Americans* in 2005. The new pyramid was, in fact, twelve individualized pyramids based upon age, sex, and physical activity. Critics have considered MyPyramid needlessly confusing, and some claim that the revised 2005 *Dietary Guidelines* were based more on lobbying efforts of the food industry than upon scientific research. In 2011 a new Food Pyramid was released—rather than a pyramid shape, however, it is a large, round plate divided into four sections (grains, fruit, vegetables, and protein) and a small plate representing dairy.

Dietary Guidelines for Americans 2010

The latest *Guidelines* were issued in December 2010. They provide authoritative advice about how good dietary habits promote health and reduce risk for major chronic diseases; this information is applicable to anyone older than two years of age. Among its recommendations are to "consume a variety of nutrient-dense foods and beverages within and among the basic food groups while choosing foods that limit the intake of saturated and transfats, cholesterol, added sugars, salt, and alcohol." Regarding weight gain, the *Guidelines* recommend making "decreases in food and beverage calories and increase[s in] physical activity."

In the preface, the *Guidelines* state: "The single most significant adverse health trend among US children in the past 40 years has been the dramatic increase in overweight and obesity." They reported that "currently, Americans consume less than 20 percent of the recommended intake for whole grains, less than 60 percent for vegetables, less than 50 percent for fruits, and less than 60 percent for milk and milk products. Inadequate intakes of nutrient-dense foods from these basic food groups place individuals at risk for lower than recommended levels of specific nutrients, namely vitamin D, calcium, potassium, and dietary fiber." Their recommendations included that Americans reduce the amount of calories that they consume and increase the amount of physical activity that they engage in. They recommend reducing sodium intake by 40 percent (from 2,300 mg to 1,500 mg), reducing the consumption of solid fats, reducing the consumption of food and beverages with added sugar, consuming foods low in fat and high in fiber, and eating a dairy- and whole grains–based diet.

The *Guidelines* note that the food industry "will need to act to help Americans achieve these goals." The food industry needs to contribute healthful food solutions to reduce the intake of solid fats and added sugar, certain refined grain products, and sodium.

Two general problems have emerged with regard to guidelines. The first is that they change frequently. Several items that were highly recommended foods during the 1950s—for example, eggs, butter, and red meats—were later discouraged. The second is that nutritional guidelines released by countries differ greatly from each other, and even differ from the guidelines of neighboring countries, and they diverge dramatically.

See also Calories; Cancer; Carbohydrates; Center for Science in the Public Interest (CSPI); Diabetes; Exercise; Fat, Dietary; Hypertension; Nutrition; Obesity; Soda/Soft Drinks; Sodium/Salt; Strokes; Sugars/Sweeteners; Transfats; U.S. Department of Agriculture

For Further Information:

Apple, Rima D. *Vitamania: Vitamins in American Culture.* New Brunswick, NJ: Rutgers University Press, 1996.

Center for Nutrition Policy and Promotion Web site: www.cnpp.usda.gov

Dietary Guidelines for Americans Web site: www.cnpp.usda.gov/DietaryGuidelines.htm

MyPyramid Web site: www.mypyramid.gov

Nestle, Marion. "Evolution of Federal Dietary Guidance Policy: From Food Adequacy to Chronic Disease Prevention." *Cadeuces* 6 (Summer 1990): 43–67.

Nestle, Marion. *Food Politics: How the Food Industry Influences Nutrition and Health.* Berkeley: University of California Press, 2002.

Nuts

Roasted chestnuts and other nuts have been sold on America's streets since colonial times. Candied nuts were typically served as desserts. They were covered with honey initially, and later with other sugar-based sweeteners. Dried nuts were often served as snacks.

Nuts require little preparation and can be easily transported. They are relatively inexpensive and are generally nutritious. The most important nuts sold in America today are almonds, walnuts, and pecans, followed by chestnuts, pistachios, and Macadamias. Most commercial nuts used in American confections are grown in California, with the exception of Macadamia nuts, which are grown mainly in Hawaii. In addition, cashews and Brazil nuts are imported. In the nineteenth century, nuts were roasted and salted, when necessary, by vendors and homemakers, but the commercial processes for salting nuts so that the salt remained on the nuts after packaging were not perfected until the early twentieth century.

Almonds

In Europe, almonds became the nut of choice and ended up in many European candy bars, such as the Toblerone. Americans imported almonds in colonial times, but they did not become an important confection in the United States until almond groves in California began to produce large quantities in the early twentieth century. Candied almonds (called Jordan almonds) and other confections that frequently contained almonds, such as English toffee and Turkish Delight, were sold in the United States in the nineteenth century, but it wasn't until Milton Hershey decided to add almonds to his Hershey's Milk Chocolate Bar in 1908 that almonds became an important junk food in America. Many other candy makers followed his lead. These included the Bit-O-Honey bar—consisting of individually wrapped blocks of taffy containing almonds—which was released in 1924; the Heath bar, made with honey and crushed almonds, which was launched in 1928; and the Almond Joy with its two almonds, first marketed in 1948.

The Hershey Company released the Golden Almond chocolate bar in 1976 and the Symphony milk chocolate bar with almonds and toffee chips in 1989. Recently, the American version of the Mars bar included almonds, but it was not a great success and it was discontinued in 2002; Mars introduced the Snickers bar with almonds as a substitute.

Mixed nuts. (Dreamstime.com)

Peanuts

The most important snack nut in America, however, is technically a legume. The peanut originated in South America but was disseminated to Africa and Asia shortly after the arrival of Europeans in the New World. From Africa, peanuts were brought into North America in colonial times. Peanuts were relatively unimportant as a snack food until after the Civil War, when vendors began selling them on city streets. One peanut vendor was Amedeo Obici, an Italian-born immigrant who lived in Wilkes-Barre, Pennsylvania. In 1906 Obici formed a partnership with another Italian immigrant to form the Planters Peanut Company. Their products then went through a packaging revolution, permitting Planters to sell fresh peanuts to a larger clientele. Planters also emphasized advertising and marketing, and the company's mascot, Mr. Peanut, quickly became an American culinary icon. The company went from a small vendor operation to a national snack food company in less than two decades. In 2005 Planters was the best-selling nut brand in the United States.

Peanuts have been a common ingredient in junk foods since the nineteenth century. They frequently found their way into peanut brittle and other homemade foods. The first commercial junk food, Cracker Jack (1896) included peanuts. The Standard Candy Company of Nashville, Tennessee, produced one of the first chocolate candy bars composed of caramel, marshmallow, milk chocolate, and roasted peanuts. The company was started by Howard Campbell in 1901, and he named his new confection Goo Goo Clusters. Thousands of other candies with peanuts have been introduced over the years. The Spangler Candy Company in Bryan, Ohio, manufactured Cream Peanut Clusters in 1911 and later produced the Jitney Bar, a maple-flavored marshmallow-peanut bar enrobed in chocolate. By far the most successful early candy bar with peanuts was the Baby Ruth, which was first manufactured in 1920.

Boston's William Schraft produced Milk Peanut Blocks, Peanut Chews, and the Peanut Crackel. Schraft's Bolo bar was a caramel, peanut fudge, and chocolate combination. Another early peanut-chocolate combination bar was produced in Pittsburgh by the D. L. Clark Company, which had been launched in 1886 by David Clark. In 1917 he produced a 5-cent bar composed of ground roasted peanuts covered with milk chocolate. It was at first simply called "Clark," but it was later renamed the Clark Bar. Clark later introduced the Zagnut bar, composed of peanut-butter crunch covered with toasted coconut. In 1922 the Goldenberg Candy Company produced Peanut Chews in Philadelphia, and they were soon popular all along the East Coast. The same company released Chew-ets, a chocolate-coated version of Peanut Chews, during the 1930s. Ernest Wilson of San Francisco manufactured Wilsonettes—chocolate-covered peanuts—in 1923. In 1925 the Hershey Company began manufacturing a chocolate-peanut-based confection called Mr. Goodbar. Mars manufactures two of America's most popular candies with peanuts, Snickers (1930) and Peanut M&M's (1954). The PayDay candy bar was manufactured by the Pratt & Langhoff Candy Company in 1932. The following year, the company changed its name to Hollywood Candy Company. The Bolster Bar, a peanut-crunch covered with milk chocolate, was manufactured by the New England Confectionery Company (NECCO). NECCO introduced the Sky Bar in 1937 with a dramatic skywriting campaign by airplanes.

The major peanut processors also introduced peanut candies. Planter's, for instance, introduced the Jumbo Block Peanut Candy Bar and the Planters Peanut Bar, composed of peanuts, sugar, corn syrup, and salt. The Tom Huston Company of Columbus, Georgia, introduced Tom's Peanut Bar during the 1920s.

Other nuts have been used to make candies. Walnettos, for instance, were combinations of walnuts and caramel, and pecans are used to make other candies and confections. Nuts are also used as toppings on ice cream and desserts.

While nuts themselves are usually considered healthy snacks compared with junk foods, nuts are filled with fat, calories, and often packagers add large amounts of sodium. When nuts were added to candy, they became important ingredient in American junk foods.

See also Advertising; Baby Ruth; Cartoon Characters; Clark Bar; Cracker Jack; Goo Goo Clusters; Heath Bar; Hershey, Milton S.; Hershey Company; Hershey's Milk Chocolate Bar; Jordan Almonds; M&M's; Mars Bar; Mars, Inc.; Mr. Peanut; New England Confectionery Company (NECCO); PayDay; Peanut Brittle; Peanuts; Snickers; Spangler Candy Company; Toblerone; Toffee; Walnettos

For Further Information:

Smith, Andrew F. *Peanuts: The Illustrious History of the Goober Pea*. Urbana: University of Illinois Press, 2002.

O

Obama, Michelle

Michelle Obama, the wife of the President Barack Obama, undertook a lead role in a national campaign to reverse the trend toward childhood obesity. In February 2009 Michelle Obama launched a campaign called Let's Move. Its purpose is "to promote making healthy choices, improving food quality in schools, increasing access to healthy, affordable food, and increasing physical activity for all youth for a healthier generation of kids."

Barack Obama created a White House Task Force on Childhood Obesity to conduct a review of every single federal program and policy relating to child nutrition and physical activity, and to develop a national action plan to maximize federal resources and set concrete benchmarks toward ending childhood obesity within a generation. The task force issued its report in May 2010. It identified its goal to return to a childhood obesity rate of just 5 percent by 2030, which was the rate before childhood obesity first began to rise in the late 1970s. The report presents a series of seventy specific recommendations, including good prenatal care for expectant mothers; improved labels on food and menus that provide clear information to help parents make healthy choices for children; reduced marketing of unhealthy products to children; healthier food in schools; and upgraded nutritional quality of other foods sold in schools.

Five days after the release of the report, sixteen corporations that manufacture junk foods announced the formation of the Healthy Weight Commitment Foundation. The corporations involved included General Mills, Kellogg Company, Kraft Foods, Mars, Inc., Nestlé USA, PepsiCo, Inc., Post Foods/Ralston Foods, Sara Lee Corporation, Coca-Cola Company, Hershey Company, Walmart, and Unilever. They agreed to eliminate 1.5 trillion calories from their products in the United States by the end of 2015 in an effort to stem obesity in America.

Michelle Obama strongly supported the passage of the Healthy, Hunger-Free Kids Act, which expanded the school lunch program and set new standards to improve the quality of school meals. It passed Congress and was signed into law in December 2010.

See also Coca-Cola Company; Exercise; General Mills; Hershey Company; Kellogg Company; Kraft Foods; Mars Inc.; Nestlé; PepsiCo; Post Foods; Sara Lee; Unilever; Walmart

For Further Information:

Healthy Weight Commitment Foundation Web site: www.healthyweightcommit.org

Let's Move Web site: www.letsmove.gov

Stolberg, Sheryl Gay. "After a Year of Learning, the First Lady Seeks Out a Legacy." *New York Times,* January 14, 2010, A20.

Task Force on Childhood Obesity Report: www.letsmove.gov/obesitytaskforce.php

Obesity

Obesity is defined as any person with a Body Mass Index (BMI), a ratio of weight to height, of 30 or higher. Overweight is defined as anyone with a BMI between 25 and 29.9.

According to studies published in 2011 in *Lancet*, the prestigious British medical journal, the global prevalence of obesity has almost doubled since 1980, "when 4.8 percent of men and 7.9 percent of women were obese. In 2008, 9.8 percent of men and 13.8 percent of women in the world were obese." An estimated 1.3 billion people worldwide are overweight or obese, and the number of people who are overweight is increasing in nearly every country in the world. For the first time in history, the number of overweight people in the world rivals that of the underfed, according to a study by the Worldwatch Institute. In 2000 a United Nations study found the incidence of obesity to be increasing rapidly in developing countries. In China, the number of overweight people jumped from less than 10 percent to 15 percent of the population in just three years. In Brazil and Colombia, the obesity rate hovers around 40 percent of the population—a level comparable to many European countries. Even in sub-Saharan Africa, where most of the world's underfed live, there has been a rapid increase in obesity and overweight.

Nowhere is this problem more acute than in the United States, where the statistics are staggering. During the past fifty years Americans have been gaining weight, such that today 61 percent of Americans are judged overweight. Obesity rates have risen from 12 percent to 20 percent of the population since 1991. Excess weight has been linked with high blood pressure, arthritis, infertility, heart disease, Type 2 diabetes, strokes, birth defects, gallbladder disease, gout, impaired immune system, liver disease, osteoarthritis, and several types of cancer (including breast, prostate, esophageal, colorectal, endometrial, and kidney cancer). It comes as no surprise that obesity is linked to a decrease in life expectancy.

In addition to increased risk for physical illness, obese people are often victims of social discrimination. Many obese and overweight Americans report job and other discrimination. Obese people have higher absentee rates and lower productivity than do normal-weight workers. Fashion lauds skinny models as the ideal body images, and obesity is a stigmatized condition. Society holds the individual responsible for obesity and believes overweight individuals lack self-control or have a moral defect. Many overweight people believe the same and feel badly about themselves.

The obesity epidemic became so alarming that in 2010 more than 130 retired American generals, admirals, and senior military leaders issued a report titled "Too Fat to Fight: Retired Military Leaders Want Junk Food Out of America's Schools." It framed the issue as a national security threat, stating that "obesity rates threaten the overall health of America and the future strength of our military." They recommended removing junk food from schools; increasing funding to improve nutritional standards and the quality of food in schools; and providing more effective programs that reduce childhood obesity.

Longevity

According to the surgeon general's Call to Action to Prevent and Decrease Overweight and Obesity (2001), obese individuals have a 50 to 100 percent increased risk of premature death from all causes. A weight gain of eleven to eighteen pounds increases a person's risk of developing Type 2 diabetes, while those with a weight gain of forty-four pounds or more have four times the risk of coronary heart disease.

A massive study conducted by the U.S. National Institutes of Health concluded in 2010 that overweight and obesity are associated with increased mortality from cardiovascular disease and certain cancers. It examined the results of nineteen long-term studies with 1.46 million subjects. It calculated the chances of premature death for individuals who were overweight and obese, and for those of normal weight. It concluded that slightly overweight individuals had 13 percent greater chance of early death, while those who were highly obese had a 250 percent chance of an early death.

The Centers for Disease Control has estimated that 248,000 Americans annually die prematurely owing to obesity; others believe that this figure is low and estimate that it is closer to 400,000. Obesity is considered the number two cause of preventable death in the United States (the primary cause is smoking). Health officials from the surgeon general to medical practitioners have identified obesity as a disease of epidemic proportions in the United States. In 1998 the World Health Organization also used the word "epidemic" to describe the global picture of obesity.

Obesity and Cancer

A large number of studies have examined the relationship between being overweight and cancer. One found that overweight people diagnosed with cancer had a poorer rate of overall survival and disease-free survival than those with the same diagnosis who had normal weights.

Obesity is associated with breast cancer. The International Agency for Research on Cancer reported in 2002 that one-third of all cases of breast cancer could be eliminated if women simply ate less, exercised more, and were more slender as a result. A 2006 study found that obese women are as much as 60 percent more likely to develop cancer of any kind than women of normal weight. Breast cancer is the second leading cause of cancer death among American women, after lung cancer.

Obesity and overweight may contribute to liver disease, as well. While drinking alcohol is the number one cause of cirrhosis and other liver diseases, studies have shown that alcohol usage and excess weight act together to reinforce the damage done to the liver. For instance, a study of men who consumed one or more glasses of wine every day were almost nineteen times more likely to suffer liver disease if they were obese than were similar normal-weight wine drinkers.

Obesity Causes

There is no single cause of obesity; genetics, environment, diet and other factors all play a role. However, the rise in obesity is correlated with the rise in the fast food and junk food industries. Junk food manufacturers and fast food operators have been particularly targeted as responsible for the obesity epidemic. Both industries have made inexpensive high-calorie and high-fat foods widely available and have promoted them through billions of dollars of advertising, much of which is targeted at children watching television. Numerous studies have linked obesity, poor nutrition, and the amount of time a person watches television. Some studies have offered specific evidence that fast food consumption is correlated with weight gain and Type 2 diabetes. For instance, a study published in 2005 in *Lancet* examined the health and eating habits of 3,031 young adults who were eighteen to thirty years old in 1985, and followed them over a fifteen-year period. The authors concluded that "fast-food consumption has strong positive associations with weight gain and insulin resistance, suggesting that fast food increases the risk of obesity and type 2 diabetes." A 2010 study published in *Diabetes Care* concluded that higher consumption of sugary-sweet beverages is associated with weight gain, obesity, and Type 2 diabetes.

Obesity Lawsuits

Many obesity lawsuits have been threatened, but only a few have been filed by variety of groups. In one instance parents threatened to bring lawsuits against school boards to force a ban on the sale of soft drinks and junk food in schools. Most school boards have agreed to changes based on increased knowledge about medical problems associated with obesity. Schools located in Chicago, Los Angeles, San Francisco, and Nashville have ended their relationships with Coca-Cola. As a result, most school districts have reduced the amount of junk foods available in their schools.

Other lawsuits have been filed against fast food chains. On July 23, 2002, Caesar Barber, a 270-pound 56-year-old, sued McDonald's, Burger King, KFC, and Wendy's, alleging that the fast food restaurants were responsible for his and the

---

Let's Go!

In 2004, pediatricians in Maine teamed up with the Maine-Harvard Prevention Research Center, community groups, medical leaders, and communities to launch a program called "Let's Go" to reduce obesity. Its slogan was "5-2-1-0," which meant five or more fruits and vegetables a day, two hours or less screen time, one hour or more of physical activity, and zero sugar-added beverages. Local businesses and health care leaders took up the cause and spread the program. Initial surveys indicate that 27 percent of students in Let's Go programs report increased physical activity and healthier lifestyles.

---

class members' poor health. Although quickly withdrawn, this suit led to a lawsuit that focused on one chain—McDonald's—with children as plaintiffs. That suit, *Pelman, et al. v. McDonald's Corporation*, alleged that the company's food was not nutritious and that the company engaged in deceptive advertising and fraud, among other things; and that McDonald's sold food that was harmful and the company was negligent in informing customers. The plaintiffs also alleged that the company injected its products with additives without informing customers; that the nutritional content of food containing those additives was changed as a result; and that their habitual consumption of food served at the restaurant made them fat. The lawsuit is still ongoing.

The National Restaurant Association has led the industry efforts to prevent such litigation by passing laws to prevent them. They supported the Personal Responsibility in Food Consumption Act in Congress to create immunity from lawsuits by preventing plaintiffs from bringing this type of action. It passed in the House but was not voted on in the Senate. Several states, however, have passed "cheeseburger laws" to prevent people from suing fast food restaurants or food manufacturers on grounds that their food is to blame for causing obesity or related illnesses such as heart disease, diabetes, or hypertension.

Over the past three decades, the rate of obesity has more than doubled among preschool children and adolescents in the United States, and has tripled among all school-age children. Obesity now affects about 12.5 million American children. According to standards established by the International Obesity Task Force, 35 percent of American children are overweight or obese. Research indicates that there is an 80 percent chance that an overweight child will become an obese adult.

In December 2010 the U.S. Department of Agriculture and the Department of Health and Human Services issued *Dietary Guidelines for Americans*, which is the cornerstone of federal nutrition policy and nutrition education activities. The *Guidelines* state that the increase in overweight and obese children is "the single most significant adverse health trend in the United States." Obesity is not only associated with adverse health effects during childhood, but evidence documents increased risk of future chronic disease in adult life.

Fast food chains and snack food purveyors have intentionally targeted youth through their advertising and promotional activities. Junk food vending machines have been installed in schools and fast food operators now participate in many school foodservice operations.

A report issued by the Institute of Medicine of the National Academies in 2006 indicated there is compelling evidence linking food advertising on television and increased childhood obesity. A study published in 2008 concluded that banning junk food advertising on children's programs would reduce the number of overweight children ages three to eleven by 18 percent, and the authors projected that this would reduce the number of overweight adolescents ages twelve to eighteen by 14 percent.

Solutions

Solutions for the obesity epidemic vary but include dieting, exercise, behavioral modification, and drug treatments. For severe obesity, gastric bypass or bariatric surgery has been recommended. This is a procedure that removes a portion of the stomach and creates a smaller stomach to which the small intestine is attached. With a smaller stomach, the patient will eat less, and thus over time weight will decrease. Surgery is always a risk, and the long-term health effects of gastric bypass surgery are unknown. Yet another surgical solution is the lap-band procedure, which implants a stomach band to limit the amount of food an individual can consume. Currently this is reserved for the morbidly obese, but a panel has recommended that the Food and Drug Administration consider this procedure for obese persons. This change will make lap-bands available to 30 million Americans or more.

Because obesity is extremely difficult to reverse, health professionals have concluded that prevention, rather than treatment, offers the best long-term solution. In 2005 the late Sen. Edward M. Kennedy, for instance, introduced a bill titled the Prevention of Childhood Obesity Act. In support of the bill, Kennedy stated, "Prevention is the cornerstone of good health and long, productive lives for all Americans. Childhood obesity is preventable, but we have to work together to stop this worsening epidemic and protect our children's future."

Other proposed solutions have included bans on the sale and promotion of junk food in schools, restrictions on junk food/fast food advertising on television targeted at youth, taxing high-calorie foods, improved labeling in food, counseling by medical professionals, and better education about nutrition in schools. Most professionals believe that no single solution will work and that multiple-intervention strategies will be necessary and more cost effective.

According to a recent study published in the *American Journal of Health Promotion*, 32 percent of nine-month-old babies are obese or overweight, as are 34 percent of two-year-olds. The Centers for Disease Control estimates that 33 percent of Americans aged twenty to seventy-four are now obese. Projections have predicted that more than 50 percent of Americans will be obese by 2050. In 1998 the medical costs of obesity were estimated to be $78.5 billion per year; estimates of the medical costs of obesity in 2008 rose to $147 billion per year, which is 9 percent of all U.S. medical costs. By 2018, costs are projected to balloon to $344 billion. Other costs of obesity include increased absenteeism rates, reduced worker productivity, and increased food and clothing costs.

See also Advertising; Cheeseburger Laws; Diabetes; Dieting; Exercise; Hypertension; Lawsuits; Nutritional Guidelines; Obesity Acceptance Movement; School Food; Strokes; Vending Machines

For Further Information:

Alderman, Jess, Jason A. Smith, Ellen J. Fried, and Richard A. Daynard. "Application of Law to the Childhood Obesity Epidemic." *Journal of Law, Medicine & Ethics* Northeastern University Public Law & Legal Theory Research Paper No. 17 (Spring 2007): 90–112.

American Obesity Association Web site: www.obesity.org

Anderson, Michael, and David Matsa. "Are Restaurants Really Supersizing America?" *American Economic Journal: Applied. Economics* 2, no. 2 (May 2010): 164–78.

Beller, Anne Scott. *Fat & Thin: A Natural History of Obesity*. New York: Farrar, Straus and Giroux, 1977.

Bray, George A., Samara Joy Nielsen, and Barry M. Popkin. "Consumption of High-Fructose Corn Syrup in Beverages May Play a Role in the Epidemic of Obesity." *American Journal of Clinical Nutrition* 79 (April 2004): 537–43.

Bray, George A., Samara Joy Nielsen, and Barry M. Popkin. *The Battle of the Bulge: A History of Obesity Research*. Pittsburgh, PA: Dorrance Publishing Company, 2007.

Brownell, Kelly D., and Derek Yach. "The Battle of the Bulge." *Foreign Policy* (November/December 2005): 27–28.

Brownell, Kelly D., and Katherine Battle Horgen. *Food Fight: The Inside Story of the Food Industry, America's Obesity Crisis, and What We Can Do about It*. Chicago: Contemporary Books, 2004.

Calories Count: Report of the Working Group on Obesity. Washington, D.C.: Food and Drug Administration, 2004.

Campos, Paul. *The Obesity Myth: Why America's Obsession with Weight Is Hazardous to Your Health*. New York: Gotham Books, 2004.

Campos, Paul, et al. "The Epidemiology of Overweight and Obesity: Public Health Crisis or Moral Panic?" *International Journal of Epidemiology* 35, no. 1 (2006): 55–60.

Cardello, Hank, and Doug Garr, *Stuffed: An Insider's Look at Who's (Really) Making America Fat*. New York: Ecco, 2009.

Chase, Chris. *The Great American Waistline: Putting It on and Taking It Off*. New York: Coward, McCann & Geoghegan, 1981.

Chou, Shin-Yi, Inas Rashad, and Michael Grossman. "Fast-Food Advertising on Television and Its Influence on Childhood Obesity." *Journal of Law and Economics* 51, no. 4 (2008): 599–618.

Critser, Greg. *Fat Land: How Americans Became the Fattest People in the World*. New York: Houghton Mifflin Company, 2003.

Currie, Janet M. *The Effect of Fast Food Restaurants on Obesity*. Cambridge, MA: National Bureau of Economic Research, 2009.

Davis, Brennan, and Christopher Carpenter. "Proximity of Fast-Food Restaurants to Schools and Adolescent Obesity." *American Journal of Public Health* 99 (March 2009): 505–10.

de Gonzalez, Amy Berrington, et al. "Body-Mass Index and Mortality among 1.46 Million White Adults." *New England Journal of Medicine* 363 (December 2, 2010): 2211–19.

Field, A. E., et al. "Snack Food Intake Does Not Predict Weight Change among Children and Adolescents," *International Journal of Obesity and Related Metabolic Disorders* 10 (October 2004): 1210-6.

Finklestein, Eric A. *The Fattening of America: How the Economy Makes Us Fat, If It Matters, and What to Do about It*. Fort Lee, NJ: Wiley, 2008.

Finucane, Mariel M. "National, Regional, and Global Trends in Body-Mass Index since 1980: Systematic Analysis of Health Examination Surveys and Epidemiological Studies with 960 Country-Years and 9·1 Million Participants." *The Lancet* 10 (February 4, 2011), as at: www.thelancet.com/journals/lancet/article/PIIS0140-6736(10)62037-5/abstract

Frank, Theodore H. "Taxonomy of Obesity Legislation." *University of Little Rock Law Review* 28, no. 3 (2006): 427–41.

Garda, Michael. "Truth, Belief and the Cultural Politics of Obesity Scholarship and Public Health Policy." *Critical Public Health* (February 2011), as at: www.informaworld.com/smpp/content~db=all~content=a931520370

Gardner, Gary. *Underfed and Overfed: The Global Epidemic of Malnutrition*. Washington, D.C.: Worldwatch, 2000.

Harris, Jennifer L., et al. "Fast Food FACTS: Evaluating Fast Food Nutrition and Marketing to Youth." New Haven, CT: Rudd Center for Food Policy & Obesity, 2010, as at: www.fastfoodmarketing.org/media/FastFoodFACTS_Report.pdf

Heaney, M. T. "Fat Politics: The Real Story behind America's Obesity Epidemic." *Journal of Health Politics Policy and Law* 32, no. 1 (February 1, 2007): 131–38.

Johnson-Down, Louise, and Grace M. Egeland. "Adequate Nutrient Intakes Are Associated with Traditional Food Consumption in Nunavut Inuit Children Aged 3–5 Years." *Journal of Nutrition* 140 (July 2010): 1311–16.

Keller, Kathleen. *Encyclopedia of Obesity*. Los Angeles: Sage Publications, 2008.

Kerr, Jim. *Diet and Obesity*. Mankato, MN: Sea-to-Sea Publications, 2010.

Kessler, David A. *The End of Overeating: Taking Control of the Insatiable American Appetite*. Emmaus, PA: Rodale; New York: Distributed to the trade by Macmillan, 2009.

Keystone Forum on Away-From-Home Foods: Opportunities for Preventing Weight Gain and Obesity Final Report. Washington, D.C.: Keystone Center, 2006; available at: key stone.org/files/file/about/publications/Forum_Report_FINAL_5-30-06.pdf

Kunkel, Dale, and Walter Gantz. "Children's Television Advertising in the Multi-channel Environment." *Journal of Communication* 42, no. 3 (1992): 134–52.

Levi, Jeffrey, Laura M. Segal, Rebecca St. Laurent, and Serena Vinter. *F as in Fat: How Obesity Threatens America's Future 2010*. Washington, D.C.: Trust for America's Health, 2010, as at: www.healthyamericans.org/reports/obesity2010/Obesity2010Report.pdf

Malik, Vasanti S., et al. "Sugar Sweetened Beverages and Risk of Metabolic Syndrome and Type 2 Diabetes: A Meta-Analysis." *Diabetes Care* 33, no. 11 (November 2010): 2477–83.

Mercola, Joseph, and Ben Lerner, *Generation XL: Raising Healthy, Intelligent Kids in a High-Tech, Junk-food World.* Nashville, TN: Thomas Nelson, 2007.

Mission: Readiness, Military Leaders for Kids, "Too Fat to Fight: Retired Military Leaders Want Junk Food Out of America's Schools," as at: http://cdn.missionreadiness.org/MR_Too_Fat_to_Fight-1.pdf

Moore, Elizabeth S. "Perspectives on Food Marketing and Childhood Obesity: Introduction to the Special Section." *Journal of Public Policy & Marketing* 26, no. 2 (Fall 2007): 157–61.

National Policy & Legal Analysis Network to Prevent Childhood Obesity (NPLAN) Web site: www.nplanonline.org/childhood-obesity/products/digital-marketing

Oliver, J. Eric. *Fat Politics: The Real Story Behind America's Obesity Epidemic.* New York: Oxford University Press, 2005.

Organisation for Economic Co-Operation and Development. *Obesity and the Economics of Prevention: Fit not Fat.* Paris: OECD, 2010.

Pereira, M. A., et al. "Fast-food Habits, Weight Gain, and Insulin Resistance (the Cardia Study): 15-year Prospective Analysis." *Lancet* 395 (January 1, 2005): 36–42.

Popkin, Barry. *The World Is Fat: The Fads, Trends, Policies, and Products That Are Fattening the Human Race.* New York: Avery, Penguin, 2009.

Rothblum, Esther, and Sondra Solovay, eds. *The Fat Studies Reader.* New York: New York University Press, 2009.

Saguy, Abigail, and Kevin R. Riley. "Weighing Both Sides: Morality, Mortality, and Framing Contests over Obesity." *Journal of Health Politics, Policy and Law* 30, no. 5 (2005): 869–923.

The Surgeon General's Call to Action to Prevent and Decrease Overweight and Obesity (2001), as at: www.surgeongeneral.gov/topics/obesity/calltoaction/toc.htm

Tao, Meng-Hua, et al. "Association of Overweight with Breast Cancer Survival." *American Journal of Epidemiology* 163, no. 2 (January 15, 2006): 101–7.

Von Behren, Julie, et al. "Obesity, Waist Size, and Prevalence of Current Asthma in the California Teachers Study Cohort." *Thorax* 65 (2010): 282–84.

Wilcox, Brian L., Dale Kunkel, Joanne Cantor, Peter Dowrick, Susan Linn, and Edward Palmer. *Report of the APA Task Force on Advertising and Children.* Washington, D.C.: American Psychological Association, 2004.

Williams, Elizabeth M., ed. *The A-Z Encyclopedia of Food Controversies and the Law.* Santa Barbara, CA: Greenwood, 2010.

Obesity Acceptance Movement

The problems associated with being obese are not just related to health, there are also the psychological, social, and economic consequences. Studies have demonstrated that obese individuals face prejudice from employers, doctors, and teachers. As a result, obese people face "social rejection, poor quality of relationships, worse outcomes and lower socio-economic status," according to the Rudd Center for Food Policy & Obesity.

Many people believe that obesity is the fault of the individuals who fail to exercise, who eat too much, and who lack self-control. They are viewed, according to many reports, as ugly, and many people feel uncomfortable when associating with obese people. As a result, obese people have more psychological problems, their earning potential is decreased, they have less opportunity for being hired or for advancement in their jobs, and their academic opportunities are more limited than individuals of average weight. This discrimination is present throughout society, and surveys of obese and overweight people document that they have faced prejudice in employment, the medical profession, and education.

As a result of the prejudice, an informal movement called the obesity (or fat) acceptance movement has emerged to end bias and to change attitudes toward overweight and obese people. Advocates support laws opposed to discrimination that are similar to the current laws against prejudice on the basis of race, age, gender, or sexual orientation. Several organizations, such as the National Association to Advance Fat Acceptance, which was formed in 1969, have emerged that have tried to channel these concerns, but they have little influence.

The Rudd Center has taken on a major research effort to document the problem and recommend solutions. One of its goals is to "reduce weight stigma by making creative connections between science and public policy." Despite this documented prejudice, according to the Center, "little has been done to stop the bias and discrimination that obese children and adults face every day."

See also Obesity; Rudd Center for Food Policy & Obesity

For Further Information:

National Association to Advance Fat Acceptance Web site: www.naafaonline.com

Rudd Center for Food Policy & Obesity Web site: www.yaleruddcenter.org

Solovay, Sondra. *Tipping the Scales of Justice: Fighting Weight-Based Discrimination.* Amherst, NY: Prometheus Books, 2000.

Wann, Marilyn. *Fat! So? Because You Don't Have to Apologize for Your Size!* Berkeley, CA: 10 Speed Press, 1998.

Occupational Safety and Health Administration (OSHA)

The Occupational Safety and Health Administration (OSHA) was created in 1970 to ensure "so far as possible every working man and woman in the nation safe and healthful working conditions and to preserve our human resources." Since then, OSHA has examined workplaces related to fast food and its suppliers and has issued guidelines related to them. For instance, in 1996 OSHA issued *Guidelines for Workplace Violence*, but restaurants opposed them. A 1999 OSHA-funded study estimated that 12 percent of all violent crimes that took place in the workplace occurred at fast food restaurants. In fact, an estimated four to five employees—most of whom are teenagers—are murdered at fast food restaurants every month. This is mainly owing to the late hours that many fast food outlets are open. In addition, the quantity of cash usually kept on hand in fast food restaurants and the minimal security that fast food chains have offered workers are also reasons for crime and violence at fast food chains. Such studies and guidelines have drawn attention to this issue, and OSHA has issued a publication to help fast food restaurants decrease the opportunities for violence.

OSHA has also levied fines on meatpacking companies for safety violations. The maximum fine that OSHA can impose, however, for a safety violation is $70,000. A 2003 study of 2,197 workplace deaths over a 20-year period revealed that OSHA had levied $106 million in civil fines for those deaths, averaging $4,823 per fatality. These fines do not strike fear into companies whose firms earn billions of dollars annually. Advocates for better safety conditions in meatpacking and other fast food operations have pushed for higher penalties, mandatory plant closures, and charges of negligence against those responsible.

See also Crime; Fast Food; Suppliers; Violence

For Further Information:

OSHA Web site: www.osha.gov

Schlosser, Eric. *Fast Food Nation: The Dark Side of the All-American Meal*. New York: Houghton Mifflin Company, 2001.

Oh Henry!

In 1914 George H. Williamson, a salesman for a candy broker in Chicago, opened his own candy store. He made candies in the kitchen in the back of the store, and he doubled as salesman during the day and janitor at night. Sales grew steadily and Williamson observed what customers liked when they bought his candy. Based on this knowledge he opened a second store, which was also successful. Rather than continue to make the candies by hand, he decided to manufacture them. In 1919 he closed both stores and began manufacturing the candies that his customers preferred most. He soon had orders from jobbers in Illinois and surrounding states for one candy bar in particular, but he needed a catchy name for it. Several stories have circulated as to how he chose the name. One story was that the candy was named after a suitor who had pursued one of the girls in Williamson's shop. Every time the man came into the candy shop to flirt, the salesgirls would squeal, "Oh,

Henry!"—or so goes the story. Another story was that Williamson liked the short stories of William Sydney Porter, whose pen name was O. Henry.

Williamson launched the Oh Henry! candy bar in 1920. It was originally a log-shaped bar with a fudge center, surrounded by a caramel and peanut layer and coated in pure milk chocolate. The Oh Henry! sold for a dime—twice the going rate of the competition. Williamson knew that he would have to convince people to pay twice as much for his product. Advertising was the answer. He first advertised in newspapers in one city, and then expanded to others. Oh Henry! ads appeared on posters in the same cities targeted by newspaper ads, and they finally hit national women's magazines, describing how women cut Oh Henry! bars into dainty slices and served them for dessert at home. The result was that by 1923, Oh Henry! was the best-selling candy bar in America.

The Williamson Candy Company moved to a larger factory in 1925, where it manufactured 500,000 Oh Henry! candy bars every nine hours. The company issued a cookbook in 1926 titled *60 New Ways to Serve a Famous Candy*, in which the candy bar (sliced, diced, chopped, or melted) was used in salads, cakes, cookies, desserts, puddings and sauces, sweet breads, and "tea dainties." It also included a recipe using Oh Henry! candy bars as a topping for sweet potatoes. By 1927, plants had been opened in Oakland, California, and New York, and millions of Oh Henry! bars were manufactured each day.

Even though sugar and chocolate were rationed during World War II, the production of Oh Henry! candy bars set a new sales record in 1943, but more than half of the candy bars went to the armed forces. The Williamson Candy Company was eventually sold to Standard Brands, and then to Nabisco. In 1990 the candy bar was acquired by Nestlé USA. It remains one of America's most popular candy bars.

See also Advertising; Cakes; Candy; Caramels; Chocolate; Cookies; Nabisco; Nestlé; Pudding; Sugars/Sweeteners

For Further Information:

Broekel, Ray. *The Great America Candy Bar Book*. Boston: Houghton Mifflin Company, 1982.

Richardson, Tim. *Sweets: A History of Candy*. New York: Bloomsbury, 2002.

Smith, Andrew F. *Peanuts: The Illustrious History of the Goober Pea*. Urbana: University of Illinois Press, 2002.

100-Calorie Snack Packs

The idea behind the 100-Calorie Snack Pack is portion control: people eat more from large package sizes than from small containers. Creating smaller sizes limits the amount of food that people eat. Snack packs were introduced in 2004, and

Keebler Right Bites and Nabisco 100 Calorie Packs. (AP/Wide World Photos)

since then their sales have skyrocketed. Many companies now produce small snack packs that contain one hundred calories or fewer. These include Almonds, Chips Ahoy!, Oreos, Ritz crackers, Ritz Snack Mix, Little Debbie, Sun Chips, Chex Cheddar Snacks, Pringles, Hershey Pretzel Bars, Cheetos, Cheese-Its, Cheese Nips, Pop Secret Popcorn, Goldfish, Shortbread Cookie Crisps, Nutribars, Rold Gold pretzels, Wheat Thins, and Hostess Snack Cakes, to name a few. Today, snack packs generate more than $200 million annually and those sales will likely be much higher in the future.

One reason is the large profits that the manufacturers generate with these small sizes. The cost per product is higher for the snack packs, mainly because more packaging is required, but the manufacturer also makes sizeable profits estimated at from 16 percent to 279 percent more per ounce, according to a study conducted by the Center for Science in the Public Interest, which also noted that "smaller portions don't make snacks good for you."

See also Calories; Center for Science in the Public Interest (CSPI); Cheetos; Chips Ahoy!; Cookies; Corporate Response to Criticism; Goldfish; Little Debbie; Oreos; Popcorn; Pretzels; Ritz Crackers

For Further Information:

Wansink, Brian. "Can Package Size Accelerate Usage Volume?" *Journal of Marketing* 60, no. 3 (1996): 1–14.

Onion Rings

Onion rings are ring-shaped slices of onion that have been battered and deep-fried. Advocates claim that onion rings were invented by the Pig Stand restaurant chain in the 1920s. No primary source evidence has been produced to support this claim, and recipes for vegetables, including onions, fried in batter were present in American cookbooks well before the twentieth century. In 1955 frozen breaded onion rings were developed by Sam Quigley in Nebraska. In 1959 he began manufacturing frozen onion rings, and he called his operation Sam's Onions. Other companies began manufacturing onion rings for home use and for fast food outlets.

Onion rings. (Dreamstime.com)

Onion rings did not become popular fast food until the 1970s. In 1973 Dairy Queen began serving onion rings, followed by Jack in the Box in 1979. Today, Burger King also serves them, as does A&W Root Beer, Carl's Jr., Sonic, and many other chains.

See also A&W; Burger King; Carl's Jr.; Dairy Queen; Jack in the Box; Sonic

For Further Information:

Whaoo! Appetizers Web site: www.appetizer.com

Orange Crush

California chemist Neil C. Ward experimented for four years before he came up with an orange soda. He partnered with Clayton J. Howell of Cleveland, Ohio, to market the new beverage in 1916. During World War I, sugar was difficult to acquire and the new beverage languished until the war ended in 1918. Ward and Howell named their company the Orange Crush Bottling Company and named their drink Ward's Orange Crush. It mainly consisted of sugar and carbonated water, with a modicum of orange concentrate. The name was subsequently shortened to Orange Crush and it became extremely successful, in part because it was promoted as a health beverage at a time when medical professionals were touting vitamin C and encouraging everyone to drink orange juice. By 1924, Orange Crush had 1,200 bottlers in the United States and Canada. It subsequently expanded to Latin America and Europe. Ward became chairman of the Orange Crush Bottling Company in 1931.

During the 1920s and 1930s, Orange Crush dominated the market for orange soda. The company added other citrus-flavored beverages, such as Lemon and Lime Crush. In 1962 Crush International was acquired by Charles E. Hires Co., maker of Hires Root Beer. In 1980 Crush International was sold to Procter & Gamble, who sold it in 1989 to Cadbury Schweppes. Today it is a brand manufactured by the Dr Pepper Snapple Group.

See also Cadbury Schweppes; Dr Pepper Snapple Group; Hires Root Beer; Soda/Soft Drinks; Sugars/Sweeteners

For Further Information:

Hogan, David Gerald. *Selling 'em by the Sack: White Castle and the Creation of American Food*. New York: New York University Press, 1997.

Oreos

In 1912 Nabisco introduced the Oreo cookie to compete with Hydrox Biscuit Bon-bons, which had been released two years earlier. Oreos were a round cookie with vanilla cream sandwiched between two chocolate sandwich biscuits. It is one of the most successful cookies in American history.

In 1994 Nabisco introduced a lower-calorie version of Oreos. In 2000 Nabisco was acquired by Kraft Foods, Inc., which expanded the Oreo cookie line. In 2001 the company created extensions to the Oreo brand, including a version with chocolate filling and Mint 'n Creme Double Delight Oreos. It added different colors and flavors to mark special events and holidays. The company has also developed many new packages for Oreos, some of which, like Oreo Barz, are no longer cookies. In 2002 the 7-Eleven convenience store chain worked with Nabisco to create plastic cups filled with Oreos. These containers fit into car cup holders so that drivers could eat them while traveling.

Perhaps because of their popularity, Oreos have been used in a number of unusual ways. Domino's Pizza chain, for instance, uses them on their Oreo Cookie Pizza. Also, deep-fried Oreos—Oreo cookies dipped in batter and deep-fried (or just fried) and dusted with powdered sugar—have recently become a favorite at carnivals, county fairs and state fairs.

Oreos have also become the subject of lawsuits. For instance, in 2003 Stephen Joseph filed a suit against Oreos, claiming that they were unhealthy because they contained transfat. When Kraft Foods, the manufacturer of Oreos, reported that it was trying to reduce transfat in Oreos, Joseph dropped the case.

Oreos are America's best-selling cookies. In 2002 Kraft boasted that 450 billion Oreo cookies had been sold since they were first manufactured in 1912. In 2010 Harris Interactive's Youth EquiTrend study on brand recognition ranked Oreos fourth among 8- to 24-year-olds.

Oreos have also become popular in other countries. In 1996 they were introduced into China, and the company had a serious problem—Chinese consumers found the Oreo to be too sweet, so they decreased the sugar content and created new forms of Oreos, such as a wafer version, and they added new flavors such as green tea ice cream and strawberry. By 2006, the Oreo was China's best-selling cookie.

See also Chocolate; Convenience Stores; Cookies; Domino's Pizza; Kraft Foods; Lawsuits; Nabisco; 7-Eleven

For Further Information:

Boland, Ed. "450 Billion Oreos to Go." *New York Times*, July 28, 2002, CY2.

Oreo Web site: www.nabiscoworld.com/oreo

Organic Junk Food

As concerns were raised with processed food, some Americans sought alternative systems of agriculture and food processing. What emerged was organic food, which was a label applied to food grown, raised, or processed without chemical pesticides, fertilizers, hormones, and food additives. The interest in organic food sprang from health food stores. Beginning in the 1970s, thousands of health food stores opened in communities across America, and many offered organic foods.

Problems emerged. There were many different definitions of the term "organic," and there was no inspection to guarantee that food was grown or raised in an organic way. The 1990 Farm Bill passed by the U.S. Congress contained the Organic Foods Production Act, which set national standards for how organic food must be produced, handled, and labeled. Organic foods could not include synthetic fertilizers or pesticides. The bill also established the National Organic Standards Board, which issues a list of prohibited substances, such as synthetic fertilizer and antibiotics, that cannot be used in organic food. After twelve years of work by the National Organic Standards Board, the National Organic Program (NOP) took effect in October 2002; it is administered by the U.S. Department of Agriculture (USDA). The NOP covers in detail all aspects of organic food production, processing, delivery, and retail sale. Under the NOP, farmers and food processors who wish to use the word "organic" in reference to their businesses and products must be certified organic by the USDA.

The term "organic" now appears on some packages of junk foods, such as cereals, potato chips, sodas (such as Coca-Cola), candies, cakes, cookies (such as Oreos and Chips Ahoy!), crackers (such as Ritz Crackers), dips, and condiments (such as ketchup). Certified Organic is defined by the U.S. Department of Agriculture, which means in part that the ingredients in the product were grown without pesticides, synthetic fertilizers, or hormones, and the product cannot have genetically modified or irradiated ingredients. Many organic foods contain high levels of calories, fat, and salt, and are low in nutrition.

See also Candy; Chips Ahoy!; Coca-Cola Company; Cookies; Dips; Ketchup; Oreos; Ritz Crackers; U.S. Department of Agriculture

For Further Information:

Schuldt, Jonathon P., and Norbert Schwarz. "The "Organic" Path to Obesity? Organic Claims Influence Calorie Judgments and Exercise Recommendations." *Judgment and Decision Making* 5 (June 2010): 144–50.

P

Packaging

Until the late nineteenth century, food was generally sold as generic commodities in barrels or sacks. The exceptions were a few specialty and luxury items. Baker's and Cadbury's chocolates, for example, had long been sold in boxes with tinfoil inner lining and the company's name printed on them.

The first general packaging revolution began in the United States during the 1870s. It was the flat-bottomed paper bag, which was initially used by grocers who scooped up the commodities and placed them in the bag. This became revolutionary when it was wed to the invention of the offset press in 1879 that permitted brands, logos, and other identifying marks to be printed on the bags. At the same time, the folding paper box began to be mass-marketed. With the cheap and rapid production of paper bags and boxes, retail life changed in America. Packing could include distinctive colors and shapes that set goods apart. Constant repetition helped consumers who had to make decisions about a vast array of commercial products. In addition, with a package, the company could develop logos and visual designs that could attract customers.

Cereal companies, such as the makers of Quaker Oats, and later those manufactured by Kellogg and Post, were among the first significant businesses to use packaging. They incorporated many of the devices subsequently employed by candy companies and fast food chains. These included color graphics, brand names, slogans, colorful images, recipes, and often spokescharacters, such as the Quaker Oats Quaker. They also included other gimmicks, such as coupons, that were intended to increase the sale of the company's products.

The first commercial snack foods, such as Cracker Jack and Marshall's Potato Chips, were sold in barrels. As soon as the barrel was opened, however, the contents went stale, which lessened their appeal. The makers of Cracker Jack solved the packing problem; they acquired a patent for a type of wax paper from Germany and packed their product in wax-paper bags. The bags were placed in a box, which was covered with a waterproof outer seal. Consumer sales soared, thanks mainly to the advertising and the new packaging that kept the confection fresh. Other snack food manufacturers followed Cracker Jack's lead to develop packaging that kept freshness in and permitted them to advertise their product.

Shelled peanuts, like those in Cracker Jack, went stale unless they were packed in airtight containers. Planters Peanuts initially sold shelled peanuts in glassine bags, but they were difficult to fill and transport and the cost of the glassine bag increased the selling price of their peanuts. So Planters, like most other peanut shellers and cleaners, sold peanuts in large tins. Planters placed glassine bags in the tin, and shopkeepers scooped out the peanuts for the customer and filled the glassine bags. This was complicated, so as the price of canning decreased, Planters Peanuts packaged many of its products in tin cans, which also made it possible for the company to advertise. The company placed the image of Mr. Peanut on virtually every package of peanuts manufactured after 1917.

The potato chip industry had a very difficult packaging problem to solve. In 1926 potato chip maker Laura Scudder of Monterey Park, California, experimented with a new potato chip-packing idea. She handpacked the chips into wax-paper bags and her employees sealed the tops with a warm iron. This created an individual serving container that kept out moisture, but it was impossible to print on the outside of wax-paper. In 1933 the Dixie Wax Paper Company introduced the first preprintable waxed glassine bag, which made it possible for manufacturers to print brand names and other information on the outside of the bag. This mode of packaging promptly became the standard in the salty snack world.

Cellophane, which was invented in 1911, was commonly used in the United States by the 1930s. It protected food and permitted customers to actually see the food that they were purchasing. Cellophane encouraged impulse buying, where the allure of visible snacks encouraged customers to buy the product. This was particularly used by bakers for packaging cookies, pies, and cakes.

Candy and chocolates have gone through numerous packaging changes. Until the late nineteenth century, candy fell into two categories: specialty chocolates, such as those made by Baker's and Cadbury's, which were sold in boxes with printed brand names; and penny candy, which was generally a generic product sold individually from large glass containers in grocery stores and in vending machines. Tootsie Rolls were the first penny candy to be individually wrapped. Wrapping enables manufacturers to create brand names and logos, which in turn leads to advertising and promotion. Since the early twentieth century, candy packaging has diversified to include a variety of shapes and sizes. Manufacturers now produce snack foods with stand-up pouches, single-serve packs, 100-calorie snack packs, and resealable bags.

Design of the packaging is vital for all food manufacturers. Research has demonstrated that customers initially recognize the color scheme on the package, then the logo, and finally the name of the product. Wrigley's gum and Hershey's Milk Chocolate Bar wrappers are frequently cited as outstanding packaging—simple designs that are readily recognized by potential customers.

Soft Drink Packaging

In the soft drink world, packaging took a different direction. At first, soft drink manufacturers produced syrup or extract that was easily transported to drugstores and soda fountains, where the syrup and carbonated water were mixed just before serving. Bottling of soda beverages began in the mid-nineteenth century, but the bottles broke easily and, owing to the lack of airtight caps, they lost carbonation. This changed in 1892 when William Painter invented the crown bottle cap, which made it possible to easily seal bottles. Bottling of soft drinks was enhanced by improved glass bottles that could keep the carbon dioxide in and would not shatter during the manufacturing process. Another packaging innovation introduced by Coca-Cola in 1915 was the contoured bottle, which became one of the most recognized bottles in the world.

Beer was distributed in cans during the 1930s, but soft drinks built up greater pressure inside and the manufacture of stronger cans for soft drinks was not perfected until 1953. Royal Crown Cola was the first soft drink distributed in a can in 1957. Five years later, pull-ring tabs were used on beer cans and, later, on soda cans. In 1965 soft drinks were dispensed from vending machines. By 1972, polyethylene terephthalate (PET) bottles were created.

Soft drink cans and bottles have been criticized because they are not biodegradable and take up considerable space in landfills. Recycling programs were begun against the wishes of many bottlers. As relatively few people return the empties, most soft drink companies have come to consider the deposit for the bottles or cans to be a profit center. Likewise, PET bottles can be recycled into other products, such as polyester carpets.

Recent Label Changes

Two recent changes in packaging have affected both snack foods and soft drink packaging. The first is the nutrition labels that are now required. The junk food manufacturers strongly opposed nutritional labeling, fearing that the lack of nutrition in most of their products would discourage customers for buying their products. Because most people do not read the labels, however, and many people who do are unable to easily understand the nutrition information, there is no evidence that sales have declined owing to the addition of these labels. In fact, there is evidence that labeling has actually increased sales: the word "nutrition" on a package implies that the contents are healthy.

The second change in labeling has been the addition of bar codes, which began to be used during the 1960s. They permit easier, faster, and more accurate checkouts and, when combined with computers, permit an immediate feedback on sales of particular snack foods and soft drinks. Using this information, manufacturers can gain a great deal of information as to who is buying their products and how successful their product advertising and promotion is in particular areas.

Fast Food

In the fast food world, packaging has taken yet another path. White Castle came up with the idea that fast food was a packaged experience. Because most customers purchased food and ate it in their cars or took it offsite to consume, White Castle needed bags to transport the food. Paper cups, bags, and coverings were used. McDonald's has carefully constructed the containers for its Happy Meals, salads, and Chicken McNuggets. Its french fry containers have been carefully designed to suggest that the fries are packed to overflowing, giving the appearance of abundance. During the 1970s, McDonald's decided to use polystyrene foam for coffee cups and food containers for its Big Macs and Quarter Pounders. Since polystyrene is not easily biodegradable, environmental groups charged McDonald's with destroying the environment. McDonald's responded by withdrawing polystyrene and replacing it with paper. Other chains have similarly packaged their food. KFC, for instance, created its large paper bucket.

Greener Packaging

KFC began to use reusable containers for some side orders, such as mashed potatoes, green beans, and coleslaw. These are replacing the styrofoam boxes. In 2010 Greener Package (GP), an organization devoted to sustainable packaging, gave KFC an award for significantly reducing their packaging's environmental footprint. The containers include the statement embossed on the lid "KFC Reusable, Microwave & Top Rack Dishwasher Safe." The container reduces the size of shipping containers, replaces the nonrecyclable containers, requires 25 percent less energy to produce than the previous package, and generates 50 percent fewer greenhouse gases, according to GP. A study indicated that customers did save and reuse the containers.

Concern with Packaging

In 2010 Canadian scientists began to express concern with the chemicals in wrappers used to line popcorn bags and fast food wrappers. A study indicated that polyfluoroalkyl phosphate esters or PAPs move into the popcorn and are ingested when the bag is heated. When PAPs enter the body, they break down to perfluorinated carboxylic acids or PFCAs, which may be harmful to humans.

See also Advertising; Beverages; Cadbury; Cakes; Carbonation; Cereals; Chicken McNuggets; Chocolate; Coca-Cola Company; Cookies; Cracker Jack; Environment; Food Labeling; French Fries; Gum; Happy Meals; Hershey's Milk Chocolate Bar; KFC; McDonald's; Mr. Peanut; Penny Candy; Pie; Popcorn; Potato Chips; Salads; Soda/Soft Drinks; Tootsie Roll Industries; Vending Machines; White Castle

For Further Information:

Greener Package Web site: www.greenerpackage.com

Hine, Thomas. *The Total Package: The Evolution and Secret Meanings of Boxes, Bottles, Cans, and Tubes.* New York: Little, Brown and Company, 1995.

Mabury, Scott, and Jessica D'eon. "Exploring Indirect Sources of Human Exposure to Perfluoroalkyl Carboxylates (PFCAs): Evaluating Uptake, Elimination and Biotransformation of Polyfluoroalkyl Phosphate Esters (PAPs) in the Rat." *Environmental Health Perspectives* published online, November 8, 2010, as at: http://ehp03.niehs.nih.gov/article/fetchArticle.action?articleURI=info%3Adoi%2F10.1289%2Fehp.1002409

Prince, Jackie. *Launching a New Business Ethic: The Environment as a Standard Operating Procedure at McDonald's and at Other Companies*. Washington, D.C.: Environmental Defense Fund, 1991.

Richardson, Tim. *Sweets: A History of Candy*. New York: Bloomsbury, 2002.

Robertson, Gordon L. *Food Packaging, Principles and Practice*. 2nd ed. Boca Raton, FL: Taylor & Francis, 2005.

Smith, Andrew F. *Peanuts: The Illustrious History of the Goober Pea*. Urbana: University of Illinois Press, 2002.

Pancakes

The pancake (also called a flapjack, slapjack, griddle cake, or hotcake) is a flat, round breadstuff made from a simple batter of flour, milk, and eggs. The batter is poured onto a lightly greased griddle or into a skillet and the cake is flipped over when the underside is done. American pancakes are most commonly made from wheat, buckwheat, or cornmeal; like other quickbreads, they lend themselves to additions such as berries and other fruits. A pat of butter along with honey, maple, or another sweet syrup are traditional accompaniments. More elaborate toppings include whipped cream and fresh fruit.

Pancakes became signature dishes at some casual restaurant chains, such as the International House of Pancakes (IHOP). They became part of fast food breakfast menus in the 1970s, when Jim Delligati, an early McDonald's franchisee in Pittsburgh, began serving a simple breakfast menu, which included pancakes. Since then other chains, such as Whataburger, have also served pancakes. The toppings, especially butter and sweet syrups, add considerable calories to the dish. In 2003 McDonald's introduced the McGriddle, which is bacon or a pork sausage wrapped in a pancake with syrup.

Several new pancake combinations have been released. Dunkin' Donuts launched Pancake Bites—sausages wrapped in maple-flavored pancakes. Burger King introduced the Ultimate Breakfast Platter, composed of scrambled eggs, hash browns, sausage, a biscuit, and three pancakes with syrup. It weighs in at 1,310 calories, 72 grams of fat, and 2,490 milligrams of sodium.

See also Dunkin' Donuts; McDonald's; Pork; Whataburger

For Further Information:

Albala, Ken. *Pancake: A Global History*. London: Reaktion Books, 2008.

Panda Express

Panda Express is a fast-casual restaurant chain launched by Andrew Cheng, who emigrated from the Yangzhou region of China to the United States in 1973. Ten years later, he launched Panda Express in Pasadena, California. It featured many Chinese-style dishes, such as Orange Chicken, Beijing Beef, Mandarin Chicken, and Kung Pao Chicken, with sides such as fried rice, steamed rice, chow mein, or mixed vegetables.

Panda Express opened its first outlet outside of California in 1988, and the company has continued to expand ever since. As of 2011, Panda Express had about one thousand outlets in thirty-four states, eight in Japan, and five in Puerto Rico. It is the largest fast food chain based on Chinese-style food, and one of the largest chains selling Asian-style food in general.

Panda Express is owned by Panda Restaurant Group, which also owns Panda Inn and Hibachi-San, a small Japanese-style chain. The company is headquartered in Rosemead, California.

See also Chinese American Fast Food; Fast Casual; Fast Food

For Further Information:

Coe, Andrew. *Chop Suey: A Cultural History of Chinese Food in the United States.* New York: Oxford University Press, 2009.

Panda Express Web site: www.pandaexpress.com

Panera Bread

Panera Bread, a fast-casual restaurant chain, specializes in bakery goods such as bread, bagels, cookies, and pastries, but it also offers a variety of other dishes, including sweets, salads, soups, macaroni and cheese, and beverages. In 2010 Zagat, the restaurant guide, rated it the most popular large chain in America. It offers some healthy choices, including options for whole grain breads and half-sized options for salads and soups. The majority of chicken used at Panera Bread is free of antibiotics and hormones.

The St. Louis Bread Company was launched in 1987 by Ken Rosenthal. Its nineteen bakery cafes in the St. Louis area were purchased by the Au Bon Pain Company in 1993. Au Bon Pain began to expand its bakery-cafe concept outside of the St. Louis area under the name Panera Bread. Seven years later, the Au Bon Pain Company sold its other chains, including its Au Bon Pain division, renamed itself Panera Bread, and began to launch and franchise outlets nationwide. In 2007 the company purchased Paradise Bakery & Café, which was based in Phoenix, with its more than 70 locations in ten mainly western and southwestern states. In 2011

Panera Bread. (AP/Wide World Photos)

the company had about 1,400 locations in 40 states and in Ontario, Canada; it is headquartered near St. Louis in Richmond Heights, Missouri.

See also Antibiotics; Au Bon Pain; Fast Casual; Hormones; Panera Bread

For Further Information:

Panera Bread Web site: www.panerabread.com

Patriotism

During wartime, many food companies have developed patriotic activities and themes for their products. During World War I, candy became an important component of military rations. The Hershey Company, for example, supplied the military with chocolate bars. Since peanuts were not rationed during the war, growing and consuming them (as opposed to rationed candy and chocolates) was viewed as patriotic. Stuart Judson's 1917 article in *The Forum*, titled "Peanuts and Patriotism," proclaimed that peanuts served valiantly in the war effort by conserving dairy products, substituting for meat, and feeding livestock.

When the United States entered World War II, Cracker Jack discontinued putting toys in its packages. Toyless Cracker Jacks were distributed to soldiers, who complained about the toys' absence, and soon prizes reappeared. Instead of the sophisticated whistles and miniature glass figures and animals that had delighted children previously, wartime prizes principally consisted of paper and tin gadgets, featuring patriotic symbols of pilots, commanders, aircraft, flags, and artillery. Perhaps the most unusual wartime prizes were paper propaganda cards, such as one with an effigy of a hanging Adolf Hitler.

During the war, many confection manufacturers lobbied the American government to guarantee that candy would be considered essential war goods. They succeeded in their efforts and 70 percent of all candy manufactured in the United States during the war was sold to the military. Although sugar was rationed, candy production continued uninterrupted through the war. It was estimated that every American serviceman consumed fifty pounds of candy during the war. In addition to one billion chocolate bars that were made for the military, Hershey manufactured D-rations and K-rations for military use. D-rations included a Hershey's Milk Chocolate Bar, greatly revised so it would not melt in hot climates. Mars, Inc., also packed rations, which included M&M's. Wrigley Company produced K-rations, each of which contained chewing gum. Tootsie Rolls, which were almost indestructible, were supplied in other rations. The Frito-Lay Company, as well as other companies, experienced shortages, rationing, and loss of manpower. Throughout the war, American armed forces at Fritos.

To make sure that the American public was aware of the patriotic activities of candy makers during the war, in 1944 the National Confectioners Association (NCA) spent $21 million on advertising that said that candy "energized" the American military. Patriotic themes, such as the American flag, soldiers, and national symbols graced all of these promotions.

When soft drink manufacturers faced the possibility that they would be declared nonessential businesses, Coca-Cola immediately presented itself as a patriotic drink. It provided free drinks for American soldiers and published patriotic-themed advertisements in magazines. As a consequence, the military permitted Coca-Cola employees to set up bottling plants behind American lines to supply the soldiers with Coke. This also gave Coca-Cola a great boost after the war, as they globalized their operations.

Many patriotic themes and activities reemerged during the Iraq wars in 1991 and 2003. On Thanksgiving Day in 1990, Mars, Inc., gave a Snickers bar to every American soldier in the Middle East. When France refused to join the American-led coalition invading Iraq in 2003, some congressional Republicans urged that the term "french fries" be changed to "freedom fries" in the congressional dining room.

Some candy manufacturers today produce candy with particular patriotic themes on their packages, especially around the Fourth of July. Tootsie Rolls, taffy, mints, and chocolate hearts have been encased in wrappings with the image of the

American flag; gummi army men, freedom rings, and airplanes are also manufactured; candy American flags are common; special jelly bean bags consist of only beans that are colored red, white, and blue; star-spangled lollipops are available on the Fourth of July, as are red, white, and blue Star Pops and Twisty Pops.

See also Advertising; Candy; Chewy Candy; Coca-Cola Company; Cracker Jack; French Fries; Frito-Lay; Gum; Hershey Company; Hershey's Milk Chocolate Bar; Jelly Beans; Lollipops/Suckers; M&M's; Mars, Inc.; National Confectioners Association; Snickers; Sugars/Sweeteners; Tootsie Roll Industries; Wrigley Co.

For Further Information:

Brenner, Joël Glenn. *The Emperors of Chocolate: Inside the Secret World of Hershey and Mars.* New York: Broadway Books, 2000.

Smith, Andrew F. *Peanuts: The Illustrious History of the Goober Pea.* Urbana: University of Illinois Press, 2002.

PayDay

In 1932 the PayDay candy bar, composed of caramel and peanuts, was invented by Frank Martoccio, founder of the F. A. Martoccio Company and later head of Hollywood Brands, Inc. Purportedly, it acquired its name because it was payday when the inventors tried to come up with a name. Hollywood Brands also made Butternut (1916), Zero (1920), and Milk Shake (1927) candy bars.

In 1967 the Martoccio family sold Hollywood Brands to Consolidated Foods Corporation, which sold it to Leaf, Inc. The North American confectionery division of Leaf, Inc., was acquired by the Hershey Company. Today, PayDay candy bars are made by Hershey. Beginning in 2003, Hershey began extending the product line with the PayDay Honey Roasted Limited Edition Bar. Two years later, it introduced PayDay Pro, an energy bar with added vitamins and minerals.

See also Candy; Caramels; Chocolate; Fudge; Hershey Company; Peanuts; Power and Energy Bars

For Further Information:

Hershey Company Web site: www.hersheys.com

Peanut Brittle

Brittles are a type of confection made by caramelizing sugar, molasses—or frequently corn syrup—along with other products, such as pecans, cashews, or shredded coconut. For peanut brittle, peanuts are used, as well as other ingredients such as peanut butter, butter, baking soda, salt, and vanilla. The hot combination is spread uniformly on a nonstick cold surface and allowed to cool. When the mixture is room temperature and hardened, the peanut brittle is broken up. One of the early manufacturers of peanut brittle in the United States was the William E. Brock Company, which first did so in 1906. Crushed peanut brittle is also added to ice cream and other confections

See also Ice Cream; Peanuts

Peanut Butter

In 1893 the vegetarian-diet advocate John Harvey Kellogg experimented with crushing various kinds of tree nuts and peanuts to produce what he called a butter or paste. Peanuts were the least expensive, so he limited his production to peanut butter. Owing in large part to his efforts, peanut butter quickly became an American food fad. Vegetarians adopted peanut butter almost immediately, and recipes for making and using it appeared in almost all vegetarian cookbooks published from 1899 on. The first major application of peanut butter among nonvegetarians was to make sandwiches. Peanut butter sandwich recipes first appeared on the scene in 1896.

Peanut butter. (Dreamstime.com)

By the 1920s, peanut butter was a major culinary product in America. Kellogg spread the good news about peanut butter's healthful qualities and was its greatest popularizer. Following the adoption of nut butters at Kellogg's Sanitarium in Battle Creek, Michigan, its popularity quickly spread among American promoters of health food and a vegetarian lifestyle. By 1899, peanut butter had also traveled across the Pacific Ocean to Australia and across the Atlantic to South Africa. The missionary zeal of vegetarians helped to introduce peanut butter into the American culinary mainstream and was instrumental in establishing the peanut butter industry.

Peanut butter did have one serious problem: peanuts contain almost 50 percent oil, and it quickly turns rancid. When the nuts are crushed to make peanut butter, the oil separates, requiring that the product be stirred before using. William Norman, an English chemist, invented a method of saturating unsaturated and polyunsaturated fatty acids, thus preventing them from turning rancid. In 1922 Joseph L. Rosefield of the Rosefield Packing Company of Alameda, California, applied these principles to peanut butter. He developed a process to prevent oil separation and spoilage in peanut butter. He removed 18 percent of the liquid oil and replaced it with an equal amount of hydrogenated oil, which was solid at room temperature. The result was a semi-solid peanut butter; no oil rose to the surface. The peanut butter was thick and creamy and did not stick to the roof of the mouth as much as previous products. Skippy was a great success and the brand ultimately ended up with Unilever, a British multinational.

The E. K. Pond Company began manufacturing peanut butter beginning in 1920, but its sales were limited. The lackluster sales encouraged the company to change the name to Peter Pan, after the popular fantasy character popularized in the 1903 James M. Barrie play. As soon as the E. K. Pond Company changed the name, sales took off. The Peter Pan brand was acquired by ConAgra in 1988.

The third peanut butter manufacturer is Procter & Gamble. In 1955 Procter & Gamble Company entered the peanut butter business. They introduced Jif in 1958 and now operate the world's largest peanut butter plant, churning out 250,000 jars every day. Peanut butter was employed in virtually every type of food, including soups, salads, sauces, and junk foods such as Snickers Bar, Clark Bar, Hershey's Peanut Kisses, and Mary Janes. In all, Americans consume about 1 billion pounds of peanut butter annually.

Having started out in the nineteenth century as a health and vegetarian food, by the 1920s peanut butter was a major national product filled with sugar. By the 1920s, children were particularly attracted to peanut butter filled with sugar. Owing to the added sugar and the fat from the peanuts, one cup of peanut butter has about 1,500 calories and contains twice as much fat (much of it transfat) as the Food and Drug Administration recommends for total daily consumption.

Several peanut butter-manufacturing plants have faced serious problems with *salmonella* outbreaks. In 2007 peanut butter was suspected in the outbreak of salmonellosis that affected 425 people in 44 states. In 2009 Peanut Corporation of America in Blakely, Georgia, was found to be infected with salmonellosis. This was "one of the nation's worst known outbreaks of food-borne disease," in which nine people are believed to have died and an estimated 22,500 were sickened, according to the *New York Times*.

See also Clark Bar; ConAgra Foods; Food and Drug Administration (FDA); Hershey Company; Mary Jane Candies; Peanuts; Transfats

For Further Information:

Moss, Michael, and Andrew Martin. "Food Problems Elude Private Inspectors." *New York Times*, March 5, 2009, as at: www.nytimes.com/2009/03/06/business/06food.html

Smith, Andrew F. *Peanuts: The Illustrious History of the Goober Pea*. Urbana: University of Illinois Press, 2006.

Peanuts

Botanically, the peanut (*Arachis hypogaea*) is classified as a legume and is related to beans and peas: the peanut's ovary is fertilized above ground, but the stem then pushes the flower underground, where the fruit matures. In the culinary world, however, the peanut is considered a nut owing to its hard outer husk and nutty taste when roasted: rarely is it prepared or served as are other legumes. Peanuts and peanut products are common ingredients in junk foods.

Peanuts originated in South America, and in pre-Columbian times they were widely disseminated in South and Central America and the Caribbean. Although Columbus likely found peanuts on his voyages to the Americas, the first reference to them was not recorded until the early sixteenth century, when Spanish settlers in what is today the Dominican Republic reported that peanuts were sown by indigenous peoples of the Caribbean. It was a common food, eaten both raw and roasted, and peanut oil was used as a substitute for olive oil.

Peanuts are easily grown and the plants are very productive. Because peanuts are protected by a hard outer shell, they are easily stored, surviving for months with minimum spoilage. In addition, they can be eaten directly from the shell without any preparation. They were an ideal food for mariners, and Spanish galleons took peanuts first to the Pacific Islands, and then to the Philippines and Indonesia. Peanuts arrived in Malaysia, Vietnam, and China before 1608 and were widely distributed in Vietnam and South China by the eighteenth century.

Simultaneously, the Portuguese introduced peanuts into their African enclaves, from which they quickly spread throughout tropical Africa. The peanut is particularly rich in oil, a characteristic that proved crucial for its adoption outside of the Americas. Perhaps its most important characteristic was its versatility. Peanuts could be cooked and served in ways that readily fit in with the culinary traditions of many different cultures.

Peanut cultivation dramatically increased in India, where peanut oil had long served as a substitute for olive oil. In the twentieth century China and India became the largest peanut oil producers in the world. Today, more than 50 percent of the worldwide peanut crop is crushed for its oil that is used in many junk foods.

During the late nineteenth century, three major peanut industries were launched in the United States. The first was started by Amedeo Obici and Mario Peruzzi, two Italian immigrants who specialized in roasted peanuts. They named their company Planters Peanuts. In 1917 they introduced their advertising mascot, Mr. Peanut, which became an American culinary icon within a few years. The second industry was initiated by the health-food advocate John Harvey Kellogg, who popularized

The Peanut Man

George Washington Carver (1864–1943) received a bachelor's degree in 1894 and a master of agriculture degree in 1896. Booker T. Washington, the founder of Tuskegee Institute (later renamed Tuskegee University) in Alabama, offered Carver a position as head of the new agriculture department. Carver accepted and remained there for the rest of his life. Carver attended a lecture by John Harvey Kellogg, in which Kellogg discussed the importance of peanuts. In late 1915, Carver published a bulletin on peanuts through the Tuskegee Agricultural Experiment Station. The bulletin was very popular, and its recipes were widely distributed. Many African Americans owned small farms, and the peanut was an ideal crop for them. Many African Americans were also employed picking peanuts, and many others worked in factories making peanut products. While Carver did not invent peanut butter, he did popularize the peanut.

peanut butter beginning in 1894. During the early twentieth century, peanut butter companies were started in many cities throughout the country. Finally, mass-produced candy bars came into their own in the mid-twentieth century, and peanuts went into several of the most popular candies, such as Goo Goo Clusters, Baby Ruth bars, Reese's Peanut Butter Cups, Butterfinger, Clark Bars, Peanut M&M's, Peanut Butter M&M's, PayDay, and Hershey's Peanut Kisses.

See also Baby Ruth; Butterfinger; Clark Bar; Goo Goo Clusters; M&Ms; Mr. Peanut; PayDay; Peanut Brittle; Peanut Butter; Reese's Peanut Butter Cups

For Further Information:

Smith, Andrew F. *Peanuts: The Illustrious History of the Goober Pea*. Urbana: University of Illinois Press, 2006.

Peeps

Peeps, three-dimensional marshmallow chicks, were invented by the Rodda Candy Company of Lancaster, Pennsylvania. The handmade process by which they were made greatly reduced the number that could be made, and increased their cost. When the Just Born candy company bought the Rodda Candy Company in 1953, the owners immediately began working on a way to manufacture Peeps. This was accomplished in 1954, and production skyrocketed.

Beginning in the 1960s, Just Born began extending the Peeps line by manufacturing Peeps with various shapes (such as bunnies and Christmas trees), colors

Peeps. (Dreamstime.com)

(pink, white, yellow, lavender, and blue), and flavors (vanilla, strawberry, and chocolate). Today, Just Born produces more than 4.2 million Peeps each day, and it is the largest marshmallow candy manufacturer in the world.

See also Candy; Chocolate; Christmas Candies; Easter Candies; Just Born; Marshmallows

For Further Information:

Marshmallow Peeps Web site: www.marshmallowpeeps.com

Penny Candy

By the mid-nineteenth century, many factories in the United States produced candy, much of which sold for a penny. It was easily produced and it was sold loose from glass jars or tins in stores. Penny candy was later sold through vending machines. Common penny candies included licorice, hard candy, lollipops, ladyfingers, pillowcases, mint patties, Jujubes, gum drops, wax candies, jelly beans, and marshmallows. The Tootsie Roll was the first penny candy to be wrapped in paper.

See also Candy; Jelly Beans; Lollipops/Suckers; Tootsie Roll Industries; Vending Machines

For Further Information:
Brenner, Joël Glenn. *The Emperors of Chocolate: Inside the Secret World of Hershey and Mars*. New York: Broadway Books, 2000.

People for the Ethical Treatment of Animals (PETA)

People for the Ethical Treatment of Animals (PETA) is an American not-for-profit animal rights organization based in Norfolk, Virginia. It was formed in 1980 by Ingrid Newkirk. One of their areas of focus is on factory farms. They carry out their work "through public education, cruelty investigations, research, animal rescue, legislation, special events, celebrity involvement, and protest campaigns."

In 2000 McDonald's became a major target of PETA, which launched a "McCruelty" campaign to change the way the corporation's suppliers treated chickens. McDonald's was targeted because it is the second-largest buyer of chicken in the world. PETA members engaged in more than four hundred demonstrations against the company, and after two years, McDonald's agreed "to make basic welfare improvements for farmed animals," according to PETA. Burger King and Wendy's followed suit. McDonald's and Wendy's also introduced vegetarian options after PETA targeted them.

In 2009 PETA once again took on McDonald's—this time for the way chickens were slaughtered. PETA believes that the method used to slaughter the chickens by the company's suppliers is outdated and that it results in needless suffering. They also believe that "McDonald's has the responsibility—and the ability—to reduce this abuse by demanding that its U.S. and Canadian suppliers use a less cruel slaughter method." In one demonstration in Chicago, Andy Dick, a comedian, dressed up as Ronald McDonald and wielded scissors to scare McDonald's into changing their policy. Afterward, Dick said, "If kids knew how chickens were mutilated for McNuggets, they'd burst into tears every time Ronald McDonald showed his face—and that may well happen when they see what this clown has to say about it."

See also Chicken McNuggets; McDonald's; Meatpacking Industry; Vegetarian/Vegan

For Further Information:
People for the Ethical Treatment of Animals Web site: www.peta.org

Pepperidge Farm

In 1937 Margaret Rudkin of Fairfield, Connecticut, began a small business baking preservative-free, whole-wheat bread. She named her company Pepperidge Farm.

After World War II, Rudkin began to expand production by opening a bakery in Norwalk, Connecticut. In addition to bread, the company manufactured dinner rolls, stuffing, and other products. Rudkin reached an agreement with Delacre Company in Brussels to produce its cookies in the United States. In 1955, Pepperidge Farm launched European-style cookies, such as Bordeaux, Geneva, and Brussels. Subsequently, the company acquired the Black Horse Pastry Company and moved into the frozen food business.

In 1961 the Campbell Soup Company acquired Pepperidge Farm. The following year, the company produced Goldfish crackers. In 1963 the company published the *Margaret Rudkin Pepperidge Farm Cookbook*, which became the first cookbook to hit the *New York Times* best-seller list. Rudkin retired in 1966.

See also Cookies; Goldfish

For Further Information:

Pepperidge Farm Web site: www.pepperidgefarm.com

PepsiCo

In the 1890s in New Bern, North Carolina, a pharmacist named Caleb D. Bradham experimented with extracts of coca leaves, kola nuts, and sugar. Bradham had purchased a pharmacy in 1893. At the drugstore's soda fountain, Bradham experimented with concocting soft drinks for his friends. One beverage based upon kola nut extract was first named Brad's Drink, but by August 28, 1898, he christened the new drink Pepsi-Cola. It was successful and its sales encouraged Bradham to incorporate the Pepsi-Cola Company in 1902. Bradham began to rapidly expand his sales. By 1907, the company had forty bottling plants across the United States. By 1910, Bradham had franchised more than three hundred bottlers in twenty-four states to produce Pepsi-Cola. But Bradham ran into financial problems and the company went into bankruptcy in 1922.

Pepsi-Cola was resurrected by a Wall Street broker, Roy C. Megarel. He controlled the company until 1931, when the company again went bankrupt. It was saved by Charles Guth, the president of the Loft Candy Company, which acquired Pepsi. The formula for Pepsi was changed at this time. The new formula eliminated pepsin, a digestive protease, as a major flavoring ingredient. By 1934, Pepsi-Cola turned the corner and began purchasing bottling operations throughout the United States. By 1939, Pepsi's net earnings had risen to more than $5.5 million.

World War II greatly affected the soft drink industry. Pepsi-Cola's operations throughout the world were disrupted by German and Japanese conquests. In the United States, sugar rationing was imposed early in 1942. Rationing drastically restricted the amount of soft drink that Pepsi-Cola could produce. After the war

Pepsi-Cola. (AP/Wide World Photos)

the sugar restrictions were removed, but Pepsi had a hard time competing with Coca-Cola, which had thrived during the war owing to government contracts. By 1950, the Pepsi Company was almost forced to declare bankruptcy for a third time, when a highly successful advertising campaign came to the rescue. Throughout the 1950s, Pepsi continued to expand aggressively abroad, particularly into Latin America and Europe. In 1959 the leader of the Soviet Union, Nikita Khrushchev, and Vice President Richard Nixon were photographed drinking Pepsi at an American exhibit in Moscow. This was later dubbed the Kitchen Debate. (Later, Coca-Cola claimed that as a result of this event, Nixon was offered the presidency of a foreign division of Pepsi and he served as a lawyer for Pepsi while practicing in New York.) By 1990, PepsiCo was producing 40 million cases of cola in 26 factories in the Soviet Union.

During the 1960s, Pepsi introduced several new products, including Mountain Dew and Diet Pepsi. In 1965 Pepsi bought Frito-Lay, Inc., and renamed the new corporation PepsiCo. During the 1970s, PepsiCo acquired several fast food chains, including Pizza Hut, Taco Bell, and KFC. PepsiCo considered its fast food chains

---

Snackified Beverages?

As part of its Tropicana brand, Pepsi introduced Tropolis, an eighty-calorie fruit puree snack that comes in squeezable pouches. Ingredients include apple puree, filtered water, banana puree concentrate, and other fruit concentrates. They come in three flavors: cherry, grape, and apple.

---

as important outlets for its soft drinks, because all of its chains sold Pepsi-Cola. However, other large fast food chains refused to carry PepsiCo beverages because of competition with Pepsi's fast food chains. In 1997 PepsiCo divested itself of its restaurant subsidiaries, creating a separate corporate entity called Yum! Brands. PepsiCo maintains the largest ownership in Yum! Brands, and all of these establishments continue to sell Pepsi beverages.

Pepsi has regularly expanded its operations by acquiring other companies. For instance, in 1998 it acquired Tropicana Products, makers of a variety of fruit juices. Tropicana was founded in 1947 by Anthony T. Rossi in Bradenton, Florida, and it is headquartered in Chicago. In 2001 PepsiCo acquired Quaker Oats, makers of Cap'n Crunch, Crunch, Life, Squares, and Honey Graham. Quaker cereals were distributed abroad and today they have a 7 percent share of the global cold cereal market.

See also Advertising; Beverages; Coca-Cola Company; Frito-Lay; KFC; Mountain Dew; PepsiCo; Pizza Hut; Soda/Soft Drinks; Soda Fountains; Taco Bell; Yum! Brands, Inc.

For Further Information:

Enrico, Roger, and Jesse Kornbluth. *The Other Guy Blinked: How Pepsi Won the Cola Wars*. New York: Bantam, 1986.

Funderburg, Anne Cooper. *Sundae Best: A History of Soda Fountains*. Bowling Green, OH: Bowling Green State University Popular Press, 2002.

Louis, J. C., and Harvey Yazijian. *The Cola Wars: The Story of the Global Corporate Battle between the Coca-Cola Company and PepsiCo*. New York: Everest House, 1980.

Smith, Andrew F. *Drinking History: Fifteen Beverages that Changed America*. New York: Columbia University Press, forthcoming.

Stoddard, Bob. *Pepsi: 100 Years*. Los Angeles, CA: General Publishing Group, 1999.

Stoddard, Bob. *The Encyclopedia of Pepsi-Cola Collectibles*. Iola, WI: Krause Publications, 2002.

Perugina

Perugina is a confectionary company that was launched in Perugia, Italy, in 1907. It did not begin to sell its products in the United States until 1960. Its products include chocolates, hard candy, nougat, biscotti, and panettone, an Italian sweet bread/cake popular during the Christmas holidays. Perugina's most popular products in the United States are its Baci (which means "kisses" in Italian), composed of chocolate and hazelnuts. Baci is similar to Hershey's Kisses, and each chocolate carries a love note on a small piece of paper. Perugina was acquired by Nestlé in 1988.

See also Chocolate; Nestlé

For Further Information:

Nestlé's Perugina Web site: www.perugina.it

Perugina Chocolate Web site: www.peruginachocolate.com

Peter Paul Candy Company

In 1919 Peter Paul Halajian and five Armenian associates founded the Peter Paul Candy Manufacturing Company in New Haven, Connecticut. One of their first products was a coconut-and-chocolate bar called Mounds, which was released in 1920. Following up this success was their Almond Joy, which was first manufactured in 1946. In 1972 Peter Paul acquired the York Cone Company, which made York Peppermint Patties, then a regional chocolate candy. Peter Paul expanded production and aggressively promoted it nationally beginning in 1975. In 1978 Cadbury acquired the Peter Paul Candy Company. Ten years later, Cadbury sold the Mounds, Almond Joy, and York Peppermint Patties brands to the Hershey Company, which markets them today.

See also Cadbury; Candy; Chocolate; Hershey Company; Mounds Bar; York Peppermint Patties

For Further Information:

Hershey's Web site: www.hersheys.com/almondjoy-mounds.aspx

Richardson, Tim. *Sweets: A History of Candy*. New York: Bloomsbury, 2002.

PEZ

In 1927 Eduard Haas, a Viennese confectioner, introduced Pfefferminze as a breath mint for smokers. It was composed of peppermint oil and sugar. When the candy was introduced into the United States, sales were dismal. In 1948 the first version of the PEZ dispenser was released; it was designed to look like a cigarette lighter. By 1952, the dispenser was improved and new images were incorporated into its design. It ejected candy from the heads of cartoon characters, such as those of Goofy or Popeye. PEZ was targeted at children and it was a hit.

PEZ. (AP/Wide World Photos)

PEZ Candy, Inc., is a private company based in Orange, Connecticut. Since 1960, McKeesport Candy Company of McKeesport, Pennsylvania, has been the distributor of PEZ dispensers. PEZ memorabilia are considered important collectibles, many of which are displayed at the Museum of PEZ Memorabilia in Burlingame, California. PEZ candies made a cameo appearance in the 1981 blockbuster movie *E.T.: The Extra-Terrestrial.*

See also Candy; Cartoon Characters; Sugars/Sweeteners

For Further Information:

Brenner, Joël Glenn. *The Emperors of Chocolate: Inside the Secret World of Hershey and Mars.* New York: Broadway Books, 2000.

Geary, Richard. *PEZ Collectibles.* 4th ed. Atglen, PA: Schiffer Publishing, 2000.

Morreale, Marie T., and E. H. Wallop. *PEZ: A Little Collectible Book.* Kansas City, MO: Andrews McMeel Publishing, 2002.

Museum of PEZ Memorabilia Web site: www.spectrumnet.com/pez

Philippines

Soda, cereal, junk foods, and hamburgers were introduced into the Philippines by Americans prior to World War II. Pepsi-Cola was imported into the Philippines beginning in 1946, and a bottling plant was established in the country the following year.

Cereal

Kellogg entered into the Filipino market early on; General Mills ventured jointly with Nestlé outside of North America to manufacture and distribute its products. Nestlé is the largest food producer in the Philippines, and it controls 70 percent of the market. Kellogg Company has licensed Alaska Milk Corporation to distribute its products; it controls 16 percent of the market. The largest sellers include Cheerios, Special K, and Frosted Flakes.

Fast Food

American fast food chains did not arrive until well after the United States recognized Philippine independence in 1946. KFC started its operation in the Philippines in 1967; as of 2011, the chain had more than sixty outlets in the Philippines.

McDonald's, called McDo by Filipinos, opened its first outlet in 1981 and was followed later by Burger King. Both companies sell burgers similar to those in the United States, but they are often accompanied by steamed rice.

See also Burger King; General Mills; Hamburger; Jollibee Foods; KFC; McDonald's

For Further Information:

Coca-Cola (Philippines) Web site: www.thecoca-colacompany.com/ourcompany/wn20060203_philippines.html

Jollibee Web site: www.jollibee.com.ph

KFC (Philippines) Web site: www.kfc.ph

McDonald's (Philippines) Web site: www.mcdonalds.com.ph

PepsiCo (Philippines) Web site: http://www.pepsiphilippines.com/

Physicians Committee for Responsible Medicine (PCRM)

Founded in 1985, the Physicians Committee for Responsible Medicine (PCRM) is a nonprofit organization based in Washington, D.C. Its president is Neal D. Barnard, a doctor who advocates a vegan diet. He has authored *Turn Off the Fat Genes*: *Eat Right, Live Longer* and *Food for Life*. PCRM's flagship publication is the quarterly magazine *Good Medicine*. PCRM is also an animal rights organization; it promotes a vegan diet and opposes medical experimentation on animals. PCRM has supported lawsuits against fast food chains and junk food manufacturers. Film director Morgan Spurlock used Barnard's addiction theories in his movie *Super Size Me* (2004). PCRM has released a number of negative advertisements against fast food corporations and other programs, such as the Atkins Diet, that it opposes.

PCRM claims that fast foods are the biggest source of unhealthy meals for children. It claimed that McDonald's Mighty Kids Meal tops the list with 840 calories, 37 grams of fat, and excessive sodium. In 2010 the organization released an anti-McDonald's television advertisement featuring a corpse in a morgue holding a partially eaten hamburger. A McDonald's golden arch logo appears on the corpse's feet, along with the words, "I was lovin' it." A voice over says, "High cholesterol, high blood pressure, heart attacks. Tonight, make it vegetarian." Few television stations permitted the commercial to air, but the advertisement received extensive visibility in television news programs, newspapers, and the Internet. Thousands have watched it on YouTube. McDonald's, the National Restaurant Association, and others condemned the advertisement as "irresponsible."

PCRM has been criticized for many of its statements, advertisements, and campaigns by the American Medical Association (AMA) and other groups. In 1991 a senior AMA leader proclaimed that PCRM members were "neither responsible nor are they physicians." A 2004 article in *Newsweek* noted that less than 5 percent of the members of the organization are physicians.

See also Addiction; Animal Rights Movement; Lawsuits; McDonald's; National Restaurant Association; Spurlock, Morgan; Vegetarian/Vegan

For Further Information:

Barnard, Neal D. *Breaking the Food Seduction: The Hidden Reasons Behind Food Cravings—And 7 Steps to End Them Naturally*. New York: St. Martin's Press, 2003.

Physicians Committee for Responsible Medicine Web site: www.pcrm.org

Super Size Me. Directed by Morgan Spurlock. Goldwyn Films, 2004.

Pie

Pies are sweet or savory dishes typically consisting of fillings enclosed in dough-based crusts. They were part of the English culinary heritage brought to America in colonial days. Savory pies, such as chicken, beef, or turkey potpies, were often served as main courses. They have survived in regional cuisines and in commercial frozen products. Sweet pies, such as cream pies or those based on various fruit, were typically served as desserts.

Bakery companies, such as Entenmann's and Sarah Lee, have marketed various types of pies, fresh and frozen. Other companies have created products that they call "pies," such as Moon Pies or fruit pies, that are completely enclosed in pastry; these are more accurately called turnovers. Hostess Brands Oatmeal Cream Pies are more accurately cookies with a cream filling between them.

Fast food companies have begun to serve some pies as desserts. McDonald's for instance, offers a baked apple pie. Burger King offers several pies, some

Apple pie. (Dreamstime.com)

co-branded with junk food companies, such as Butterfinger Creme Pie and Hershey's Sundae Pie.

See also Branding; Burger King; Entenmann's; Hershey Company; Hostess Brands; McDonald's; Moon Pie; Sarah Lee Corporation

For Further Information:

Clarkson, Janet. *Pie: A Global History*. London: Reaktion Books, 2009.

Pillsbury

The precursor to the Pillsbury Company was created in 1872 by C. A. Pillsbury in Minneapolis. The company mainly milled flour. In the mid-twentieth century Pillsbury began to make other products, such as cake mixes, frosting, crescent rolls, and croissants. Beginning in the 1960s, Pillsbury began to expand by acquiring other companies. These included Burger King (1967), Totino's frozen pizzas (1971), Häagen-Dazs (1983), Godfathers Pizza (1984), and Old El Paso Mexican-style foods (1995).

In 1989 Pillsbury was acquired by Grand Metropolitan and its successor, Diageo; Godfathers Pizza was sold in 1990 and Burger King was sold in 2000. In 2001

Pillsbury Doughboy. (AP/Wide World Photos)

Pillsbury was acquired by General Mills. As part of the acquisition, General Mills licensed another company to make Pillsbury's bakery products; it also licensed Häagen-Dazs products to Nestlé's subsidiary, Dreyer's. General Mills continues to produce Totino's and El Paso brands.

See also Burger King; Cakes; Croissants; Dreyer's/Edy's Ice Cream; General Mills; Häagen-Dazs; Nestlé; Pizza; Pizza, Frozen

For Further Information:

Powell, William J. *Pillsbury's Best: A Company History from 1869.* Minneapolis: Pillsbury Co., 1985

Pixy Stix

Pixy Stix is a flavored, powdered sugar packed into strawlike containers of varying length. It started as a "fru tola" syrup used by druggists in the early twentieth century to flavor ices. In 1934 Sunline, Inc., a candy manufacturer in St. Louis, Missouri, began producing "Lik-M-Aid," a Kool-Aid–like powdered candy that was marketed to the 4–8-year-old age group. In 1950 Sunline began manufacturing Pixy Stix in a straw for the 8–12-year-old group. Sunline was eventually acquired by Nestlé, which continues to manufacture Pixy Stix through its Willy Wonka Candy Company brand.

See also Candy; Kool-Aid; Nestlé; Wonka Brand

For Further Information:

"NVA Adds to Exhibitor List; Sunline, Inc., Newest Entry." *Billboard*, April 27, 1968, CMW-6.

Pizza

Leavened and flattened breads with various toppings have been common in the Mediterranean region for hundreds, if not thousands, of years. Pizza can be traced to nineteenth-century Naples, Italy. It had a variety of toppings, including tomato sauce and cheese. Pizza migrated to the United States late in the nineteenth century. The first known pizzeria in the United States was established by Italian bakers in New York in 1902. By the 1920s, pizza was a common food served in small outlets and at Italian festivals.

Pizza became an American mainstream food after World War II. It meshed well with casual dining and could easily be eaten in automobiles or around the television in the home. It was not negatively affected by delays between cooking and eating, which made it ideal for drive-ins and take-home places. The day's supply of pizza dough was rolled out in the morning and refrigerated in ten-inch pans, ready to be quickly topped and baked in the same pan when ordered. It drastically reduced

Pizza. (Dreamstime.com)

labor costs and made the mealtime rush more manageable. This new method was a boon for franchised chains.

Pizza was distinctly different from other fast foods. Before the 1950s, pizza was considered a foreign food. A 1953 song sung by Dean Martin, "That's Amore," with the lyrics "When the moon hits your eye like a big pizza pie" helped popularize it. The first pizza franchises opened in 1954 with the creation of Shakey's Pizza chain, which grew to more than one hundred outlets by 1960. Most of Shakey's pizza was eaten in the restaurant. Pizza Hut was the first true fast food pizza chain. Tom Monaghan made it into the Fortune 500 with his Domino's Pizza, founded in 1960. Frozen pizza was introduced in the early 1960s. There are two claims to having been the first to sell commercially frozen pizza in 1962: Tombstone Pizza in Medford, Wisconsin, and Rose Totino of Totino's Italian Kitchen in Minneapolis.

There are many other makers of pizza, such as Red Baron Pizza, founded in 1979, Godfather's Pizza, founded in 1973 in Omaha, Nebraska, and Papa John's, founded in 1984 in Jeffersonville, Indiana. Today, Papa John's also has almost three thousand outlets in forty-nine states and twenty countries. There are thousands of local and regional pizza parlors. In 2011, Papa John's introduced a six-cheese, double bacon pizza as a promotional item.

See also Automobiles; California Pizza Kitchen; Chicken Wings; Chuck E. Cheese's Pizza; Domino's Pizza; Kraft Foods; Little Caesars Pizza; Monaghan, Tom; Pizza, Frozen; Pizza Hut; Sbarro; Shakey's Pizza; Tombstone Pizza

For Further Information:

Food Franchise Web site: www.foodfranchise.com/pizzafranchise.asp

Godfather's Pizza Web site: www.godfathers.com

Helstosky, Carol. *Pizza: A Global History*. London: Reaktion Books, 2008.

Jakle, John A., and Keith A. Sculle. *Fast Food: Roadside Restaurants in the Automobile Age*. Baltimore: Johns Hopkins University Press, 1999.

Levenstein, Harvey. *Paradox of Plenty: A Social History of Eating in Modern America*. New York: Oxford University Press, 1993.

Levine, Ed. *Pizza: A Slice of Heaven. The Ultimate Pizza Guide and Companion*. New York: Universe Publishing, 2005.

Pizza, Frozen

Pizza became popular in America during the late 1950s. In the early 1960s frozen pizza was introduced, and pizza became the most popular of all frozen foods. Precisely who was the first to develop a commercial frozen pizza is unknown. Rose Totino of Totino's Italian Kitchen in Minneapolis, Minnesota, claims to have done so in 1962. By the late 1960s, Totino's Finer Foods was the top-selling frozen pizza. Pillsbury bought the company in 1971.

Joseph, Ronald, Frances, and Joan Simek, who owned the Tombstone bar, a small country tavern across the street from a cemetery in Medford, Wisconsin, also claimed to have produced frozen pizza in 1962. Kraft Foods bought the Tombstone Pizza enterprise in the 1990s and, after a major promotional campaign, it quickly became the top seller of frozen pizza in supermarkets. Kraft Foods also bought the rights to California Pizza Kitchen's frozen pizza.

In 1975 the Schwan Food Company introduced frozen Red Baron Pizza. When Kraft Foods introduced DiGiorno's pizza, Schwan introduced Freschetta frozen pizza. Kraft Foods promoted its pizza using the slogan, "It's not delivery, it's DiGiorno!" As of 2010, the best-selling frozen pizza brand was DiGiorno, followed by Tombstone, Red Baron, and Freschetta. Americans eat an estimated 1.8 billion slices of frozen pizza annually. Total annual sales of frozen pizza are about $2.4 billion out of an estimated $30 billion in total pizza sales.

In 2010 Kraft Foods sold Tombstone Pizza, DiGiorno's, and California Pizza Kitchen's frozen pizza to Nestlé for $3.7 billion. Since then, DiGiorno's has released some unusual frozen pizza combinations. One was Pizza & Boneless Wyngz, nuggets of chicken containing no bones, and no wing meat, either. Others included various pizzas packaged with Nestlé's chocolate chip cookie dough.

See also Chicken Wings; Kraft Foods; Nestlé; Pillsbury Company; Pizza; Tombstone Pizza

For Further Information:

Helstosky, Carol. *Pizza: A Global History*. London: Reaktion Books, 2008.

Kraft Foods Web site: www.kraftfood.com

Schwan Food Company Web site: www.theschwanfoodcompany.com

Pizza Hut

Frank Carney, an eighteen-year-old student at the University of Wichita, read an article about pizza in the *Saturday Evening Post* and decided to open a pizza parlor in 1958. With his brother, Dan Carney, he opened a pizza parlor in Wichita, Kansas. They named it Pizza Hut because they believed that the small brick building they rented resembled a hut. Their main product was a small, thin, pan pizza with cheese, sausage, or pepperoni. Initially, it came in two sizes: small, which sold for 95 cents, and large, which sold for $1.50.

At the time there were other pizzerias in Wichita and in many other cities; these were mainly family-owned shops. Six months after the Carneys opened their first restaurant, the brothers opened a second one. Within a year there were six Pizza Hut outlets. The brothers began franchising Pizza Hut in 1959. Pizza Hut popularized pizza as a fast food in America.

In 1963 Pizza Hut designed a building style that was adopted for all restaurants throughout the chain. It had a large dining room with seating for eighty people, and an expanded menu was introduced. The company shifted to a thicker-crust pizza and added several additional types of pizzas, including Chicago pan-style pizza. About 50 percent of their operation was take-out. The company also began its first national advertising campaign with the jingle "Putt-Putt to Pizza Hut."

PepsiCo purchased Pizza Hut in 1977. Pizza Hut began a process to American-ize its image. Its initial logo—an Italian chef tossing a pizza—was changed to the red roof that symbolized their "hut." By 1990 Pizza Hut ranked fourth in sales among all chain restaurants.

In 1997 Pizza Hut was spun off from PepsiCo into Tricon Global Restaurants, now Yum! Brands, Inc. As of 2011, the chain had nearly 10,000 restaurants in 90 nations. Pizza Hut has rapidly expanded in China, where it has nearly 500 Pizza Hut restaurants in more than 120 cities, and an additional 106 Pizza Hut Home Service delivery units. Pizza Hut franchisees added buffalo wings to their menu in 1995. Yum! Brands launched The WingStreet brand in 2003. Almost all outlets are in Pizza Hut restaurants.

As the company has opened outlets in other countries, it has had to add foods to make the menus more palatable. In Japan, for instance, Pizza Hut offers Golden Fortune (shrimp, crab stick, fish, pineapple, lime, and cheesy dough-bite pizza).

See also Advertising; China; Fast Food; Franchising; PepsiCo; Pizza; Yum! Brands, Inc.

For Further Information:

Helstosky, Carol. *Pizza: A Global History*. London: Reaktion Books, 2008.

Jakle, John A., and Keith A. Sculle. *Fast Food: Roadside Restaurants in the Automobile Age*. Baltimore: Johns Hopkins University Press, 1999.

Langdon, Philip. *Orange Roofs, Golden Arches: The Architecture of American Chain Restaurants*. New York: Knopf, 1986.

Pizza Hut Web site: www.pizzahut.com

Spector, Robert. *The Pizza Hut Story*. Wichita, KS: IPHFHA, 2008.

Politics of Junk Food

Food-related matters have been political issues for more than a century. The controversies surrounding pure food were legion. Legislation promoting pure food was introduced into Congress for thirty years before the Pure Food and Drug Act was finally passed in 1906. This and other acts created an administrative structure to enforce the laws and prevent adulteration of food. This series of legislative acts created federal mechanisms to research food issues and, where necessary, take action against products or their ingredients that are determined to be a danger to health. Federal agencies also have the ability to spotlight serious food-related problems, such as obesity and foodborne illnesses.

Many federal laws and regulations affect the quality and price of foods Americans eat. Price supports for agricultural commodities, for instance, stabilize prices for farmers and consumers.

These laws, however, are not made in a political vacuum. During the early part of the twentieth century, food corporations formed associations, many of which had lobbying arms in Washington, D.C. When World War II broke out, junk food manufacturers pressed the federal government to declare their products essential for the war effort. Through lobbying, the Coca-Cola Company won the right to sell its beverages to the military. Other soda companies, such as PepsiCo, almost went out of business owing to the rationing of sugar during the war.

Food companies lobby the political system to convince Congress that their products promote health and should not be subject to restrictive regulations. To gain support for their positions, corporations contribute to congressional campaigns and lobby officials in federal agencies. They fund nutrition research, sponsor journals, and conduct conferences, and they support nutritional organizations that espouse their own views. Food company lobbyists often pressure political leaders to make compromises regarding nutritional recommendations.

In addition, food companies join trade associations. Many fast food and junk food businesses have formed alliances, such as American Council for Fitness and Nutrition (ACFN), which opposes creating national standards for school food. Fast food chains, such as McDonald's, have opposed increasing the minimum wage at both the federal and state levels. They have also encouraged the passage of legislation that would exempt teenagers under eighteen from the minimum wage.

Food corporations also try to prevent lawsuits against them through passage of favorable federal legislation. When Samuel Hirsch sued McDonald's, Wendy's, KFC, and Burger King for contributing to obesity, the fast food and junk food manufacturers and their associations began to lobby for the introduction and passage of the Personal Responsibility in Food Consumption Act in Congress that would exempt fast food chains from such lawsuits. This did not pass, but fast food and junk food companies have pressured states into passing "cheeseburger laws" intent on protecting the companies from similar lawsuits.

Nonprofit organizations, such as the Center for Science in the Public Interest, have attempted to counter the lobbying efforts of food manufacturers by also lobbying Congress, supporting bills, and trying to influence federal agencies. CSPI has presented studies and research supporting its position and has lobbied Americans to contact their representatives on matters before Congress.

See also Beverages; Burger King; Center for Science in the Public Interest (CSPI); Chains; Cheeseburger Laws; Coca-Cola Company; Fast Food; Junk Foods; KFC; Lawsuits; Lobbying; McDonald's; Obesity; PepsiCo; School Food; Soda/Soft Drinks; Sugars/Sweeteners; Vegetarian/Vegan; Wendy's

For Further Information:

Lien, Marianne Elisabeth, and Brigitte Nerlich, eds. *The Politics of Food*. New York: Berg, 2004.

Nestle, Marion. *Safe Food: Bacteria, Biotechnology, and Bioterrorism*. Berkeley: University of California Press, 2003.

Nestle, Marion. *Food Politics: How the Food Industry Influences Nutrition and Health*. Berkeley: University of California Press, 2007.

Pollan, Michael

Michael Pollan (1955–) is a professor of journalism at the University of California, Berkeley, and the author of three major works on food: *The Botany of Desire* (2001), *The Omnivore's Dilemma* (2006), and *In Defense of Food* (2008). His latest work, *Food Rules: An Eater's Manual* (2009), largely summarizes the rules in his previous work, *In Defense of Food*. In his writing he has opposed large agribusinesses, fast food, and junk foods, while supporting small farmers and the consumption of nutritionally sound foods.

See also Factory Farms; Fast Food; Junk Foods

For Further Information:

Pollan, Michael. *The Botany of Desire: A Plant's-Eye View of the World*. New York: Random House, 2001.

Pollan, Michael. *The Omnivore's Dilemma: A Natural History of Four Meals*. New York: Penguin, 2006.

Pollan, Michael. *In Defense of Food: An Eater's Manifesto*. New York: The Penguin Press, 2008.

Pollan, Michael. *Food Rules: An Eater's Manifesto*. New York: Penguin Books, 2009.

Pollo Campero

Pollo Campero ("the country chicken" in Spanish) is a fast food restaurant chain that was started by Dionisio Gutiérrez in Guatemala in 1971. The restaurant served breaded fried chicken and grilled chicken flavored with lime and orange juices, red bell peppers, and a blend of herbs and spices. Chicken is available on the bone, in sandwiches, or in Caesar salads. It also serves chicken bowls, burritos, and chicken tenders, which are accompanied by beans, rice, yuca fries, sweet plantains, coleslaw, french fries, horchata, tamarindo, and mashed potatoes. Some outlets also sell salads, wraps, gluten-free cupcakes, and other bakery goods.

Today, Pollo Campero is the largest restaurant chain in Guatemala and the largest chicken fast food chain in Latin America. In 2002 Pollo Campero opened a franchise in Los Angeles, its first restaurant in the United States. As of 2010, Pollo Campero had more than fifty restaurants in the United States, and three hundred more restaurants in Costa Rica, Ecuador, El Salvador, Guatemala, Honduras, Indonesia, Mexico, Nicaragua, and Spain.

See also Chicken; Cupcakes; French Fries; Mexican American Food; Salads

For Further Information:

Pollo Campero Web site: www.campero.com

El Pollo Loco

In 1975 El Pollo Loco ("the crazy chicken" in Spanish) began as a roadside chicken stand in Guasave on Mexico's Pacific Coast. The company expanded to northern Mexico and, in 1980, opened its first outlet in the United States in Los Angeles. The menu featured marinated flame-grilled chicken, which was popular across much of Latin America and with U.S. Latinos. El Pollo Loco expanded its menu to include burritos, tacos, salads, and other products. In 1995 it launched a joint venture with Fosters Freeze, so that the latter's soft-serve ice cream desserts could be sold in many El Pollo Loco outlets.

In 2009 El Pollo Loco challenged KFC to a public taste test. KFC declined to accept the challenge, and this brought forth a number of televised El Pollo Loco commercials and videos dubbed "Chicken Wars."

Corporate

In 1983 the El Pollo Loco chain was purchased by the Denny's restaurant chain, which in turn was bought by Flagstar (now Advantica Restaurant Group, Inc.) in 1987. In 1999 American Securities Capital Partners, a private equity investment firm, acquired El Pollo Loco, only to sell it in 2005 to Trimaran Capital Partners, a private equity firm. As of 2011, the company had 380 outlets in Arizona, California, Illinois, Nevada, Georgia, Texas, and other states. It is headquartered in Costa Mesa, California.

See also Chicken; Fosters Freeze; Ice Cream; KFC; Mexican American Food; Mexico

For Further Information:

Jakle, John A., and Keith A. Sculle. *Fast Food: Roadside Restaurants in the Automobile Age*. Baltimore: Johns Hopkins University Press, 1999.

El Pollo Loco Web site: www.elpolloloco.com

Pop Rocks

General Foods acquired the company that made Kool-Aid in 1953. Kool-Aid's sales were impressive, but nowhere near the sales of soft drinks such as Pepsi and Coke. The reason for this difference, believed William A. Mitchell, a scientist at General Foods, was that soft drinks had carbonation, and Kool-Aid didn't. Mitchell had an idea—what if the company carbonated Kool-Aid? Mitchell created a solid substance at room temperature in which carbon dioxide was trapped. When the solid was mixed with water, the trapped carbon dioxide escaped, creating a popping or cracking noise. Unfortunately, the resulting beverage had much less carbon dioxide than did soft drinks. While it wouldn't work as a soft drink, Mitchell proposed it as a candy. But here was another problem: General Foods did not have other candies, so there was no obvious place for it in the company. Besides, management at General Foods was unimpressed with his discovery and considered it a joke and novelty. Mitchell continued to make batches of Pop Rocks for children at company events.

Zotz, hard candies that fizzed when chewed, were introduced by an Italian confectioner in 1968 and were an immediate success. When General Foods acquired a snack food company in the 1970s, the manager of that division was interested in Pop Rocks. Technical production problems were solved, and the company began giving away Pop Rocks with other snack foods as a promotional tool. The product was first released in Canada, where it generated an incredible buzz.

Pop Rocks began to be released in the United States in 1975. In 1978, 500 million packages were sold. As General Foods was unable to manufacture enough candy to meet demand, it took almost three years before they were generally available through the country. Soon production increased to 2.5 billion packages, but then sales began to slide.

From their first introduction, Pop Rocks generated a series of myths. At first, it was said that they would destroy one's taste buds. Then rumors spread that a kid ate some Pop Rocks, drank some soda, and his stomach exploded. It was claimed that the kid was John Gilchrist, the young actor who played "Mikey" in the commercials for Quaker Oats' Life Cereal. As these myths spread, sales declined. Pop Rocks were no more than a fad. In 1979 General Foods began to unload excess inventory in Australia, England, and Korea. General Foods discontinued manufacturing Pop Rocks in 1982. The Koreans were particularly interested in the product, and the American manufacturing equipment was shipped to that country in 1984.

Kraft Foods purchased the rights to Pop Rocks in 1985 and manufactured them under the name Action Candy. A Spanish company has manufactured a similar product called Fizz Whiz, and a Turkish company released Hleks Popping Candy and currently dominates the market. In the United States Pop Rocks were revived, and as of 2011, they were manufactured by Pop Rocks, Inc., headquartered in Atlanta. The company produced five standard flavors: blue razz, strawberry, tropical, watermelon, and strawberry sugar free, but also numerous special flavors.

An unusual use of Pop Rocks has been invented in Japan, where some Baskin-Robbins franchisees offered Popping Shower—an ice cream alternative with white chocolate and crème de menthe studded with Pop Rocks.

See also Carbonation; General Foods Corporation; Kool-Aid; Kraft Foods; Zotz

For Further Information:

Pop Rocks Web site: www.pop-rocks.com

Rudolph, Marv. *Pop Rocks: The Inside Story of America's Revolutionary Candy.* Sharon, MA: Specialty Publishers, 2006.

Pop-Tarts

In the 1960s Post Cereals developed the process for making a breakfast food that could be heated in the toaster. They released their first product, Country Squares, to the public in 1963. The Kellogg Company immediately began a crash development program to counter Post Cereal's Country Squares. After six months of work, Kellogg came up with a product that was initially called a Fruit Scone. The name was changed to Pop-Tart, which was a pun on the then-popular Pop Art movement. Pop-Tarts have sugary fillings, which are sealed inside two layers of a pastry crust. They are thin enough to fit into normal toasters. Post Cereal's Country Squares failed to take off, but Pop-Tarts sales were extremely successful when they were released in 1964. They are mainly sold in supermarkets, but online sales have increased. In 2010 the Kellogg Company opened a retail outlet called Pop-Tarts World in Times Square, New York.

As of 2011, Kellogg produced thirty flavors of Pop-Tarts. The most popular flavors are frosted strawberry and frosted brown sugar cinnamon. The Kellogg Company sells more than 2 billion Pop-Tarts annually. They are distributed mainly in the United States, the United Kingdom, and Canada.

See also Kellogg Company

For Further Information:

Pop-Tart Web site: www.poptarts.com

Popcorn

Popcorn appeared on the American culinary scene during the mid-nineteenth century after the invention of the wire-over-the-fire popper. This device made it possible to contain the popped corn in an enclosed space without having to chase

Popcorn. (Dreamstime.com)

after the kernels as they scattered around the cooking area. By the late nineteenth century, low-cost popcorn was America's favorite snack. Cracker Jack, a combination of popcorn, peanuts, and molasses, became America's first commercial snack food during the early twentieth century.

During World War I, popcorn became a patriotic snack food. It was not rationed during the war and it was not imported. The Depression did not hurt popcorn sales because it was a luxury that most Americans could afford. Movie theaters and World War II catapulted popcorn into the mainstream as sugar-based snacks vanished from grocers' shelves. The invention of the microwave oven and the release of hybrid kernels with tremendous popping volume created popcorn mania during the 1950s and 1960s.

Popcorn Mania

In 1988 the Wyandot Popcorn Company claimed that it had produced enough popcorn to fill the Empire State Building thirty times over. It issued videocassettes of the original 1933 version of King Kong and gave its personnel Popcorn Mania T-shirts. Mania was the appropriate word to describe what was then under way in the popcorn world. Magazines reinforced the upward spiral of popcorn mania. In 1984 *Reader's Digest* ran an article titled "Popcorn! It's No Flash in the Pan." The popularity of popcorn exploded for a variety of reasons, but particularly because of the boosterlike efforts of Orville Redenbacher on behalf of gourmet popping corn and of the successful marriage of popcorn with microwave technology.

Consolidation

Since World War II, the popcorn industry has consolidated. In 1963 the Cracker Jack Company was sold to Borden, Inc. Borden, based in New York City, embarked on an acquisition drive that resulted in the purchase of twenty-three companies during the 1980s. With the acquisition of Laura Scudder's snack food company and the Snacktime Company in Indianapolis, Borden became the number two marketer of snack foods in the nation, behind Frito-Lay, a subsidiary of PepsiCo. Borden developed Cracker Jack Extra Fresh Gourmet Quality Popping Corn. In

1997 Borden sold Cracker Jack to Frito-Lay, which also marketed Cheetos Cheddar Cheese Flavored Popcorn and Smartfoods popcorn. By the 1980s, the Wyandot Popcorn Company had become the nation's second-largest processor of popcorn. It was acquired by Vogel Popcorn, which in turn was sold to ConAgra Foods. ConAgra had previously purchased Orville Redenbacher's Gourmet Popping Corn during the mid-1970s, and it had acquired other snack food brands, such as Crunch 'N Munch, a Cracker Jack competitor.

Globalization

Popcorn may be a mature industry in America, but it has begun to expand abroad. Canada consumes one-third of U.S. popcorn exports. Europeans consider popcorn a sweet snack, and most consume it in caramelized form. The Japanese have acquired a taste for snack food, and popcorn sales there have risen steadily. Popcorn consumption in the United Kingdom takes place mainly at movie theaters, carnivals, and (to a much lesser extent) at home. Many observers believe that there is a potentially explosive market for popcorn in the United Kingdom and other Western European countries. With the fall of the Soviet Union and the end of the Cold War, popcorn processors began looking to Eastern Europe and Russia as emerging markets.

Popcorn is easily grown, inexpensive to buy, and accessible to most people. It is readily processed and almost effortlessly prepared for consumption. Without salt and butter, popcorn is a healthy food.

Health Issues

Popcorn is unquestionably nutritious. It consists of approximately 71 percent carbohydrates, 14 percent water, 10.5 percent protein, 3 percent fat, and small amounts of minerals. One cup of plain popcorn contains only twenty-seven calories. Popcorn by itself does not contain the ingredients that other snack foods are criticized for—salt, sugar, and chemical additives. It has been highly recommended by the National Cancer Institute as "a high-fiber food to choose more often." The Illinois division of the American Cancer Society praised popcorn as one of the "eleven things that don't cause cancer." The American Heart Association has recommended it as "low in saturated fat and fairly low in calories." The American Dental Association recommended sugar-free popcorn as a food that does not promote tooth decay, but does remove tartar from teeth. These recommendations were all based on plain, hot-air popped popcorn without additives.

However, most people do not consume popcorn without oil and additives. The Center for Science in the Public Interest (CSPI) issued a warning in 1988 about the high fat content of most microwave and prepared popcorns. Their message was that most microwave popcorn makers (as well as ready-to-eat popcorn producers) loaded their products with high levels of salt, saturated fats, and artificial butter flavor consisting of hydrogenated oils, saturated fats, artificial colorings, flavorings, and other preservatives.

The first company to produce a low-fat, low-salt popcorn was Weight Watchers. A serving of Weight Watchers brand microwave popcorn contained 9 percent fat, 150 calories, and 8 milligrams of sodium. Other manufacturers have followed suit. Redenbacher's Gourmet Light Microwave Popping Corn contained one-third less salt, one-third fewer calories, and two-thirds less fat than Redenbacher's regular popcorn. Other companies produced so-called light popcorn: Deli Express, Wise Foods, and the Boston Popcorn Company.

Despite these new products, the popcorn industry, swept up in a period of frenzied expansion, largely ignored the initial Center for Science in the Public Interest (CSPI) report. At the depths of the popcorn slump in 1994, CSPI again appalled popcorn lovers when it revealed that theater popcorn cooked in coconut oil was extraordinarily high in saturated fat. Saturated fat raises blood cholesterol and increases the risk of heart disease. Specifically, CSPI proclaimed that a tub of movie theater popcorn that had been popped in coconut oil without imitation butter contained 80 grams of fat—more than in six Big Macs. If imitation butter were added, the fat was boosted to 130 grams (the same as in eight Big Macs).

The report shocked theater owners even more than the general public, because more than half of their revenues derived from their food concessions. Some movie chains switched to oils low in saturated fats. After the CSPI report was issued, AMC Entertainment, Inc., one of the largest U.S. movie chains, and the Toronto-based Cineplex Odeon started popping with canola oil. The same-sized bucket of popcorn popped in canola oil had one-sixth the previous amount of saturated fat. "It's very positive press," said Dwight More, president of the Canola Council of Canada. His euphoria was short-lived, however. A week later, scientists at Howard University reported that hydrogenated canola oil was full of transfats that clogged arteries even faster than butter.

In 2010 Canadian scientists expressed concern with the chemicals in the coating used to line popcorn bags. A study indicated that polyfluoroalkyl phosphate esters (PAPs) move into the popcorn and are ingested when the bag is heated. When PAPs enter the body, they break down to perfluorinated carboxylic acids (PFCAs), which may be harmful to humans.

See also Carbohydrates; Center for Science in the Public Interest (CSPI); Cheetos; Cholesterol; ConAgra Foods; Cracker Jack; Fat, Dietary; Frito-Lay; Movie Theaters; Packaging; PepsiCo; Redenbacher, Orville; Snack Foods; Sodium/Salt; Sugars/Sweeteners; Transfats

For Further Information:

Mabury, Scott, and Jessica D'eon. "Exploring Indirect Sources of Human Exposure to Perfluoroalkyl Carboxylates (PFCAs): Evaluating Uptake, Elimination and Biotransformation of Polyfluoroalkyl Phosphate Esters (PAPs) in the Rat." *Environmental Health Perspectives* published online, November 8, 2010, as at: http://ehp03.niehs.nih.gov/article/fetchArticle.action?articleURI=info%3Adoi%2F10.1289%2Fehp.1002409

Smith, Andrew F. *Popped Culture: A Social History of Popcorn in America.* Columbia: University of South Carolina Press, 1999.

Popeyes

In the early 1970s Al Copeland owned a Tastee Donut franchise that had been started by his brother in New Orleans. Copeland decided to shift from doughnuts to fast food chicken when KFC started opening outlets in New Orleans. He opened his own chicken outlet in 1972 and called it Chicken on the Run. It served traditional mild chicken and it was not successful. Copeland shifted to spicy fried chicken and renamed it Popeyes, supposedly after the Popeye Doyle character in the then-popular movie *The French Connection.* His new fast food chicken operation was a success and Copeland began to franchise it. Its first franchise restaurant was opened in Baton Rouge, Louisiana, in 1976. By 1981, there were more than three hundred Popeyes. He began to advertise Popeyes with slogans such as "Love that Chicken from Popeyes." In 1987 consumers preferred Popeyes over KFC in a blind taste test, which encouraged Copeland to employ the slogan: "America's Fried Chicken Champ—The Spicy Taste That Can't Be Beat." Popeyes regularly added new products to its menu: buttermilk biscuits in 1985, Cajun Popcorn Shrimp four years later, and Cajun Crawfish in 1988.

Nine years later, Popeyes opened its five hundredth restaurant. Popeyes bought the Church's Chicken restaurant chain in 1989. The Popeyes Independent Franchise Association (PIFA) was formed in 1991 with the mission to protect the interests of the franchisees. In the same year, Popeyes opened its first international restaurant in Kuala Lumpur, Malaysia, and later opened an outlet in Schweinfurt, Germany. In 1993 America's Favorite Chicken Company, now known as AFC Enterprises, Inc., became the new parent company of Popeyes and Church's. The brand's headquarters moved to Atlanta. Popeyes developed new restaurants through conversions, mass-merchandisers, convenience stores, and grocery stores. The brand continued to grow internationally as it opened its fiftieth restaurant in Korea. In 1996 Popeyes opened its one thousandth restaurant worldwide. In 1998 Pop-eyes acquired sixty-six former Hardee's restaurants and converted them into Popeyes restaurants.

In 1999 Popeyes opened the Cajun Kitchen in a Chicago suburb. Cajun Kitchen provided food associated with a traditional casual restaurant with the speed of a fast food restaurant. In the same year, the company opened the Popeyes Cajun Café, intended for shopping malls, food courts, and other entertainment venues. In 2000 Popeyes achieved worldwide sales of approximately $1.2 billion. As of 2011, Popeyes had more than 1,977 restaurants in the United States and 27 international markets, including Puerto Rico, Japan, Germany, Korea, and the United Kingdom.

See also Advertising; AFC Enterprises; Chicken; Church's Chicken; El Pollo Loco; Hardee's; KFC; Pollo Campero; Slogans/Jingles

For Further Information:

Jakle, John A., and Keith A. Sculle. *Fast Food: Roadside Restaurants in the Automobile Age*. Baltimore: Johns Hopkins University Press, 1999.

Popeyes Web site: www.popeyesgulfcoast.com/history.htm

Poppycock

Howard Vair, a proprietor of a Detroit candy store, is credited with inventing Poppycock, which consists of clusters of glazed popcorn and nuts. In 1960 Wander, a Swiss company that manufactured Ovaltine, bought the rights to the product and began manufacturing Popycock. In 1967 Wander launched Fiddle Faddle, a combination of perfectly popped popcorn mixed with caramel, butter toffee, Heath toffee bits, and honey nuts. Two years later, it launched Screaming Yellow Zonkers!, a sweet popcorn without nuts. It was reportedly inspired by the Beatles' movie *Yellow Submarine*. By 1986, Wander was annually manufacturing 14 million pounds of Poppycock, Fiddle Faddle, and Screaming Yellow Zonkers! In that year, the company was purchased by Sandoz, creating Sandoz-Wander. Its name was changed to Lincoln Snacks, which was eventually acquired by ConAgra Foods in 2007. ConAgra discontinued making Screaming Yellow Zonkers! Popycock and Fiddle Faddle are junk foods averaging about 140 to 180 calories per cup.

See also Candy; ConAgra Foods; Nuts; Popcorn

For Further Information:

ConAgra Popycock Web site: www.conagrafoods.com/consumer/brands/getBrand.do?page=poppycock

Popsicle. (Dreamstime.com)

Popsicle

Street vendors sold Hokey-Pokies (frozen fruit juices) as early as the 1870s in New York and other cities, but it was Frank Epperson, a lemonade salesman from Oakland, California, who began the commercial manufacture of them in 1923. Epsicles, as he first called them, were ice pops on wooden sticks. He trademarked the name, which was later changed to Popsicle. In 1925, Epperson sold the rights to the Joe Lowe Company of New York. By 1928, more than 60 million Popsicles were sold annually. Consolidated Foods Corporation acquired the company in 1965. Twenty-one years later, the Gold Bond Ice Cream Company of Green Bay, Wisconsin, purchased Popsicle's American operations. In 1989 Unilever purchased Gold Bond. Unilever also owned Good Humor, Dove, Klondike, and Breyers.

See also Breyers; Dove Bar; Good Humor; Ice Cream; Klondike Bar; Unilever

For Further Information:

Funderburg, Anne Cooper. *Chocolate, Strawberry, and Vanilla: A History of American Ice Cream.* Bowling Green, OH: Bowling Green State University Popular Press, 1995.

Pork

Pigs were likely domesticated in Southeast Asia. They quickly spread throughout Asia and Europe, where they have been an important food source since ancient times. Pigs were brought to the Americas by European colonists, and they thrived, particularly in the American South. Pork became an important food source, especially in the making of barbecue, sausages, and bacon. Fast food has employed pork in breakfast sausages, and bacon has been used as a side for breakfast meals and for hamburgers. In 2003 McDonald's introduced the McGriddle, which is bacon or a pork sausage wrapped in a pancake. Dunkin' Donuts responded with its Pancake Bites—sausages wrapped in maple-flavored pancakes.

Bacon is also an option on many hamburger sandwiches. Five Guys offers four hamburgers with bacon: Bacon Burger, Bacon Cheeseburger, Little Bacon Burger, and the Little Bacon Cheeseburger. Wendy's offers eight hamburgers with bacon, such as the Baconator Single, Double, and Triple. Hardee's offers the Texas Toast Bacon Cheese Thickburger. Checker's offers its Baconzilla burger, Jack in the Box its Bacon Ultimate Cheeseburger, and McDonald's its Angus Chipotle BBQ Bacon.

Pork is used as an ingredient in some tacos. Pepperoni, usually made from pork and beef, and pork sausage have also been employed on pizza. In other countries, particularly in Asia, pork is more prominent on the menu of American fast food chains. McDonald's in Thailand, for instance, serves Samurai Pork Burgers. In 2009 McDonald's Japan introduced Mega Teriyaki, with two jumbo pork patties.

Bacon. (Dreamstime.com)

Ribs do appear on some fast food menus. Chicken Delight, for instance, has served barbecue ribs. Pork has also been used for limited time offers, such as the McRib (a ground pork patty with condiments on a roll) sold by McDonald's. Burger King responded with real ribs as a limited time offer. Pork products, such as pork rinds, have also been used as snack food, and SPAM has been used in a variety of ways, including for making sandwiches and salads.

In Israel and Islamic countries, or countries with large Muslim populations, pork is not served in fast food chains owing to religious prescriptions. Additionally, some fast food outlets that cater to Muslim populations in Europe often have no pork products on their menu.

See also Burger King; Checker's Drive-In Restaurants; Chicken Delight; Dunkin' Donuts; Five Guys Burgers & Fries; Hardee's; Japan; Limited Time Offers; McDonald's; Pancakes; Pizza; Pork Rind; SPAM; Tacos; Wendy's

For Further Information:

Horowitz, Roger. *Putting Meat on the American Table*. Baltimore: Johns Hopkins University Press, 2006.

Kaminsky, Peter. *Pig Perfect: Encounters with Remarkable Swine and Some Great Ways to Cook Them*. New York: Hyperion, 2005.

Lee, Paula Young, ed. *Meat, Modernity, and the Rise of the Slaughterhouse*. Durham; University of New Hampshire Press; Hanover: published by University Press of New England, 2008.

Mizelle, Brett. *Pig*. London: Reaktion Books, 2011.

Rogers, Katherine. *Pork: A Global History*. London: Reaktion Books, forthcoming.

Pork Rind

Pork rinds are crispy snacks made from small pieces of the tough layer of pigs' skins. Rinds are salted and then fried, roasted, baked, microwaved, and/or dehydrated. They can be spiced with a variety of flavorings, including barbecue spices, cheese, sour cream, chives, lime, vinegar, pepper, or chili pepper. They are high in salt and fat content. Pork rinds are one of the smaller-selling foods in the junk food world, but there are scores of producers of pork rinds, including Utz Quality Foods and Evans Food, Inc., the largest producer of pork rinds in the world.

See also Pork; Utz Quality Foods

For Further Information:

Evans Food Web site: www.evansfood.com

Severson, Kim. "For the Big Game? Why, Pigskins." *New York Times*, February 2, 2010, as at: http://www.nytimes.com/2010/02/03/dining/03skin.html?_r=1

Post Foods

After serious financial reversals in the late 1880s, Texan businessman Charles W. Post suffered a series of breakdowns. In 1891, hoping to strengthen his health, Post and his wife moved to Battle Creek, Michigan, which was little more than a village at the time. The family lived in a small cottage near the sanitarium that Dr. John Harvey Kellogg directed. According to legend, each day for nine months, Charles Post's wife, Ella, pushed him in his wheelchair up to the sanitarium, where he endured a treatment regimen. Dr. Kellogg told Ella Post that her husband did not have long to live, so Post discontinued his visits.

The Posts ran into Mrs. Elizabeth Gregory, a Christian Scientist who lived in Battle Creek. Gregory insisted that Post had the power to heal himself. Encouraged to give faith a try, Post was moved into Gregory's home, where he ate food she prepared for him and read *Science and Health,* the textbook of Christian Science written by the church's founder, Mary Baker Eddy. Post's health recovered and he almost immediately established a health institute, which he named La Vita Inn. He wrote *I am Well!*, which told of his miraculous recovery and the importance of "natural suggestion," or what would later be called the "power of positive thinking."

Post also began to manufacture health foods. He particularly liked the Caramel Coffee served at the Kellogg Sanitarium. He began to experiment with foods and beverages made at Kellogg's Sanatarium, one of which was a coffee substitute he called Postum, which proved to be a success. Post incorporated the Postum Cereal Company to manufacture and sell his grain-based coffee substitute. At the time, medical professionals had been warning about the dangers of drinking coffee, and Post divulged that his beverage was just the thing for "jangled nerves." Also helpful was Post's Battle Creek address, which led Americans to believe that his operation was somehow connected with Kellogg's Sanitarium.

With a major success under way, Post began experimenting with other products. In January 1898 he started marketing Grape Nuts, made from wheat and malted barley, which served to sweeten the cereal. Grape Nuts was a variation on Jackson's granula and Kellogg's granola, made by the same method. Post's advertisements touted Grape Nuts as a "scientific health food" containing "vitalizing" elements, and health food advocates promptly endorsed it. In 1906 C. W. Post introduced a new cereal, which he called Elijah's Manna. It was his version of the corn flakes made at the Battle Creek Sanitarium. After Bible Belt ministers complained that the name was "sacrilege," Post rechristened the cereal Post Toasties.

C. W. Post died in 1914, and his daughter, Marjorie Merriweather Post, inherited her father's estate and continued to build the company. It acquired several other companies, such as Jell-O, in 1925, and it was renamed General Foods Company in 1929. General Foods was acquired by Philip Morris, the cigarette manufacturer, in 1985, which merged General Foods with Kraft Foods in 1987. The cereal brands of Nabisco were acquired by Kraft Foods in 1993.

On November 15, 2007, Kraft announced that it would spin off Post Cereals and merge that business with Ralcorp Holdings, a manufacturer of breakfast cereals, cookies, crackers, chocolate, snack foods, and peanut butter. The official name of the company became Post Foods, LLC; it is headquartered in St. Louis. The new Post Foods now manufacturers a number of cereals, including Shredded Wheat, Grape Nuts, Golden Crisp, Honeycomb Alpha-Bits, and Pebbles. It has a 15 percent share of the global market for cold cereals.

In 2010 Post Foods announced that it was lowering the sugar content of its Fruity and Cocoa Pebbles cereals to make a healthier cereal option for kids.

See also Cereals; Coffee; General Foods Corporation; Granola; Jell-O; Kraft Foods; Nabisco

For Further Information:

Bruce, Scott, and Bill Crawford. *Cerealizing America: The Unsweetened Story of American Breakfast Cereal*. Boston: Faber and Faber, 1995.

Major, Nettie Leitch. *C. W. Post—The Hour and the Man: A Biography with Genealogical Supplement*. Washington, D.C.: Judd & Detweiller, 1963.

Post Cereals Web site: www.postcereals.com

Smith, Andrew F. *Eating History: Thirty Turning Points in the Making of American Cuisine*. New York: Columbia University Press, 2009.

Potato Chips

By popular tradition, one George Crum, a cook at the Moon's Lake House in Saratoga, New York, was the first to fry thin potato slices into ultra-crisp chips, which came to be called Saratoga potatoes; these were served as an accompaniment to meat or game. In fact, though, recipes calling for fried "shavings" of raw potatoes had appeared in American cookery books since 1824—and thin Saratoga potatoes were served with ice cream or sold in paper bags from confectioneries at Moon's Lake House before Crum was employed there. Regardless of who invented them, recipes for Saratoga potatoes and potato chips appeared regularly in American cookbooks beginning in the 1870s.

Potato chips were first mass-produced during the 1890s by a number of manufacturers, including John E. Marshall of Boston and William Tappendon of Cleveland, Ohio. They were sold in barrels to grocery stores. Proprietors dished out the chips into paper bags for customers, who warmed them in the oven before serving. Unfortunately the chips were often stale, and the product never really caught on. The packaging problem was not solved until the 1930s, when potato chips were sold in vacuum-sealed bags. By that time, potato chips were a snack food rather than a side dish.

In 1937 Herman W. Lay, an ambitious businessman from Nashville, Tennessee, bought Barrett Foods, a snack food company with plants in Atlanta and Memphis. The first product to bear the Lay's brand name was popcorn; the company began manufacturing potato chips in 1938.

When World War II began, potato chips were initially declared a nonessential food in the United States, which meant that production would have to stop for the duration. Manufacturers lobbied the War Production Board to change this designation, and their efforts were successful. Potato chip sales increased throughout the war, in part because sugar and chocolate were rationed, limiting the availability of candy bars and other sweet snacks.

Herman Lay's firm had become a major regional producer of snack foods by the war's end. After the war, Lay automated his potato chip manufacturing business and diversified its products. In 1945 he met Elmer Doolin,

Potato chips. (Dreamstime.com)

who manufactured Frito Corn Chips in San Antonio. Doolin franchised Herman Lay to distribute Fritos. The two companies cooperated on other products. In 1958 Lay acquired the rights from Frito-Lay to the new creation called Ruffles, a thick, "corrugated" potato chip made especially for dipping. Frito-Lay is the largest potato chip manufacturer in the world. Frito-Lay's brands include Lay's, Walkers, Smith's, Stax, Ruffles, and many more. Frito-Lay is a subsidiary of PepsiCo and has nearly 60 percent of the potato chip market.

Pringles

In the 1960s Procter & Gamble introduced Pringles, which are made from dehydrated and reconstituted potatoes. Unlike potato chips, Pringles are a uniform size and shape, making possible their packaging in a long tube. The potato chip industry went to court to prevent Procter & Gable from calling Pringles "potato chips." It was resolved in 1975, when the U.S. Food and Drug Administration defined Pringles as "potato chips made from dehydrated potatoes." In 2011 Pringles was acquired by Diamond Foods.

Kettle Potato Chips

Seventy years ago, most potato chips were made by batch method. Each batch would be made separately and operators moved the chips from one machine to another. This was an inefficient way of manufacturing and most companies shifted to continuous processing, which operated at great speed with the minimum of operator involvement. In 1982 the Kettle Food Company began producing "kettle potato chips" which were made by batch processing. They were thicker and had a harder surface. They also contained more oil and calories. They became popular as a "natural" food in the last two decades of the twentieth century, and virtually every major potato chip maker jumped in and began to produce their own brands of kettle chips.

Chips Abroad

American-style potato chips began to be manufactured in Great Britain in the 1920s. To avoid confusion with "chip potatoes," British manufacturers called their product "potato crisps" or simply "crisps." As American-style potato chips flooded the world market, the English word "crisp" fell by the wayside, although Walker's Crisps is the largest-selling brand in England. New flavors emerged as indigenous manufacturers developed their own flavors. Tayto Chips, for instance, sold in the United Kingdom, come in flavors such as Pickled Onion, Prawn Cocktail, and Roast Chicken.

In 1994, following interviews with 100,000 people in 30 countries, PepsiCo decided to establish the potato chip as the world's most popular snack. They decided to increase sales and advertising in other countries using the Lay brand name. They built plants in foreign markets, conducted consumer research, and created different flavors, such as shrimp chips for the Korean market and a squid-peanut flavor for Southeast Asia.

Healthy Chips

One major problem with potato chips has been that they are high in fat (particularly transfats), sodium, and calories. As concern with obesity and other food-related issues have emerged, some potato chip manufacturers have begun to make products with less fat and sodium. Frito-Lay introduced Baked Lays into the "healthy-chip market" in 1996, and Baked Lays has dominated this market segment. In 2010 Frito-Lay began using a "designer salt" that reduces sodium levels in Lay's potato chips but keeps the same taste.

Other healthy-chip manufacturers include Alexia, Flat Earth's baked veggie crisps, Quaker Tortillaz, Smartfood, Stacy's Pita Chips, and Terra Chips. Popchips, Inc., was co-founded by Keith Belling and Pat Turpin in 2007. As no oil is used in the manufacturing process, Popchips have fewer calories and less than half the fat of fried potato chips.

Every year Americans purchase $6 billion of potato chips and shoestring potatoes, which works out to about seventeen pounds per person. An additional $6 billion are spent on potato chips in other countries.

See also Breakfast; Diamond Foods; Frito-Lay; PepsiCo; Potatoes; Pringles

For Further Information:

Burhans, Dirk E. *Crunch!: A History of the Great American Potato Chip*. Madison, WI: Terrace Books, 2008.

Fox, William S., and Mae G. Banner. "Social and Economic Contexts for Folklore Variants: The Case of Potato Chip Legends." *Western Folklore* 42 (May 1983): 114–26.

Smith, Andrew F. *Potato: A Global History*. London: Reaktion Books, 2011.

Potatoes

The potato originated in western South America. It was domesticated by indigenous peoples at least eight thousand years ago. When Europeans ran into the potato in the mid-sixteenth century, they exported it to Europe, where it thrived in mountainous, arid, and rocky areas where grain crops, such as corn or wheat, could not be grown efficiently. Europeans brought the potato to North America, and by the early eighteenth century it was a common field crop in New England. The potato plant is prolific—a single plant produces an average of 4.4 pounds of potatoes, but productivity can be much greater. According to the *Guinness Book of World Records*, the record for the most potatoes grown on a single plant is 370 pounds.

The potato is inexpensive and it can be used for a wide variety of dishes that feature all sorts of tastes, textures, and aromas. Potatoes have been prepared in a wide variety of ways—boiled, baked, fried, roasted, steamed, sautéed, mashed, hashed, souffléed, and scalloped. They are used in pancakes, dumplings, salads, soups, stews, chowders, and savory puddings. Owing to this versatility, more potatoes are consumed than any other vegetable, and in terms of international production, potatoes rank behind only wheat and rice as the most important foods in the world.

Many junk foods and fast foods, including french fries, tater tots, hash browns, and potato chips, are made from potatoes. In addition, potato products are ingredients in many other junk foods and fast foods.

See also French Fries; Potato Chips; Tater Tots

For Further Information:

Smith, Andrew F. *Potato: A Global History*. London: Reaktion Books, 2011.

Poutine

La poutine (French-Canadian for "mess") is a Canadian dish composed of french fries topped with cheese curds and brown gravy. Other ingredients, such as tomato puree or even foie gras, are frequently added to this basic mix. Credit for inventing poutine is given to Fernand Lachance's Café Ideal in Warwick, Québéc, in 1957, but the gravy wasn't added until 1964. It is now available throughout Canada, where it is sold in national restaurant chains, such as Burger King, New York Fries, and A&W. Recently, poutine has become an item offered by restaurants in the United States.

See also A&W; Burger King; Canada

For Further Information:

Allemang, John. "Poutine: Québec's Accidental Delicacy Becomes Global Haute Cuisine." *Québec Globe and Mail,* May 22, 2010, as at: www.theglobeandmail.com/life/food-and-wine/poutine-quebecs-accidental-delicacy-becomes-global-haute-cuisine/article1578242/

Roy, Suman and Brooke Ali. *From Pemmican to Poutine: A Journey through Canada's Culinary History from Coast to Coast*. nl: Key Publishing House, Inc., 2010.

Surhone, Lambert M., Miriam T. Timpledon, Susan F. Marseken, eds. *Poutine: French Fries, Fast Food, Carne Asada, Carne Asada Fries, Guacamole, Sour Cream, Pico de Gallo, Cheese Fries, List of Accompaniments with French Fries New York Fries*. nl: Betascript Publishers, 2009.

Trillin, Calvin. "Funny Food." *New Yorker* (November 23, 2009): 68.

Powdered Mixes

Powdered mixes, such as those used to make hot and cold beverages, have been around since the mid-nineteenth century. Commercial powdered mixes, such as Nestlé's Instant Chocolate and Ovaltine, were common in the United States by the early twentieth century. Kool-Aid, which was launched in 1927, dominated the children's beverage market throughout the 1930s and 1940s. Instant coffee was invented in 1901 but was not a commercial success until 1938, when Nescafe released its freeze-dried coffee. Instant tea was introduced in 1953, and Lipton's Instant Tea came out five years later. The diet craze spawned many powdered mixes, including Crystal Light and Country Time.

The powdered mixes industry received a jolt in 1957 when General Foods released Tang, a powdered orange-flavored mix composed of sweeteners and artificial flavorings. All customers had to do was mix the powder with water for an easy-to-prepare breakfast drink. It became popular during the 1960s and 1970s. Today, Tang is the best-selling powdered mix. It is owned by Kraft Foods and is currently sold in sixty countries.

See also Beverages; Chocolate Beverages; General Foods Corporation; Kool-Aid; Kraft Foods; Nestlé; Tang

For Further Information:

Tang Web site: www.kraft.com/archives/brands/brands_tang.html

Turback, Michael. *Hot Chocolate*. Berkeley, CA: 10 Speed Press, 2005.

Power and Energy Bars

In 1986 Brian Maxwell and nutritionist Jennifer Biddulph in Berkeley, California, founded PowerBar. Their product was intended to be used by long distance runners to supply carbohydrates during endurance events. PowerBar was a success and it was acquired by Nestlé in 2000.

PowerBar created a new field of energy bars. Other companies, such as Clif Bar, Inc., began to manufacture similar products in 1992. Gatorade manufactured its Energy Bar in 1999. During the early twenty-first century, the Atkins Advantage and the Atkins Endulge were successfully marketed, as was the Zone Perfect. Today, hundreds of energy bars (also known as snack bars, granola bars, food bars, nutrition bars, and cereal bars) are available for purchase at grocery stores. In 2005 the Hershey Company introduced PayDay Pro, an energy bar with added vitamins and minerals.

Most power and energy bars are high in calories, which come from carbohydrates. Often the main ingredient is sugar, such as high-fructose corn syrup, dextrose, and fructose. They may also contain chocolate, Kellogg's Rice Krispies, and caramel. Concentrated doses of sugar may give the consumer an immediate burst of energy or sugar rush, which is the same as if one ate a candy bar. The rush is often followed by the crash, and often consumers may end up more tired than before eating the bar. The energy bar market is projected to grow more than 27 percent, from $962 million in sales in 2003 to an estimated $1.23 billion in sales in 2013.

See also Caramels; Carbohydrates; Chocolate; Granola; Hershey Company; High-Fructose Corn Syrup; Kellogg Company; Nestlé; PayDay; Sugars/Sweeteners

For Further Information:

The U.S. Market for Food Bars. New York: Packaged Facts, 2003.

Pregnancy and Early Childhood

Animal and human studies have developed evidence that the foods females eat during pregnancy affect their offspring. In one experimental study, pregnant rats were divided into two groups: fourteen were fed healthy, nutritional food, and twenty-eight were fed a junk food diet with open access to biscuits, muffins, and doughnuts. The junk-fed pregnant rats had lower birth weight offspring. Researchers found that offspring in the junk food-eating group, when given the opportunity to consume protein-rich foods, preferred eating food rich in fat and sugar. Subsequent studies demonstrated that the offspring of rats who ate junk food during pregnancy were overweight by comparison to the control groups, and this held even for the offspring of the offspring.

To the extent that junk food and fast food contribute to obesity, many studies indicate complications for pregnant women who are obese, and maternal obesity's long-term adverse outcomes for the health of offspring in later life. Maternal obesity increases the risk for the offspring to develop obesity, and also has an impact on the offspring's cardiometabolic health, hypertension, vascular dysfunction, and such. Recent studies have also suggested that there is a link between the father's diet prior to conception and his child's chances of medical conditions like diabetes and heart disease.

A study published in 2011 in the *Journal of Epidemiology and Community Health* suggests that there may be a link between diet and intelligence. The study showed that 20 percent of children who ate food high in fats, sugars, and processed foods had an average IQ of 101 points, compared with 106 for the 20 percent of children who ate healthy food. The research examined 14,000 children whose health was monitored at the ages of three, four, seven, and eight. A predominantly junk food diet at the age of three was associated with a lower IQ at the age of eight and a half, regardless of whether the diet improved after the age of three. This small positive correlation does not necessarily mean a cause-and-effect relationship, as

IQ can be influenced by many factors, including economic and social background. However, the brain grows fastest during the first three years of life, and as one of the study's co-authors concluded, "A junk food diet is not conducive to good brain development."

See also Diabetes; Junk Foods; Obesity

For Further Information:

Bayol, Stéphanie A., et al. "A Maternal 'Junk Food' Diet in Pregnancy and Lactation Promotes an Exacerbated Taste for 'Junk Food' and a Greater Propensity for Obesity in Rat Offspring." *British Journal of Nutrition* 98 (2007): 843–51.

Bayol, Stéphanie A., et al. "Evidence That a Maternal "Junk Food" Diet During Pregnancy and Lactation Can Reduce Muscle Force in Offspring." *European Journal of Nutrition* 48, no. 1 (2009): 62–65.

Bayol, Stéphanie A., et al. "A Maternal 'Junk Food' Diet in Pregnancy and Lactation Promotes Nonalcoholic Fatty Liver Disease in Rat Offspring." *Endocrinology* 151, no. 4 (2010): 1451–61.

Carone, Benjamin R., et al. "Paternally Induced Transgenerational Environmental Reprogramming of Metabolic Gene Expression in Mammals." *Cell* (December 23, 2010): 1084–96.

Drake, Amanda J., and Rebecca M. Reynolds. "Impact of Maternal Obesity on Offspring Obesity and Cardiometabolic Disease Risk." *Reproduction* 140 (2010): 387–98.

Northstone, Kate, et al. "Are Dietary Patterns in Childhood Associated with IQ at 8 Years of Age? A Population-based Cohort Study." *Journal of Epidemiology and Community Health*, as at: http://jech.bmj.com/content/early/2011/01/21/jech.2010.111955?q=w_jech_ahead_tab

Ong, Z. Y., and B. S. Muhlhausler. "Maternal 'Junk-food' Feeding of Rat Dams Alters Food Choices and Development of the Mesolimbic Reward Pathway in the Offspring." *The FASEB Journal*, as at: www.fasebj.org/content/early/2011/03/20/fj.10-178392.abstract

Pret a Manger

Pret a Manger (French for "ready to eat") is a British-based fast-casual restaurant chain. Its signature menu items are sandwiches, but it also sells wraps, baguettes, soups, salads, and bakery goods. The company was launched in 1986 by Sinclair Beecham and Julian Metcalfe. Its menu includes the Turkey Club and the Italian BMT (bacon, mozzarella, tomato). The company prides itself on using natural, preservative-free, and hormone-free ingredients and proclaims that the food is made fresh each day.

Environmental impact and sustainability have been important corporate concerns. Pret a Manger has reduced waste and its UK operations now acquire much of its electricity from renewable energy sources. The company has also been experimenting with recyclable containers, which it hopes to recycle into usable materials and decrease waste going into landfills. In 2009 the company stopped stocking bluefin tuna, owing to the methods of fishing and the rapid depletion of the Atlantic bluefin population, and they switched to skipjack, a more sustainable type of tuna, which is caught by the pole-and-line method.

Pret a Manger opened its first restaurant in the United States in 2000. As of 2011, Pret a Manger was headquartered in Westminster, London, with more than two hundred restaurants in the United Kingdom, Hong Kong, Singapore, and the United States.

See also Environment; Fast Casual; Salads; Sandwiches

For Further Information:

Pret a Manger U.S. Web site: www.pret.com/us

Pretzels

Pretzels are glazed, salted baked goods that are shaped into long tubes and often twisted into knots. The word derives from German, but the Dutch probably first introduced them to America. Homemade pretzels were sold by street vendors, but it wasn't until 1861 that the first commercial pretzel company was launched by

Pretzels. (Dreamstime.com)

Julius Sturgis in Lititz, Pennsylvania. His pretzels were twisted by hand and sales remained local. The first automatic pretzel-twisting machine was developed by the Reading Pretzel Machinery Company in 1933. Pretzel manufacturers remained concentrated in Pennsylvania and pretzels did not emerge as a national snack until the 1960s.

Pretzels are made in two ways: the large, soft pretzel and the hard, crisp pretzel. The soft pretzel is perishable and must be sold as a fresh-baked item (usually by vendors) or as a frozen food. Several chains sell soft pretzels, such as Auntie Anne's, Wetzel's Pretzels, and Pretzel Time. The smaller, crisp pretzels have a long shelf life and are sold in plastic barrels or bags. The two best-selling pretzel brands were Frito-Lay's Rold Gold and Snyder's of Hanover.

Recent Developments

Several companies produced chocolate-covered pretzels; in 2010 Mars, Inc., produced M&M's with pretzels inside. A German-owned company, Swissmaker, began selling pretzels, including such treats as Italian Salami Soft Pretzel and a pretzel with Swiss chocolate, in the United States. They also sold a large selection of sugar glazed nuts. In 2011, the company opened a large store in New York.

See also Auntie Anne's; Chocolate; Frito-Lay; M&M's; Mars, Inc.; Snyder's of Hanover; Street Vendors

For Further Information:

Bartlett, Virginia K. *Pickles and Pretzels: Pennsylvania's World of Food.* Pittsburgh: University of Pittsburgh Press, 1980.

Pricing

In the United States the pricing for fast food and junk food has rapidly changed over the years. White Castle, the first fast food chain, initially targeted working people and intentionally kept its prices low. Subsequent fast food chains have targeted different groups, and consequently had different pricing patterns. McDonald's, Jack in the Box, KFC, Pizza Hut, and Burger King started off targeting suburban families, and their goal was to keep the price of the food down. Others targeted different groups. Bob's Big Boy launched a large hamburger that cost three times as much as the hamburgers offered by other fast food chains. It worked. Big Boys sold and fast food chains got the picture. Burger King released the Whopper in 1957 at the price of 37 cents—more than twice as much as McDonald's burgers. McDonald's responded with its Big Mac and Quarter Pounder. Eventually, most fast food chains began offering deluxe products with higher prices. As the disposable income of suburban families increased, so did the offerings and prices of fast food operations. Likewise, junk foods, such as penny candy, were offered at low cost. As disposable income increased in the United States, prices for potato chips, candy, and chocolate bars, for example, greatly increased. Part of the increase is related to supply; chocolate prices have increased over the years, while sugar prices have sharply declined.

The category with the greatest price flexibility is soda. Because the cost of water and sugar is very low, great profits can be generated. The problem is that the competition can (and has) offered lower-priced soft drinks. Major soda companies—Coca-Cola, PepsiCo, and Dr Pepper Snapple Group—have responded by acquiring as many of their competitors as possible and by advertising their products extensively.

See also Advertising; Big Boy; Burger King; Candy; Chocolate; Coca-Cola Company; Dr Pepper Snapple Group; Hamburger; KFC; McDonald's; Penny Candy; Pizza Hut; Potato Chips; Soda/Soft Drinks; Sugars/Sweeteners; White Castle

For Further Information:

Jakle, John A., and Keith A. Sculle. *Fast Food: Roadside Restaurants in the Automobile Age*. Baltimore: Johns Hopkins University Press, 1999.

Schlosser, Eric. *Fast Food Nation: The Dark Side of the All-American Meal*. New York: Houghton Mifflin Company, 2001.

Pringles

In 1969 Procter & Gamble introduced Pringles Potato Chips, made from dehydrated and reconstituted potatoes. They were named after Pringle Street in Finneytown, Ohio. Unlike potato chips, Pringles are a uniform size and shape, making it possible to package them in a long tube. The potato chip industry went to court to prevent Procter & Gamble from calling Pringles "potato chips." This was resolved in 1975, when the U.S. Food and Drug Administration defined Pringles as "potato chips made from dehydrated potatoes."

Pringles are one of Procter & Gamble's biggest brands and they are sold in more than 140 countries. Procter & Gamble has extended the Pringle product line to now include Sour Cream & Onion, Salt & Vinegar, and Hot & Spicy. In 1998 Fat-Free Pringles, made with olestra, were introduced. The Center for Science in the Public Interest (CSPI) claimed that olestra disrupted some people's digestive tracts, but Proctor & Gamble argued that Pringles posed no health threat. Nevertheless, the product was withdrawn from the market.

One reason for Pringles' success has been their extensive advertising. For instance, in 2005 Proctor & Gamble arranged a movie tie-in with *Star Wars Episode III—Revenge of the Sith*. Pringle cans featured special *Revenge of the Sith*–themed characters, such as Anakin Skywalker, Yoda, and Darth Vader. In April 2011, Diamond Foods acquired Pringles.

See also Advertising; Center for Science in the Public Interest (CSPI); Diamond Foods; Food and Drug Administration (FDA); Movie Tie-Ins; Potato Chips

For Further Information:
Pringles Web site: www.pringles.com

Product Placement

Since the 1970s, movie producers have approached fast food and junk food companies with offers to include their products in movies for a fee or in exchange for advertising and other promotions. The classic example was Universal Studios' approach to Mars, Inc., to use M&M's in its movie *E.T.: The Extra-Terrestrial.* Mars turned them down, and Universal then approached the Hershey Company, which produced Reese's Pieces. Universal and Hershey's came to an agreement in which Reese's Pieces were used in the movie, and Hershey agreed to promote *E.T.* with $1 million. In turn, Hershey was granted rights to use the film to promote its own products. When the movie was released, sales of Reese's Pieces skyrocketed.

Product placements have been common elements in many movies. In 1982 the Coca-Cola Company purchased Columbia Pictures to generate publicity through Coke product placements in its films. (Coca-Cola later sold Columbia Pictures.) McDonald's appears in *Bye, Bye Love* (1995), *George of the Jungle* (1997), and *Clear and Present Danger* (1994). In the movie *Richie Rich* (1994) Macaulay Culkin, playing Richie Rich, has a McDonald's restaurant in his home. Product placement costs run between $50,000 and $100,000, depending upon the prominence of the placement. Filmmakers typically receive advertising estimated to be valued between $25 million and $45 million.

Product placement is but one relationship between movies and junk food and fast food. Product placements have been so successful that they are now included in books, music videos, comic strips, and songs. Cooperative marketing relationships have developed that include the manufacturing of toys and other merchandise. Even more unusual relationships have been created. For instance, Hostess produced Hostess Turtle Pies prior to the release of the movie *Teenage Mutant Ninja Turtles II* (1991). The pies were advertised as "Fresh from the sewers to you!"

In addition to movies, fast food and junk food have had close relationships with television programs. Burger King, for instance, has had a relationship with Nickelodeon and McDonald's has one with the Fox Kids Network.

See also Advertising; Burger King; Coca-Cola Company; Hershey Company; Hostess Brands; M&M's; Mars, Inc.; McDonald's; Movies; Pie; Television

For Further Information:

Brownell, Kelly D., and Katherine Battle Horgen. *Food Fight: The Inside Story of the Food Industry, America's Obesity Crisis, and What We Can Do about It.* Chicago: Contemporary Books, 2004.

Gupta, P. B., and S. J. Gould. "Consumers' Perceptions of the Ethics and Acceptability of Product Placement in Movies: Product Category and Individual Differences." *Journal of Current Issues and Research in Advertising* 19 (1997): 37–50.

Save Harry campaign Web site: www.SaveHarry.com

Shrek Web site: www.shrek.com

Protests

Protests against junk food and fast food have been growing since the 1970s for a variety of reasons. Animal rights and vegetarian activists have protested against the consumption of meat and meat products, and the conditions at the feedlots and slaughterhouses that supply meat to fast food operations. Leftists, anarchists, and nationalists have protested against the globalization of fast food. Environmentalists have protested against the loss of rainforests owing to activities of fast food suppliers, and against the amount of waste needlessly generated by fast food chains and their suppliers.

Nutrition activists have protested about the empty calories and the high levels of salt, fat, and sugar present in most junk and fast foods. Recent concern has focused on the size of portions offered in fast food operations, particularly supersized meals. Consumer advocates and educators have protested against the targeting of children through advertising and the sale of junk food and fast food in schools. Labor unions have protested the anti-union activities of fast food chains. Groups have engaged in boycotts against junk food manufacturers, as well as fast food chains. Because fast food operations are often considered synonymous with the United States, people in other countries have protested against policies and actions of the U.S. government by destroying, trashing, and bombing fast food outlets.

Fast food chains and junk food manufacturers have responded to these protests in a variety of ways. McDonald's eliminated beef tallow and other beef products from its french fry oil, and Burger King placed signs in its outlets reporting that its french fries were made with beef products to alert vegetarians as to the contents of its products. Fast food operations in other countries have intentionally localized their suppliers. The McDonald's outlets in France buy 95 percent of the food they serve from local farmers and processors. All fast food chains have offered special foods and beverages appropriate to local sensibilities. For instance, McDonald's does not sell hamburgers in India, but it does sell veggie burgers. When environmentalists attacked McDonald's for destruction of rainforests, the company shifted to suppliers in countries without rainforests.

Protests have also targeted fast food chains for political reasons. When the McDonald's outlets in Norway released the McAfrika Burger in August 2002, protestors attacked the company for profiting from a name when there were millions of people starving in South Africa. (At the time, South Africa was in the midst of massive famine owing to natural disasters—heavy floods, then drought.) KFC became a target during the uprising in Egypt in early 2011.

McDonald's has become a symbol of American prosperity and creativity. Simply because of the size, visibility, and impact of fast and junk food operations around the world, fast food companies attract protesters. Many people believe that they threaten national cultures by shifting how, where, and what people eat.

See also Advertising; Animal Rights Movement; Anti-Unionization; Boycotts; Burger King; Calories; Consumerism; Environment; Fat, Dietary; French Fries; KFC; McDonald's; "McLibel"; School Food; Sodium/Salt; South Africa; Sugars/Sweeteners; Supersizing; Suppliers; Vegetarian/Vegan

For Further Information:

Bové, José, François Dufour, and Gilles Luneau. *The World Is Not for Sale: Farmers Against Junk Food.* New York: Verso, 2001.

McSpotlight Web site: www.mcspotlight.org

Pudding

Historically, the word "pudding" has a variety of meanings. In America the term is less diverse, but it still encompasses many different products, such as sweet desserts, tapioca pudding, hasty puddings, bread puddings, Christmas puddings, rice puddings, custards, flans, mousses, and even Jell-O. They are commercially available in mixes, frozen products, and ready-to-eat cups.

General Foods, makers of Jell-O, introduced its chocolate pudding mix in 1926. Royal Desserts, manufactured by Standard Brands, produced similar mixes shortly thereafter. Some puddings can also be used for pie fillings. General Foods eventually expanded their Jell-O product line to include ready-to-eat pudding.

Banana pudding. (Dreamstime.com)

Frozen puddings were introduced by Birds Eye in 1968 and were soon available throughout the United States. In 1970 McCain Foods, Ltd., a Canadian company, released its frozen pudding. Shortly thereafter, other companies released similar products. Frozen pudding usually came in four flavors—chocolate, vanilla, butterscotch, and tapioca. During the 1980s, General Foods released Jell-O Pudding Pops, which was frozen pudding on a stick.

Room-temperature puddings are also available in supermarkets. They are sold in "snack packs," which contain multiple cups and are geared for children's lunches.

See also Chocolate; Jell-O; Vanilla

Push-Ups

During the 1980s, Push-Ups, also known as Rocket Pops, became popular. Push-Ups were composed of many different ingredients, from ice cream to sherbet to yogurt. The mechanism varied by brand: some used axles, wheels, and cylinders; others used a stick in a tube. The consumer pushed up the bottom and licked the product at the top. Today, Push-Ups continue to be made by a number of companies, including Nestlé. Their product line includes vanilla-flavored sherbet with chocolate, strawberry, or caramel.

See also Caramels; Chocolate; Ice Cream; Nestlé

For Further Information:

Funderburg, Anne Cooper. *Chocolate, Strawberry, and Vanilla: A History of American Ice Cream*. Bowling Green, OH: Bowling Green State University Popular Press, 1995.

Q

Qdoba Mexican Grill

Qdoba (an invented name) is a fast-casual restaurant chain in the United States serving Mexican-style food. Its signature dish is the burrito. It was launched by Anthony Miller and Robert Hauser in Denver, Colorado, in 1995.

ACI Capital acquired and expanded the company and sold it to Jack in the Box in 2003. As of 2011, Qdoba had more than five hundred locations in forty-three states.

See also Burrito; Fast Casual; Jack in the Box; Mexican American Food

For Further Information:

Qdoba Web site: qdoba.com

Quesadillas

Quesadillas, a food of Mexico, are typically composed of melted cheese inside a folded corn or wheat tortilla with other ingredients added. Mexican-style quesadillas are sold in many fast food chains in America, such as Del Taco, Moe's Southwest Grill, Rubio's Fresh Mexican Grill, Taco Bueno, and Taco Bell.

See also Del Taco; Mexican American Food; Moe's Southwest Grill; Rubio's Fresh Mexican Grill; Taco Bell; Taco Bueno

For Further Information:

Smith, Andrew F. "Tacos, Enchiladas and Refried Beans: The Invention of Mexican-American Cookery." In Mary Wallace Kelsey and ZoeAnn Holmes,

Quesadillas. (Dreamstime.com)

eds., *Cultural and Historical Aspects of Foods*. Corvallis: Oregon State University, 1999, 183–203; also at: http://food.oregonstate.edu/ref/culture/latinamerica/la_smith.html

Quick-Service Restaurants (QSR)

"Quick-service restaurant" (QSR) is the term used by many restaurant chains as an alternative to the term "fast food," which now has pejorative connotations.

See also Fast Food

For Further Information:

Quick Service Magazine Web site: www.qsrmagazine.com

Quiznos

Quiznos is a fast food chain specializing in toasted submarine sandwiches, soups, chips, and desserts. The first Quiznos Subs restaurant was opened Denver, Colorado, in 1981. Rick Schaden ate at the restaurant and liked the sandwich so much that in 1987 he bought a franchise in Boulder, Colorado. He subsequently purchased additional franchises, and in 1991 he and his father bought the entire franchise operation, which then had eighteen restaurants.

While the company did not invent the toasted sub sandwich, it did popularize the concept. It was so successful selling toasted subs that Subway began offering customers a toasted option in 2004. Quiznos offers a wide variety of unusual types of subs, such as their Chicken Carbonara, Spicy Monterey Club, and Turkey Bacon Guacamole subs.

Under Schaden's leadership, the chain expanded rapidly. By 1996 there were 100 outlets; by 2000 it reached more than 1,000 outlets; four years later, it topped 3,000 outlets. By 2005, the number of Quiznos outlets passed those of the Blimpie chain. As of 2011, it had 3,400 outlets in the United States—and almost 500 in Canada and 200 in 13 other countries. Quiznos ranks second in the sub sandwich category of fast food chains, while Subway remains the leader. Quiznos is a privately held company and it is headquartered in Denver.

See also Blimpie International; Sandwiches; Subs/Grinders; Subway

For Further Information:

Quiznos on Facebook: www.facebook.com/Quiznos
Quiznos on Twitter: twitter.com/Quiznos
Quiznos Web site: www.quiznos.com

R

Radio

Since the 1920s, snack food and fast food have been advertised on radio. From the manufacturers' standpoints, radio has immense power in its advertising potential and its relatively low cost. Products advertised on the radio sell. When radio programs became popular in the 1920s, food companies commissioned celebrities, such as Jack Benny, to promote their products. Some of the earliest food companies to advertise effectively on radio were cereal makers. In 1926 General Mills (Wheaties) was the first radio advertiser to use a jingle. In 1933 Wheaties sponsored the program *Jack Armstrong, the All-American Boy* on the radio. The fast food chain White Castle began advertising on radio by the 1930s. Beginning in the 1950s, most fast food chains and junk food manufacturers advertised on radio. For instance, the chocolate drink Ovaltine sponsored the *Little Orphan Annie* and *Captain Midnight* radio programs.

Studies have indicated that Americans spend more time listening to the radio than watching television. Because radio advertising is low cost compared with television advertising, it is frequently used by fast food chains at the local level. Radio advertising is particularly effective during commute times, when many people listen to the radio in their cars. It is estimated that food companies (mainly fast food) expend about 7 percent of their advertising budget on radio advertising.

See also Advertising; Cereals; General Mills; Television; White Castle

For Further Information:

Hogan, David Gerald. *Selling 'em by the Sack: White Castle and the Creation of American Food.* New York: New York University Press, 1997.

Smith, Andrew F. *Popped Culture: A Social History of Popcorn in America.* Columbia: University of South Carolina Press, 1999.

Rally's

Rally's was founded in Louisville, Kentucky, in 1985; the following year, the company began to franchise. Its signature menu items are the Rallyburger and Big Buford (a double-patty cheeseburger). Most stores have a "double drive-thru order and pickup service," and few of its stores have indoor seating. Rally's expanded rapidly, both by franchising and by buying smaller chains such as Maxie's of America, Snapps Drive-Thru and Zipps Drive-Thru, and West Coast Restaurant Enterprises.

In 1996 CKE Restaurants, the parent company of Hardee's and Carl's Jr., owned a 30 percent share in Rally's; CKE sold this to Checker's Drive-In Restaurants in 1999, when Rally's and Checkers merged. Rally's is a division of Checkers Drive-In Restaurants, headquartered in Clearwater, Florida. As of 2011, there were more than eight hundred Rally's and Checkers stores in thirty states.

See also Checker's Drive-In Restaurants

For Further Information:

Rally's Web site: www.rallys.com

Razzles

Razzles are a confection that starts as a candy but turns into gum when chewed. It was advertised as: "First it's a candy, then it's a gum. Little round Razzles are so much fun," and it's a "whole candy store in a package." Razzles were introduced in 1966 but they became particularly popular in the 1980s, when the confection was manufactured by Concord Confections, headquartered in Toronto, Canada. It was acquired by Tootsie Roll Industries in 2004. Razzles come in a variety of flavors, including raspberry, lime, and tangerine; Sour Razzles and Tropical Razzles were later added to the product line.

See also Candy; Gum; Tootsie Roll Industries

For Further Information:

Tootsie Roll Industries Web site: www.tootsie.com

Red Robin Gourmet Burgers

Gerald Kingen opened the first Red Robin restaurant near the campus of the University of Washington in Seattle in 1969. The company's menu includes burgers made with "beef, chicken, fish, turkey, pot roast, and vegetarian substitutes, as well as salads, soups, appetizers, and other entrees such as rice bowls and pasta." As of 2011, Red Robin had more than 450 fast-casual restaurants in the United States and Canada. The company is headquartered in Greenwood Village, Colorado.

See also Fast Casual; Hamburgers

For Further Information:
Red Robin Web site www.redrobin.com

Redenbacher, Orville

Popcorn entrepreneur Orville Clarence Redenbacher (1907–1995) was born in Brazil, Indiana. He grew up on a farm and studied agronomy and genetics at Purdue University, where he conducted research on popcorn hybrids. Upon graduation in 1928, he was hired as a high school vocational agricultural teacher, a position he held until 1929. He was then employed as an assistant county farm agent in Terre Haute, Indiana. When the senior agent moved to Indianapolis, Redenbacher took over his position and conducted a five-minute daily radio program beginning in 1930. He was the first county agricultural agent in the country to broadcast live from his office and the first to interview farmers in the field with a mobile unit.

In January 1940 Tony Hulman, owner of the Indianapolis 500 racetrack, hired Redenbacher to manage his 12,000-acre farm in Princeton, Indiana, which produced seed for farmers. Redenbacher built a hybrid seed-corn plant and began experimenting with popcorn hybrids. Under Redenbacher's management, Princeton Farms' operations grew by 50 percent.

While at Princeton Farms, Redenbacher met Charles Bowman, the manager of the Purdue Ag Alumni Seed Implement Association in Lafayette, Indiana. Redenbacher and Bowman went into partnership in 1951 and purchased the George F. Chester Seed Company at Boone Grove, Indiana. Popcorn was part of their hybrid field-seed operation, and within a few years Redenbacher and Bowman became the world's largest supplier of hybrid popcorn seed. They reportedly crossed 30,000 popcorn hybrids to find the right mix. In 1965 their popcorn experimentation created a variety that expanded to nearly twice the size of existing commercial brands. It was fluffier and left few unpopped kernels. They called the new variety Red Bow, after the first three letters in Redenbacher's and Bowman's last names. For five years Redenbacher tried to sell his new hybrid to the major processors. However, it cost more to harvest and its yields were smaller than traditional popcorn. Because popcorn was then considered a commodity, processors were not interested.

Redenbacher hawked popcorn out of the backseat of his car to stores in northern Indiana. In 1970 Redenbacher quit producing popcorn seed for other processors and concentrated on selling Red Bow. Redenbacher and Bowman consulted a Chicago public relations firm that convinced them to change the name from Red Bow to Orville Redenbacher's Gourmet Popping Corn. Because its price was higher than that of other popcorn, consumers needed to be convinced that Redenbacher's popcorn was of a better quality than its competitors. The advertising tag "The

World's Most Expensive Popcorn" emerged. Redenbacher and Bowman achieved regional success through word-of-mouth promotion and virtually no advertising, but they needed assistance to expand nationally. In 1973 they teamed up with Blue Plate Foods, a subsidiary of Hunt-Wesson Foods based in Fullerton, California, to market their gourmet popcorn. This connection enabled national advertising and a widespread distribution system.

When Hunt-Wesson sold Blue Plate Foods in 1974, Redenbacher's gourmet popcorn was so successful that Hunt-Wesson kept the rights to it. In 1976 Orville Redenbacher's Gourmet Popping Corn business operations and property were sold to Hunt-Wesson, which launched a massive advertising campaign, starring Redenbacher himself, for their newly acquired product. He made hundreds of personal presentations a year and appeared in scores of television commercials. Redenbacher was one of America's most unlikely television stars, with his folksy image (bow tie, dark-framed spectacles, and midwestern accent). The image worked. Consumers easily recognized the label adorned with Redenbacher's image. In 1984 he wrote *Orville Redenbacher's Popcorn Book*, which was mainly a promotion piece for his popcorn.

In 1990 Hunt-Wesson (along with the Redenbacher brand) was acquired by ConAgra Foods. Redenbacher's contract for television commercials was not renewed in 1994. While lounging in a whirlpool in his condominium in Coronado, California, Redenbacher suffered a heart attack and drowned in 1995.

After his death, *Time* magazine called Redenbacher "the Luther Burbank of popcorn." His gourmet popping corn stands as his shining legacy. Because his was one of the first foods called "gourmet," it can be said that the naming of his popcorn launched a new category of foods and created gourmet sections in grocery stores.

See also Advertising; ConAgra Foods; Entrepreneurs; Popcorn; Television

For Further Information:

Redenbacher, Orville. *Orville Redenbacher's Popcorn Book*. New York: St. Martin's Press, 1984.

Sherman, Len. *Popcorn King: How Orville Redenbacher and His Popcorn Charmed America*. Arlington, TX: The Summit Publishing Group, 1996.

Smith, Andrew F. *Popped Culture: A Social History of Popcorn in America*. Columbia: University of South Carolina Press, 1999.

Reese's Peanut Butter Cups

Harry Burnett Reese, a former employee of the Hershey Company, founded the H. B. Reese Candy Company in 1917. Reese experimented with molasses and coconut candies called Johnny Bars and Lizzie Bars. Reese moved his operation

Reese's Peanut Butter Cups. (Dreamstime.com)

to Hershey, Pennsylvania, in 1923 and began purchasing chocolate from Hershey. In 1928 he came out with chocolate-covered peanut butter cups, which were packaged in five-pound boxes for sale in candy assortments. Ten years later, Reese marketed these cups separately for a penny apiece. These subsequently became known as Reese's Peanut Butter Cups, and they were extremely popular. Increased demand meant factory expansion, and Reese's became the second-largest buyer of chocolate in the United States. During World War II, difficulties in acquiring sugar and chocolate prompted Reese to discontinue his other lines to concentrate on the peanut butter cups, because peanuts were not rationed during the war. After the war, the peanut-candy market boomed. Reese's Peanut Butter Cups, distributed through wholesale jobbers, vending machine operators, and syndicated stores, gained popularity and the company constructed an even larger facility in 1957.

When Harry Reese died in 1956, the company went through a bitter battle for control among the six brothers who inherited it. With annual sales at $14 million, the company was acquired by Hershey Chocolate Company in 1963 for $23.3 million. Under the ownership of Hershey Chocolate Company, Reese's Peanut Butter Cups were sold nationally. The advertising slogan "Two great tastes that taste great together" was developed by Ogilvie & Mather in 1970. In 1976 Hershey expanded the product line by launching Reese's Crunchy Peanut Butter Cup, with a different flavor and a texture of chopped peanuts.

The remarkable success of the Reese's chocolate–peanut butter combination encouraged Hershey to test-market a small peanut butter candy in 1979. While the product was under development, PB was its proposed name. Because Mars, Inc., already held the trademark on PB, Hershey decided on Reese's Pieces, which were released nationally in 1978. Within four years, they were so successful that a new production line was established in Stuart's Draft, Virginia. Mars, Inc., released Peanut Butter M&M's to counter Reese's Pieces. Their sales peaked in 1991 at $78 million, then dropped to $34 million in 1993. Mars purportedly then tried to relaunch the brand by copying the coloring and styling of Hershey's Reese's Pieces. This resulted in a lawsuit, with Hershey claiming that Mars was capitalizing on Hershey's goodwill and substantial investment in Reese's Pieces. Hershey won, and Mars changed the candy's appearance so that it looked less like Reese's Pieces.

In 1981 Hershey was approached by Universal Studios for assistance with making a new film. The main character in the film was a lovable alien, and the filmmakers wanted to have the children in the film lure the creature with a trail of candy. The producers had previously contacted Mars, Inc., requesting the use of M&M's, but Mars refused. So Universal turned to Hershey for permission to use Reese's Pieces, instead, and Hershey agreed. Reese's Pieces consequently received national visibility in *E.T.: The Extra-Terrestrial*, which was a blockbuster film. This was considered an inexpensive marketing triumph, and advertisers have tried to duplicate it ever since.

The Hershey Company has continued to expand its successful Reese's Peanut Butter Cup line by releasing White Chocolate Reese's Peanut Butter Cups in 2003. Reese's Peanut Butter Cups remain one of America's most popular candies. In 2010 Harris Interactive's Youth EquiTrend study of brand recognition ranked Reese's Peanut Butter Cups third among 8- to 24-year-olds.

See also Advertising; Candy; Chocolate; Hershey Company; Lawsuits; M&M's; Mars, Inc.; Peanut Butter; Sugars/Sweeteners; Vending Machines

For Further Information:

Broekel, Ray. *The Great America Candy Bar Book*. Boston: Houghton Mifflin Company, 1982.

Hershey's Web site: www.hersheys.com/products/reese/index.html

Richardson, Tim. *Sweets: A History of Candy*. New York: Bloomsbury, 2002.

Smith, Andrew F. *Peanuts: The Illustrious History of the Goober Pea*. Urbana: University of Illinois Press, 2006.

Refried Beans

Refried beans were "Mexico's commonest dish." However, the earliest known American recipe was not published until 1888. Under the title of "Trijoles," Mrs.

Joseph Warner Maddox of San Antonio boiled the beans first, then fried them in lard. Restaurants and cantinas likely offered refried beans on their menus well before this time. Several observers reported that meals were seldom served without them. For the poor, frijoles were "the mainstay of their diet both winter and summer." Frijoles were served "in a large dish from which you help yourself, dashing a spoonful of the nutty pellets on the side of your *enchilada.* Occasionally you will find them fried dry, and always you must flavor them with chile." Frijoles were, said John G. Bourke, prepared "in a half dozen different ways; stewed or boiled to a pulpy paste, it appears at almost every meal, and well deserves its title of 'El plato nacional,' the national dish." Virtually all Mexican American restaurant chains, such as Taco Bell or Taco Bueno, serve some form of refried beans.

See also Mexican American Food; Taco Bell; Taco Bueno

For Further Information:

Smith, Andrew F. "Tacos, Enchiladas and Refried Beans: The Invention of Mexican-American Cookery." In Mary Wallace Kelsey and ZoeAnn Holmes, eds., *Cultural and Historical Aspects of Foods.* Corvallis: Oregon State University, 1999, 183–203; also at: http://food.oregonstate.edu/ref/culture/latinamerica/la_smith.html

Regional Fast Foods

Major national chains dominate the American fast food world, but there are many local and regional operations that serve fast food hamburgers, pizza, and chicken, as well as various ethnic foods. Large regional hamburger chains include Big Boy and In-N-Out Burger. Whataburger, founded in Corpus Christi, Texas, in 1950, sells burgers, chicken, and salads, and mainly operates in Alabama, Arizona, Florida, Louisiana, New Mexico, Oklahoma, and Texas. Fatburger and Tommies Burgers mainly operate in Southern California. Wolfe Burger sells the Big Bad Wolfe burger mainly in Pasadena, California. Krystal, which started in 1932, operates in southeastern states only, offering breakfasts and hamburgers. Blake's Lotta Burger has seventy-five locations in New Mexico. The Happy Chef has outlets in Iowa, Minnesota, South Dakota, and Wisconsin.

Many regional chains specialize in chicken. Bojangles, with its chicken and biscuits, has locations mainly in the South. Chester Fried Chicken was launched in Chester County, Pennsylvania, in 1974. By 2002, the Chester Fried Chicken brand was sold in more than 1,700 licensed locations throughout the country.

Most communities in the American southwest have Mexican American fast food outlets. Regional Mexican American fast food restaurant chains include El Pollo Loco and Del Taco. There are many more: Taco Del Mar Mexican Food, launched in 1992, is headquartered in Seattle and has outlets in western and midwestern states. In 1959 Taco Time began in Eugene, Oregon, and today has more than three hundred outlets. Taco John's started in 1969 and today operates in twenty-seven states. Pepe's was launched in Chicago in 1967; Taco Maker was launched in Ogden, Utah, in 1968.

American cities and most towns usually have at least one pizza parlor, and there are many regional chains. Boston Pizza, a sports bar and fast food chain, was launched by a Greek immigrant in Edmonton, Canada, in 1964. As of 2011, the chain had 325 outlets mainly in Canada and 54 outlets in the United States. In 1971 Jim Fox launched Fox's Pizza Den in Pitcairn, Pennsylvania. Vocelli Pizza, launched in 1988, has 100 outlets today.

Many American communities have Chinese-style fast food outlets. Chinese-style fast food chains include Panda Express; Manchu Wok, which started in Peterborough, Ontario, and today has two hundred outlets; and Tasty Goody, which has eight locations in southern California, mainly in the area between Los Angeles and Riverside. Mr. Chau's Fast Food is in the San Francisco Bay/Silicon Valley area of California.

In addition to local chains, national and regional chains serve different foods in various regions. McDonald's, for instance, serves veggie burgers in New York. Regional chains serve regional favorites, such as barbecue or chicken fried steak in the South.

Commercial regional snack foods and soft drinks are quickly disappearing, but some have survived. Moxie soda, for instance, remains a favorite drink in New England. Moon Pies remain a favorite in Tennessee and the South, and Tasty Kakes are still made in Philadelphia.

See also Big Boy; Chicken; Hamburger; In-N-Out Burger; McDonald's; Moon Pie; Moxie; Panda Express; Pizza; El Pollo Loco; Wienerschnitzel

For Further Information:

Jakle, John A., and Keith A. Sculle. *Fast Food: Roadside Restaurants in the Automobile Age.* Baltimore: Johns Hopkins University Press, 1999.

Religion

Historically, religion has played a part in junk food and fast food and, as American fast food and junk foods have globalized, religion has increasingly become a matter of importance. For instance, fast food operations in India do not serve beef and have extensive vegetarian options in deference to Hinduism. Likewise, many fast food outlets in Israel, or in other countries that have large Jewish populations, are kosher. Fast food operations in Muslim countries or areas of countries that have large Muslim populations do not serve pork and they frequently serve halal food. McDonald's restaurants in Islamic countries do not display statues of Ronald McDonald, which would be considered a prohibited "idol."

In the United States some fast food operations serve halal or kosher products. Fortune cookies in their earliest versions included quotations from the New Testament, not the common Chinese proverbs. This tradition of including quotes from the New Testament was continued by two fast food operations; In-N-Out Burger, a privately owned fast food company, continued this tradition by offering similar verses from the New Testament on various pieces of packaging.

Religion has played an important role in some fast food operations. Chick-fil-A's corporate purpose, for instance, is "to glorify God by being a faithful steward of all that is entrusted to us, and to have a positive influence on all who come in contact with Chick-fil-A." The company has also required that outlets remain closed on Sunday as "our way of honoring God and of directing our attention to things that mattered more than our business." When the company contributed free food to a marriage seminar sponsored by the Pennsylvania Family Institute, an organization opposed to gay marriage, gays became upset. The resulting uproar on Facebook and the Internet resulted in Chick-fil-A pulling its sponsorship from the Pennsylvania Family Institute.

The founders of several fast food operations have used their private money to fund religious organizations. Tom Monaghan, who launched Domino's Pizza, sold his controlling interest in the company and now directs the Ave Maria Foundation, which supports "a variety of organizations which bring Catholic life and culture to the world." It has publicly championed conservative causes and opposed abortion. Carl Karcher, founder of Carl's Jr., invested in Catholic-based philanthropy and was passionately outspoken against abortion and gay rights.

Religious groups have attacked fast food chains for various reasons. The Christian Leaders for Responsible Television, a media watchdog group affiliated with the American Family Association, for instance, charged that Burger King sponsored 18.85 instances of sex, violence, or profanity for every thirty seconds of each commercial that they broadcast on primetime television. They offered no specific examples of how Burger King advertising had done this, but they did call for a national boycott of the company. Burger King defended its advertising policies, but then supposedly came to some understanding with the group. The American Family Association later attacked McDonald's for its membership in a gay rights organization.

Many soda and junk food manufacturers put out special packaging or special products around religious holidays, especially at Christmas or at Easter. As American junk foods and fast foods globalize, it is likely that religion will increasingly become a more important component in their preparation and packaging.

See also Carl's, Jr.; Chick-fil-A; Fortune Cookies; Halal; In-N-Out Burger; Israel; Kosher

Rice Cakes

Rice cakes are small, round snacks made from puffed rice. They are common in the cuisines of many Asian nations, and in the United States they are available commercially from many processors. Typically, rice cakes are considered healthy snacks, containing from thirty to seventy calories per cake and very low in fat. For these reasons, they are frequently consumed by dieters.

That being said, very few of the cakes have any nutritional value and have minimal fiber, and others consider them empty calories. Commercial manufacturers add salt and other preservatives; they may also add a wide variety of flavorings, including apple, butter, caramel, cinnamon, cheddar cheese, chocolate, herbs, nacho, onion, peanut butter, and sour cream.

Rice cakes. (Dreamstime.com)

See also Cakes; Chocolate; Nachos; Peanut Butter

Ritz Crackers

In November 1934 the National Biscuit Company (later renamed Nabisco) test-marketed Ritz Crackers. They were so successful that the company released them nationally the following year. Their name, Ritz, originated with César Ritz, the Swiss hotelier who established luxury hotels in Europe and the United States. By 1920, the term "ritzy" had commonly come to mean classy and glamorous. Ritz Crackers were released in the midst of the Depression, when few people could afford the luxuries of fancy foods. Ritz Crackers quickly became a staple American junk food. They were also exported to Europe, South America, and Australia, where they have maintained significant sales.

Ritz Crackers are usually consumed right out of the box. As appetizers, they have been used as a base for other foods, such as cheese and ham. Beginning in the 1930s, the National Biscuit Company began promoting the use of Ritz Crackers with sugar and spices to make mock apple pie, which had previously been made with soda crackers. Their recipe found its way into cookbooks by the 1960s.

Crushed Ritz Crackers have also been used for toppings for many dishes, from casseroles to creamed corn.

Nabisco has continued to expand the Ritz product line, releasing smaller versions (Ritz Bits and Mini Ritz), a stick version (Ritz Sticks), and versions with different flavors, such as BBQ Chicken and Sweet Chili & Sour Cream. Ritz Crackers are sold in boxes and, up to the 1970s, were also sold in round tins. Today, they are also sold in bags.

Ritz Crackers have maintained their popularity; in 2010 they were identified as the most popular American salty snack.

See also Crackers; Kraft Foods; Nabisco; Sodium/Salt

For Further Information:

Ritz Crackers Web site: www.kraft.com.au/nabisco/products_ritz.cfm

Ronald McDonald

In 1960 John Gibson and Oscar Goldstein acquired the McDonald's franchise for the Washington, D.C., area. To gain visibility for their fast food outlets, Gibson and Goldstein sponsored a local children's television program about a clown, called *Bozo's Circus*. In the program, Willard Scott played Bozo. It was a successful combination and Scott encouraged children watching the program to ask their parents to take them to McDonald's. Subsequently, Scott dressed as a clown and appeared at the grand openings of local McDonald's outlets. Sales in Washington grew by a whopping 30 percent per year. In 1963 the Washington television station dropped *Bozo's Circus*, which lagged in ratings. The local McDonald's franchise decided to produce television commercials starring another clown.

Gibson, Goldstein, and Scott debated about what to name the clown, and an advertising agency proposed Archie McDonald, which offered an allusion to McDonald's golden arches symbol. This was rejected because there was a sportscaster in the Washington area named Arch McDonald. Using a simple rhyme, Scott came up with the name Ronald McDonald. Scott played Ronald McDonald in the first television commercials broadcast in October 1963. It was the first commercial sponsored by a local McDonald's franchisee.

In 1965 the national McDonald's Corporation decided to sponsor the broadcast of the Macy's Thanksgiving Day Parade. They chose to feature Ronald McDonald, but they did not select Willard Scott to play him because they wanted someone thinner to play the part. Coco, a Hungarian clown from the Barnum & Bailey Circus, was selected. (Willard Scott went on to become the weatherman on NBC's *Today Show*.) Previously, no fast food chain had advertised on national television, and it was a financial risk because McDonald's major sales were in the summertime, not in November or January. As a result of this promotion, McDonald's national sales increased by 22 percent.

The reason for the tremendous success was clear. Ronald McDonald appealed to children, who were not previously considered an important audience for fast food chains. These commercials produced immediate nationwide results, which convinced McDonald's to expend more funds advertising on television, giving McDonald's an edge in the children's market.

Ronald McDonald became McDonald's official spokesman in 1966. He subsequently appeared in a McDonald's commercial at the first Super Bowl in January 1967. He also became the centerpiece of a number of other advertising activities: his image appeared on a vast array of products, including book covers, coloring books, comic books, cups, dolls, masks, Frisbees, games, calendars, mugs, napkins, postcards, puppets, records, toy parachutes, trains, glasses, trucks, and the famous Flying Hamburger.

In addition, McDonald's Playlands featured Ronald McDonald and a cast of other mythical characters. While none of the other characters achieved the prominence of Ronald McDonald, the Playlands strengthened McDonald's dominance in the children's fast food market. When McDonald's signed a contract to open three hundred outlets at military bases, Ronald McDonald posed for pictures in front of an aircraft carrier. The first Ronald McDonald House, a residence located adjacent to a hospital to provide free or low-cost room and board for families with children requiring extended hospital care, was set up in Philadelphia in 1974. Since then, two hundred more have been constructed in the United States and eleven in other countries. All are sponsored by local McDonald's operations. Ten years later, Ronald McDonald's Children's Charities was founded in honor of Ray Kroc. Today, it is one of the largest organizations financially devoted to the welfare of children. They have provided housing and meals for the families of more than two million seriously ill children.

Ronald L. McDonald has "authored" three books: *The Complete Hamburger: The History of America's Favorite Sandwich* (1997); *Ronald McDonald's Franchise Buyers Guide: How to Buy a Fast Food Franchise* (2003); and *Ronald McDonald's International Burger Book* (2004). Other books have used his name in their title, such as Marshall Fishwick's *Ronald Revisited: The World of Ronald McDonald* (1983) and *The Ronald McDonald House of NYC Cookbook* (1994).

As McDonald's expanded to other countries, so did Ronald McDonald. In some countries, adjustments were necessary. In Japan, for instance, the name was changed to Donald McDonald, because of the difficulty in pronouncing the "r" in Ronald. In Islamic countries there are no statues of Ronald McDonald because it would be considered a prohibited "idol."

Because Ronald McDonald is a symbol of the company, it also has been a target for protestors who are upset with the company's policies and products. In 2000 Hong Kong protestors dressed like Ronald McDonald carried signs that said that the company was exploiting workers in China, owing to alleged use of child laborers by McDonald's suppliers. When it became public in 2001 that McDonald's had used beef tallow in making its french fries in the United States, hundreds of enraged Hindus ransacked a McDonald's in Bombay and smeared cow dung on a statue of Ronald McDonald because they thought the same practice was followed in India. It wasn't.

Ronald McDonald has also become a symbol of the fast food industry, and he has been targeted by various groups. Corporate Accountability International (CAI), for instance, has launched a campaign to retire Ronald McDonald. They believe that as a promotional tool for McDonald's he contributes to childhood obesity. CAI is opposed to any in the fast food industry who advertise to children. They have set up a Web site titled "Retire Ronald" for youth and issued a report, *Clowning with Kids' Health: The Case for Ronald McDonald's Retirement.*

The McDonald's Corporation has responded by proclaiming that Ronald McDonald is "the heart and soul of Ronald McDonald House Charities, which lends a helping hand to families in their time of need, particularly when families need to be near their critically ill children in hospitals." Another response to these attacks has been for McDonald's to promote a healthier image for Ronald McDonald. His Web site has been revamped to include games not tied to McDonald's foods or brand, and the new games involve physical activity, such as juggling fruit, jumping rope, and playing football. Spokespersons for McDonald's proclaimed Ronald McDonald's mission to be to "promote joy, fun and the spontaneity of the brand."

In 2011 anti-McDonald's extremists stole a statue of Ronald McDonald and imitated an al-Qaeda video, threatening to behead the statue unless McDonald's answered questions such as, "Why are you not open about the manufacturing process, raw materials, and additives used in your products? What are you afraid of?" If they did not receive an answer before a certain deadline, they threatened to decapitate the statue by guillotine. Some culprits were apprehended before the beheading occurred and the statue was liberated, but other activists beheaded a replica of the statue and spread the video on the Internet. McDonald's declared the stunt to be "in very poor taste."

Despite the opposition to Ronald McDonald, his image can be found in most McDonald's outlets, and he is among the most popular children's characters in the world. He speaks in twenty-five languages, including Cantonese, Portuguese, Russian, and Hindi. Ninety-six percent of American children recognize Ronald McDonald, slightly less than the number who recognize Santa Claus. *Advertising Age* rated Ronald McDonald as the second-most-successful icon of the twentieth century. (Their number one pick was the Marlboro Man.)

See also Advertising; Corporate Accountability International; Corporate Charities; Japan; Marketing to Children; McDonald's

For Further Information:

Clowning with Kids' Health: The Case for Ronald McDonald's Retirement. Boston: Corporate Accountability International, 2010), available at: www.stopcorporateabuse.org/current-publications-and-reports

Fishwick, Marshall. *Ronald Revisited: The World of Ronald McDonald.* Bowling Green. OH: Bowling Green University Popular Press, 1983.

Losonsky Terry, and Joyce Losonsky. *McDonald's Happy Meal Toys around the World.* Atglen, PA: Schiffer Publishing, Ltd., 1995.

Losonsky, Joyce, and Terry Losonsky. *McDonald's Pre-Happy Meal Toys from the Fifties, Sixties, and Seventies.* Atglen, PA: Schiffer Publishing Ltd., 1998.

Love, John F. *McDonald's Behind the Arches.* Rev. New York: Bantam Books, 1995.

McDonald, Ronald L. *The Complete Hamburger: The History of America's Favorite Sandwich.* Secaucus, NJ: Carol Publishing Group, 1997.

McDonald, Ronald L. *Ronald McDonald's Franchise Buyers Guide: How to Buy a Fast Food Franchise.* Philadelphia, PA: Xlibris, 2003.

McDonald, Ronald L. *Ronald McDonald's International Burger Book.* Tucson, AZ: Hats Off Books, 2004.

Retire Ronald Web site: www.retireronald.org

Ronald McDonald's Web site: www.ronald.com

YouTube "Rare First Ever Ronald McDonald Commercial," as at: www.youtube.com/watch?v=QIuXv7Y8QA4&feature=related

YouTube "Ronald McDonald Commercial from the 1970s," as at: http://www.youtube.com/watch?v=bnP8vfR9Ph4&feature=related.

Root Beer

Root beer has been a commonly consumed beverage in America since at least the eighteenth century. It was made in various ways with roots, bark, flower buds, seeds, and leaves of plants such as wintergreen, sassafras, ginger, nutmeg, cinnamon, sarsaparilla, wild cherry, licorice, birch, and vanilla. Usually these are dried and converted into essential oils, which were then used to make the syrup. Each company maintained its proprietary secret formula for making root beer. Throughout the nineteenth century, root beer was a health beverage and was frequently made in the home. It was frequently served as a hot tea. By the 1840s, commercially bottled root beer in stoneware was sold in confectionery and general stores. Recipes for root beer appeared in cookbooks by the 1860s.

Precisely when root beer syrup was combined with carbonated water to form a cold soft drink is unclear. The earliest known record of commercial root beer production is of George Twitchell of Philadelphia, who manufactured a syrup for a root beer tonic that was intended to be combined with soda in 1850. Root beer was first mass-produced commercially by a Philadelphia pharmacist, Charles E. Hires. Hires Root Beer was one of America's most popular beverages during the late nineteenth and early twentieth centuries. In 1919 A&W Root Beer originated in Lodi, California. Dad's Old-Fashioned Root Beer was launched in 1937; Barq's Root Beer was created in 1898 and remained a family-owned business based in Biloxi, Mississippi, until the company was purchased by the Coca-Cola Company in 1995. Owing to this connection, it is today one of the nation's leading root beers.

See also A&W; Barq's Root Beer; Beverages; Coca-Cola Company; Hires Root Beer; Secret Formulas; Soda/Soft Drinks; Soda Fountains

For Further Information:

Enkema, L. A. *Root Beer: How It Got Its Name; What It Is; How It Developed from a Home-brewed Beverage to Its Present Day Popularity.* Indianapolis, IN, Hurty-Peck & Co., 1952.

Hires brand Web site: www.dpsu.com/brands_hires_root_beer.html

Morrison, Tom. *Root Beer Advertising: A Collector's Guide.* Atglen, PA: Schiffer Publishing, 1992.

Morrison, Tom. *More Root Beer Advertising and Collectibles.* Atglen, PA: Schiffer Publishing, 1997.

Yates, Donald, and Elizabeth Yates, eds. *American Stone Ginger Beer & Root Beer Heritage, 1790 to 1920: Written by Numerous Authors and Historians.* Homerville, OH: Donald Yates Publishers, 2003.

Rowntree's of York

William Tuke and Sons of York, England, owners of a grocery business, began selling cocoa in 1785. In 1862 Henry Isaac Rowntree acquired the Tukes' cocoa business. In 1881 the company introduced Rowntree's Fruit Pastilles, and in 1893 they released Rowntree's Fruit Gums. Four years later, Rowntree & Co. was officially launched. The company was instrumental in creating what were then novel programs for employees, including a pension scheme, unemployment benefits, dining and other facilities, workers' councils, and annual paid holidays. Joseph Rowntree helped create the Industrial Welfare Society in 1919, and B. Seebohm Rowntree wrote a book on poverty, advocating higher pay for all workers.

During the early twentieth century, Rowntree's introduced many new chocolate products, but none were as successful as those of its major competitor, Cadbury. In 1931 the company began an aggressive development program. One key to its success was the relationship between Rowntree and Forrest Mars, whose company had successfully launched the Mars Bar in England in 1932. Until then, combination bars had not been successful in England. One result of the collaboration was the

Chocolate Crisp, which was launched in 1935. Two years later, it was renamed Kit Kat. It was the company's most popular and successful chocolate candy. In 1969 the Hershey Company bought rights to manufacture the Kit Kat bars in America. Hershey's changed the formula because American taste in chocolate differed from that of the English.

Another likely result of the collaboration between Forrest Mars and Rowntree was Smarties, which were launched in England in1937. They were a colorful, sugar-coated chocolate confection packaged in a round tube, which remain popular today in the United Kingdom, South Africa, Canada, and Australia. It is believed that Forrest Mars took the Smarties idea and developed M&M's, which were launched in 1940.

In 1988 Nestlé acquired Rowntree; subsequently, many new chocolate candies under the Rowntree brand have been introduced. The Kit Kat line, for instance, was extended to include dozens of different flavors and a variety of different shaped products, such as Kit Kat Chunkies (1999) and Kit Kat Kubes (2003). In the United States, Hershey developed Kit Kat Bites for the 7-Eleven convenience store chain. These were packaged in containers that fit into car cup holders so that they could be consumed by drivers while traveling.

See also Cadbury; Candy; Chocolate; Hershey Company; Kit Kat; M&M's; Mars, Forrest; Mars, Inc.; Nestlé; South Africa

For Further Information:

Richardson, Tim. *Sweets: A History of Candy*. New York: Bloomsbury, 2002.

Roy Rogers

In 1967 Roy Rogers, the famous television Western actor, agreed to permit the Marriott Corporation to use his name on a fast food outlet chain. The Marriott executive in charge of the Roy Rogers chain was Jim Plamondon Sr. The following year, the first Roy Rogers Western Roast Beef Sandwich restaurant was opened in Falls Church, Virginia. The chain quickly expanded the number of its outlets through franchising, and the company expanded its menu to include chicken and hamburgers.

In 1982 the Marriott Corporation bought Gino's, another fast food chain, and converted many of them into Roy Rogers outlets. Three years later, Marriott bought Howard Johnson's restaurants and converted some of them into Roy Rogers outlets. By 1990, Roy Rogers had 894 outlets. In that year Imasco, the parent company of Hardee's, purchased the Roy Rogers chain from Marriott. Hardee's converted 220 Roy Rogers outlets into Hardee's restaurants, but then reconverted them into Roy Rogers two years later. Other Roy Rogers outlets were sold to Boston Chicken (later renamed Boston Market), Wendy's, and McDonald's. Only 13 Roy Rogers franchises survived, one of which was Plamondon Enterprises, Inc., which was controlled by Jim Plamondon's children. In 2002 Imasco sold the Roy Rogers trademark to Plamondon Enterprises, Inc., which then created a new company called Roy Rogers Franchise Company, Inc.

See also Boston Market; Chicken; Hamburger; Hardee's; Marriot Corporation; McDonald's; Sandwiches; Wendy's

For Further Information:

Jakle, John A., and Keith A. Sculle. *Fast Food: Roadside Restaurants in the Automobile Age*. Baltimore: Johns Hopkins University Press, 1999.

Roy Rogers Web site: www.royrogersrestaurants.com

Royal Crown Cola

In 1905 Claud A. Hatcher, a pharmacist, launched the Union Bottling Works in the basement of his family's grocery store in Columbus, Georgia. Chero-Cola was the first of his Royal Crown line of beverages, and it was followed by ginger ale and strawberry- and root beer–flavored sodas. In 1912 Hatcher changed the name of the company to the Chero-Cola Company. The company struggled throughout World War I, when sugar was difficult to obtain, and it had financial difficulties during the early 1920s, but in 1924 it was strong enough to bring out a new line of fruit-flavored sodas called Nehi. By 1925, the Chero-Cola Company had 315 plants located primarily in the southern states. In 1928 Hatcher again changed the name of the company to the Nehi Corporation. Hatcher died in 1933 and his successor, H. R. Mott, streamlined operations, reformulated Chero-Cola, and shortened the brand name, Royal Crown Cola, to RC. By 1940, the company's products were available in forty-seven of the forty-eight states. The company continued to expand and aggressively advertised in national publications, such as *Saturday Evening Post* and *Good Housekeeping.*

The Nehi Corporation was a major innovator in the soft drink world. In 1954 the company became the first to nationally distribute soft drinks in cans. Four years later, the company introduced the sixteen-ounce bottle, which contrasted favorably with Coca-Cola's small eight-ounce bottle. In 1958 the company released the first diet cola, called Diet Rite, on a local basis, and then launched it nationally in 1962. At this time, the company changed its name from Nehi Corporation to the Royal Crown Company. In 1980 the company released RC 100, the first caffeine-free cola, and the first diet cherry cola, Diet Cherry RC.

In 1998 the company introduced RC Edge, the first maximum-power cola containing a synergistic blend of spices and caffeine. In 2000 the RC Cola brand was acquired by Cadbury Schweppes, located in Plano, Texas. Today, RC is manufactured by Dr Pepper Snapple Group.

See also Advertising; Caffeine; Cola; Dr Pepper Snapple Group; Ginger Ale; Root Beer; Soda/Soft Drinks

For Further Information:

RC Cola's Web site: www.drpeppersnapplegroup.com/brands/rc-cola

Rubio's Fresh Mexican Grill

Rubio's is a fast-casual Mexican American restaurant chain launched in 1983 by Ralph Rubio in San Diego, California. It features fresh ingredients in its burritos, soft-shell tacos, fish tacos, quesadillas, salads, chicken, steak, and seafood. As of 2011, Rubio's had 180 locations in California, Arizona, Colorado, Utah, and Nevada. It is headquartered in Carlsbad, California.

See also Burrito; Chicken; Fast Casual; Mexican American Food; Quesadillas; Tacos

For Further Information:

Rubio's Web site: www.rubios.com

Rudd Center for Food Policy & Obesity

The Rudd Center for Food Policy & Obesity at Yale University was created by Kelly D. Brownell with financial support from the Rudd Foundation. Brownell serves as director of the center. The center's primary mission is to fund research and education in the fight against obesity, to reduce weight stigma, and to promote positive change in the world's diet.

Since the center's launch in the fall of 2005, it has received widespread recognition for its leading-edge research and expertise in this field. It has convened conferences, such as the Food & Addiction Conference on Eating and Dependence held in July 2007. It was the first time that leading researchers, clinicians, and policymakers gathered to discuss food addiction.

The center also conducts studies, such as the "Trends in Television Food Advertising: Progress in Reducing Unhealthy Marketing to Young People?" and "Fast Food FACTS: Evaluating Fast Food Nutrition and Marketing to Youth," which was released in November 2010. The report gathered and examined evidence regarding the effects of marketing fast food to children and adolescents.

The center also issues policy briefs on important topics related to food policies and obesity, such as "Soft Drink Taxes" (2009), "Weight Bias, A Social Justice Issue" (2009), and "School Food: Opportunities for Improvement" (2009).

See also Advertising; Nutrition; Obesity; Soda/Soft Drinks; Soda Tax

For Further Information:

Friedman, Roberta R. "School Food; Opportunities for Improvement; a Policy Brief." New Haven, CT: Rudd Center for Food Policy & Obesity, 2009, as at: www.yaleruddcenter .org/resources/upload/docs/what/reports/RuddBriefSchoolFoodPolicy2009.pdf

Harris, Jennifer L., et al. *Cereal Facts: Evaluating the Nutrition Quality and Marketing of Children's Cereal.* New Haven, CT: Rudd Center for Food Policy & Obesity, 2009, at: www.cerealfacts.org/media/Cereal_FACTS_Report.pdf

Harris, Jennifer L., et al. "Fast Food FACTS: Evaluating Fast Food Nutrition and Marketing to Youth." New Haven, CT: Rudd Center for Food Policy & Obesity, 2010, as at: www.fastfoodmarketing.org/media/FastFoodFACTS_Report.pdf

Rudd Center for Food Policy & Obesity Web site: www.yaleruddcenter.org.

Rules

Many fast food restaurants have explicit rules, such as patrons must wear shirts and shoes to enter, and only customers can use the restrooms. These and other rules are usually posted on public display in the outlets.

All fast food chains also have unwritten rules. In the United States, for instance, customers are expected to line up to order food. Customers expect rapid service. Employees are expected to smile. Customers usually take their own orders to their tables. Customers are expected to eat and leave promptly, thus permitting other customers to sit down. Customers are also expected to clean up their own messes. In other countries, these unwritten rules have led to confusion and some have been rejected. For instance, in East Asia, youth expect to spend considerable time in fast food chains, believing that the "fast food" refers to the delivery time and not the time spent eating the meals.

See also Fast Food

For Further Information:

Watson, James L. *Golden Arches East: McDonald's in East Asia.* Stanford, CA: Stanford University Press, 1997.

Russia

For much of the twentieth century, the United States and the Soviet Union were engaged in the Cold War and had relatively few economic relationships. This began to change in the 1960s and expanded rapidly after the collapse of the Soviet Union and the emergence of Russia in the 1990s. American soda companies and fast food and junk food companies have rapidly expanded their operations in Russia during the twentieth century.

Soda

In 1959 the leader of the Soviet Union, Nikita Khrushchev, and the American vice president, Richard Nixon, were photographed drinking Pepsi-Cola in front of an American exhibit in Moscow. As a result, this was later dubbed the Kitchen Debate. Perhaps owing to this incident, PepsiCo opened operations in Eastern Europe in 1966 and in the Soviet Union in 1974. In 2010 PepsiCo acquired Wimm-Bill-Dann Dairy & Juice Co., a Russian-owned and operated food and beverage company. This deal made Pepsi the biggest food-and-beverage company in Russia.

Coca-Cola got off to a slower start. It began selling its Fanta brand in 1979 and set up a plant for bottling Coca-Cola in 1987. In 1992 Coca-Cola established a subsidiary in Russia and began to manufacture and establish a distribution system for its products.

Fast Food

Since the collapse of the Soviet Union in 1991, American fast food companies have expanded throughout that region. In 1990 McDonald's opened its first outlet in Pushkin Square, Moscow; it is their largest outlet, with 900 seats, and it serves an estimated 40,000 people per day. It was not easy to operate in Russia during the early years. George Cohon's *To Russia with Fries* (1997) describes how he set up McDonald's in Russia.

Other chains with operations in Russia include Johnny Rockets and Baskin-Robbins. Burger King opened its first restaurant in Russia in 2010, and Wendy's was planning to do so in 2011.

Junk Food

Mars, Inc, also rapidly expanded its operations in Russia and Eastern Europe in 1991. They set up a distribution system through kiosks and began an aggressive advertising campaign. By 1994, Mars was selling Snickers, Mars Bars, M&M's, ice cream, Skittles, Bounty, and fourteen other products in Russia. Snickers became a symbol of success and the market reforms then under way in the country. Mars was so successful that Snickers became a symbol of Western-style reforms, and the Communists accused Russian president Boris Yeltsin and his reformers of trying to "Snickerize" Russia. Since then, Mars has continued to expand its operations in Russia.

Other junk food companies, such as Cadbury and Nestlé, also opened operations in Russia. Hershey began to export its candies to Russia in the mid-1990s, but it made the decision not to open a manufacturing facility there. By 2002, Mars, Cadbury, and Nestlé had invested more than $1 billion in Russia.

See also Baskin-Robbins; Burger King; Cadbury; Coca-Cola Company; Hershey Company; Johnny Rockets; Mars, Inc.; McDonald's; PepsiCo

For Further Information:

Cohon, George. *To Russia with Fries*. Toronto: McFarlane, 1997.

S

Salads

Salads began appearing on fast food menus in the 1990s, but they became common in the early twenty-first century when chains introduced or upgraded their salad offerings. These salads were promoted as healthy alternatives to their main menu, and they promoted their salads as containing fresh, "high quality ingredients." Some promoted their "preservative-free dressings."

Salads are considered one of the more healthy items on fast food menus. Taco Bell's Chicken Ranch Taco Salad (Fresco Style) contains beans, salsa, lettuce, rice, southwest chicken, and tomatoes. It has 240 calories, 6 grams of fat, and 1,110 milligrams (mg) of sodium. Jack in the Box's Grilled Chicken Salad contains salad greens, grilled chicken, cheese, tomatoes, onions, cucumbers, and carrots. If a consumer used their low-fat balsamic dressing, the entire salad would contain 286 calories, 10.5 grams of fat and 1,140 mg sodium. KFC's Grilled Chicken BLT Salad contains lettuce, roasted chicken, tomatoes, and bacon bits. If their Hidden Valley Ranch Fat-Free dressing is used, the salad weighs in at 255 calories, 7 grams of fat and 1,160 mg sodium.

Salads, however, can have more calories, fat, and salt than other items on the menu, such as chicken, hamburgers, tacos, or hot dogs. McDonald's Premium Southwest Salad with Crispy Chicken and Ranch Dressing contains 600 calories, 35 grams of fat, and 1,450 mg of sodium. Burger King's Tendercrisp Garden Salad contains 670 calories, 45 grams of fat, and 1,740 mg of sodium. Wendy's Chicken BLT Salad with croutons and honey dijon dressing contains 790 calories, 53.5 grams of fat, and 1,665 mg of sodium; and their Southwest Taco Salad with ranch dressing contains 640 calories, 36 grams of fat, and 1,200 mg of sodium. Taco Bell's Chicken Ranch Taco Salad contains 910 calories, 54 grams of fat, and 1,660 mg of sodium, which exceeds the total amount of sodium most adults should consume in an entire day.

Most of the calories are in the croutons and salad dressing (some of which may have as many as 190 to 290 calories). By not consuming the croutons, by using light or no dressing, and by ordering grilled rather than crispy chicken, the calories and fat contents of salads can be lowered, but not necessarily the sodium.

See also Burger King; Calories; Chicken; Fat, Dietary; Jack in the Box; KFC; McDonald's; Sodium/Salt; Taco Bell; Wendy's

For Further Information:

Kamp, David. *The United States of Arugula: How We Became a Gourmet Nation.* New York: Broadway Books, 2006.

Salmonella

Salmonella poisoning is caused by a rod-shaped bacterium that takes its name from Daniel Salmon, an American veterinarian who discovered it in 1885, and it is one of the most common foodborne illnesses in America. More than 2,200 varieties have been identified, but food poisonings are caused mainly by *Salmonella enteritidis* and *S. typhimurium*. *Salmonella* produces fever, abdominal pain, diarrhea, nausea, vomiting, and general weakness, usually within twelve to seventy-two hours after infection. The U.S. Department of Agriculture estimates that *Salmonella* is present in 35 percent of turkeys, 11 percent of chickens, and 6 percent of ground beef. It is also present in many eggs. About 40,000 cases of *Salmonella* are reported each year, but it is likely that many more cases go unreported.

Salmonella contamination has been found in a number of food products. In 2007 peanut butter was suspected in the outbreak of *Salmonella* poisoning that affected 425 people in 44 states. The recall cost the manufacturer, ConAgra Foods, an estimated $50 million. In 2010 more than 500 million eggs were recalled after dangerous levels of *Salmonella* were detected in the eggs of two Iowa producers. These may have caused about 1,300 illnesses in 14 states. *Salmonella* can also be spread easily to other foods by improper handling.

In 2009 Peanut Corporation of America in Blakely, Georgia, was found to be infected with *Salmonella*. According to the *New York Times*, this was "one of the nation's worst known outbreaks of food-borne disease," in which nine people are believed to have died and an estimated 22,500 were sickened.

The Centers for Disease Control estimates that *Salmonella* causes about one-third of the 48 million foodborne illnesses each year, and about 180 people die from *Salmonella* poisoning. Most people infected with it are unaware of the cause of their illness, placing the blame on the flu or some other ailment. The potential for *Salmonella* poisoning can be reduced by cooking meat to 165°F, by proper hygiene, by appropriate handling of all food, and by preventing infected individuals from working around food.

See also ConAgra Foods; Foodborne Illnesses; U.S. Department of Agriculture

For Further Information:

Brands, Danielle A. *Salmonella*. Philadelphia: Chelsea House Publishers, 2005.

Moss, Michael, and Andrew Martin. "Food Problems Elude Private Inspectors." *New York Times*, March 5, 2009, as at: www.nytimes.com/2009/03/06/business/06food.html

Salty Junk Foods

Salty junk foods, such as potato chips, popcorn, and nuts, have been part of the American diet since the nineteenth century, but it wasn't until the following century that these products became important commercially. Potato chips led the field, as new packaging made it possible to manufacture bags of chips without spoiling. Fritos were the first successful commercial corn chips. Pretzels did not become important nationally until the 1960s.

As of 2011, the salty junk food manufacturing industry in the United States includes about five hundred companies, but the top fifty companies generate 90 percent of the $24 billion annual revenue. Major companies include PepsiCo's Frito-Lay; Kettle Foods; Kraft's Nabisco subsidiary, Diamond Foods; and ConAgra Foods. Major salty junk foods include potato chips (which generate about 30 percent of sales), tortilla chips (20 percent of sales), and bulk nuts. Other products include canned nuts, corn chips, popcorn, and hard pretzels. Americans eat salty snacks five times a week and families expend about $80 on salty snacks each year. In 2010 the most popular American salty junk food brands were Orville Redenbacher Popcorn, Snyder's Pretzels, Rold Gold Pretzels, Doritos, Fritos, SunChips, and Cheez-Its

In Europe there are almost four hundred salty food manufacturers. Among the top ten are American multinationals Kraft Foods, PepsiCo, and Proctor & Gamble. The largest market for salty snacks in Europe is the United Kingdom, followed by Germany, Spain, France, and Italy. The salty snack with the greatest European sales is potato chips, followed by extruded snacks.

Salty junk foods have been increasing in sales for the past seventy years. They suffered a slight decline in sales during the global economic downturn in 2008–2009, but they quickly made a recovery and sales have been increasing since then. The concern with the amount of salt in foods has led to attempts by manufacturers to lower the sodium content of their products. The concern with transfats has led to the reduction or elimination of these from many salty snacks. The concern with obesity has led to the creation of salty snacks with lower calorie levels.

See also ConAgra Foods; Corn Chips; Diamond Foods; Doritos; Extruded Snacks; Frito-Lay; Fritos; Junk Foods; Kraft Foods; Nabisco; Nuts; Peanuts; PepsiCo; Popcorn; Potato Chips; Pretzels; Pringles; SunChips

Saltwater Taffy

See Taffy

Sanders, Harland

Fried chicken entrepreneur Harland Sanders (1890–1980) was born in Henryville, Indiana. He left school when he completed the sixth grade, and for the next twenty-five years he worked at odd jobs, including farmhand, insurance salesman, railroad fireman, ferry operator, and tire salesman, and he served in the Army. In 1929 he opened a service station on Route 25 in Corbin, Kentucky. At the time, the highway was a major thoroughfare from the Midwest to Atlanta and Florida, so his business thrived. He added a small lunch counter to serve home-cooked food to travelers. He expanded the counter into a restaurant, which was such a success that in 1936 the governor of Kentucky honored him with the title of honorary colonel, and in 1939 Duncan Hines recognized it in his book *Adventures in Good Eating.*

In 1939 Sanders' restaurant burned down. He decided to rebuild it, and he added a motel to his operation. His newly rebuilt restaurant seated 142 people. By then, Sanders had worked out a method for cooking chicken quickly in a pressure cooker and had developed a secret seasoning. Sanders claimed to have worked on the recipe for nine years before he perfected it. Convinced that he had made an important discovery that could be commercialized, he attended a seminar on food promotion in Chicago, where he met Pete Harmon, a hamburger restaurant operator from Salt Lake City. In 1952 Harmon used Sanders' recipe for chicken, and his business boomed.

Meanwhile, Sanders' own restaurant in Corbin was not doing well. Mounting debts required its sale at public auction in 1956. At the age of sixty-five Sanders hit the road, selling his secrets for making fried chicken to restaurateurs and the right to use the name Kentucky Fried Chicken (KFC). In exchange, franchisees paid him a 5-cent royalty on every chicken they sold. To gain visibility, Sanders dressed up like a Kentucky colonel, complete with a white suit, goatee, and black string tie. In the first two years he sold five franchises, but then the franchising business picked up steam. By 1964, when he sold his company to John Y. Brown and Jack Massey for $2 million, there were more than six hundred KFC franchises. Sanders became a spokesman and goodwill ambassador for the company, and his image became synonymous with the company. In 1974 he wrote a memoir; its title summed up his views: *Life as I Have Known It Has Been Finger-Lickin' Good.* Sanders died at the age of ninety in 1980. Sanders' image, however, has survived, and through KFC it has become one of the most-recognized images in the world.

See also Chicken; Entrepreneurs; Franchising; Fried Chicken; KFC

For Further Information:

Hogan, David Gerald. *Selling 'em by the Sack: White Castle and the Creation of American Food.* New York: New York University Press, 1997.

Jakle, John A., and Keith A. Sculle. *Fast Food: Roadside Restaurants in the Automobile Age.* Baltimore: Johns Hopkins University Press, 1999.

Pearce, John Ed. *The Colonel: The Captivating Biography of the Dynamic Founder of a Fast-Food Empire.* Garden City, NY: Doubleday, 1982.

Sanders, Harland. *Life as I Have Known It Has Been Finger Lickin' Good.* Carol Stream, IL: Creation House, 1974.

Sandwiches

The Fourth Earl of Sandwich was probably not the first person to place food between two pieces of bread and consume it by holding it in his hand, but his doing so launched a culinary revolution. British immigrants introduced sandwiches into the United States, where they have thrived ever since. By the Civil War, sandwiches were extremely common. They were constructed of very thin slices of bread, day-old spongecake, or small rolls cut in bite-sized squares or triangles. These dainty pieces were used for luncheons, teas, supper, picnics, or the convenience of travelers. They were subsequently sold in fancy teahouses. For the working class, large rolls were often used to house diverse fillings. These substantial sandwiches were served at taverns and bars. Sandwich-meat spreads started as a byproduct of the meat canning industry. They were composed of cuttings of minced ham, tongue, and seasonings. Sandwich condiments included shredded and leaf lettuce, ketchup, mayonnaise, and mustard, as well as a variety of sliced and minced pickles. Other common sandwich condiments included spices, chopped and sliced onions, mushrooms, chili peppers, tomatoes, salad dressings, and many types of relishes.

Until the late nineteenth century, most sandwiches were served cold because bread could not easily contain the juices from hot meat or sausage. The solution was simple: use rolls or buns. But these were not considered delicate enough to be consumed easily in polite company. However, large, hot sandwiches were sold by vendors and in delicatessens and bars. Sandwiches based on sausages or ground meat, such as hot dogs and hamburgers, appeared in the late nineteenth century but did not become popular until the early twentieth century.

Commercial sandwiches took off in three different directions. Hamburgers were popularized by White Castle, White Tower, McDonald's, Burger King, and Wendy's; hot dogs were popularized by Wienerschnitzel and Nathan's Famous; roast beef sandwiches were popularized by Arby's and Roy Rogers; and large hoagies or submarine sandwiches have been popularized by Subway, Blimpie, and Quiznos. Through the American military and American fast food establishments, the Anglo-American sandwich went global during the second part of the twentieth century. Sandwiches are now consumed in some form in almost every country in the world.

See also Arby's; Blimpie International; Breakfast Fast Foods; Burger King; Condiments; Hamburger; Ketchup; Nathan's Famous; Quiznos; Roy Rogers; Subs/Grinders; Subway; Wendy's; White Castle; White Tower; Wienerschnitzel

For Further Information:

Mercuri, Becky. *American Sandwich: Great Eats from All 50 States.* Layton, UT: Gibbs Smith, 2004.

Wilson, Bee. *Sandwich: A Global History.* London: Reaktion Books, 2010.

Sara Lee

In 1939 Nathan Cummings, a Canadian, purchased the C. D. Kenny Company, a small wholesale distributor of sugar, coffee, and tea in Baltimore. He expanded the company's reach by rapidly acquiring other companies. By the 1940s, he was able to distribute packaged goods nationwide. The company changed its name to Consolidated Grocers Corporation, later shortened to Consolidated Foods.

In 1956 Cummings acquired The Kitchen of Sara Lee, a small bakery in Chicago started by Charles Lubin and Arthur Gordon in 1950. The company made many products, including pound cake and pecan coffee cake. In 1952 Lubin launched a product line of cheesecakes and fruit cakes, which he named after his daughter, Sara Lee.

Consolidated Foods rapidly expanded into frozen foods that could be distributed nationwide through supermarkets. Although the company sold a large variety of goods, its most famous product was its Sara Lee bakery goods. In 1985 Consolidated Foods changed its name to Sara Lee Corporation. It is one of America's largest manufacturers and packagers of branded goods and is headquartered in Chicago. In 2010 the Sara Lee Corporation sold its North American fresh bakery business to Mexico's Grupo Bimbo.

See also Bakery Goods; Cakes

For Further Information:

Sara Lee Bakery Web site: www.saraleebakery.com.

Sbarro

In 1959 Gennaro and Carmela Sbarro opened an Italian grocery store called Salumeria Italiana in Brooklyn, New York. They served homemade food and mozzarella, imported cheeses, sausages, and salamis. They expanded their ready-to-eat foods to include pastas, salads, and sandwiches, but their best-selling product was pizza. Pizza by the slice was not a new concept in New York, but it was unique in other parts of the country. They focused on their pizza and opened additional locations in the New York City area and then throughout the northeast. Unlike other fast food operations, Sbarro featured thirty-five-foot, cafeteria-like counters at its outlets.

In 2007 Sbarro was acquired by MidOcean Partners, an American private equity firm. Its corporate headquarters are located in Melville, New York. In 2011 Sbarro operated nearly one thousand restaurants in forty-eight states and twenty-six countries, including the United Kingdom, Puerto Rico, Canada, Russia, and Israel. Sbarro is the largest shopping mall–based restaurant chain in the world, and it now has outlets in airports, hospitals, travel plazas, movie theaters, toll-road rest stops, universities, and train stations.

See also Movie Theaters; Pizza

For Further Information:

Sbarro Web site: www.sbarro-rus.com

Schlosser, Eric

Eric Schlosser (1959–) is an investigative journalist. He worked for *Atlantic Monthly* and wrote *Fast Food Nation: The Dark Side of the All-American Meal* (2002). It was an exposé of the American fast food industry, and a film of the same name was based on the book and released in 2006. He also co-authored *Chew On This: Everything You Don't Want to Know About Fast Food* (2006). He was interviewed in Morgan Spurlock's *Super Size Me*, in the movie *McLibel*, and he narrated with Michael Pollan the movie *Food, Inc.* (2008).

See also Fast Food Nation; *Food, Inc.*; "McLibel"; Pollan, Michael; *Super Size Me*

For Further Information:

Fast Food Nation (2007) DVD.

Food, Inc. (2009) DVD.

McLibel (2005) DVD.

Schlosser, Eric. *Fast Food Nation: The Dark Side of the All-American Meal*. Boston & New York: Houghton Mifflin Company, 2001.

Schlosser, Eric, and Charles Wilson. *Chew On This: Everything You Don't Want to Know About Fast Food*. Boston: Houghton Mifflin, 2006.

Super Size Me. Directed by Morgan Spurlock. Goldwyn Films, 2004.

School Food

Schoolchildren eat one-third of their meals at school during the academic year. American schools are therefore in a unique position to help improve youth dietary behaviors and prevent and reduce obesity. As childhood obesity has dramatically increased over the past few decades, the food offered in schools and the school environment has been carefully examined. The nutritional quality of these meals has been challenged, as has the wide variety of foods that are sold in vending machines, school stores, and by other means. Most researchers conclude that schools are contributing to the obesity crisis, rather than trying to control it.

School Meals

Some states had school lunch programs in the 1920s, and the federal government began supporting some lunch programs in the 1930s. In 1946 the School Lunch Act was first passed, which established federally subsidized lunches for the nation's schoolchildren. Since then, other programs have been established that also assist in supporting meals for students.

The National School Lunch Program (NSLP) and the School Breakfast Program (SBP) provide food at no charge for students whose families are 130 percent below the federal poverty level, and they provide reduced-price meals for students whose families are 131–185 percent below the federal poverty level. Nationwide, 18 percent of states and 74 percent of school districts offer breakfast to students, while 45 percent of states and 96 percent of school districts offer lunches to students. In addition, many states and school districts have special programs for disadvantaged students. Despite all of these programs, not all eligible students take advantage of them. It is estimated that only a little more than half of those eligible eat subsidized lunches, and only 40 percent of those eligible take advantage of subsidized breakfasts.

The Child Nutrition Act of 1966 transferred all school food programs to the U.S. Department of Agriculture (USDA), which sets nutritional standards and controls the types of food offered or sold through its programs, such as the School Breakfast Program, the National School Lunch Program, and the Summer Food Service Program. The USDA also controls the environments in which these meals are served, during the time they are being served. The USDA bans offering "Foods of Limited Nutritional Value," which include some sodas, gum, popsicles, jelly beans, and a few other candies; but Snickers, M&M's, potato chips, Dove Bars, Snapple, Coca-Cola, Pepsi, and most other junk foods are permitted. In addition, school meals can include many fast foods that are high in calories and low in nutrition, such as hamburgers, hot dogs, french fries, nachos, chicken nuggets, smoothies filled with sugar, and pizza. Some schools and school districts have contracted with fast food companies to offer their food at lunch in the schools. The American School Food Service Association estimates that 30 percent of public high schools offer branded fast food in their cafeterias. These include streamlined menus from companies such as McDonald's, Taco Bell, KFC, and Pizza Hut. One school district in California became the largest purveyor of Pizza Hut pizzas in the world—they served more than one thousand pizzas at lunch every day.

Concern about the nutritional content of the meals remains. In 2006 the Centers for Disease Control examined food served in schools and found that breakfasts and lunches contained more fat, saturated fat, sugar, and salt than was recommended by the USDA's dietary reference intakes (DRI). They concluded that schools and school districts need to reduce the total fat, saturated fat, sodium, and added sugar content of school meals. Some school districts have banned junk foods and replaced them with healthier foods, such as fruits and vegetables. These programs have not always been successful, as students refuse to eat the healthy food and bring junk food from home, buy junk food at school, or consume junk food before and after school hours.

In 2011 the USDA proposed new nutrition standards in the National School Lunch and School Breakfast Programs. These new standards were intended to bring school meals—33 million lunches and 9 million breakfasts per day—into line with the *Dietary Guidelines for Americans* released in 2010. These standards lower the calorie requirements at breakfast and lunch, lower sodium levels, decrease saturated fat, and reduce starchy foods such as potatoes and corn.

Advertising Junk Food in Schools

Public schools have been targeted by fast food and junk food manufacturers. Commercial messages are conveyed in the schools through posters, billboards, corporate-sponsored educational materials, ads, and product placement in textbooks. About 12,000 schools show Primedia's Channel One, which features advertisements for junk food such as Coca-Cola, Pepsi-Cola, M&M's, Doritos, Hostess cakes, Mountain Dew, and Nestlé's Crunch. Advertisements for junk foods or fast food on school grounds convey the message to students that schools endorse these products. Parents' criticisms of these products at home become less credible.

Fast Food Outlets around Schools

As children and adolescents are important targets of fast food chains, many outlets have been opened near schools so that students will visit them for breakfast, lunch, where possible, and after school. Several studies have been conducted with regard to location of fast food establishments. A 2005 study of fast food locations in Chicago found that 78 percent of the city's schools had at least one fast food restaurant within easy walking distance, and that there were three to four times as many fast food restaurants within a mile of schools "than would be expected if the restaurants were distributed throughout the city in a way unrelated to school locations." The conclusion of those researchers was that "fast-food restaurants are concentrated within a short walking distance from schools, exposing children to poor-quality food environments in their school neighborhoods." Recently, local building commissions have refused to approve the construction of fast food outlets near schools.

Educational Materials and Programs

Many fast food and junk food corporations in America produce educational materials for use in schools. These materials minimally advertise the company and its products, but often the content in the materials reflects corporate views on issues related to health and nutrition. In addition, fast food companies offer specific school programs. Pizza Hut, for instance, has run a reading club, while McDonald's has run a spelling club. While the effectiveness of corporate materials has been questioned, there is no question that American youth are consuming increasing amounts of junk and fast food on and off campus, and to some extent these materials contribute to this consumption.

Corporate Sponsorships

Corporations sponsor school sports teams and sport contests, and schools permit corporations to advertise their products (in many cases, exclusively) on school grounds and at school events.

Some schools generate tens of thousands of dollars through corporate sponsorships and sales of products. Beginning in the late 1990s, soda companies began signing agreements with schools and school districts for exclusive sales of its products to students in schools. For these rights, schools may receive an up-front payment, a percentage of sales, or financial compensation when revenues exceed a specified amount. By 2000, about 150 school systems in 29 states had entered exclusive "pouring rights" agreements with cola companies. Supporters argue that schools need the money. Other schools have fought back and refused to sell or promote junk food and fast food.

Competitive Foods and Beverages

Competitive foods are those foods and beverages sold at a school separately from the USDA school meal programs. The USDA's ban on "Foods of Limited Nutritional Value" does not include the sale of candy bars, soda, potato chips, cookies and other high-fat snack foods in à la cart lines. Neither does it prohibit the sale of junk food for fundraising purposes on campus. A Centers for Disease Control study found that 33 percent of elementary schools, 71 percent of middle schools, and 89 percent of high schools had vending machines, à la cart lines, school stores, canteens, or snack bars where students could buy food, most of which was junk food.

Eric Schlosser, author of *Fast Food Nation* (2001), urged a boycott of all fast food, soda, and junk food operations in schools, no matter how much corporate money is offered to schools to sell or advertise their products there. In 2001 the USDA's report *Foods Sold in Competition with USDA School Meal Programs* expressed considerable concern about foods sold in competition with school meals. The authors believed that competitive foods jeopardize the nutritional effectiveness of the USDA's meal programs, as those buying and eating junk food tended not to eat school meals. They also believed that junk foods sold in schools may contribute to unhealthy eating practices among children, and subsequent health risks. A 2010 study funded by the USDA found that banning all junk food in schools resulted in an 18 percent reduction in overweight or obese students, and they recommended that the sale of junk food during mealtimes be banned.

Vending Machines

It is estimated that 68 percent of the nation's schools now sell soda and junk food in vending machines on campus. These machines generate as much as $700 profit each month from some schools. But money isn't the only reason why soda companies and junk food companies want to see their products at schools—they also want to create brand loyalty. As soft drink companies sign exclusive rights contracts with schools, students are exposed to products from only Coca-Cola, PepsiCo, or Dr Pepper Snapple Group. Young people form a commitment to branded beverages and junk foods and keep this loyalty long after they leave school.

Bills have been introduced into some state legislatures to require that schools stock their vending machines with healthy snacks and postpone soft drink sales until after lunch. In 2002 the Texas legislature restricted the sale of fast food in public schools. The Los Angeles Unified School District voted to ban the sale of soft drinks in schools during school hours, but permitted them to be sold thirty minutes after school lets out and at sports and other events. In 2006 Connecticut banned the sale of soda and other sugary drinks in the state's public schools. Similar bans are under discussion in other states and school districts. In 2006 a bill was introduced into the Arizona legislature that would pay school districts $50,000 for forgoing junk food sales on campus. New York City's Department of Education has banned the sale of nonnutritious soda and junk food in vending machines. In May 2006 the major soft drink manufacturers agreed to remove sweet drinks from schools. The American Beverage Association claimed an 88 percent reduction in the sale of sugar-added beverages through vending machines in schools. A study published in 2010 in the *Archives of Pediatrics & Adolescent Medicine*, however, surveyed schools and found that almost half of the nation's public elementary school students could purchase unhealthy beverages such as sodas, sports drinks, and higher-fat milk. The article concluded that, "as of the 2008–2009 school year, high-calorie beverages and beverages not allowed by national guidelines were still widely available in elementary schools."

Anti–Junk Food Bans and Legislation

At the federal level, anti–junk food bills have also been introduced. In 2004 Susan Combs, the Texas agricultural commissioner, banned many junk foods from schools in the state. In the same year, Senator Tom Harkin introduced the Healthy Lifestyles and Prevention America Act, and in 2005 Senator Ted Kennedy introduced the Prevention of Childhood Obesity Act. Both bills, had they passed, would have restricted the marketing of junk foods in schools and encouraged improved nutritional education in schools.

In December 2010 Congress passed and the president signed the Healthy, Hunger-Free Kids Act, which requires the secretary of agriculture to use science-based nutrition standards for all foods sold in schools, including vending machines, snack bars, and school stores. The act is expected to greatly reduce the amount of junk food in schools, including sugary beverages, and increase the amount of organic food available in schools. The act also restricts the frequent sale of junk foods for school fundraising activities during school hours. The legislation does not apply to events held after school.

Healthy Food Problems

As many observers have pointed out, large amounts of healthy food served in school cafeterias go to waste. Garbage cans are often filled with half-eaten or uneaten fruits and vegetables and partially consumed milk cartons. So the problem isn't just what food to serve, but how to get students to eat it. One nutrition expert pointed out that drinking chocolate milk is better than drinking no milk at all. Uneaten foods and beverages are often thrown out, rather than given to centers to feed homeless or hungry people, owing to state and federal laws.

See also American Beverage Association (ABA); *Fast Food Nation*; U.S. Department of Agriculture; Vending Machines

For Further Information:

Brownell, Kelly D., and Katherine Battle Horgen. *Food Fight: The Inside Story of the Food Industry, America's Obesity Crisis, and What We Can Do about It*. Chicago: Contemporary Books, 2004.

Consumers Union Education Services. *Captive Kids: A Report on Commercial Pressures on Kids at School*. Yonkers, NY: Consumers Union, 1998.

Consumers Union Education Services. *Selling America's Kids: Commercial Pressures on Kids of the 90's*. Mount Vernon, NY: Consumers Union, 1990.

Consumers Union Web site: www.consumersunion.org

Foods Sold in Competition with USDA School Meal Programs: a Report to Congress. Washington, D.C.: USDA, 2001.

Friedman, Roberta R. "School Food; Opportunities for Improvement; A Policy Brief." New Haven, CT: Rudd Center for Food Policy & Obesity, 2009, as at: www.yaleruddcenter.org/resources/upload/docs/what/reports/RuddBriefSchoolFoodPolicy2009.pdf

Hawkes, Corina. "The Worldwide Battle against Soft Drinks in Schools." *American Journal of Preventative Medicine* 38, no. 4 (2010): 457–61.

Lankford, Ronnie D., ed. *Junk Food*. Detroit: Greenhaven Press, 2010.

Levine, Susan. *School Lunch Politics: The Surprising History of America's Favorite Welfare Program*. Princeton, NJ: Princeton University Press, 2008.

McMurray, Coleen. "Are Schools Havens for Junk Food Junkies?" *Gallup Poll Tuesday Briefing* (September 2003): 103–4 J.

Miura, Marlo R., Jason A. Smith, and Jess Alderman. *Mapping School Food: A Policy Guide*. Boston: Public Health Advocacy Institute, 2007.

O'Toole, Terrance P., et al. "Nutrition Services and Foods and Beverages Available at School: Results from the School Health Policies and Programs Study 2006." *Journal of School Health* 77, no. 8 (2007): 500–21.

Piehl, Norah, ed. *Should Junk Food Be Sold in Schools?* Detroit: Greenhaven Press, 2011.

Poppendieck, Janet. *Free for All: Fixing School Food in America*. Berkeley: University of California Press, 2010.

Rossi, Peter H. *Feeding the Poor: Accessing Federal Food Aid*. Washington, D.C.: AEI Press, 1998.

Samuels, Christina A. "Lawmakers Pass Junk-Food Curbs." *Education Week*, (May 4, 2005): 31.

School Breakfast Program Web site: www.fns.usda.gov/cnd/breakfast/AboutBFast/bfast facts.htm

School Meals: Building Blocks for Healthy Children. Report of the Institute of Medicine of the National Academies Web site: www.iom.edu/Reports/2009/School-Meals-Building-Blocks-for-Healthy-Children.aspx

Smarter School Lunches Web site: smarterlunchrooms.org

"Soda Ban Spreads in California." *Journal of Physical Education, Recreation & Dance* 73 (November/December 2002): 9.

"Texas Restricts Junk Food Sales in Schools." *Journal of Physical Education, Recreation & Dance* 73 (August 2002): 18.

Turner, Lindsey, and Frank J. Chaloupka. "Wide Availability of High-Calorie Beverages in US Elementary Schools." *Archives of Pediatrics & Adolescent Medicine* 164, no. 11 (November 1, 2010), as at: http://archpedi.ama-assn.org/cgi/content/abstract/arch pediatrics.2010.215v1

Yallop, Jacqueline, and Bill Campbell. "Junk Food." *Times Educational Supplement* (June 10, 2005): F11–F14.

Schweppes

In 1783 Johann Jacob Schweppe improved the process for manufacturing carbonated water and formed the Schweppes Company in Geneva, Switzerland. Shortly thereafter, he set up a factory in England for production of soda water and seltzers. In the aftermath of the French Revolution in 1789, Schweppes moved his company to England. In 1870 the company began manufacturing Schweppes Tonic Water, which included quinine and ginger ale. Schweppes opened its first factory in America in 1884. Schweppes continued to expand its global operation, particularly after World War II. In 1969 Schweppes and Cadbury merged to form Cadbury Schweppes. In 2008 the two companies demerged. Schweppes became a brand name and it is produced by different companies in various countries. In the United States, Mexico, and Canada, for instance, Schweppes brands are manufactured by the Dr Pepper Snapple Group and its subsidiary, Canada Dry Motts. In the United Kingdom and many other countries, Schweppes brands are manufactured by Coca-Cola Company.

See also Cadbury; Coca-Cola Company; Dr Pepper Snapple Group; Ginger Ale

For Further Information:
Schweppes Web site: www.schweppes.com

Seasonal Candy

Commercial seasonal candies have been sold at least since the mid-nineteenth century in America and Europe, when candy canes were mass-produced for Christmas and Cadbury offered boxed chocolates for Valentine's Day. Sale of seasonal candy was strongly promoted by the National Confectioners Association. Today, seasonal candy has become a multibillion-dollar industry with heavy sales at Christmas, Chanukah, Easter, Mother's Day, and Valentine's Day. Patriotic candies are also sold, particularly around the Fourth of July.

See also Candy; Candy Canes; Chanukah Candies; Chocolate; Christmas Candies; Easter Candies; National Confectioners Association; Valentine's Day Candies

For Further Information:

Richardson, Tim. *Sweets: A History of Candy*. New York: Bloomsbury, 2002)

Seattle's Best Coffee

In 1970 Jim Stewart and his brother opened an ice cream parlor and coffeehouse, named Stewart Brothers Wet Whisker, on Seattle's waterfront. They roasted their own beans and began to serve a variety of coffee beverages, including espressos, eventually expanding their operation to communities in the Seattle area. They entered their coffee into a local contest and won first place. Based on the contest results, the brothers changed the name of their establishment to Seattle's Best Coffee. AFC Enterprises acquired the company in 1998 and began franchising the brand in other states and Canadian provinces. Five years later, the brand was sold to Starbucks, and some international franchise rights ended up with Roark Capitol Group. Beginning in 2008, the brand began to franchise coffee for sale in a variety of ways, such as through J. C. Penny's department stores, movie theaters, airlines, Taco Bell, Subway, Borders, and Barnes & Noble Cafes. In 2010 Burger King also agreed to sell Seattle's Best Coffee in more than seven thousand of its restaurants. Another move into mass market coffee occurred in 2009, when Starbucks introduced Via, a new instant coffee, which is sold in its stores and grocery stores.

As of 2011, Seattle's Best Coffee was distributed in more than 40,000 locations. It is also expanding sales through convenience stores and vending machines.

See also AFC Enterprises; Burger King; Convenience Stores; Movie Theaters; Starbucks; Subway; Taco Bell; Vending Machines

For Further Information:

Seattle's Best Web site: www.seattlesbest.com

Seattle's Best Coffee. (AP/Wide World Photos)

Secret Formulas

Many fast food and junk food manufacturers have proudly announced that they use so-called secret ingredients and secret ways of making their products. As chemists can easily determine what's in food products, the main reason for secret sauces and ingredients is to increase sales. In addition, the proclamations of secret ingredients discourage consumers from trying to make similar products in their homes, thus depriving manufacturers of potential sales. Finally, there are secrets in every industry, and companies do not want to give their competitors any hint of what goes into their successful products or product lines, since manufacturers try to duplicate the competition's success.

White Castle founder Walter Anderson proclaimed that White Castle's secret had been to flatten the meat into thin patties and then sear them on both sides "to seal in the natural juices." Harland Sanders figured out a way to cook chicken quickly in a pressure cooker, and he developed a secret seasoning featuring a blend of eleven herbs and spices, which Sanders sold to franchisees. McDonald's claimed to have a secret sauce that made their hamburgers taste better. Today, McDonald's maintains its lead in french fry taste by adding secret ingredients to its flavorings.

The chocolate industry has been notorious for maintaining its secrets. Nestlé's formula for making milk chocolate was a carefully guarded secret beginning in the nineteenth century. The secret formula for Cadbury's chocolate is purportedly known by only six people, and the formula itself is stored in a vault. Perhaps the longest-held secret in American chocolate manufacturing is how the Hershey Company processes the milk that gives their chocolate its flavor. Mars, Inc., is supposedly one of the most secretive companies in the world, requiring employees to sign nondisclosure statements that they will not impart any information about Mars to outsiders.

Soda manufacturers are also famous for their secret formulas. Roy Allen, who launched A&W Root Beer, reportedly purchased the formula from a pharmacist in Arizona. To this day, its unique blend of herbs, spices, barks, and berries remains a proprietary secret. The Coca-Cola Company has long maintained the secret formula for making its beverages, and purportedly only a handful of people know it. It is claimed that the original copy of the formula is held in SunTrust Bank in Atlanta. When the company tried to change the formula in 1985 to create New Coke, it turned out to be a public relations disaster.

Today, it is relatively easy to analyze the make-up of food products. The real secrets generally remain in how products are manufactured and the technology that companies use to make them.

See also A&W; Cadbury; Coca-Cola Company; Hershey Company; Mars, Inc.; Sanders, Harland; Soda/Soft Drinks; White Castle

For Further Information:

Allen, Frederick. *Secret Formula: How Brilliant Marketing and Relentless Salesmanship Made Coca-Cola the Best-Known Product in the World*. New York: Harper Business, 1994.

Brenner, Joël Glenn. *The Emperors of Chocolate: Inside the Secret World of Hershey and Mars*. New York: Broadway Books, 2000.

Pendergrast, Mark. *For God, Country and Coca-Cola*. New York: Scribner's, 1993.

See's Candies

In 1921 Charles See, an immigrant from Canada, opened up a candy shop in Los Angeles. See used the image of his wife, Mary See, to serve as his store's icon. By the mid-1920s, See's had opened twelve stores in the Los Angeles area. The company then expanded throughout California.

Warren E. Buffett's investment group, Berkshire Hathaway, Inc., purchased See's Candies in 1972. Today, See's Candies sells about one hundred different types of candy. It is headquartered in South San Francisco, and as of 2011, had about two hundred stores in western states.

See also Candy; Chocolate

For Further Information:

Pick, Margaret Moos. *See's Famous Old Time Candies: A Sweet Story.* San Francisco: Chronicle Books, 2005.

See's Candies Web site: www.sees.com

Service Stations

Historically, gas stations sold services and products directly related to the automobile. As major highways and the interstate system were constructed beginning in the 1950s, gas stations began to offer motorists a variety of junk foods, such as candy, cookies, packaged bakery goods, and soda. Many service stations became convenience stores. ARCO stations with these stores sell a variety of junk foods, including The Beast, a soda that weighs in at eighty-eight ounces.

Service stations have co-branded with convenience stores. For instance, Pennzoil stations in Pennsylvania developed a relationship with 7-Eleven. Others have co-branded with fast food operations. Texaco, for instance, has co-branded with Blimpie and Carl's Jr. Hess Corporation began to sell Dunkin' Donuts products in its gas stations. Many Canadian Esso gas stations now sell Tim Horton's doughnuts and other products. McDonald's began co-branding with service stations in 1993, and since then has established relationships with Texaco, Exxon, Amoco, Mobil, and Citgo. Taco Bell has more than 1,500 restaurants in gas stations.

Service stations have had some unusual connections with fast food and junk food. Ben and Jerry's ice cream, for instance, began in a converted gas station. Harlan Sanders opened a gas station before he constructed a restaurant to feed travelers. At the restaurant, Sanders featured his special chicken recipe. When the gas station and the restaurant folded, Sanders hit the road, selling his recipe and in the process creating Kentucky Fried Chicken (KFC).

See also Bakery Goods; Ben and Jerry's; Blimpie International; Candy; Carl's Jr.; Convenience Stores; Cookies; Doughnuts/Donuts; Dunkin' Donuts; KFC; McDonald's; Sanders, Harlan; 7-Eleven; Soda/Soft Drinks; Taco Bell; Tim Horton's, Inc.

For Further Information:

7-Eleven Web site: www.7-eleven.com

7-Eleven

7-Eleven is a convenience store chain that was launched in 1927 by Southland Ice Company in Dallas, Texas, which sold milk, eggs, and bread, and then expanded to sell packaged and canned items. The company also began to increase its geographic reach, first in Texas, then in the United States, and finally throughout the world.

Southland Ice called these Tote'm stores, since customers toted away their purchases. In 1946, the company changed the name of the stores to 7-Eleven, which reflected their hours of operation, 7 AM to 11 PM. The company did not change its corporate name to 7-Eleven until 1999.

Beginning in 1964, 7-Eleven began selling coffee to go. Two years later, 7-Elevens began selling Slurpees. Today, the company sells about 144 million Slurpees annually, the most popular being Coca-Cola with cherry flavor.

7-Eleven began selling the thirty-two-ounce Big Gulp in 1980. At that time, it was the biggest fountain soda on the market. Eight years later, 7-Eleven introduced the giant sixty-four-ounce Double Gulp. It was the first retailer to introduce self-serve fountain drinks, and today it sells almost 33 million gallons of fountain drinks per year. In 1988 7-Eleven also began selling Big Bite hot dogs; today the chain sells 100 million hot dogs every year. In 1991 the company introduced its World Ovens pastries; the company sells an estimated 60 million fresh-baked doughnuts and pastries annually. The blueberry muffin is its best-selling pastry. As a bow to the growing concern about obesity in the 1990s, in 1999 7-Eleven introduced the Früt Cooler, which was a low-fat, smoothie-like beverage, and they followed it up with sugar-free Slurpee drinks in 2002.

In 2000 7-Eleven introduced gummi candies in a clear plastic cup, called the Candy Gulp. It fits nicely into car cup holders and it promptly became the chain's best-selling candy. The company also worked with Nabisco to produce cups filled with Nabisco's Chips Ahoy! and Mini Oreos. Likewise, 7-Eleven worked with the Hershey Company to produce cups filled with Reese's Pieces and Kit Kat Bites, and with Frito-Lay to launch Go Snacks—plastic containers shaped like water bottles but filled with Doritos, Cheetos, and Fritos. These foods are highly profitable and gross margins on some junk foods, such as chips, presweetened cereals, and soft drinks, run between 70 to 90 percent.

7-Eleven is one of the world's largest purveyors of fast food and junk food. 7-Eleven also sells fast foods, such as hot dogs, pizza, burritos, chicken wings, chicken tenders, and corn dog rollers, which are traditional corn dogs without the stick. For breakfast, many 7-Eleven outlets sell pretzel/croissant breakfast sandwiches, energy drinks, hash browns, and fresh and packaged bakery goods.

As of 2011, 7-Eleven was the world's largest convenience store chain, with more than 7,100 outlets in the United States and 40,200 stores worldwide, 11,000 of which are in Japan. Other countries with large numbers of 7-Elevens include Canada, Taiwan, Thailand, South Korea, China, Hong Kong, Malaysia, Mexico, Singapore, Australia, the Philippines, Indonesia, Norway, Sweden, and Denmark. Nearly 7 million consumers visit a 7-Eleven store each day. 7-Eleven, Inc., is headquartered in Dallas, Texas; it is a subsidiary of Seven & I Holdings Company, a Japan-based multinational corporation.

See also Burrito; Cheetos; Chicken Tenders; Chicken Wings; Chips Ahoy!; Coca-Cola Company; Convenience Stores; Corn Dogs; Doritos; Frito-Lay; Fritos; Hershey Company; Hot Dog; Japan; Nabisco; Obesity; Oreos; Pizza; Slurpee

For Further Information:

Ishikawa, Akira. *The Success of 7-Eleven Japan: Discovering the Secrets of the World's Best-Run Convenience Chain Stores.* River Edge, NJ: World Scientific Publishing, 1998.

7-Eleven Web site: www.7-eleven.com

7-Up

In 1919 Charles Leiper Grigg of St. Louis, Missouri, was an advertising executive promoting Whistle, an orange soda manufactured by Vess Jones. After a dispute with Jones, Grigg went to work for the Warner Jenkinson Company, which developed flavoring agents for soft drinks. While there, he invented an orange-based soft drink called Howdy.

To promote his soft drink, Grigg, along with Edmund G. Ridgway, created the Howdy Company in St. Louis. Grigg's Howdy drink competed with many other sodas, such as Orange Crush, which then dominated the market. Grigg began experimenting with lemon-lime flavors. After two years of work, he came up with a beverage that blended seven different flavors; he introduced this as Bib-Label Lithiated Lemon-Lime Soda in 1929. Shortly thereafter, the name was changed to a less cumbersome one, "7-Up," and Grigg created a winged logo.

It was the right time for the drink to be marketed. Prohibition ended a few years later and 7-Up was marketed as a mixer for alcoholic drinks. Sales were so successful that in 1936 Grigg changed the name of the Howdy Company to the Seven-Up Company. Within ten years, 7-Up was the third-best-selling soft drink in the world. In 1967 the Seven-Up Company began an advertising campaign positioning the beverage as the "uncola," which greatly increased sales. Later it launched a campaign stressing the fact that it had no caffeine. This campaign was one reason why other soda companies began manufacturing decaffeinated drinks of their own.

The Seven-Up Company has regularly diversified its product line. In 1970 the company introduced sugar-free 7-Up; its name was changed to Diet 7-Up in 1979. The company introduced Cherry 7-Up and Diet Cherry 7-Up in early 1987. All three diet drinks received flavor enhancements in 2000.

In 1978 Philip Morris USA acquired the company, but it was sold again in 1986, when the company was merged with the Dr Pepper Company. In turn, Dr Pepper/ Seven-Up Companies, Inc., was acquired by Cadbury Schweppes in 1995. The brand 7-Up is now part of Dr Pepper Snapple Group, located in Plano, Texas. In 2006 the company removed several chemical additives and launched a major promotional campaign proclaiming that 7-Up was all natural. The Center for Science in the Public Interest (CSPI) threatened to take the manufacturer to court, claiming that one 7-Up ingredient, fructose, was not a natural ingredient.

See also Advertising; Caffeine; Center for Science in the Public Interest (CSPI); Diet Soda; Dr Pepper Snapple Group; Orange Crush; Soda/Soft Drinks

For Further Information:

Rodengen, Jeffrey L. *The Legend of Dr. Pepper/Seven-up*. Ft. Lauderdale, FL: Write Stuff Syndicate, 1995.

7-Up Web site: www.dpsu.com/seven_up.html

YouTube "7 Up Commercial 1970s" at: www.youtube.com/watch?v=3tAiEFhNHZk&feature=related

Shakey's Pizza

In 1954 Sherwood Johnson and Ed Plummer opened the first Shakey's restaurant in Sacramento, California. "Shakey" derived from Johnson's nickname, which he received after suffering from malaria during World War II. The second Shakey's Pizza Parlor opened in Portland, Oregon, in 1956, and two years later Shakey's began franchising its restaurant. The chain spread to more than 272 outlets by 1967. The first franchise in Canada was established in 1968, and by 1975 outlets had reached Japan and the Philippines. Johnson was a banjo player and frequently played at his restaurants to entertain the customers. Johnson encouraged other franchisees to hire banjo players, and this became one of the chain's trademarks.

Shakey's was the first franchised pizza chain. It pioneered the concept of the chain pizza parlor and popularized pizza in the United States. It was not truly a fast food operation because most of its food was consumed inside the restaurant and it had very little carry-out business and no home delivery. Owing to stiff competition, in 1978 Shakey's shifted to buffets, with pizza as an important adjunct.

Shakey Johnson retired in 1967 and sold his half of the company to Colorado Milling and Elevator Co., which acquired Plummer's half the following year. The company changed hands several times thereafter and suffered as a result. In 2004 Shakey's was sold to Jacmar Companies of Alhambra, California. At that time, the chain had only 63 Shakey's restaurants in the United States and about 350 in the Philippines.

See also Pizza

For Further Information:

Helstosky, Carol. *Pizza: A Global History*. London: Reaktion Books, 2008.

Hogan, David Gerald. *Selling 'em by the Sack: White Castle and the Creation of American Food.* New York: New York University Press, 1997.

Schremp, Gerry. *Kitchen Culture: Fifty Years of Food Fads, from Spam to Spa Cuisine.* New York: Pharos Books, 1991.

Signage

Since the 1920s, signage for fast food restaurants has been particularly important. Automobiles traveled quickly down highways, and drivers and passengers could easily miss restaurants unless they were clearly marked with signs. Another means of visually attracting customers was through unusual architecture, such as upside-down ice cream cones, so that the building itself became a sign for a particular restaurant. White Castle was the first to recognize the importance of having all of its outlets similar in appearance so passersby would easily recognize them.

Other chains, such as A&W, did not have a common architecture, and hence relied on signs to convey the fact that they indeed sold A&W root beer. Likewise, KFC franchises at first did not have a common appearance. All that franchises were required to do was put up a sign stating that they were a KFC restaurant and display a likeness of Colonel Sanders. Because small signs were hard to read from a passing automobile, large signs were the rule. At night, signs were difficult to read regardless of the size, so neon signs became common.

Many fast food signs were so large and outlandish that they alienated local residents who had to look at them regularly. President Lyndon B. Johnson successfully lobbied Congress to pass the Highway Beautification Act in 1965, which greatly restricted signs along highways paid for with federal funds. This and other local and state ordinances encouraged fast food chains to decrease the size and flamboyance of their signage, as well as their building architecture.

See also A&W; Advertising; Architecture/Design; Automobiles; Fast Food; White Castle

For Further Information:

Schremp, Gerry. *Kitchen Culture: Fifty Years of Food Fads, from Spam to Spa Cuisine.* New York: Pharos Books, 1991.

Slim Jim

Slim Jim was started by Adolph Levis, who sold pickles, sausages, and other popular snacks and condiments in Philadelphia during the 1930s. Levis experimented with different ways to serve sausages, and in 1928 he hit on a success—spicy cured beef sausage, dried and shaped into sticks. On the back of the beef stick jar was a

Slim Jim beef sticks. (AP/Wide World Photos)

picture of a tall man who Levis called "Slim Jim," which became the name of the product. Levis sold his company in 1967, and three years later it was acquired by GoodMark Food, Inc. The Slim Jim product line was expanded and today it includes about twenty varieties, including meat sticks, beef jerky, beef steak, and beef and cheese. GoodMark Foods (and Slim Jims) was sold to ConAgra Foods in 1998.

See also Beef Jerky; ConAgra Foods

For Further Information:

ConAgra Web site: www.conagrafoods.com

Slogans/Jingles

In the junk food and fast food world, slogans are usually short, striking phrases intended to encourage consumers to purchase products. Typically, slogans are used repeatedly in advertising. Soda manufacturers have used slogans since the late nineteenth century. Dr Pepper used "King of Beverages" and, more recently, "Be a Pepper!" Mountain Dew used the slogan "Get That Barefoot Feelin' Drinkin' Mountain Dew." Pepsi-Cola and Coca-Cola have had some of the most memorable slogans. Coca-Cola's slogans include "The Pause that Refreshes," "It's the Real Thing," "I'd Like to Buy the World a Coke," "Coke Is It," and "Things Go Better with Coke." Pepsi has countered with some slogans that were just as memorable, such as "Come Alive! You're in the Pepsi Generation," and "Pepsi-Cola Hits the Spot," which *Advertising Age* rated as one of the most successful advertising campaigns of the twentieth century.

Snack food manufacturers have regularly used slogans in advertising. M&M's uses "The milk chocolate that melts in your mouth, not in your hand." The Mounds and Almond Joy jingle, "Sometimes You Feel Like a Nut, Sometimes You Don't," remains a classic. The National Confectioners Association slogan, "Eat Candy, the Energy Food," implies that anyone who needs energy should buy their members' products. Fritos popularized the slogan "Munch a Bunch of Fritos Corn Chips." Ruffles potato chips were popularized with the slogan "R-R-Ruffles Have R-R-Ridges," and Lay's potato chips with "Bet You Can't Eat Just One." Dunkin' Donuts' commercial with "Fred the Baker," played by Michael Vale, first aired in 1983. His line, "Time to Make the Donuts," popularized the chain.

Fast food chains have used slogans from their earliest days. White Castle's slogan, "Buy 'em by the Sack," was copied by White Tower—"Take Home a Bagful." Chicken Delight's slogan, "Don't Cook Tonight, Call Chicken Delight," was a popular refrain. KFC's "Finger-lickin' Good" has been used for decades. Taco Bell's commercials starred a talking Chihuahua who squealed "Yo Quiero Taco Bell!" Burger King jumped from one slogan to another, but their more popular include: "Hold the pickles, hold the lettuce, special orders don't upset us, all we ask is that you let us serve it your way. Have it your way, have it your way at Burger King," "Battle of the Burgers" and "Aren't You Hungry for a Burger King Now?" McDonald's has also been extremely successful with their slogans, such as "Billions and Billions Served." Their most recent slogan, "I'm Lovin' It," was the company's first global advertising campaign. It was launched in Germany in 2003, using the slogan "Ich liebe dich," and then it was extended to other languages. Other McDonald's jingles, such as "Two all-beef patties, special sauce, lettuce, cheese, pickles, onions on a sesame seed bun," have been particularly popular. The company's "You Deserve a Break Today" jingle has been identified by *Advertising Age* as the most successful jingle of the twentieth century.

Perhaps the most famous fast food slogan was Wendy's "Where's the Beef?" which aired in 1984 and starred actress Clara Peller. It captured America's attention and was picked up by Democratic presidential candidate Walter Mondale as a criticism of Ronald Reagan's tenure as president. For years, "Where's the beef?" was the question that challenged any idea, event, or product. Recently, *Advertising Age* rated it as one of the top ten slogans of the twentieth century.

Slogans have occasionally backfired. The McDonald's company's penchant for prefixing its products with "Mc," such as McNuggets, has encouraged others to use the prefix for a range of less-enticing themes, such as McDollars, McGreedy, McCancer, McMurder, McProfits, McGarbage, and McCrap. The McSpotlight Web site is focused on anti-McDonald's issues.

See also Advertising; Burger King; Chicken Delight; Coca-Cola Company; Dr Pepper; Dunkin' Donuts; Frito-Lay; KFC; M&M's; Marketing to Children; McDonald's; Mounds Bar; Mountain Dew; PepsiCo; Taco Bell; Wendy's; White Castle; White Tower

For Further Information:

Cross, Mary, ed. *A Century of American Icons: 100 Products and Slogans from the 20th Century Consumer Culture*. Westport, CT: Greenwood Press, 2002.

McSpotlight Web site: www.mcspotlight.org

YouTube Wendy's Advertisement "Where's the Beef?" at: www.youtube.com/watch?v=Ug75diEyiA0&feature=related

Slow Food

Slow Food is an international organization dedicated to preserving local food traditions, protecting biodiversity, and serving as an alternative to fast food culture. It was launched by Carlo Petrini, who was deeply concerned when the first McDonald's restaurant opened in Rome, Italy, in 1986. He believed that the industrialization of food was standardizing taste and leading to the loss of thousands of local and regional foods. In 1986 he launched the Slow Food movement in Barolo, Italy. Slow Food International was started in Paris three years later. Its international office is located in Bra, Italy.

Today, Slow Food is active in 50 countries and has a worldwide membership of more than 80,000. Slow Food USA is a nonprofit education organization with 12,000 members, which is divided into 140 local "convivums." It is dedicated to preserving endangered foodways, celebrating local food traditions (such as dwindling animal breeds and heirloom varieties of fruits and vegetables), and promoting artisanal products. It advocates economic sustainability and biodiversity through educational events and public outreach programs.

Slow Foods works with Terra Madre (Mother Earth), which is "an international network of food producers, cooks, educators and students from 150 countries who

---

Slow Food Founder

Carlo Petrini (1949–) was born in Bra, Italy. When McDonald's opened a restaurant in the 1980s near the Spanish Steps in Rome, Petrini protested the move, and in 1986 he founded the "Slow Food Movement" in Barolo, Italy. He remains the organization's president. Petrini also helped create the University of Gastronomic Sciences in Northern Italy in 2004, and he is the editor, author, or co-author of five books.

are united by a common goal of global sustainability in food." Terra Madre convenes a conference every two years in Torino, Italy. It is held in conjunction with Slow Food's fair, Salone del Gusto.

Slow Food founded the University of Gastronomic Sciences, an international academic institution with campuses in Colorno and Pollenzi, Italy. Its mission is to be an "international research and education center for those working on renewing farming methods, protecting biodiversity, and building an organic relationship between gastronomy and agricultural science."

See also McDonald's

For Further Information:

Petrini, Carlo, ed., with Ben Watson and the Slow Food Editors. *Slow Food; Collected Thoughts on Taste, Tradition, and the Honest Pleasures of Food*. White River Junction, VT: Chelsea Green Publishing Company, 2001.

Petrini, Carlo. *Slow Food: The Case for Taste*. New York: Columbia University Press, 2003.

Petrini, Carlo, and Gigi Padovani. *Slow Food Revolution: A New Culture for Eating and Living*. New York: Rizzoli, 2006.

Petrini, Carlo. *Slow Food Nation: The Creation of a New Gastronomy*. New York: Rizzoli Ex Libris: Distributed in the U.S. by trade by Random House, 2007.

Petrini, Carlo. *Terra Madre: Forging a New Global Network of Sustainable Food Communities*. White River Junction, VT.: Chelsea Green Publishing Company, 2009.

Slow Food USA Web site: www.slowfoodusa.org

Terra Madre Web site: www.terramadre.info

Slurpee

Omar Knedlik, an operator of a Kansas Dairy Queen, placed bottled soft drinks in his freezer; the result was a slushy beverage. In 1959 Knedlik contacted the John E. Mitchell Company, a Dallas machinery manufacturer, to construct a machine to make the slushy beverage. Mitchell experimented with automobile air conditioners to create a machine that would freeze carbonated soft drinks that could be served in a slushy form and could be consumed through a straw. Mitchell's machine reduced the temperature of soda to 28°F.

The drink was not a huge success with retailers. However, 7-Eleven tested the machines in 1965, and within two years they were installed in every 7-Eleven store. The name Slurpee was selected because it makes a slurping sound when it is consumed through a straw. The Slurpee product line has been regularly extended by 7-Eleven, such as Slurpee Liquid-Filled Bubble Gum and the Slurpee Ice frozen treat. Today, the company sells about 144 million Slurpees annually, the favorite being Coca-Cola with cherry flavor.

The Slurpee machine inspired the frozen margarita, an alcoholic beverage containing salt, lime, tequila, Triple Sec, and crushed ice, which was invented in 1971 by Dallas restaurant owner Mariano Martinez.

See also Beverages; Coca-Cola Company; Dairy Queen; 7-Eleven

For Further Information:

Slurpee Web site: www.slurpee.com

Smoothie King

In the 1960s Steve Kuhnau worked as a soda jerk selling malts, shakes, and other products. As he suffered from lactose intolerance, he was unable to consume many of the products he served. At home he began experimenting with blending fruit, nutrients, and proteins. In 1973 Kuhnau opened a health food store in Kenner, Louisiana. He began selling the beverages he had made and used the name "smoothies" to identify them. His health food store was a success, particularly the smoothies. He concentrated on making smoothies and he began to franchise his operation in 1989. Its menu consists of dozens of different combinations of smoothies and snacks, some of which are very high in calories. For instance, its large Peanut Power Plus Grape weighs in at 1,498 calories. The Smoothie King's main competition is Jamba Juice and Dairy Queen.

Smoothie King has more than six hundred locations in the United States, Korea, and Japan. In 2010, the company signed an agreement to open outlets in the Middle East. Smoothie King is headquartered in New Orleans.

See also Calories; Dairy Queen; Jamba Juice; Smoothies

For Further Information:

Smoothie King Web site: www.smoothieking.com

Smoothies

Smoothies are nonalcoholic, chilled beverages that include a mixture of usually healthful ingredients, such as fruit, fruit juice, ice, yogurt, milk, and occasionally ice cream. They began to appear in the 1960s, and they usually consisted of a blend of fresh fruit and yogurt. Smoothies began to be sold commercially in the early 1970s. As smoothies use many fresh ingredients, they are usually made to order. They are also usually relatively expensive and are typically sold to those interested in health foods.

Bottled or frozen smoothies are sold in supermarkets, as well as in many food chains. Today, prebottled smoothies are available for home use. For instance, PepsiCo sells smoothies in its Naked Juice line.

Smoothies have also become signature beverages of several fast food chains. The largest smoothie chains are Jamba Juice, launched in 1990, and Smoothie King, launched in 1973. Other chains that sell smoothies are Dairy Queen, Froots, and Tropical Smoothie Café. In 2010 McDonald's began to sell smoothies, much to the consternation of smoothie chains. Other fast food chains are also serving smoothies, such as Jack in the Box.

As of 2010, an estimated three thousand juice bars sold smoothies, as did tens of thousands of fast food outlets. Smoothies are occasionally sweetened, and some contain chocolate. Light smoothies are often sweetened with artificial sweeteners, such as Splenda. While smoothies have many healthful ingredients, many blends are also high in calories, varying from 190 calories to 400 calories, but with a few special combinations hitting 1,000 calories. They are often hailed as meal replacements, however, when smoothies accompany meals or are consumed as snacks between meals, they add calories to the diet.

See also Calories; Dairy Queen; Froots; Ice Cream; Jack in the Box; Jamba Juice; McDonald's; PepsiCo.; Smoothie King; Sugars/Sweeteners; Yogurt; Yogurt, Frozen

For Further Information:
Brown, Ellen. *The Complete Idiot's Guide to Smoothies.* New York: Alpha Books, 2005.

Snack Foods

Snacking—eating foods between meals—has always been a part of America's diet. Until the mid-nineteenth century, snacks mainly consisted of natural foods: fruit, such as apples, peaches, pears, and (when available) bananas and citrus; nuts, such as walnuts, chestnuts, and pecans; grain-based products, such as bakery desserts, biscuits, and cookies; and occasionally cheese. Even though it was common to snack in nineteenth-century America, many medical practitioners spoke out against this practice, as they believed that eating between meals promoted indigestion. More important, snacking also took away one's appetite for upcoming meals, which contained what medical practioners considered to be more nutritious and healthful food. Despite these concerns, pretzels, peanuts, ice cream, candy, popcorn and derivative products such as popcorn balls, were commonly sold at fairs, circuses, sporting contests, amusement parks, and other venues by the mid-nineteenth century. These were made and sold mainly by individuals in small kiosks, stands, or by vendors on the streets.

During the twentieth century, natural foods were replaced with commercially branded foods. For many people, snacking has become a continuous process indulged in at all times. Studies have demonstrated that almost 75 percent of Americans derive at least 20 percent of their calories from snacks. Snacking has replaced meals for many Americans. By the beginning of the twenty-first century, Americans annually consumed almost $22 billion of salted nuts, popcorn, potato chips, pretzels, corn chips, cheese snacks, and other salty snacks.

Commercial snack foods—foods manufactured and distributed over wide geographic areas—burst onto the American scene around the turn of the twentieth century. Some commercial snack foods were based on foods previously prepared in homes, restaurants, and by vendors, such potato chips, gum, taffy, and chocolates. In these cases, manufacturers had to convince the public that their commercial products were better than existing products. Whether or not these products were better, in many cases they were less expensive because they were usually mass-produced.

Other commercial snack foods had no antecedents, such as chocolate bars and soft drinks, and manufacturers struggled to attract potential consumers. Introductions of new snack foods therefore required extensive advertising. The first new commercial snack food was Cracker Jack, a combination of popcorn, peanuts, and molasses. It was formulated in Chicago, marketed at the Chicago Columbian Exposition in 1893, and perfected in the years following. In 1896 it was advertised broadly in many cities in America. Subsequent snack foods thrived because of extensive advertising. Planter's Peanuts, founded in 1906 in Wilkes-Barre, Pennsylvania, became successful through promotion and the invention of the Mr. Peanut icon. Baby Ruth candy bars were dropped by parachute over the city of Pittsburgh to gain visibility.

From the early beginnings, snack foods rapidly charmed their way into American life. Many social conditions contributed to their success. The temperance movement and Prohibition, for instance, encouraged the creation of soda fountains as gathering places and distribution centers for soft drinks and ice cream. The rapid growth of grocery stores and supermarkets helped disseminate snack foods and sodas. The advent of advertising convinced Americans to buy these new products. This was particularly important with the invention of radio and television, which could be used to market their products easily and effectively. The ambition and drive of snack food moguls, such as Milton S. Hershey, built snack food and drink empires. The vast increase in disposable wealth in the United States during the twentieth century meant that most Americans could purchase snack foods, at least on occasion.

Commercial snack foods fall into two major categories. The most prominent is sweet snacks. America's craving for sugar blossomed after the Civil War. As sugar prices declined in the nineteenth century, candy manufacturers mass-produced candies that average Americans could afford. World War I brought attention to chocolate bars, when the U.S. Quartermaster Corps ordered forty-pound blocks of chocolate and sent them to the American soldiers in Europe. In the post–World War II era, sweets continued their relentless drive to stardom.

A second category is salty snacks. America's first salty snacks were popcorn and peanuts. These products appealed to children and both were associated with children's holidays, especially Halloween and Christmas. During the late nineteenth century, potato chips were added to the salty snack list. Many factors contributed to the rise of salty snack foods in America; important ones were packaging and marketing revolutions. Prior to 1900, snack foods such as peanuts, popcorn, and potato chips were sold from barrels or large glass jars. Grocers scooped them and placed them in a twist of paper or a paper bag. Not only was this time-consuming, but the snacks often went stale before they were sold. During the early twentieth century, manufacturers began experimenting with cans, wax paper, glassine, cellophane, and other packaging materials that made possible the sale of individual portions that could be examined easily by customers. The package also kept snacks fresh until the customer opened it. Other factors that contributed to the increase in consumption of salty snacks were the end of Prohibition in 1933 and food rationing during World War II. Bars reopened after Prohibition ended, and salty snacks were given free to customers to increase drink orders. The interest in salty snacks increased even more during World War II, because rationing caused a severe shortage of sugar, sweets, and chocolates, making many familiar candies unavailable. Salty snacks based on corn, potatoes, and peanuts were abundant during the war. Other salty snack foods include extruded snacks.

After World War II, the sale of sweet and salty snacks soared, greatly promoted by television advertising beginning in the 1950s. As the twentieth century progressed, the quantity and diversity of sweet and salty snack foods proliferated until every grocery store, kiosk, newspaper stand, and corner shop in America was heavily stocked with bags and packets of candies, chips, chocolates, crackers, pretzels, and much more. Thousands of snack foods have been manufactured in the United States. Collectively, these snack foods comprise a market niche generating billions of dollars of annual sales. Most are high in calories, fat, and sodium, and low in nutritional content.

Snack foods have greatly increased in popularity and diversity. As the category has grown, the line between meals and snacks has blurred. Snack foods, such as breakfast bars or diet bars, are offered as meal replacements. As concern with obesity has increased, natural snacks, such as fruit, nuts, and seeds, have reemerged. Health concerns have driven the invention of new snacks that are lower in fat, sodium, and calories. Other snacks are organic, fiber-rich, and fortified with vitamins and minerals. Interest in high protein diets increased the demand for meat-based snacks. Concern with allergies has sparked snacks that are gluten free. Even for the traditional snacks, manufacturers have begun to lower caloric and sodium content.

See also Advertising; Baby Ruth; Candy; Chocolate; Cookies; Corn Chips; Cracker Jack; Extruded Snacks; Gum; Hershey, Milton S.; Ice Cream; Junk Foods; Mr. Peanut; Nuts;

Packaging; Peanuts; Popcorn; Potato Chips; Pretzels; Radio; Soda Fountains; Sugars/ Sweeteners; Supermarkets; Television

For Further Information:

Fox, William S., and Mae G. Banner. "Social and Economic Contexts for Folklore Variants: The Case of Potato Chip Legends." *Western Folklore* (May 1983) 42: 114–26.

Jacobson, Michael F., and Bruce Maxwell. *What Are We Feeding Our Kids?* New York: Workman Publishing, 1994.

Matz, Samuel A. *Snack Food Technology*. 3rd ed. New York: AVI Van Nostrand Reinhold, 1993.

Smith, Andrew F. *Popped Culture: A Social History of Popcorn in America*. Columbia: University of South Carolina Press, 1999.

Smith, Andrew F. *Peanuts: The Illustrious History of the Goober Pea*. Urbana: University of Illinois Press, 2006.

Snack Food Association. *Fifty Years: A Foundation for the Future*. Alexandria, VA: Snack Food Association, 1987.

"State of the Industry: For Your Eyes Only." *Snack Food & Wholesale Bakery* (June 2002): SI-1–SI71.

Snickers

Snickers was created in 1929 by Frank Mars and his family. It built on the success of earlier peanut and chocolate products, including the Goo Goo Cluster (1913), Goldenberg's Peanut Chews (1922), and Reese's Peanut Butter Cups (1928). Snickers was first sold to the public the following year. Named for the Mars' horse, it was composed of peanut butter nougat, peanuts, and caramel encased in milk chocolate. The nougat was made by whipping egg whites until they were light and frothy, then stabilizing them with sugar syrup, which was added along with flavoring ingredients. The caramel was made with milk, sugar, fat, and flavorings. Snickers were wrapped by hand until 1944, but thereafter machine wrapped.

Snickers quickly became the most popular candy bar in America, a position it has held ever since. The target of its advertising was children, and Snickers was a sponsor of the *Howdy Doody Show* on television from 1949 until 1952. Building upon the success, Mars, Inc., has introduced new types of Snickers: In 1984, for instance, it introduced the Snickers Ice Cream bar; it has also introduced Snickers Cruncher and Snickers Almond, a replacement for the American Mars Bar, which was discontinued in 2002. In 2008 Mars introduced Snickers Charged, a candy bar with caffeine, taurine, and other stimulants added.

When the Center for Science in the Public Interest (CSPI) criticized junk food for having empty calories, consumption of many snack foods declined. Mars, Inc., responded with an advertising campaign that announced that "Snickers Really

Satisfies." According to another advertisement, eating a Snickers bar relieves tension and helps a consumer enjoy life: "A Snickers a Day Helps You Work, Rest and Play." The company also used creative opportunities to promote its product. On Thanksgiving Day in 1990, Snickers bars were given to every American soldier in the Middle East, and during the first Gulf War, frozen Snickers bars were sent to the American military.

Mars, Inc., has expanded its sales of Snickers abroad, and the chocolate bar is now sold throughout the world. In the United Kingdom, its name was changed to the Marathon bar because Snickers rhymed with "knickers," a British colloquialism for women's panties. In 1990 Mars made the decision to use uniform names throughout the world for its confections, and the Marathon bar was changed back to Snickers. Some customers had such an attachment to the old name that they refuse to buy Snickers bars, even though they are made in the same way as the old Marathon bar, but in general the shift occurred without many problems. Snickers is very popular in other countries, particularly Russia and Eastern Europe, where it has been one of the best-selling candy bars. Snickers has remained America's best-selling chocolate bar for almost seventy years.

See also Caffeine; Candy; Caramels; Center for Science in the Public Interest (CSPI); Chocolate; Mars Bar; Mars, Frank; Mars, Inc.; Nougat; Peanut Butter

For Further Information:

Brenner, Joël Glenn. *The Emperors of Chocolate: Inside the Secret World of Hershey and Mars*. New York: Broadway Books, 2000.

Broekel, Ray. *The Great America Candy Bar Book*. Boston: Houghton Mifflin Company, 1982.

Pottker, Janice. *Crisis in Candyland: Melting the Chocolate Shell of the Mars Family Empire*. Bethesda, MD: National Press Books, 1995.

Richardson, Tim. *Sweets: A History of Candy*. New York: Bloomsbury, 2002.

Smith, Andrew F. *Peanuts: The Illustrious History of the Goober Pea*. Urbana: University of Illinois Press, 2006.

Snickers Web site: www.snickers.com

Snyder's-Lance, Inc.

Snyder's-Lance, Inc., was created in 2010 by the merger of Snyder's of Hanover and Lance, Inc. The merged company is the second-largest salty snack food company in the United States. The company is headquartered in Charlotte, North Carolina. The brands of the merged companies include Snyder's of Hanover, Lance, Cape Cod, Grande, Tom's, Jays, O-Ke-Doke, Stella D'oro, Krunchers, Archway, and Naturals.

See also Lance; Snyder's of Hanover; Stella D'oro

Snyder's of Hanover

Harry V. Warehime of Hanover, Pennsylvania, founded the Hanover Pretzel Company in 1909, but he shifted his interest to canning in 1924 when he founded the Hanover Canning Company, which canned peas, beans, and tomatoes in the summer and made sauerkraut in the winter. After World War II, the company thrived and began acquiring other companies, which it operated under a variety of brand names. One such company was Snyder's Bakery, which was acquired in 1961. It had been launched in 1924 by William V. Snyder and his wife, Helen. They initially sold cakes and egg noodles. Potato chips were added to their product line during the 1930s. The company was incorporated in 1948. Their potato chip business thrived, and the company stopped making cakes and egg noodles.

Reflecting its broader interests, the Hanover Canning Company changed its name to Hanover Foods in 1962. The following year, Hanover acquired the Bechtel Pretzel Company and added pretzel making to its manufacturing portfolio. Hanover expanded its sales of chips and pretzels under the Snyder's brand name into southeastern Pennsylvania, but then it ran into problems. There was another company named Snyder's in Berlin, Pennsylvania, and the two names caused confusion. A court settlement was reached in which Snyder's Hanover brand changed its name to Snyder's of Hanover. With its new brand name, the company thrived and extended is product line to include prepopped popcorn, cheese twists, and tortilla chips. Snyder's of Hanover was spun off as a private company in 1980.

Snyder's acquired Jay's Food, Inc., in 2008 and took over the brands Krunchers!, Kettle Chips, O-Ke-Doke Popcorn, and Jays Potato Chips. When it attempted to acquire Utz Quality Foods in 2008, the Federal Trade Commission stepped in and began asking questions. Rather than answer them, Snyder's discontinued discussions with Utz. In 2010 Snyder's merged with Lance, Inc., to create Snyder's-Lance, Inc.

See also Cakes; Lance; Popcorn; Potato Chips; Pretzels; Snyder's-Lance, Inc.

Social Media

According to the *Pew Report* "Social Media & Mobile Internet Use Among Teens and Young Adults" (2010), 47 percent of the adults online and about 73 percent of teenagers and young adults belong to at least one social networking Web site, such as Facebook, Twitter, MySpace, Foursquare, LinkedIn, and YouTube.

Fast food restaurants are active social networkers as well, maintaining dedicated pages on most social media Web sites, and engaging in extensive promotion through social media sites. According to emarketer.com, online promotional expenditures through social networking has increased from $1.4 billion in 2009 to $1.68 billion in 2010, and expenditures are projected to increased even more in 2011. These expenditures include Facebook at $835 million, MySpace at $323 million, and social games and apps at $142 million. Promotional campaigns include developing fan pages on Facebook, conducting contests, offering discount coupons, sending e-mails and mobile phone updates, and producing YouTube commercials.

In addition to promotion, companies also receive informal feedback via social networks, which is useful in informing companies of what's working and what's not.

Companies also respond to public relations problems with heavy social networking responses. For instance, Taco Bell's response to the charge of false advertising related to its seasoned beef, which a lawsuit claimed contained only 35 percent beef, was a major campaign on Facebook that offered a free "crunchy seasoned beef taco" to users. It became the largest promotion involving complimentary tacos in fast food history.

See also Facebook; Internet; Taco Bell; Twitter; YouTube

For Further Information:

Elad, Joel. *LinkedIn for Dummies*. Indianapolis, IN: Wiley Pub., Inc., 2008.

Funk, Tom. *Social Media Playbook for Business: Reaching Your Online Community with Twitter, Facebook, LinkedIn, and More*. Santa Barbara, CA: Praeger, 2011.

Lenhart, Amanda, Kristen Purcell, Aaron Smith, and Kathryn Zickuhr. "Social Media & Mobile Internet Use Among Teens and Young Adults." *Pew Report*, February 3, 2010, as at www.pewInternet.org/Reports/2010/Social-Media-and-Young-Adults/Summary-of-Findings.aspx

Miller, Michael. *Introduction to Social Networking*. Boston: Prentice Hall, 2011.

Soda/Soft Drinks

Mineral waters have long been considered therapeutic, and water with carbon dioxide (CO_2) was considered to have medicinal attributes. European spas and resorts built at natural springs frequently included drinking bubbly mineral waters as part of their health regimens. During the eighteenth century, several scientists, including Joseph Priestly and Antoine-Laurent Lavoisier, are credited with the discovery that carbon dioxide was the source of the bubbles in natural springs, beer, and champagne. Priestly constructed an apparatus for manufacturing the gas, and reports of his invention were sent to the Earl of Sandwich, the same person credited with inventing the sandwich, who was then the Lord of the Admiralty. He requested that Priestly demonstrate his apparatus before the Royal College of Physicians. Priestly did so, and one person in the audience was Benjamin Franklin, the prominent American who lived in London at the time. Others constructed different systems for producing soda water. In 1783 Jean Jacob Schweppes improved a process for manufacturing carbonated water and formed the Schweppes Company in Geneva, Switzerland. During the French Revolution and its aftermath, Jacob Schweppes moved his operation to England, where his soda water was approved for medicinal use by the royal family.

By 1800, manufacturers found they could produce the same bubbly effect by placing a solution of sodium bicarbonate in water. Carbonated water, however, was generally made under high pressure with sulfuric acid. Operators could be burned easily by the acid, and containers did explode. Apparatuses for making the water were patented beginning in 1810, but because of the complexity of the process and the medicinal use of the resulting product, they were only operated by trained technicians.

In 1819 Samuel Fahnestock, a Pennsylvanian, patented the first soda fountain, which looked like a beer keg. By 1824, soda fountains were in use, although they did not become commonplace until just before the Civil War. Because the apparatus was expensive and the resulting beverage was considered medicinal, soda water was generally dispensed only in drugstores.

It was a small step from soda water to flavored soda water. Ginger ale is usually credited with being the first carbonated commercial beverage. Commercial ginger ale appears to have been first marketed in 1866 by James Vernor, a Detroit pharmacist, who created Vernor's Ginger Ale.

Another early soft drink was root beer, which was made most commonly from the leaves, roots, and other parts of aromatic plants and trees. In its early years, root beer was also a health beverage. By the 1840s, many root beers were manufactured locally and they were sold in confectionery and general stores. Precisely when it was combined with carbonated water to form a cold soft drink is unclear. The first mass-produced root beer was manufactured in 1876 by a Philadelphia drugstore operator, Charles E. Hires. Hires Root Beer became extremely popular and was advertised at the Centennial Exposition held in Philadelphia in 1876. Alcoholic beverages had been banned at the exposition, and the summer proved to be extremely hot. Many fairgoers liked what they drank and demanded soda drinks when they returned home. Soda fountains, which sold combinations of ice cream and drinks composed of fruit syrups, sugar, and soda water, sprung up around the nation.

The first cola-flavored beverage was created in 1881. It may have inspired John S. Pemberton of Atlanta, Georgia, to invent Coca-Cola in 1886. Its success did encourage others to develop cola beverages, including Caleb Bradham, who invented Pepsi-Cola in 1898. Chero-Cola, later reformulated and released as Royal Crown Cola, was created in Columbus, Georgia, in 1905.

Many other soft drinks were manufactured during the late nineteenth and early twentieth centuries. Moxie, for instance, was introduced in 1884; Dr Pepper was invented in Waco, Texas, in about 1885; Orange Crush was first manufactured in Chicago in 1906; and Charles Leiper Grigg created 7-Up in 1929.

Early soft drinks were generally bottled in stoneware, which was much stronger than glass and would not explode like early glass bottles did, owing to the pressure of fermentation. It was much easier and cheaper to produce syrup or extract, which could be sold to drugstores where it would be combined with carbonated water. This began to change in 1892 when William Painter invented the crown bottle cap, which made it possible to seal bottles easily and cheaply. At the same time, bottling technology improved such that the new glass bottles could keep the carbon dioxide in, and the bottles would not shatter during the manufacturing process. In 1919 there were more than five thousand soda bottlers in the United States, and the industry was large enough that it needed an organization to represent it. The result was the formation of the American Bottlers of Carbonated Beverages, later renamed the National Soft Drink Association.

Since their origin, soft drinks have gone through regular changes in the way they are dispensed and bottled. Vending machines dispensed soft drinks into paper cups by the 1920s. Bottled Coca-Cola was sold in vending machines after World War II. Iron cans were used in the 1950s, and in 1957 aluminum cans were developed. Five years later, pull-ring tabs were first used on beer cans, and later on soda cans. By 1965, canned soft drinks were dispensed in vending machines. In the same year, plastic bottles were used for soft drinks, but soda stored in plastic often exploded. In 1972 polyethylene terephthalate (PET) bottles were invented by Nathan Wyeth (brother of the artist Andrew Wyeth), who worked for DuPont Corp. Wyeth developed a stronger system of molding plastic, enabling DuPont to produce a light-weight, clear, and resilient bottle.

Diet soda was launched in 1952, when Kirsch Beverages began marketing No-Cal ginger ale and root beer. It was followed by many other diet sodas, including Diet Rite Cola (1958), Tab (1963), and Diet 7-Up (1979). Coca-Cola and Pepsi released their diet colas in 1982. In 1980 Royal Crown Company released its decaffeinated cola, RC 100, and other soda manufacturers followed with caffeine-free colas of their own. About the same time, soda companies began marketing decaffeinated sodas. As a backlash, in 1985 C. J. Rapp created Jolt Cola, and other similar sodas, such as Surge and Josta, came on the market with 30–60 percent more caffeine than Coke or Pepsi.

There are many reasons why soft drinks have been so successful in America. The growth of the temperance movement encouraged soft drinks. Soft drinks were served in soda fountains, which competed with saloons and bars. Women's groups, such as the Women's Christian Temperance Union, supported soda fountains and the sale of soft drinks. Soft drinks greatly profited during Prohibition, when manufacturing and selling alcoholic beverages was illegal. It was also during the 1920s that fast food chains emerged, and virtually all of them sold soft drinks. When Prohibition was repealed in 1933, soft drinks and fast food outlets were already well-established American institutions.

To sell more soda, the industry has greatly increased the size of soda containers. Serving size has increased from a standard six-and-a-half-ounce bottle to a twenty-ounce bottle. At movie theaters, 7-Eleven stores, and some fast food restaurants, the most popular size is now sixty-four ounces.

Beginning in the 1990s, soft drinks were roundly condemned by many nutritionists. They have been called "liquid candy" and are full of sugar, salt, and caffeine. Soft drink manufacturers spend billions of dollars on promotion and advertising. Marketing efforts are aimed at children through cartoons, movies, videos, charities, and amusement parks. In addition, soft drink companies sponsor contests, sweepstakes, games, and clubs via television, radio, magazines, and the Internet.

In *Fast Food Nation* (2001), Eric Schlosser reports that soft drink companies are increasingly making deals with public schools for exclusive sales rights on campus and for other promotional activities in schools. He states that a school district in Colorado Springs, Colorado, signed an $11 million deal with Coca-Cola that specifies annual sales quotas, so that school administrators encourage students to drink Coke. He also reported that a high school in Beltsville, Maryland, made nearly $100,000 in one year on a deal with a soft drink company. Some school districts, such as the New York Department of Education, have banned soda drinks from schools, but other school districts respond by stating that they need the funds that sponsorships provide.

Soft drink manufacturers have spent as much as 25 percent of their entire revenues on advertising, much of it targeting youth. In 1998 the Center for Science in the Public Interest (CSPI) study *Liquid Candy* reported that soft drink companies had targeted schools for their advertising and sales of their products. It also reported that soft drinks "provided more than one-third of all refined sugars in the diet." Soft drinks, according to CSPI, are the single greatest source of refined sugar, providing 9 percent of calories for boys and 8 percent for girls. CSPI states that at least 75 percent of teenagers drink soda every day.

Through advertising, soft drinks helped shape our lifestyles. When one quaffs a Coke or Pepsi, thirst-quenching is not the only matter at stake. Advertisements have associated soft drinks with new tastes and new status. Drinking the beverage makes the consumer feel young, sexy, strong, smart, cool, athletic, and fun loving.

Advocates for limiting soda consumption have linked soda with tooth decay, delayed bone development, obesity, and diabetes. Diet sodas are not much better, according to critics, because sugar substitutes also have potential risks. Aspartame, for instance, has been linked to a range of chronic disorders such as cramps, seizures, vertigo, and multiple sclerosis. There is particular concern with the amount of soft drinks consumed by children and youth. Soda companies have advertised extensively on children's television. With vending machines in schools, soft drinks are more accessible today than ever. If soda consumption means that youth are not drinking milk, then they may not be getting enough calcium and other vitamins and minerals.

High-fructose corn syrup, manufactured from corn starch, was widely introduced into food in the 1970s. During the last ten years, federal subsidies to corn growers in the United States amounted to $40 billion, so that corn syrup is cheaper than sugar. Today, most soft drink manufacturers use less-expensive sweeteners, such as fructose, rather than cane sugar for sweeteners.

The cost of soft drink production is low since water, carbon dioxide, sweeteners, colorings, and flavorings are inexpensive. The sales of soda are now more popular than coffee, tea, and juice combined. According to the American Beverage Association, soft drink companies gross almost $93 billion in sales in the United States alone, and the industry employs 211,000 people. Coca-Cola and PepsiCo sell more than 70 percent of the carbonated beverages in the world. Worldwide, these companies sell 1.3 billion glasses of soda every day.

Recent Developments

While adult consumption of soft drinks has declined over the last three decades, American children from the ages of six to seventeen have tripled their consumption. Between the late 1970s and 2006, the per capita consumption of sugary soda beverages increased from 64.4 to 141.7 calories per day. A 2005 study by the Center for Science in the Public Interest (CSPI) said that soft drinks were the single biggest source of calories consumed by Americans. On average, children and adults consume about 175 calories daily from these beverages. Another study published in the *American Journal of Public Health* in 2008 examined eighty-eight research studies on soft drinks and concluded that there are "clear associations of soft drink intake with increased energy intake and body weight. Soft drink intake also was associated with lower intakes of milk, calcium, and other nutrients and with an increased risk of several medical problems, e.g., diabetes." The researchers reported that recommendations for a reduction in soft drink consumption "are strongly supported by the available science." According to a National Cancer Institute report, sugary soft drinks contribute about 7 percent of the total calories in the average American diet, and many nutritionists consider them to be the primary source of added sugars in the American diet.

Concern about obesity has led schools and cities to ban the sale of soda and soft drinks. In 2010 Massachusetts required schools to provide healthy options, such as nonfried fruit and vegetables. It also gave the power to regulate foods sold in school vending machines to the state health officials. In Kansas, the Kansas City School District banned the sale of junk foods in vending machines during the school day. The Kansas State Board of Education banned the sale of candy and junk food in vending machines. It also limited the sale of beverages to water, 100 percent fruit juice, low-sugar sports drinks, and low-fat or skim milk. Thanks in part to the soft drink industry, there has been an estimated 88 percent reduction in sugar-added beverages sold through vending machines in schools, according to the American Beverage Association.

Likewise, cities such as San Francisco, San Antonio, Los Angeles, New York, and Boston have banned or restricted the sale of sugary beverages on city property. Seattle University in Washington banned sugary beverages and even bottled water—the latter case for environmental reasons.

Despite the bans, sales of soda and soft drinks have continued at a brisk pace. In 2010 Americans bought approximately $18.7 billion of carbonated beverages, $5 billion more than total milk sales.

See also Advertising; Barq's Root Beer; Beverages; Caffeine; Carbonation; Center for Science in the Public Interest (CSPI); Coca-Cola Company; Diabetes; Diet Soda; Dr Pepper; *Fast Food Nation*; Ginger Ale; High-Fructose Corn Syrup; Hires Root Beer; Movie Theaters; Moxie; Obesity; Orange Crush; PepsiCo; Root Beer; Royal Crown Cola; Sandwiches; Schweppes; 7-Eleven; 7-Up; Soda Fountains; Sports Sponsorships; Vernor's Ginger Ale

For Further Information:

American Beverage Association Web site: www.ameribev.org

Emerson, Edward. *Beverages, Past and Present: An Historical Sketch of their Production, Together with a Study of the Customs Connected with Their Use.* Two vols. New York and London: G. P. Putnam's Sons, 1908.

Hawkes, Corina. "The Worldwide Battle against Soft Drinks in Schools." *American Journal of Preventative Medicine* 38, no. 4 (2010): 457–61.

Jacobson, Michael F. *Liquid Candy: How Soft Drinks Are Harming Americans' Health.* 2nd ed. Washington, D.C.: Center for Science in the Public Interest, 2005.

Riley, John J. *A History of the American Soft Drink Industry. Bottled Carbonated Beverages 1807–1957.* Washington, D.C.: American Bottlers of Carbonated Beverages, 1958.

Schlosser, Eric. *Fast Food Nation: The Dark Side of the All-American Meal.* New York: Houghton Mifflin Company, 2001.

Smith, Andrew F. *Drinking History: Fifteen Beverages that Changed America.* New York: Columbia University Press, forthcoming.

Vartanian, Lenny R., et al. "Effects of Soft Drink Consumption on Nutrition and Health: A Systematic Review and Meta-Analysis, *American Journal of Public Health* 97, no. 4 (April 2007): 667–75.

Woodroof, Jasper Guy, and G. Frank Phillips. *Beverages—Carbonated and Noncarbonated.* Rev. ed. Westport, CT: AVI Publishing Co., 1981.

Yates, Donald, and Elizabeth Yates, eds. *American Stone Ginger Beer & Root Beer Heritage, 1790 to 1920: Written by Numerous Authors and Historians.* Homerville, OH: Donald Yates Publishers, 2003.

Soda Fountains

Soda fountains, selling soda water in combination with other products, were an important part of American social life from the late nineteenth century to the mid-twentieth century. At first, the term "soda fountain" referred to the machine that produced carbonated water. The first patent for such a machine was granted to Samuel Fahnestock in 1819, and other patents followed. No evidence has surfaced that soda fountains were commonly used until just before the Civil War, when Gustavus D. Dows operated a marble soda fountain. He continued to improve his design and is considered the inventor of the soda fountain. It was not until after the Civil War that soda fountains, serving a variety of beverages composed of soda water and syrups, became common in drugstores. Many products under a variety of names, such as birch beer, pepsin, ginger ale, and sarsaparilla, were sold at soda fountains, as was ice cream, which required the construction of ice boxes to store it. Since customers consumed their sodas in the drugstores, stools and counters were constructed for seating them.

Soda fountains proliferated rapidly. Beginning in the 1880s, many stores with soda fountains began to add light food, especially sandwiches. In 1883 James Tufts patented a soda fountain that he called the Arctic. Tufts went on to become a major soda fountain manufacturer. In 1903 the soda fountain prototype emerged with its two units, a large, high-back section with a mirror or painting, and a low front section with stools for customers, permitting them to watch their order being prepared. They mimicked fixtures common in bars and saloons at the time. They became an important social center, particularly in small towns, by the end of the nineteenth century, and as Prohibition was adopted in local counties and in states, soda fountains became important meeting places. It was from soda fountains that several of today's popular soft drinks emerged, including Dr Pepper, Coca-Cola, and Pepsi-Cola.

By 1908, there were an estimated 75,000 soda fountains in the United States. Operators began expanding their menus to include sandwiches, cakes, and other items, so that by 1912 many soda fountains had evolved into luncheonettes. When the Eighteenth Amendment to the U.S. Constitution passed, and the manufacture and sale of liquor became illegal, soda fountains were a major beneficiary. During the 1940s, soda fountains became places for teenagers to hang out. Soda fountains greatly declined in importance during the 1950s, owing to competition from bottled drinks and fast food chains.

See also Cakes; Carbonation; Coca-Cola Company; Dr Pepper; Fair Food; Ginger Ale; Ice Cream; Pepsi-Cola; Sandwiches; Soda Tax

For Further Information:

Funderburg, Anne Cooper. *Sundae Best: A History of Soda Fountains*. Bowling Green, OH: Bowling Green State University Popular Press, 2002.

Jakle, John A., and Keith A. Sculle. *Fast Food: Roadside Restaurants in the Automobile Age*. Baltimore: Johns Hopkins University Press, 1999.

Langdon, Philip. *Orange Roofs, Golden Arches: The Architecture of American Chain Restaurants*. New York: Knopf, 1986.

Soda Tax

Thirty-three states impose sales taxes on soft drinks. The taxes vary depending on the state and whether the soft drinks are acquired through grocery stores or vending machines. Recently governors and state legislatures have proposed greatly increasing these taxes in order to raise revenue. In 2009 Kelly Brownell, director of the Rudd Center on Food Policy & Obesity, and others proposed in an article in the *New England Journal of Medicine* a one cent tax on sugary beverages, with the monies raised to be dedicated to health care.

In 2009 many states, such as California, Connecticut, Florida, Iowa, Indiana, and several others, did tax soda from four to six cents. A few states taxed sweetening syrup, mainly high-fructose corn syrup. These moves have been strongly opposed by the soda industry, including PepsiCo, Coca-Cola, Kraft Food, as well by those who wholesale and distribute the beverages, and those who sell the beverages in supermarkets and restaurants. The American Beverage Association (ABA) and its state affiliates have opposed efforts to tax soda, and it has created a coalition, Americans Against Food Taxes, consisting of the beverage industry and restaurant chains, to lobby against such efforts. The Maine legislature, for instance, passed a tax of 42 cents per gallon of soda; the funds were to go to health care. In 2008 the soft drink industry pumped $4 million into a referendum that repealed the tax. In 2010, when the legislature in the state of Washington passed a soda tax and a tax on some junk foods, the ABA pumped $16 million into a campaign to defeat the tax in a referendum and won.

In 2009 New York governor David Paterson proposed an 18 percent sales tax on nondiet sodas and sugary juice drinks. His reason for proposing the tax was an attempt to reduce the state's budget deficit. His proposal did not include taxing bottled water, diet soda, coffee, tea, or milk. His proposed tax, had it been enacted, had been estimated to raise more than $400 million, at least for the first year. As it was anticipated that sales of sugared beverages would decline by 18 percent, it was not projected that the proposal would generate as much income during the second year. Nutrition and health groups supported the proposal, hoping that the tax would reduce the number of people, especially children, who drank sugared beverages, whose consumption is associated with poor diet, increased rates of obesity, and risk for diabetes, but bottling companies and other business associations strongly opposed the bill and it was not seriously considered by the state legislature.

Opponents have raised the concern that soda taxes are regressive—they will disproportionately hurt the poor and minorities who spend a larger proportion of their income on food and may buy more soda that do other segments of the American population. Those opposed to the tax also believe that the government should stay out of private behavior, and that it should not try to regulate what people drink. To gain general support for their opposition, these groups have framed the issue as a tax on food, not a tax on soda. They have paid for numerous television commercials in their opposition.

Proponents believe that large increases in soda taxes raise the relative price of unhealthy beverages, thereby discouraging consumption and hopefully encouraging manufacturers to reformulate their products. They also believe that such taxes could raise revenue that could be used to finance nutrition initiatives, such as those that improve school food. Responding to the concern that soda taxes are regressive, proponents argue that sodas are filled with calories and therefore contribute to obesity, which is a regressive disease that disproportionately affects poor and minority populations. While everyone must eat, sugared beverages are not a necessary part of the diet and generally deliver many calories with little or no nutrition, and there is a low-cost alternative easily available—water. If the soda tax will decrease consumption of soda, proclaim those who favor the tax, the poor will benefit most by reducing consumption.

See also American Beverage Association (ABA); High-Fructose Corn Syrup; Soda/Soft Drinks; Vending Machines

For Further Information:

Brownell, Kelly D., et al. "The Public Health and Economic Benefits of Taxing Sugar-sweetened Beverages." *New England Journal of Medicine* 361 (2009): 1599–605.

Chriqui, Jamie F., et al. "State Sales Tax Rates for Soft Drinks and Snacks Sold through Grocery Stores and Vending Machines, 2007." *Journal of Public Health Policy* 29 (July 2008): 226–49.

Sodium/Salt

Sodium is a necessary component of the human body. It allows for the transmission of nerve impulses, and therefore is essential for life. Sodium is a metal that is soluble in water, and it easily combines with other elements, especially chloride, creating common table salt (sodium chloride). Consuming salt is the most common way humans acquire sodium. Approximately 40 percent of uniodized table salt is sodium by weight.

For millennia, humankind ate a diet low in salt. About five thousand years ago humans figured out that salt acts as a preservative. This discovery made it possible to preserve food over the winter that would otherwise have gone to waste. Salt became extremely important as an economic product, and humans began consuming more salt in the foods they ate.

In addition to serving as a preservative, large amounts of salt are added to processed foods for a variety of other reasons. Salt is inexpensive, and it makes otherwise tasteless food palatable at virtually no cost. As foods with high salt content are routinely consumed today, the salt taste receptors are suppressed and a preference for highly salted foods increases, which causes greater demand for highly salted processed foods. It also decreases the preference for unsalted foods, such as fruits and vegetables, and low-salt processed foods.

Salt has two other important properties from a commercial standpoint. Salt, when combined with other chemicals, increases the amount of water that can be bound into a gel, thus increasing the weight of meat products by the addition of 20 percent water. This increases the value of the meat at very little added expense. Salt is also a major determinant of thirst. The consumption of salty foods increases the sales of beverages and water. Decreasing salt consumption will have the opposite effect in beverage sales. Some soda manufacturers are also manufacturers of salty snacks, and it is in their financial interest to keep salt consumption high.

Salt Problems

Salt is the most common condiment in America. Since colonial times, salt was commonly used as a preservative and a seasoning in a wide range of foods. During the past forty years, the consumption of salt among Americans has risen by 50 percent, according to the American Heart Association. According to the Mayo Clinic, Americans get 77 percent of their sodium from processed foods, not the salt shaker. About 35 percent of the sodium Americans consume comes from cereals, breads, and pastries. Salty junk foods, such as potato chips and pretzels, also contribute to salt consumption.

The National Academy of Sciences recommends that Americans consume a minimum of 500 milligrams (mg) per day of sodium to maintain good health, but most Americans consume about 3,500 mg per day of sodium. The 2005 *Dietary Guidelines for Americans*, prepared jointly by the U.S. Department of Health and Human Services and the USDA, recommends that young adults consume fewer than 2,300 mg (approximately one teaspoon) of sodium per day. People with hypertension, African Americans, the middle-aged, and the elderly are advised to consume no more than 1,500 mg per day.

It is generally believed that consuming excessive quantities of salt causes a rise in blood pressure (hypertension), which increases the risk of cardiovascular disease, strokes, heart attacks, and kidney failure, and it has been associated with stomach cancer and other diseases. CSPI executive director Michael F. Jacobson proclaimed: "Excess sodium in the diet causes tens of thousands of preventable heart attacks and strokes each year. This salt assault is probably good for funeral directors and coffin makers, but it is a disaster for shoppers and restaurant patrons."

Cardiovascular events are a major cause of premature death, and cost Americans billions of dollars every year in increased medical costs and lost productivity. Reducing blood pressure can reduce the risk of a heart attack or stroke. A review of many studies on salt and hypertension in the *British Medical Journal* concluded in 2002 that "restricting sodium intake in people with hypertension reduces blood pressure," although the long-term effects on blood pressure, mortality, and morbidity of reduced salt intake in people with and without hypertension were unclear.

Most medical practitioners and health advocates have argued for decreased salt consumption. The Center for Science in the Public Interest (CSPI) has lobbied Congress to require food labeling on high-salt foods, and the U.S. Food and Drug Administration (FDA) launched a series of initiatives aimed at encouraging Americans to reduce their salt consumption. In 2005 CSPI urged Congress to create a new Division of Sodium Reduction.

Fast foods, such as french fries, chicken, pizza, and hamburgers, are also high in sodium content. A Fresco Burrito Supreme–Chicken from Taco Bell, for instance, packs 1,290 mg of sodium; a Spicy Chicken Sandwich from Carl's Jr. has 1,260 mg of sodium. A New York study examined the salt content of fast food chains, including Au Bon Pain, Burger King, Domino's Pizza, KFC, McDonald's, Papa John's, Pizza Hut, Subway, Popeye's, Taco Bell, and Wendy's. It found that 56 percent of meals contained more sodium than should be consumed by adults during an entire day. Chicken fast food had the worst sodium levels, with almost 84 percent of the meals exceeding the daily recommended level. The highest levels of sodium were found in Popeye's fried chicken, with an average of 2,497 mg. Domino's Pizza came in second with 2,465 mg per serving on average.

Removing Salt

Owing to concern with overconsumption of sodium, a number of companies have pledged to reduce the amount of salt in their products. For instance, Heinz has lowered the amount of salt in its ketchup. Campbell's has reduced salt in 110 products and plans to double that number. Hormel Foods, the maker of SPAM, cut out 560,000 pounds of salt from its products in 2007. Taco Bell reduced sodium by 20 percent during 2008–2010. KFC has reported removing a million pounds of salt annually from its menu.

Despite the announcements, reducing salt is not easy. It affects food safety, its flavor, texture, preservation, color, and nutritional properties. Some companies have just reduced the salt content; others have tried replacing salt with other spices; and still others are engaged in trying to develop molecules that can replace or enhance salt.

National Salt Reduction Initiative

In 2009 New York City launched the National Salt Reduction Initiative (NSRI), a coalition of cities, states, and health organizations that helps food manufacturers and restaurants voluntarily reduce the amount of salt in their selected product categories by 25 percent over a period of five years. The initiative has received extensive support from the W. K. Kellogg Foundation and the U.S. Department of Health and Human Services. Companies that have signed on to the NSRI include Au Bon Pain, Hostess, Kraft Foods, Mars, Inc., McCain Foods, Snyder's of Hanover, Starbucks, Subway, and Unilever. Independently, other manufacturers have announced their plans to reduce salt in their products. General Mills, for instance, announced a goal of reducing sodium by 20 percent across multiple product categories by 2015. PepsiCo, the parent company to Frito-Lay, announced it would cut on average 25 percent of the salt in its products; Nestlé has pledged to slash sodium in its products by 10 percent by 2015.

The World Health Organization has set a global target for maximum intake of salt for adults at 2,000 mg per day. Eleven countries in the European Union have agreed to reduce salt intake by 16 percent over the next four years. The *Dietary Guidelines for Americans* issued by the U.S. Department of Agriculture and the Department Health and Human Services in 2010 recommend that Americans consume fewer than 1,500 mg of sodium daily.

The group with the highest salt consumption, according to a study funded by the American Heart Association, is teenagers who consume more than 9–10 grams of salt (4,000 mg of sodium) daily. According to the National Center for Health Statistics, pizza is the biggest culprit for teens. If teenagers reduced the amount of salt they consumed by just 3 grams (the equivalent of one-half teaspoon) per day, researchers concluded it would decrease the number of hypertensive teenagers and young adults by somewhere between 44 percent and 63 percent. Decreasing salt consumption would have a long-term effect of decreasing by 30–43 percent the number of hypertensives at ages 35–50. A study published in the *New England Journal of Medicine* concluded that reducing dietary salt by 3 grams per day for adults could also substantially reduce cardiovascular events and medical costs.

Excessive salt consumption is a dietary habit that can be changed by gradual reduction of sodium intake. It takes one to two months of consuming lower levels of salt for the salt taste receptors to become readjusted, and then foods with a high sodium content taste too salty.

See also Au Bon Pain; Center for Science in the Public Interest (CSPI); Condiments; Corn Chips; Domino's Pizza; Food and Drug Administration (FDA); French Fries; Fritos; Hamburger; Heart Attack; Hostess Brands; Hypertension; Jacobson, Michael F.; KFC; Kraft Foods; Mars, Inc.; McCain Foods; McDonald's; Nutritional Guidelines; Pizza; Pizza Hut; Popeye's; Potato Chips; Pretzels; Salty Junk Foods; Snyder's of Hanover; Soda/Soft Drinks; SPAM; Starbucks; Subway; Taco Bell; Unilever; U.S. Department of Agriculture; Wendy's

For Further Information:

Bibbins-Domingo, Kirsten, et al. "Projected Effect of Dietary Salt Reductions on Future Cardiovascular Disease." *New England Journal of Medicine* 362 (2010): 590–99.

"Dietary Approaches to Stop Hypertension Diet" (DASH) at the Web site: www.nhlbi.nih .gov/health/public/heart/hbp/dash/new_dash.pdf

Dietary Guidelines for Americans Web site: www.healthierus.gov/dietaryguidelines

Feldman, Stanley A., and Vincent Marks, eds. *Panic Nation: Unpicking the Myths We're Told about Food and Health.* London: Blake, 2005.

Gratzer, Walter. *Terrors of the Table: The Curious History of Nutrition.* New York: Oxford University Press, 2005.

He, F. J., and G. A. MacGregor. "A Comprehensive Review on Salt and Health and Current Experience of Worldwide Salt Reduction Programmes." *Journal of Human Hypertension* 23 (December 2008): 363–84.

Hooper, Lee, et al. "Systematic Review of Long Term Effects of Advice to Reduce Dietary Salt in Adults." *British Medical Journal* 325, no. 7365 (September 21, 2002): 628–32.

Jacobson, Michael F., with Jessica Emami and Stephanie Grasmick. *Salt Assault: Brand-Name Comparisons of Processed Foods.* Washington, D.C.: Center for Science in the Public Interest, 2005.

Jacobson, Michael F. *Salt: The Forgotten Killer.* Washington, D.C.: Center for Science in the Public Interest, 2005.

Kurlansky, Mark. *Salt: A World History.* New York: Walker and Company, 2002.

Laszlo, Pierre. *Salt: Grain of Life.* New York: Columbia University Press, 2001.

Multhauf, Robert P. *Neptune's Gift: A History of Common Salt.* Baltimore: Johns Hopkins University Press, 1978.

New York City Department of Health and Mental Hygiene. "Cutting Salt, Improving Health" Web site: www.nyc.gov/html/doh/html/cardio/cardio-salt-initiative.shtml

Taubes, Gary. "The (Political) Science of Salt." *Science* 281 (August 14, 1998): 897–906.

Sonic

In 1953 Troy Smith opened a root beer and hot dog stand called the Top Hat Drive-In in Shawnee, Oklahoma. He installed a speaker system at his drive-in and used the slogan "Service with the Speed of Sound." He also hired carhops to deliver food directly to customers in their cars, and it became a success. In 1956 Smith franchised his first operation to Charlie Pappe of Woodward, Oklahoma, who later acquired the chain. Pappe changed its name to Sonic Drive-In.

When Charlie Pappe took over in 1967, Sonic had 41 outlets; within six years, the company expanded to 165 stores. In 1973 the company was restructured into Sonic Systems of America, which was later changed to Sonic Industries. Ownership of the company shifted to its franchisees and it became a publicly traded company. By 1978, Sonic had expanded to more than 800 outlets in thirteen southern and southwestern states.

Sonic confronted many problems in the early 1980s. Its profits fell and unprofitable outlets were closed. The chain survived mainly because its strength was in small towns, where real estate costs were lower and competition was less intense.

The first Sonic television advertisement appeared in 1977. By 2000, Sonic's media spending approached $64 million. Sonic's "retro-future" logo was introduced and the entire system adopted a consistent new look and menu. As of 2011, the company had 3,500 Sonic Drive-Ins across the United States; it is the only national fast food chain to retain carhops as an integral part of its operation.

See also Advertising; Carhops; Drive-Ins; Hamburger; Root Beer; Television

For Further Information:

Langdon, Philip. *Orange Roofs, Golden Arches: The Architecture of American Chain Restaurants.* New York: Knopf, 1986.

Sonic Web site: www.sonicdrivein.com

South Africa

American junk food and soda companies have been operating in South Africa since the 1920s. It wasn't until the late twentieth century that American fast food companies began to launch major operations in South Africa.

Cereals

Kellogg Company began distributing its cereals in South Africa in 1923. In 1948 the company launched a manufacturing plant there; today, the company manufacturers all of the cereals that it sells it South Africa, including Coco Pops, Chocolate Corn Flakes, Froot Loops, and Honey O's.

Fast Food

Wimpy was an American company in origin, but it sold international rights to a company in the United Kingdom. Wimpy's greatest success outside of the United States and the United Kingdom was in South Africa, where the company opened its first outlet in Durban in 1967. The chain has thrived in South Africa ever since.

It was not until the end of apartheid (white rule) in South Africa in 1992 that McDonald's began considering opening an outlet, which it did in Johannesburg in 1995. Like all of its operations outside the United States, McDonald's has tried to localize its products. Happy Meal options, for instance, include corn cups in South Africa. McDonald's has 132 outlets in South Africa and it is slowly expanding operations throughout Africa.

The largest American fast food operation in South Africa is KFC, with more than 500 restaurants. It opened its first restaurant in 1971, and by 1987 the company had 180 stores. It divested itself of the company-owned stores as a means of protesting against apartheid. When apartheid ended, KFC began to expand again throughout the country. It plans to expand its number of outlets to 850 by 2014.

Nando's

Nando's is a restaurant chain launched by Robert Brozin and Fernando Duarte that started in South Africa in 1987. It specializes in Portuguese-Mozambique foods, such as flame-grilled Peri Peri (a chili grown in Africa) dishes, but it also serves burgers, chicken, pitas, salads, chicken wings, and wraps. Nando's now has franchises in twenty-six countries in Africa, Asia, Europe, and Australia, and the company has opened four restaurants in the United States. In addition to its restaurants in South Africa and the United States, Nando's has restaurants in Australia, Canada, Malaysia, Mauritius, Pakistan, Singapore, United Kingdom, and Zimbabwe.

Other fast food companies are considering opening restaurants in South Africa, including Starbucks.

Soft Drinks

Coca-Cola was the first American soft drink to begin operating in Africa when they opened a bottling facility there in 1928. In 1986 Coca-Cola divested itself of its operations owing to the apartheid policies of the South African government and the threat of a global boycott of Coca-Cola products by many groups opposed to apartheid. When apartheid ended, Coca-Cola jumped back into South Africa, and it has just its operations there as a wedge for entry into the rest of the continent.

See also Chicken; Chicken Wings; Coca-Cola Company; Hamburger; KFC; McDonald's; Salads; Wimpy

For Further Information:

Coca-Cola (South Africa) Web site: www.coke.co.za

Kellogg's (South Africa) Web site: www.kelloggs.co.za

KFC (South Africa) Web site: www.kfc.co.za

McDonald's (South Africa) Web site: www.mcdonalds.co.za

Nando's Web site: www.nandos.com

Southeast Asia

American junk foods entered Southeast Asia first through the Philippines, which was an American Commonwealth until 1946. The United States maintained military bases in the Philippines for decades afterward, and fast food establishments opened up initially around them. When the United States expanded its military operations throughout Southeast Asia during the Vietnam War, American junk foods, such as Pepsi, Coca-Cola, Cheetos, and potato chips, and some fast foods were spread throughout the region. After the war ended in 1972, American fast food chains began to open outlets. This accelerated rapidly toward the late twentieth and the early twenty-first centuries.

McDonald's opened its first outlet in Southeast Asia in 1979, and it has rapidly expanded into other Southeast Asian nations since then, with large presences in Malaysia, the Philippines, and Singapore.

KFC also has a large presence in Southeast Asia. It opened its first outlet in the Philippines in 1967. Since then it has rapidly expanded. Its success is based in part on its "local" menu items. For instance, the company introduced Hot and Spicy Shrimp, Shrimp Stix, and Shrimp Hearties into many of its outlets.

Pizza Hut has also expanded its operations and it is the largest pizza chain in most countries of the region. Other fast food operations that are opening outlets in the region include Dairy Queen, Arby's, Carl's Jr., Krispy Kreme Doughnuts, Long John Silver's, 7-Eleven, and Wendy's.

See also Burger King; Carl's Jr.; Cheetos; Coca-Cola Company; Jollibee Foods; KFC; Krispy Kreme; Long John Silver's, McDonald's; PepsiCo; Philippines; Potato Chips; 7-Eleven

For Further Information:

Smith, Andrew F. *Eating History: Thirty Turning Points in the Making of American Cuisine*. New York: Columbia University Press, 2009.

Spaghetti Tacos

Spaghetti tacos were invented by Spencer, an eccentric character on the hit Nickelodeon series *iCarly*. On a program that first aired in November 2007 Spencer made a dinner consisting of pasta with red sauce in a hard shell taco. It was intended as a joke, but the young viewers of the program thought otherwise.

Reruns of the program caused a wave of interest in spaghetti tacos, as children across the country began asking their parents to make them. Recipes for the dish went viral on the Internet, and today there are hundreds of different spaghetti taco recipes available online. Spaghetti tacos now have two Facebook pages, hundreds of recipes, and thousands of references on the Internet.

See also Internet; Tacos

For Further Information:

Stapinski, Helene. "Spaghetti Tacos: Silly Enough for Young Eaters." *New York Times*, October 5, 2010.

SPAM

SPAM—the food, not the e-mail variety—is a low-cost canned meat product made by the Hormel Foods Corporation. It consists of chopped pork shoulder and ham and was first marketed in 1937 during the Depression. SPAM is a made-up name, and how it acquired its name is a matter of conjecture; Hormel offers no definitive answer.

SPAM was popularized during World War II when it was consumed by Americans, particularly those in the U.S. military. During the war, it was widely distributed throughout the Pacific and in the United Kingdom and the Soviet Union. Edward R. Murrow, an American correspondent in England during the war, reported in December 1942 that the Christmas dinner "will not be lavish, but there will be SPAM for everyone." In all, 100 million pounds of SPAM were shipped abroad during the war. After the war, Hormel introduced the SPAM girls, who went around the United States promoting the product.

SPAM continued to be sold after the war, and in 1959 Hormel claimed that they had sold the 1 billionth can of SPAM. It was particularly popular in Hawaii, Guam, Saipan, and the Philippines, where it remains so today. The annual per capita consumption of SPAM in Guam, for instance, is eight pounds; the McDonald's restaurant in that territory serves SPAM with fried eggs and rice as a breakfast dish. The McDonald's franchise in Saipan sells SPAM burgers, as do the McDonald's and Burger King restaurants in Hawaii. In 1970 SPAM was featured in Monty Python's Flying Circus, which is most likely the source for the word meaning "junk mail."

Spam. (AP/Wide World Photos)

Extending the Product Line

In 1963 Hormel introduced SPAM spread; eleven years later, smoked SPAM with cheese was introduced. Subsequently Hormel introduced a variety of other SPAM products, including SPAM Oven Roasted Turkey in 1997 and Hot and Spicy SPAM in 2000. SPAM with bacon was introduced four years later, and SPAM hot dogs in 2008. Classic SPAM is high in calories, fat, and salt, and low in most nutrients, although low-sodium and low-fat varieties are available today.

SPAM Contests

In 1991 the State Fair Best SPAM Recipe contest was launched and continues today, and participants from more than forty states compete. Since 2003, Hawaii has hosted an annual SPAM JAM, which includes a contest for the best SPAM recipe.

Today, SPAM is sold in more than forty countries. In 2007 Hormel reported that it had sold its seven billionth can. Several SPAM cookbooks have been published and many cookbooks contain SPAM recipes. Carolyn Wyman's *Spam: A Biography* (1999) looked at the history and iconic status of SPAM. In 2001 Hormel opened a SPAM Museum in Austin, Minnesota. It documents the history of SPAM and also sells ephemera in the museum store. In addition to its culinary attributes, SPAM is an iconic American food.

See also Japan; Pork; Sodium/Salt

For Further Information:

Armstrong, Dan, and Dustin Black. *The Book of Spam: A Most Glorious and Definitive Compendium of the World's Favorite Canned Meat.* New York: Atria Books, 2007.

Great-Tasting Recipes with Spam Luncheon Meat. Lincolnwood, IL: Publications International, 1996.

Patten, Marguerite. *Spam: The Cookbook.* London: Hamlyn, 2009.

SPAM Web site: www.spam.com

Wyman, Carolyn. *I'm a Spam Fan: America's Best Loved Foods.* Stamford, CT: Longmeadow Press, 1993.

Wyman, Carolyn. *Spam: A Biography.* San Diego, CA: Harcourt Brace, 1999.

Spangler Candy Company

Arthur G. Spangler of Bryan, Ohio, launched the Spangler Manufacturing Company in 1906. It made baking soda, baking powder, starch, spice, and flavorings. When Arthur's brother, a candy salesman, joined the company two years later, the company began to manufacture candy. It made Cream Peanut Clusters in 1911, and by 1914 the company was producing chocolates, chocolate bars, ice cream cones, and soft drinks. The candy business was a tremendous success, and the company slowly phased out its other products. In 1920 the company changed its name to the Spangler Candy Company.

Spangler began making Circus Peanuts in the 1930s. These are chewy marshmallow-based candies shaped like a peanut. Today, Spangler makes about 32,000 pounds of this treat daily, most of which is sold in bulk to repackagers. It has also extended the product line to include candies shaped like hearts for Valentine's Day and candies shaped like chicks and bunnies for Easter.

Spangler acquired Dum Dum Pops, a lollipop, from the Akron Candy Company in 1953 and quickly geared up production. The following year, Spangler purchased A-Z Christmas Candy Canes of Detroit, Michigan, and today Spangler produces about 45 percent of all the candy canes made in the United States. It also makes Saf-T-Pops. The Spangler Candy Company is headquartered in Bryan, Ohio, and it remains privately owned.

See also Candy Canes; Chocolate; Dum Dum Pops; Ice Cream; Lollipops/Suckers; Valentine's Day Candies

For Further Information:

Culbertson, William L. *A Sweet Century: The 100-year History of Spangler Candy Company and the Spangler Family, Bryan, Ohio.* Bryan, OH: Spangler Candy Co., 2006.

Gilmore, Paul E. "A Special Tribute to Spangler Dum Dum Pops on the Occasion of their 50th Anniversary." Wallace E. Evans, *Congressional Record*, June 17, 2003, 15097.

Spangler Candy Company Web site: www.spanglercandy.com

Sports Drinks

Sports drinks are beverages intended for athletes to improve their performance. The first sports drink was Gatorade, which was formulated in 1965 by Robert Cade and Dana Shires of the University of Florida to solve rehydration problems faced by football players. It is a noncarbonated drink consisting of water, electrolytes, and carbohydrates. It is believed that the beverage prevents heat stress and heat stroke during heavy workouts. Gatorade was used by the University of Florida football team in 1967, when the team won the Orange Bowl. This gave the drink extensive national visibility, and Gatorade began to be manufactured and sold in stores. Since 1986, coolers filled with Gatorade and ice have traditionally been emptied over the heads of coaches after victories.

Gatorade created an industry focused on sports drinks. Powerade was launched in 1990 and it has been heavily promoted by the Coca-Cola Company. In 2001 Coca-Cola introduced new formulas in the Powerade line. PepsiCo created All-Sport athletic drinks, which have been promoted as the "Official Sport Drink" of the top soccer leagues. Stokely-Van Camp, Inc., of Indianapolis, Indiana, secured the rights to Gatorade and marketed it nationally. In 1983 Stokely-Van Camp was acquired by Quaker Oats, which was acquired by PepsiCo in 2003.

For those actively engaged in athletics, consuming sports drinks helps rehydration, improves electrolytes, and increases energy levels. Three problems have been associated with sports drinks, though. Consuming sports drinks while exercising can cause cramps and heat-related illnesses. Most people lose few electrolytes during exercise and don't need sports drinks. An even more serious problem is that sports beverages are more often consumed as a snack beverage. As many sports drinks are high in calories and sugar, when consumed they simply add unneeded calories. Consuming sports drinks when not exercising can produce weight gain.

See also Carbohydrates; Coca-Cola Company; PepsiCo; Sugars/Sweeteners

For Further Information:

Ranjit, N., M. H. Evans, C. Byrd-Williams, A. E. Evans, and D. M. Hoelscher. "Dietary and Activity Correlates of Sugar-Sweetened Beverage Consumption Among Adolescents." *Pediatrics* 126 (October 1, 2010): e754–e761.

Rovell, Darren. *First in Thirst: How Gatorade Turned the Science of Sweat into a Cultural Phenomenon.* New York: American Management Association, 2006.

The 2009–2014 World Outlook for Sports and Energy Drinks. San Diego: ICON Group International, 2008.

Sports Sponsorships

In 1928 Coca-Cola became the first sponsor of the International Olympic Games; it has been an Olympics sponsor ever since. At the 1984 Olympics in Los Angeles, Coca-Cola was the second-leading advertiser, having spent $29 million on promotion. When the Olympics were hosted in Atlanta in 1996, the Coca-Cola Company spent $73 million on advertising. At the 2000 Olympics in Sydney, Australia, Coke spent an estimated $55 million on advertising. Pepsi-Cola cans were confiscated from spectators per the agreement with Coca-Cola. At the 2004 Olympic games in Athens, Greece, Coca-Cola spent $145 million on sponsorship and advertising. The Coca-Cola Company sponsors numerous athletic sports, including Major League Baseball, the National Basketball Association, the National Football League, and the National Hockey League. It has also sponsored collegiate and high school teams and contests. Other soft drink manufacturers have engaged in similar activities. Dr Pepper sponsors collegiate bowls and football title games.

Fast food chains have also found that sports sponsorships are an excellent venue for gaining visibility for their brands. National brands sponsor sporting events and franchises often support local events, such as high school teams. McDonald's has sponsored high school basketball tournaments, such as high school all-star games. It also has sponsored the National Basketball Association on four continents and sponsors the International Olympics. Pizza Hut, Taco Bell, and KFC have had contracts with the National Collegiate Athletic Association; Wendy's has sponsored the National Hockey League's All-Star Fan Balloting in the United States, while McDonald's sponsors the All-Star Fan Balloting in Canada. Burger King has supported youth programs such as the President's Challenge Physical Activity and Fitness Awards Program. Del Taco has sponsored the National Hockey League's Anaheim Mighty Ducks. Many fast food chains, soda manufacturers, and junk food makers also place advertisements in stadiums, on cars in automobile races, and on clothes that athletes wear. These advertisements are seen by those in attendance and then are viewed by those who watch the broadcast of the sporting event.

More important than the direct advertising message is the underlying one: dieting is not the answer to obesity and other health problems—a "healthy lifestyle" is. Sports sponsorships offer the mechanism for junk food, fast food, and sodas to be associated with exercise, athletics, and an active lifestyle.

See also Automobiles; Burger King; Coca-Cola Company; Del Taco; Dr Pepper; KFC; McDonald's; Pizza Hut; Soda/Soft Drinks; Taco Bell; Wendy's

For Further Information:

McAllister, M. P. "Sponsorship, Globalization, and the Summer Olympics." In Katherine Toland Frith, ed. *Undressing the Ad: Reading Culture in Advertising*. New York: Peter Lang, 1997.

Schlosser, Eric. *Fast Food Nation: The Dark Side of the All-American Meal*. New York: Houghton Mifflin Company, 2001.

Spurlock, Morgan

Morgan Spurlock (1970–) is a New York–born journalist and filmmaker best known for the documentary film *Super Size Me* (2004), in which he consumed only food served at McDonald's for twenty-eight days. According to the film, he gained twenty-four pounds and suffered depression and had problems with his liver. *Super Size Me* was nominated for an Academy Award in 2009. Morgan Spurlock is the author of two books: *Don't Eat This Book: Fast Food and the Supersizing of America* (2005) and *Where in the World Is Osama bin Laden?* (2008). In 2011 Morgan Spurlock spearheaded the writing of a humorous graphic novel titled *Supersized: Strange Tales from a Fast-Food Culture*, which was intended as a companion to the film *Super Size Me*.

See also Addiction; McDonald's; *Super Size Me*; Supersizing

For Further Information:

Spurlock, Morgan. *Don't Eat This Book: Fast Food and the Supersizing of America*. New York: G. P. Putnam's Sons, 2005.

Spurlock, Morgan, et al. *Supersized: Strange Tales from a Fast-Food Culture*. Milwaukie, OR: Dark Horse, 2011.

Super Size Me. Directed by Morgan Spurlock. Goldwyn Films, 2004.

Starbucks

Historically, coffee was a low-cost, mass-market beverage. This began to change in the 1960s when coffee stores began selling premium coffee beans, roasters, and other related equipment. One such retail store was Peet's Coffee & Tea in Berkeley, California. It was founded in 1966 by Alfred Peet, a Dutch immigrant, who sold coffee beans and equipment to many students from the nearby University of California. Three customers who were particularly impressed with Peet's coffee were Jerry Baldwin, Zev Siegl, and Gordon Bowke. In 1971 they opened a similar coffee retail store in Seattle, which they called Starbucks, a name derived from the first mate in Herman Melville's novel *Moby Dick*. They acquired beans from Alfred Peet and sold them along with related coffee equipment, such as a drip coffeemaker that was manufactured by the Swedish firm Hammarplast.

Starbucks coffee. (AP/Wide World Photos)

Howard Schultz, the American general manager for Hammarplast, visited Starbucks in 1981, and he liked what he saw. A year later, Schultz joined Starbucks as the director of marketing. In 1983 Schultz visited Italy, where he became enamored with Italian coffee bars and espresso. He believed that Starbucks should sell coffee beans and espresso, but he found little interest from the owners. He left Starbucks in 1985 and started a coffee bar chain of his own. The owners of Starbucks purchased Peets in 1984, and they decided to focus their efforts on Peets rather than Starbucks, so they sold Starbucks to Schultz and his coffee chain in August 1987.

Schultz converted Starbucks into a coffee bar that sold premium coffee, and he rapidly expanded the operation. In addition to selling premium coffee, Starbucks also sells a variety of other products, including pastry.

Mass-Market Expansion

Starbucks traditionally focused on selling premium coffees. However, it began to move into mass-market coffee in 2003, when it acquired Seattle's Best Coffee and began to sell lower-priced coffee in a variety of stores, such as J. C. Penny's department stores, movie theaters, Taco Bell, Subway, Borders, and Barnes & Noble Cafes. In 2010 Burger King announced that it would sell Seattle's Best Coffee in more than 7,000 of its restaurants. As of 2011, Seattle's Best Coffee is distributed in more than 40,000 locations. It is also expanding into convenience stores and vending machines. Another move into mass-market coffee occurred in 2009, when Starbucks introduced Via, a new instant coffee, which is sold in its stores and grocery stores.

Nutrition

Many products sold at Starbucks are filled with calories. Its Grande White Hot Chocolate, for instance, adds up to 410 calories; a flavored latte comes to 250 calories; and a simple mocha contains 260 calories. As for baked goods, a blueberry scone at Starbucks has 460 calories—the same as a ten-piece Chicken McNugget meal, and a chocolate chunk cookie is equivalent to an order of medium fries.

Fair Trade Coffee

In 1998 Starbucks began partnering with Conservation International, a nonprofit organization, to develop a plan to responsibly source coffee from the Chiapas region of Mexico. The result was Fair Trade coffee, which Starbucks offered as one of its options in 2003. This is a voluntary certification program that guarantees the buyer that coffee farmers and workers labor under decent conditions, have access to health care, receive a fair wage, and that the coffee is grown in an environmentally responsible manner. Fair Trade coffee costs more, but proponents believe that paying the extra price for Fair Trade coffee is socially and environmentally responsible. Today, Starbucks is the largest single purchaser of certified Fair Trade coffee.

Globalization

Beginning in 1987, Starbucks began to expand abroad to Canada, Japan (1996), the United Kingdom (1998), and then continental Europe and the Middle East. As of 2011, Starbucks had one thousand stores in Canada, and it is Europe's largest coffee chain.

Starbucks opened its first store in China in 1999. By 2010, the company had four hundred stores in China, and four hundred more in Hong Kong, Macao, and Taiwan. It offers black sesame green tea and Frappuccinos with coffee jelly pieces in Asia. By 2015, Starbucks plans to have one thousand outlets in China alone.

Recent Developments

Starbucks offers free, unlimited Wi-Fi in all its U.S. company-operated stores. Starbucks also has a consumer product division, which sells items such as coffee beans and Via. It also sells Starbucks ice cream to specialty grocery stores.

In March 2007 *Consumer Reports* proclaimed McDonald's Premium Roast to be "cheapest and best" coffee, beating Starbucks coffee, which it considered "strong, but burnt and bitter enough to make your eyes water instead of open."

Starbucks has had a major Internet presence. In 2010 the media measurement firm General Sentiment identified Starbucks as the company with the most successful online media promotion. The company's Fall 2010 Fast Food Industry Report highlights the brands that made the "most significant" online media impact between September and November. That impact—loosely defined as the sentiment and volume of all the buzz, content, and conversations generated online about a brand—is then assigned a dollar value. Starbucks is the largest retailer of specialty coffee in the world with more than 15,000 stores in 55 countries. It is headquartered in Seattle.

See also Burger King; Coffee; Convenience Stores; Dunkin' Donuts; Fair Trade; McDonald's; Movie Theaters; Seattle's Best Coffee; Subway; Taco Bell

For Further Information:

Clark, Taylor. *Starbucked: A Double Tall Tale of Caffeine, Commerce, and Culture*. New York: Little, Brown and Co., 2007.

Michelli, Joshep. *The Starbucks Experience: 5 Principles for Turning Ordinary into Extraordinary*. New York: McGraw-Hill, 2007.

Moore, John. *Tribal Knowledge: Business Wisdom Brewed from the Grounds of Starbucks Corporate Culture*. Chicago: Kaplan, 2006.

Pendergrast, Mark. *Uncommon Grounds: The History of Coffee and How It Transformed Our World*. New York: Basic Books, 1999.

Schultz, Howard, and Dori Jones Yang. *Pour Your Heart into It: How Starbucks Built a Company One Cup at a Time*. New York: Hyperion, 1997.

Seattle's Best Web site: www.seattlesbest.com

Smith, Andrew F. *Drinking History: Fifteen Beverages that Changed America*. New York: Columbia University Press, forthcoming.

"Starbucks War." *Consumer Reports* Web site: www.consumerreports.org/cro/food/bever ages/coffee-tea/coffee-taste-test-3-07/overview/0307_coffee_ov_1.htm

Starbucks Web site: www.starbucks.com

Stella D'oro

The Stella D'oro Biscuit Company was formed in 1932 in New York by a baker named Joseph Kresevich, an immigrant from Trieste, Italy, and his wife, Angela. In 1992 the company was sold to Nabisco. In 2009 it was acquired by Lance, Inc., which merged with Snyder's of Hanover in 2010 to form Snyder's-Lance, Inc. The brand includes forty different products, including bread sticks, biscotti, cookies, and breakfast treats.

See also Cookies; Lance; Nabisco; Snyder's-Lance, Inc.; Snyder's of Hanover

For Further Information:

Stella D'oro Web site: www.stelladoro.com

Stick Food

Several different types of stick foods were developed in the late nineteenth and early twentieth centuries. The first stick foods were lollipops and suckers, which have been impaled on sticks since the late nineteenth century. They were easy to sell, easy to eat, and sticks were cheap. Several claims have been made for the inventor of the machine that automatically inserted the stick into the lollipop. One was Samuel Born, a Russian immigrant, who arrived in New York in 1910. He moved to San Francisco, where he invented the Born Sucker Machine. He subsequently launched Just Born, a candy company that is today headquartered in Bethlehem, Pennsylvania.

A second stick food emerged in 1896 when Thomas Patton invented a machine that liquefied sugar and forced it through small holes in a spinning machine. It was then collected on a stick or paper cone. It was popularized as cotton candy or cotton floss in 1904, and it quickly became a children's favorite at circuses, amusement parks, and state and local fairs.

Another stick food was invented by Frank Epperson, a lemonade salesman from Oakland, California, who in 1923 began the commercial manufacture of Epsicles when he placed ice pops on wooden sticks. This avoided the necessity of giving customers dishes and utensils and made it easier for customers to eat the ice pops standing up. As ice cream trucks became common in American cities, sticks were added to ice cream to make it easier to sell. Many other companies began to produce similar items. Stick ice cream was so successful that General Foods expanded their Jell-O product line to include Jell-O Pudding Pops, which was frozen pudding on a stick.

In 1927 Stanley S. Jenkins filed a patent for a "Combined Dipping, Cooking, and Article Holding Apparatus." This patent was for impaling "wieners, boiled ham, hard boiled eggs, cheese, sliced peaches, pineapples, bananas and like fruit, and cherries, dates, figs, strawberries, etc.," on a stick, dipping them in a batter, and deep-frying them. What initially emerged from this idea was the corn dog, a popular food at fairs and amusement parks. Corn dogs were popularized during the 1940s, and they quickly became a national stick food.

Stick foods had several advantages: There was no need for a seating area, and no need for plates, napkins, spoons, knives, or forks. Simultaneously with the development of commercial stick foods there was also a surge of interest in the home and office—appetizers were frequently served on toothpicks. Then kabobs became popular. These were chunks of meat and vegetables skewered on a stick.

After World War II, vendors at state fairs saw the convenience of stick food and slowly began to add to the list of foods served on a stick. During the last twenty years, state fair stick food has dramatically expanded to include hundreds of foods, including Frito pies, frozen Mars bars, and Twinkies. Many state fairs have fifty or sixty different types of stick foods, including some very unusual foods: macaroni and cheese, chocolate-covered Key limes, SPAM, meatballs, Irish stew, chocolate-covered cheesecake, fudge brownies, pies, mashed potatoes, caramel apples, hard-boiled eggs, pizza, french fries, fried pickles, deep-fried Tootsie Rolls, Livermush (composed of pig liver, head parts, and cornmeal), deep-fried cheese, and even a salad on a stick. Virtually all are high in calories, fats, and salt, and low in nutrition.

An exception to most stick food was McDonald's special promotion in Italy in 2010. For a couple of months, McDonald's Italian stores offered kiwi on a stick as part of its effort to buy and sell local Italian fruit in its outlets.

See also Calories; Cheese; Chocolate; Corn Dogs; Cotton Candy; Deep Fried; Fair Food; Fat, Dietary; French Fries; Ice Cream; Jell-O; Lollipops/Suckers; Mars Bar; McDonald's; Pizza; Pudding; SPAM; Street Vendors; Tootsie Roll Industries; Twinkies

Street Vendors

Vendors have sold food on streets since the founding of American cities. The products sold by vendors have changed, as has their mode of operation. Initially, street foods included milk, dairy products, corn, oysters, clams, yams, and a wide range of staples. The type of goods sold shifted in the early nineteenth century when staples were replaced by snack foods and fast foods. Among the first snack foods sold by vendors were nuts. Although many Americans ate fruit and other foods between meals, nuts needed to be roasted before they could be consumed. The advantage of nuts was that they were inexpensive, particularly when compared with other types of sweets or desserts.

Popcorn followed a similar path. Popcorn had to be processed, either by popping or by conversion into popcorn balls and other confections, before it could be sold. Vendors sold popcorn and other snacks at public gatherings by the 1840s. Street hawkers in Boston peddled popcorn balls by the wagonloads. One entrepreneurial seller, Daniel Fobes, decided to use maple syrup rather than the more costly molasses as the binder for popcorn balls. During the presidential election of 1848, he sold his product at political rallies for Zachary Taylor and Millard Fillmore. He expanded his business through a series of partnerships and ever-increasing sales of candy products. The firm Fobes founded was one of the three constituents of the New England Confectionery Company, which still survives.

Snacks vended at fairs, circuses, and expositions attracted crowds to their stands. By the 1890s, vendors prowled the streets with steam-driven wagons, and many made an excellent living. In 1907 the *Chicago Tribune* reported that sympathy was wasted on vendors. While most people thought of a vendor "as an unfortunate individual, aged or decrepit, cut off from the legitimate lines of trade, and barely eking out a scanty living," the average vendor cleared about $150 per week, which was good pay in those days.

Vendors also frequented amusement parks. One such pushcart vendor was Charles Feltman, who sold sausages on white rolls at Coney Island, New York. He is credited with inventing the hot dog, a treat that became the rage of street vendors in the late nineteenth century—and remains a staple of street food today. Other street vendors, most likely in Chicago, invented hamburgers in the late nineteenth century, and they quickly spread throughout American cities. Both the hot dog and the hamburger moved indoors and eventually became central ingredients in the fast food movement that began in the 1920s.

Snack Food

Frederick Rueckheim and his brother sold popcorn and peanut confections on the streets of Chicago. They made all their confections by hand until 1884, when they shifted to steam-powered machinery. Like many other vendors, the Rueckheim brothers experimented with sugar-coated popcorn. They tested different sweeteners and tried a variety of combinations with marshmallows, nuts, and other products. They were satisfied with a new product that they introduced at Chicago's Columbian Exposition in 1893. It was a great success, and three years later the brothers launched their new product, which they called Cracker Jack. Cracker Jack moved into indoor distributors, but many other snack foods, such as pretzels and potato chips, continued to be sold by vendors.

Mobile wagons became popular during the late nineteenth century. They created a new class of mobile street vendors who traversed America's streets for almost a half century. As automobiles began to clog the streets of America, many cities passed laws licensing street vendors to prevent congestion. The result was that many vendors moved indoors. Cities required that vendors be licensed and they restricted a limited number to sell their foods on the streets or, more frequently, sidewalks or other public space.

Immigrants

Twentieth-century street foods included pretzels, coffee, soda, ice cream, popsicles, cookies, donuts, and sandwiches. As new waves of immigrants arrived, vendors have introduced new foods, such as hummus, falafels, gyros, burritos, tacos, pizza, Italian ices, and many others. Some street vendors launched businesses that became quite successful. For instance, Amedeo Obici and Mario Peruzzi founded Planters Peanuts. Joseph Kraft, a Canadian street cheesemonger, created what would become Kraft Foods. Another Italian immigrant who started as a street vendor, Joseph Kresevich, created Stella D'oro Biscuit Company.

During the early twenty-first century, a new type of street vendor emerged—the food truck. First in New York, and then in Washington, D.C., and Los Angeles, and then in many American cities, trucks began parking on streets offering fast food for sale. These offered a wide variety of food, including hamburgers, pizza, hot dogs, french fries, and many other goodies. Many trucks maintain an active social media presence, and many inform customers where they will be at particular times via Twitter or Facebook.

See also Automobiles; Candy; Coffee; Corn Dog; Cracker Jack; Entrepreneurs; Food Trucks; Hamburger; Hot Dog; Immigrants; Kraft Foods; Mexican American Food; Nachos; New England Confectionery Company (NECCO); Nuts; Peanuts; Popcorn; Popsicle; Pretzels; Stella D'oro

For Further Information:

Kraig, Bruce. *Hot Dog: A Global History*. London: Reaktion Books, 2008.

Smith, Andrew F. *Popped Culture: A Social History of Popcorn in America*. Columbia: University of South Carolina Press, 1999.

Smith, Andrew F. *Peanuts: The Illustrious History of the Goober Pea*. Urbana: University of Illinois Press, 2006.

Smith, Andrew F. *Hamburger: A Global History*. London: Reaktion Books, 2008.

Smith, Andrew F. *Eating History: Thirty Turning Points in the Making of American Cuisine*. New York: Columbia University Press, 2009.

Stress

Stress is a physical, mental, or emotional state of tension. It can be caused by social pressures and anxiety. Stress may contribute to overeating, especially of junk foods and fast foods. Some studies have suggested that there may be a relationship between social stress, such as public speaking, tests, and relationship pressures, and overeating and weight gain. When people are stressed by social conditions, they tend to eat "comfort foods," such as brownies, doughnuts, candy, ice cream, pizza, or french fries. This connection is in part psychological: people associate junk foods with fun and good times. When people face difficult situations, they often don't worry about the long-term consequences of overeating.

There may also be a biological reason. Judith Wurtman and Nina Frusztajer Marquis, in their book *The Serotonin Power Diet* (2008), have argued that consuming food with high carbohydrates, such as junk foods and fast foods, triggers the release of insulin, which ultimately stimulates the production of serotonin. Serotonin levels affect moods, sleep, and appetites. Elevated serotonin levels are associated with feelings of well-being and this helps people relax. Consuming foods high in sugar and fat releases these feel-good hormones in the brain, and the more one indulges, the more one needs to get that same level of satisfaction, and this often leads to overeating and obesity.

Scientific studies on the relationship between stress and long-term weight gain, however, have produced mixed results. A recent review of research studies that have examined the relationship between stress and weight gain, however, has indicated that there is little association between people's stress levels and their weight gain over several years.

While stress may or may not contribute to obesity, what is clear is that children who are obese do suffer more stress. A survey conducted by the Yale University's Rudd Center for Food Policy & Obesity demonstrated that children and adolescents who are overweight or obese (ages 8–17) report much more stress, headaches, sleep problems, anger, and fighting than do children who are normal weight.

See also Dieting; Obesity; Rudd Center for Food Policy & Obesity

For Further Information:

Talbott, Shawn. *The Cortisol Connection: Why Stress Makes You Fat and Ruins Your Health—And What You Can Do About It*. 2nd ed. Alameda, CA: Hunter House, 2007.

Wardle, Jane, et al. "Stress and Adiposity: A Meta-Analysis of Longitudinal Studies." *Obesity* (October 14, 2010), as at: www.nature.com/oby/journal/vaop/ncurrent/full/oby2010241a .html

Wurtman, Judith, and Nina Frusztajer Marquis. *The Serotonin Power Diet*. New York: Rodale, 2008.

Strokes

When blood flow to any part of the brain is interrupted and brain cells in that area quickly die because of lack of oxygen and nutrients, a stroke has occurred. Strokes

---

Mr. Bigg's

United African Company of Nigeria, PLC, headquartered in Lagos, began selling fast food in the 1960s. In 1986 the company launched Mr. Bigg's, which sells fast food chicken and hamburgers, although the popular items—meat pies, scotch eggs, and jollof rice—are more closely connected with Nigerian culinary traditions. As of 2011, Mr. Bigg's had 180 restaurants in Nigeria and Ghana and had recently opened outlets in the United States.

---

are the leading cause of disability in America: they may cause paralysis, speech impairment, blurred vision, dizziness, and loss of memory. Strokes are the third-largest cause of death in the United States, and about 160,000 Americans died of one each year.

There are many risk factors for a stroke, but unhealthy diet is one. According to the American Heart Association, "Diets high in saturated fat, trans fat and cholesterol can raise blood cholesterol levels. Diets high in sodium (salt) can contribute to increased blood pressure. Diets with excess calories can contribute to obesity." As junk foods and fast foods are frequently high in empty calories, saturated fat, transfats, cholesterol, and salt, the consumption of these foods increase the risk factors for strokes.

See also Calories; Cholesterol; Fat, Dietary; Sodium/Salt; Transfats

For Further Information:

American Heart Association's "Risk Factors for a Stroke" Web site: www.americanheart .org/presenter.jhtml?identifier=4716

Subs/Grinders

Sandwiches made with long loaves of Italian bread were developed in several different cities in the United States. In Philadelphia, street vendors began serving antipasto such as sliced meats, salami, cheese, fish, and vegetables on long, submarine-shaped loaves of bread. They called the sandwich a Hoagie. It usually included luncheon meats, lettuce, tomato, onion, cheese, and mayonnaise.

In New Orleans, Clovis Martin, owner of Martin Brothers Grocery, asked his cook to come up with a sandwich that would keep those "poor boys" who were unemployed during the Depression satisfied for an entire day but cost only a nickle. The result was the Po'Boy, a hefty cross section of French bread stuffed with roast beef and cheese. Today, Po'Boys may contain a fried fish fillet, fried oysters or shrimp, or thinly sliced roast beef or other cold cuts. If lettuce, tomatoes, and/or

Turkey, ham, and salami sandwiches. (Dreamstime.com)

chopped cabbage are added, the sandwich is referred to as "dressed." A variation is La Mediatrice ("The Peacemaker" in French), which contains fried oysters.

In Chicago, Italian Beef Sandwiches were sold by street vendors after World War I. They consisted of thin slices of beef roasted in broth with garlic, oregano, and spices, along with mozzarella and roasted green peppers, stuffed into Italian bread and then drenched with beef broth. It remains a hit, but today there are many different ways of making it. It can be bought on the streets through vendors or in most Italian restaurants in Chicago. Similar sandwiches developed in other cities across America.

The first fast food chain featuring these sandwiches was launched in 1964 by Tony Conza, Peter DeCarlo, and Angelo Baldassare in Hoboken, New Jersey. They called it Blimpie. The second sub sandwich chain was created in 1965 by Frederick DeLuca and Dr. Peter Buck of Bridgeport, Connecticut, who called their chain Subway; it is the nation's largest sub chain today. Quiznos Subs restaurants were launched in 1981 and quickly surpassed other sandwich shops to become the second-largest sandwich chain.

See also Blimpie International; Ice Cream; Quiznos; Sandwiches; Street Vendors; Subway

For Further Information:

Mercuri, Becky. *American Sandwich: Great Eats from All 50 States.* Layton, UT: Gibbs Smith, 2004.

Subway

In 1965, seventeen-year-old Frederick DeLuca of Bridgeport, Connecticut, borrowed $1,000 from family friend Dr. Peter Buck and they opened Pete's Submarine Sandwiches restaurant in Milford, Connecticut. Their first shop floundered, but they opened a second one. It succeeded, and the partners began expanding their operation. Its flagship product was the "sub" sandwich, composed of a variety of cold cuts, including ham, turkey, and salad vegetables. They changed the name of the restaurant to Subway, although its corporate name is Doctor's Associates, Inc. DeLuca and Buck began franchising in 1974. Subway expanded its operation through development agents who sold Subway franchises—a system that has led to abuses and numerous lawsuits. The costs of setting up a Subway outlet, however, are comparatively low, as are the franchising fees. By 1979, Subway had one hundred stores. A large number of franchisees are immigrants, who work long hours to make a success of their outlets.

Subway expanded its menu to include new creations, such as Sweet Onion Chicken Teriyaki and Southwest Chipotle Cheese Steak. In 1993 Subway began opening outlets in convenience stores, truck stops, and Walmarts. Subway increased its expansion abroad in the 1990s. Subway's products are considered more healthful because the main products are not fried, as are most hamburgers and chicken sold at other fast food outlets. Recently, Subway has begun to offer breakfasts.

In 1999 Jared Fogle, an Indiana University student, claimed to have lost 245 pounds with a diet composed mostly of Subway sandwiches and walking. He has become a spokesperson for Subway, promoting their healthy image. In 2010 Harris Interactive's Youth EquiTrend study ranked Subway seventh in brand recognition among 8–24-year-olds, and it was the top-ranked fast food chain in the study.

As of 2011, Subway was the largest fast food chain in the world and the second-largest fast food franchise in the world, with more than 23,000 stores in the United States and an additional 10,600 locations in 92 other countries. Subway has more stores than does any other fast food chain in the world.

See also Chicken; Hamburger; Menus; Sandwiches Subs/Grinders

For Further Information:

Jakle, John A., and Keith A. Sculle. *Fast Food: Roadside Restaurants in the Automobile Age*. Baltimore: Johns Hopkins University Press, 1999.

Subway Web site: www.subway.com

Sugars/Sweeteners

Sugars are simple carbohydrates, which are broken down by metabolic reactions to monosaccharides glucose and fructose. Both are metabolized in the body, where they are used for energy and stored as fat. Glucose is an essential nutrient and the

Splenda sweetener. (AP/Wide World Photos)

brain needs constant access to it. Most foods consumed by humans have carbohydrates that can be broken down. The human preference for sweetness is inborn, and this preference contributed to early survival. The U.S. Department of Agriculture (USDA) reports that each American consumes, on average, 152 pounds of sugar annually.

Historically, humans have sought sugar from many sources. In Europe, the main sweetener until the eighteenth century was honey, a product made by bees. It is composed of fructose, glucose, and a variety of other components. It is about as sweet as common table sugar. Honey production was unable to keep up with the rapidly increasing European populations in the sixteenth and seventeenth centuries, and Europeans began to seek new sources for sugar. They found it in sugarcane.

Cane Sugar

The plant with the highest concentration of sucrose is sugarcane, which contains up to 17 percent sucrose. Sugarcane likely originated in New Guinea but was cultivated in ancient times in Southeast Asia, India, and China. The word "sugar" derives from the Sanskrit *sarkara*, and it dates back at least 2,500 years. Sugarcane was cultivated in China at about the same time, but, surprisingly, China did not develop sugar-based sweets, instead preferring maltose, an extract from sorghum.

In the ancient Mediterranean, the very small quantities of sugar from cane that arrived from South Asia were mainly used for medicinal purposes. The process of extracting or refining sugar is complex and requires considerable technological expertise, which was probably first developed in Persia (today, Iran). Sugarcane cultivation did not reach the Mediterranean until the Middle Ages, when conquering Arabs brought it to southern Italy and Spain.

Christopher Columbus introduced sugarcane into the Caribbean, but it did not become an important crop until the mid-seventeenth century, when Europeans figured out the complex process of making sugar, and with it the process of making rum. Sugarcane thrived in the favorable climate and soil of the Caribbean. Along with sugarcane came slavery; estimates vary, but approximately 15 million Africans were brought to the New World, mainly to work in sugarcane fields. During this time Europe's demand for sugar soared, owing to the simultaneous introductions of tea, coffee, and cocoa. Sugarcane cultivation began in North America in the middle of the eighteenth century, when it was planted in French-controlled New Orleans.

To make sugar, sugarcane must be crushed and the juice extracted. The juice is heated and, when cooled, some of it crystallizes: this is considered raw sugar. Left behind is a sweet residue called treacle or molasses, which could not be further refined by traditional methods. Its advantage was that it was much less expensive than white crystallized sugar. In colonial times, molasses was mainly used to make rum. The British passage of the Molasses Act and the Sugar Act, which imposed very unpopular taxes, contributed to the American Revolutionary War.

Molasses was also used as a sweetener, particularly for confections, such as molasses candy. America's first national commercial confection, Cracker Jack, was sweetened with molasses, but virtually all subsequent sweet snacks were made with sugar. As manufacturing processes became more efficient and the price of sugar declined in the mid-nineteenth century, the amount of sweeteners in American cookery ballooned.

Increasing demand for imported sugar contributed to the conquest of Puerto Rico and the Philippines during the Spanish-American War and led to the annexation of the Hawaiian Islands. These additions and increased access to sugar meant that during the period from 1880 to 1915, the per-capita consumption of sugar doubled and the use of molasses declined.

Sugar was easily transported and stored and quickly became the major ingredient of candy. It was first used to make hard candy in the eighteenth century, then for making penny candy and chocolates during the nineteenth century. During and since the twentieth century, in addition to candy and other commercial confections, large quantities of sugar are consumed in many processed foods, baked goods (including cakes and cookies), and nondiet soft drinks.

Beet Sugar

Sucrose is also produced from sugar beets, but it requires a complicated process to extract, and the system to do this was not devised until the late eighteenth century. Production of sucrose from sugar beets is more expensive. In the United States, sugar beet farmers in Utah and other states have lobbied Congress to maintain price supports for their beet sugar, which means that Americans pay almost twice as much for sugar as do people outside the United States.

Sugar Critics

Sucrose has no nutritional value (no minerals, vitamins, protein, or fiber) other than providing calories. Natural and refined sugars are identical, but natural sugars are usually accompanied by some vitamins and minerals, and fruit contains fiber and other healthy contents.

Concern with sugar consumption was voiced beginning in 1942 when the American Medical Association's (AMA) Council on Food and Nutrition stated that it "would be in the interest of the public health for all practical means to be taken to limit consumption of sugar in any form in which it fails to be combined with significant proportions of other foods of high nutritive quality." The attack on sugar intensified during the 1970s when nutritionists proclaimed that sugar was a cause of many diseases, including diabetes, hyperactivity, heart disease, and obesity. This campaign started with John Yudkin's book *Pure, White and Deadly* (1972), which proclaimed that sugar consumption was linked with heart disease. Yudkin's ideas received extensive publicity in the United Kingdom and the United States, and many other writers joined his crusade against sugar. Studies purportedly demonstrated that rats became sugar dependent, and when sugar was removed from their diet they suffered in a way that was similar to withdrawal from morphine or nicotine. One result of the sugar scare was a great demand for diet foods, diet programs, and diet sodas, which became more popular during the 1970s and 1980s.

The only disease that has been directly tied to sugar consumption is dental caries. Refined sugar, however, is high in calories, and consumption of high levels of sugar is associated with obesity. The Center for Science in the Public Interest (CSPI) points out that consumption of products with high sugar content and empty calories is frequently associated with the failure to consume other foods that are nutritious. The CSPI report *Liquid Candy: How Soft Drinks Are Harming Americans' Health* (2005) stated that if people fill up with soda and junk food, rather than consuming fruit juice or fruit, then they are "missing a chance to cut [their] risk of osteoporosis, cancer, or heart disease." A major European study that involved 65,000 adults over the age of 13 concluded in 2010 that women with elevated blood sugar levels have a significant risk of suffering cancers of the pancreas, skin, and urinary tract.

Sugar Substitutes

Concern with increasing obesity in America led to the invention of low- or no-calorie artificial sweeteners. These had similar sweetness to table sugar, but their taste differed considerably, thus requiring the addition of other products to create a similar taste. The first marketed artificial sweetener was saccharin, which was originally synthesized in 1879, but it was not used commercially as a sweetener until 1950. Saccharin has 300–500 times the sweetness of sugar, and small amounts of it were added to diet foods as a substitute for sugar.

A second artificial sweetener, calcium cyclamate, was used in diet soda beginning in 1952. Variations of it were used in a variety of other products. Cyclamates were banned by the U.S. Food and Drug Administration (FDA) in 1970. They were generally replaced by saccharin. In 1977 a Canadian study confirmed that saccharin caused cancer in test animals and the FDA placed a moratorium on its use. That ban was lifted in 1991. By that time, diet products had shifted mainly to a third sugar substitute, aspartame (marketed under the names NutraSweet and Equal).

Stevia is a zero-calorie natural sugar substitute that derives from varieties of plants in the sunflower family. It has been widely used for centuries in South America. An extract from the plant has three hundred times the sweetness of table sugar. The sweetener has been widely used as a natural sweetener in Japan since 1970. Since then, has become popular in many countries in Asia and South America. In the United States, stevia was also used as an artificial sweetener, but in 1991 the Food and Drug Administration (FDA) banned its importation. The ban was lifted three years later, when the FDA proclaimed it to be an herbal supplement that had to be listed on the labels of products using it. In 2006 the World Health Organization's Joint Experts Committee on Food Additives has approved, based on long-term studies, an acceptable daily intake of steviol glycoside of up to 4 milligrams per kilogram of body weight. In 2008 the FDA approved two sweeteners derived from stevia: Truvia, which had been developed by Cargill and Coca-Cola Company, and PureVia, which had been developed by PepsiCo and the Whole Earth Sweetener Company. The following year, the FDA placed a purified form of stevia on the "Generally Recognized as Safe" list.

Sucralose is an artificial sweetener that is six hundred times as sweet as table sugar. It was first approved for use in Canada in 1991, and seven years later in the United States. It is found in thousands of diet products and it is marketed under several brand names, such as Splenda, SucraPlus, Candys, Cukren, and Nevella.

Acesulfame potassium is a zero-calorie artificial sweetener that is two hundred times as sweet as table sugar. It is approved for use in the United States and the European Union.

Neotame, an artificial sweetener made by NutraSweet, is between 7,000 and 13,000 times sweeter than table sugar. The FDA approved it for use in the United States in 2002, but to date it has not been widely used.

Little evidence has surfaced about negative short-term effects of approved artificial sweeteners; the long-term health risks, if any, remain under debate.

High-Fructose Corn Syrup

High-fructose corn syrup, manufactured from corn starch, was widely introduced into the beverage industry in the 1970s. Since the mid-1990s, federal subsidies to corn growers in the United States have amounted to $40 billion, so that corn syrup is now cheaper than sugar. Most carbonated beverages use less-expensive sweeteners, such as fructose, rather than cane sugar for sweeteners. Today, high-fructose corn syrups account for almost half the sweeteners used industrially in the United States, particularly in the beverage industry and in the confectionery industry.

Sugar Reduction

Owing to criticism, some junk food companies have begun to decrease the amount of sugar in their foods. For instance, the Kellogg Company announced plans to reduce the sugar content of its cereals by 15 percent, and General Mills, which produced six of the ten unhealthiest cereals and did more child-focused marketing of any cereal company, announced that it intended to lower the sugar content of its cereals that it marketed to children.

See also Cancer; Candy; Carbohydrates; Center for Science in the Public Interest (CSPI); Chocolate; Diabetes; Diet Soda; Food and Drug Administration (FDA); High-Fructose Corn Syrup; U.S. Department of Agriculture

For Further Information:

Aronson, Marc, and Marina Bidhos. *Sugar Changed the World: A Story of Magic, Spice, Slavery, Freedom and Science*. Boston: Houghton Mifflin Harcourt, 2010.

Bishop, Marlene R., ed. *Chocolate, Fast Foods, and Sweeteners: Consumption and Health*. New York: Nova Science Publishers, 2010.

Brownell, Kelly D., and Katherine Battle Horgen. *Food Fight: The Inside Story of the Food Industry, America's Obesity Crisis, and What We Can Do about It*. Chicago: Contemporary Books, 2004.

Chen, Joanne. *The Taste of Sweet: Our Complicated Love Affair with Our Favorite Treats*. New York: Crown Publishers, 2008.

De la Peña, Carolyn. *Empty Pleasures: The Story of Artificial Sweeteners*. Chapel Hill: University of North Carolina Press, 2010.

Duffy, William. *Sugar Blues*. New York: Warner Books, 1975.

Harris, Jennifer, et al. "Effects of Serving High-Sugar Cereals on Children's Breakfast-Eating Behavior." *Pediatrics* 127 (2011): 71–76.

Jacobson, Michael F. *Liquid Candy: How Soft Drinks Are Harming Americans' Health.* Washington, D.C.: Center for Science in the Public Interest, 2005.

Kalamaras, Paula M., and Paul T. Kraly. *Sugar and Sweeteners: Trends and Developments in Foods and Beverages.* Norwalk, CT: Business Communications Co., 2003.

MacInnis, Peter. *Bittersweet: The Story of Sugar.* Crows Nest, Australia: Allen & Unwin, 2002.

Mintz, Sidney W. *Sweetness and Power: The Place of Sugar in Modern History.* New York: Elisabeth Sifton, Viking, 1985.

de la Peña, Carolyn. *From Saccharin to Splenda.* Chapel Hill: University of North Carolina Press, 2010.

Richardson, Tim. *Sweets: A History of Candy.* New York: Bloomsbury, 2002.

Smith, Andrew F. *Sugar: A Global History.* London: Reaktion Books, forthcoming.

Sugar Association Web site: www.sugar.org

Warner, Deborah Jean. *Sweet Stuff: An American History of Sweeteners to Sugar to Sucralose.* Washington, DC: Smithsonian Institutional Press, 2011.

Woloson, Wendy A. *Refined Tastes: Sugar, Confectionery and Consumption in Nineteenth-Century America.* Baltimore: Johns Hopkins University Press, 2002.

Yudkin, John. *Pure, White and Deadly: The Problem of Sugar.* London: Davis-Poynter Ltd, 1972.

Sun Capital Partners, Inc.

Sun Capital Partners is a private equity firm based in Boca Raton, Florida. In the food world, Sun Capital owns Boston Market, Captain D's, and Friendly's restaurant chains.

See also Boston Market; Captain D's Seafood Kitchen

For Further Information:
Sun Capital Partners Web site: www.suncappart.com

SunChips

Frito-Lay introduced a brand of fried, multigrain chips called SunChips in 1991. The chips are made from corn, wheat, oats, and rice, and they are variously flavored with herbs, cheese, and seasonings. SunChip flavors include cheddar, onion, salsa, peppercorn ranch, and chipotle. Frito-Lay marketed SunChips as a healthier alternative to other chips. They contain 30 percent less fat than potato chips and they have no cholesterol and no transfats.

Frito-Lay also positioned SunChips as an eco-friendly product. One factory in Modesto, California, that manufactures them has solar collectors that reduce the amount of nonrenewable energy going into the production of the chips. To decrease waste, Frito-Lay announced in 2009 that the packaging for the 10.5-ounce bags of SunChips were completely biodegradable. The bags were made from plant products. As few people compost, Frito-Lay encouraged people to do so through the SunChips Web site.

Their bioplastic bags were noisier than traditional bags, and SunChips received considerable criticism for them. A Facebook group called "Sorry But I Can't Hear You Over This SunChips Bag" sprang up and had more than 44,000 followers. As a consequence of the criticism, Frito-Lay quietly yanked the bag, but the company is in the process of developing new types of eco-friendly bags.

SunChips. (AP/Wide World Photos)

See also Cholesterol; Facebook; Frito-Lay; Potato Chips; Transfats

For Further Information:

Sun Chips Web site: www.sunchips.com

Super Size Me

Super Size Me is a documentary film directed by Morgan Suprlock, who also stars in the film. It follows Spurlock, who, for twenty-eight days, ate large amounts of food—about five thousand calories per day including breakfast, lunch, and dinner—at McDonald's. During this time he gained twenty-four pounds, among other problems. The film was intended as an attack on fast food in America. McDonald's removed the "supersize" option from its menu before the movie was released in 2004. It was nominated for an Academy Award for Best Documentary Feature.

The movie was based on the addiction theories of Neal D. Barnard, author of *Turn Off the Fat Genes: Eat Right, Live Longer*, and *Food for Life*.

See also Addiction; McDonald's; Spurlock, Morgan; Supersizing

For Further Information:

Spurlock, Morgan. *Don't Eat This Book: Fast Food and the Supersizing of America*. New York: G. P. Putnam's Sons, 2005.

Spurlock, Morgan, et al. *Supersized: Strange Tales from a Fast-Food Culture*. Milwaukie, Oregon: Dark Horse, 2011.

Super Size Me. Directed by Morgan Spurlock. Goldwyn Films, 2004.

Supermarkets

The growth of supermarkets paralleled the growth of fast food chains. The term "supermarket" likely originated in Southern California during the 1920s. Los Angeles was a sprawling metropolis highly dependent upon the automobile. Two chains—Ralph's Grocery Company and Alpha Beta Food Markets—constructed large stores that were organized into food departments. The major difference from other grocery stores of the time was size: typical supermarkets covered five thousand square feet, ten times larger than grocery stores of the day. Because land was inexpensive in Los Angeles at that time, large parking lots could be constructed around the supermarkets.

Supermarket chains had advantages similar to those of large fast food chains. Their great strength lay in their enormous purchasing power. Buying wholesale reduced retail prices and increased volume of sales, meaning increased profits. Also, centralized warehousing systems allowed supermarkets to get price concessions from manufacturers and save on distribution costs.

The success of the early supermarkets in Southern California encouraged grocery store chains to close smaller stores and open supermarkets. In addition, independent grocers did not have access to capital, as did large chains, and they were unable to make the conversion; tens of thousands went out of business during the late 1930s and early 1940s.

The post–World War II growth of supermarkets was tremendous. Chain stores abandoned inner-city grocery stores and expanded into the suburbs with supermarkets. As a result, large chains increased their share of the nation's grocery business from 35 percent to 62 percent during the decade after the war. The variety of inventory grew with the number of supermarkets. In the 1940s, an average store carried 3,000 different items; by the late 1950s, this had increased to 5,800; and by the 1970s, supermarkets stocked more than 10,000 items. Because supermarkets made large profits on junk foods, these were stocked and sold extensively.

During the 1970s and 1980s, supermarket industry leaders became concerned as many Americans shunned their kitchens and began eating out at fast food chains. Supermarkets countered by expanding their offerings of ready-to-eat foods to take home, and some supermarkets constructed places for customers to eat their food in the stores. Supermarkets supply a large percentage of fast food and sell vast quantities of junk food.

Supermarkets use a variety of techniques to get customers to buy junk food. Companies such as PepsiCo, Coca-Cola Company, and Kraft Foods pay fees for prominent displays and their location on shelves. They also pay for standalone displays. One estimate was that 52 percent of the standalone displays were for junk foods, including cookies, potato chips, and doughnuts.

Typically, presweetened cereals, such as Frosted Flakes, Fruit Loops, Honey Smacks, and Frosted Mini-Wheats, are placed at children's eye levels (two shelves above the bottom). When young children accompanied adults to the supermarket, the adults spent up to 50 percent more money. These products produce 70 percent margins for their manufacturers. In 2010 supermarket chains sold $4.9 billion worth of candy, gum, and chocolates, and Walmart sold an additional $4 billion.

See also Cereals; Junk Foods; Soda/Soft Drinks; Walmart

For Further Information:

Kahn, Barbara E., and Leigh McAlister. *Grocery Revolution: The New Focus on the Consumer.* Reading, MA: Addison Wesley Longman, 1997.

Levinson, Marc. *The Great A&P and the Struggle for Small Business in America.* New York: Hill and Wang, 2011.

Mayo, James M. *The American Grocery Store: The Business Evolution of an Architectural Space.* Westport, CT: Greenwood Press, 1993.

Smith, Andrew F. *Eating History: Thirty Turning Points in the Making of American Cuisine.* New York: Columbia University Press, 2009.

Zimmerman, M. M. *The Super Market: A Revolution in Distribution.* New York: McGraw-Hill Book Company, 1955.

Supersizing

Portion sizes (the amount of food being eaten at one time) have grown considerably. During the 1950s, the typical size for soft drinks was about eight ounces; today, a small-sized beverage (when one can be found) is twelve ounces. A large-sized cola has graduated to thirty-two ounces, with an estimated 310 calories, and ARCO service station stores have come out with The Beast, which weighs in at eighty-eight ounces. Twenty years ago, cheeseburgers would have weighed in at about 333 calories; many cheeseburgers now contain 590 calories.

In the 1950s McDonald's served only one size of french fries. In 1972 the company added a large size for its fries, but the large-sized fries of the late 1970s are the small size today. In 1994 McDonald's added Super Size Fries, with 610 calories and 25 grams of fat. Supersized fries were three times the size of the 1950s french fries. The company also created supersized meals, which consisted of a sandwich, supersized french fries (seven ounces), and a supersized beverage (forty-two ounces). McDonald's signs encouraged customers to "Super Size It!" as did their employees, who were directed to ask customers if they wanted to supersize their order. Supersized meals were less expensive than ordering the three items separately, but even at this reduced price McDonald's made more profit on each supersized order.

Subsequently, the term "supersized" was used in many other retail establishments to mean the largest size. Other fast food chains created their own names for supersized portions. Burger King, for instance, created portions similar to McDonald's supersized portions, but called them King Size. Other fast food chains made similar offers.

Supersizing was not only limited to fast food outlets, though. Junk food manufacturers jumped on board with large sizes of their own. For instance, Frito-Lay put out its Big Grab size. Supersized items offered better value for bigger portions. These supersized items generate hefty profits and they draw customers in who purchase other products. When Hardee's introduced its Monster Thickburger, its sales increased by 20 percent.

Obesity and fast food became linked, and "supersized" became a symbol of this relationship. The filmmaker Morgan Spurlock filmed his experiences eating three meals a day from McDonald's (supersized, if available) for twenty-eight days, and he documented the effects on his body. According to the film, Spurlock gained twenty-four pounds and reported serious health problems at the end of the twenty-eight days. The release of the film, *Super Size Me* (2004), generated bad publicity for McDonald's throughout the world. Prior to its release, McDonald's phased out supersizes from its meal options. Spurlock's film was nominated for an Academy Award for Best Documentary Feature. He subsequently wrote a book, *Don't Eat This Book: Fast Food and the Supersizing of America* (2005), describing his experiences while making the movie and criticizing fast food restaurants and the food they serve.

See also Calories; Cholesterol; Convenience Stores; Fat, Dietary; Frito-Lay; Hardee's; McDonald's; Obesity; Service Stations; Soda/Soft Drinks; Spurlock, Morgan; *Super Size Me*

For Further Information:

Ingram, Scott. *Want Fries With That? Obesity and the Supersizing of America.* New York: Franklin Watts, 2006.

Spurlock, Morgan. *Don't Eat This Book: Fast Food and the Supersizing of America.* New York: G. P. Putnam's Sons, 2005.

Spurlock, Morgan, et al. *Supersized: Strange Tales from a Fast-Food Culture.* Milwaukie, OR: Dark Horse Books, 2011.

Suppliers

Today, most fast food chains generally do not grow their own potatoes, raise their own cattle or chickens, or make their own bread. These are all acquired from suppliers. The size of chains such as McDonald's or KFC gives these companies purchasing power, such that they influence which varieties of potatoes are grown and which animals are raised and how they are fed and processed. McDonald's is the largest purchaser of potatoes, beef, and pork in America and is second only to KFC in the purchasing of chickens. Fast food chains place massive orders for quantities of a specific variety of potato (Russet Burbank), for instance, and for specific breeds of cattle, pigs, and chickens. This has led to dependence upon a limited number of varieties and breeds and has led to the near-extinction of some heritage potatoes and breeds of animals. As fast food chains have moved overseas, the companies have preferred to purchase from local suppliers, but these, too, must meet company standards. Thus, homogenization of foods has increased globally.

Because fast food chains order vast amounts of food, they acquire what they order at a greatly reduced price. As suppliers compete for fast food orders, they try to keep their costs down. Because a major cost is labor, many suppliers have sought immigrant employees who will work for lower wages. This has led to problems, particularly in slaughterhouses, as Eric Schlosser points out in *Fast Food Nation* (2001). Because fast food chains do not own suppliers, they maintain that they are not responsible for the behavior of their suppliers or for the effects their suppliers have upon the environment. This has particularly become a problem in developing countries, which often do not have protections for workers or proper working conditions.

Some fast food chains have begun to be concerned about the actions of their suppliers. McDonald's, for instance, formed an alliance with Environmental Defense Fund and announced that it would switch from plastic to paper packaging. In addition, McDonald's stopped purchasing beef from Brazil in order to prevent the destruction of the rainforests. In 2000 McDonald's said it would no longer accept genetically modified (GMO) potatoes, and its suppliers had to change their potatoes. In response to protests by People for the Ethical Treatment of Animals (PETA), McDonald's imposed rules on its suppliers specifying how livestock should be raised and slaughtered, stressing the humane treatment of animals.

In 2004 PETA released a video taken at a chicken supplier for KFC. As a result of the animal cruelty depicted in the film, Pilgrim's Pride fired several employees and began a workforce training program to prevent animal cruelty.

See also Beef; Chicken; Environment; Factory Farms; *Fast Food Nation*; Genetically Modified Food; KFC; McDonald's; People for the Ethical Treatment of Animals (PETA)

For Further Information:

Schlosser, Eric. *Fast Food Nation: The Dark Side of the All-American Meal.* New York: Houghton Mifflin Company, 2001.

Sweet Candy Company

In 1892 Leon Sweet began selling licorice, lollipops, and jawbreakers in Portland, Oregon. He moved to Salt Lake City, Utah, in 1900 and incorporated the Sweet Candy Company. One reason for the move was the closer proximity to Utah Sugar Company, which made sugar from locally grown beets. The company grew slowly, in part by acquiring smaller candy makers. It widened its distribution to eleven western states.

Over the years, the company added more products to their offerings. Saltwater taffy, for instance, was added in 1908, and it became the company's best-selling product.

Traditionally candy was packaged in wooden and metal boxes. In the 1920s Sweet began packaging its products in cellophane, a new technology at the time.

The Sweet Company manufactured a wide variety of products with affectionate names, such as the Brown Bomber (named in honor of the boxer Joe Lewis), Cinnamon Bears, Chocolate Orange Sticks (1945), Rodeo Bars, Razzle Dazzle, and Pink Lady Chocolates.

Today the Sweet Candy Company produces about 250 items. It claims to be the world's largest manufacturer of saltwater taffy. It is one of the few family-owned candy companies in America.

See also Candy; Chocolate; Licorice; Lollipops/Suckers; Taffy

For Further Information:

International Directory of Company Histories. Vol. 60. Chicago: St. James Press, 2004.
Sweet Candy Company's Web site: www.sweetcandy.com

Sweet Popcorn

Throughout the first half of the twentieth century, Cracker Jack dominated the sweet popcorn field. In the 1950s, others began producing similar products. Howard Vair, a proprietor of a Detroit candy store, is credited with inventing Poppycock, which were clusters of glazed popcorn and nuts. In 1960 Wander, a Swiss company, bought the rights to Poppycock, and seven years later launched Fiddle Faddle, a combination of popcorn mixed with caramel, butter toffee, Heath toffee bits, and honey nuts. In 1969 the company released Screaming Yellow Zonkers, a sweet popcorn without nuts. The company was purchased in 2004 by Chicago-based, privately held Ubiquity Brands.

Meanwhile, American Home Products, owners of Jiffy Pop, launched Franklin's Crunch'n Munch in 1966. It was eventually purchased by ConAgra Foods, which shortened the product name to Crunch'n Munch.

By the end of the 1980s, Cracker Jack was still the leader in the sweet popcorn field in the United States, but it was losing market share to a pack of competitors. By the early 1990s, Crunch'n Munch had toppled Cracker Jack as the nation's number one ready-to-eat sweet popcorn confection. Fiddle Faddle is the number three sweet popcorn.

See also Candy; ConAgra Foods; Popcorn; Poppycock

For Further Information:

Smith, Andrew F. *Popped Culture: A Social History of Popcorn in America.* Columbia: University of South Carolina Press, 1999.

T

Taco Bell

During the early 1950s, few Americans outside of California knew what a taco was. Today, Mexican American food is one of America's fastest-growing cuisines. While there are many reasons for this upsurge, the Taco Bell fast food chain launched by Glen Bell played an important role in this national shift.

During World War II, Glen Bell served in the Marines, working in foodservice. In 1948 he operated a one-man hamburger and hot dog stand in San Bernardino, California. However, Bell preferred to eat Mexican take-out food. Taco stands dotted the Southern California landscape, but none offered fast food and most had poor reputations. Bell developed ways to improve the efficiency of preparing and serving Mexican food. At the time, taco shells were made by frying a soft tortilla for a few minutes. Bell invented a prefabricated hard taco shell that did not have to be fried, thus saving time on each order. Bell also developed procedures he believed would make for speedier service. As taco sales at his stand increased, he dropped hamburgers and hot dogs altogether.

With a partner, in 1954 Bell opened three Taco Tia outlets in San Bernardino—the same city where Richard and Maurice McDonald opened their revolutionary fast food establishment, McDonald's. Like the McDonald brothers, Bell opened more restaurants in the surrounding area, but when he wanted to expand to Los Angeles his partner refused. Bell sold out his interest in Taco Tia. In 1958, with new partners, Bell launched another chain, El Taco, in Long Beach, California.

Bell sold out to his new partners in 1961. He invested in and helped develop a new restaurant chain called Der Wienerschnitzel. In 1962 he opened his first Taco Bell in Downey, California. Bell targeted college students, traveling salesmen, and the military. The menu specialized in tacos, burritos, and a few other items. Bell opened three additional outlets, which generated $50,000 per year. In 1964 he began franchising his operation, and soon eight additional outlets were launched in the Long Beach, Paramount, and Los Angeles areas. The resulting Taco Bell chain used the symbol of a Mexican man sleeping under a sombrero, and the chain's buildings had a California mission–style architecture. The company prospered and continued to grow.

In 1975 Glen Bell resigned as chairman of the company, but he retained a controlling interest. By 1978, Taco Bell had grown steadily for 16 years and had 868 restaurants. Both H. J. Heinz and PepsiCo wanted to purchase Taco Bell. PepsiCo won the bidding war, spending $130 million to acquire the chain. Management of the PepsiCo subsidiary was placed in the hands of John Martin, who had previously worked for several fast food companies. He popularized Taco Bell's Mexican-style food nationally through heavy discounting and value meals, which combined foods and drinks for cost savings. By 1980, Taco Bell had 1,333 outlets and was rapidly expanding. One reason for the expansion was the continual introduction of new products, such as fajitas, wraps, Gorditas, and Chalupas.

While these names of Mexican foods might have been new to many Americans, their contents were not. Their components were similar to hamburgers—ground beef, cheese, tomatoes, lettuce, and sauce. The main difference was the tortilla, which most customers could easily understand as a substitute for the hamburger bun. Others who tried to imitate Taco Bell did not stray too far from this traditional American combination, either.

Taco Bell learned from other fast food chains. Like other companies, most of its food is prepared outside and is assembled at the outlet. Its guacamole, for instance, is made at a factory in Mexico. The taco meat arrives frozen, ready for heating. Beans are dehydrated and employees just add water. Taco Bell also innovated by installing double drive-thru windows, which decreased waiting time for customers, increased the volume of sales, and increased profits.

Taco Bell has had both success and failure in its promotional efforts. For example, its original sleeping Mexican symbol was considered a negative stereotype by many Mexican Americans, and it was replaced with a mission bell when PepsiCo took over. Likewise, the architecture for the outlets had been a red-tiled mission style; PepsiCo changed it to a mainstream mansard style. These changes worked, and by 1990 there were more than 3,500 Taco Bell outlets throughout the United States. In addition, the company licensed Taco Bell Home Originals dinner kits to Kraft Foods in 1996. These were sold in supermarkets. Taco Bell launched a major promotional drive with television commercials featuring a talking Chihuahua that squealed, "Yo Quiero Taco Bell!"

In 2011 Taco Bell introduced new items on its breakfast menu, including a double ham and cheddar melt and a sausage skillet burrito. Taco Bell has co-branded with Cinnabon and sells that company's products for breakfast, as well.

Seasoned Beef

In 2011 an Alabama law firm, Beasley Allen Crow Methvin Portis & Miles, filed a class action lawsuit against Taco Bell for false advertising. What Taco Bell calls "seasoned beef" was actually just 36 percent meat, according to the law firm's analysis. The rest consisted of extenders, binders, and preservatives, including wheat oats, water, modified corn starch, sodium phosphate, soy lecithin, autolyzed yeast extract, maltodextrin, soy bean oil, flavorings, and other ingredients. If true, it would have violated U.S. Department of Agriculture guidelines that require "beef" products to be at least 70 percent beef. Taco Bell denied that their advertising was misleading and claimed that their seasoned beef was 88 percent beef, and the rest was a "secret formula" consisting of water, sugar, and spices. Taco Bell has threatened to counter-sue the law firm and its client. Taco Bell responded with a major campaign on Facebook that offered a free "crunchy seasoned beef taco" to customers. It became the largest promotion involving complimentary tacos in fast food history.

Globalization

In 1997 Taco Bell was spun off from PepsiCo and is now a division of Yum! Brands, Inc., which also owns KFC, Pizza Hut, Long John Silver's, and A&W Restaurants. Yum! Brands has rapidly expanded Taco Bell's operations outside the United States. In 2010 Taco Bell opened its first restaurant in the United Kingdom. Taco Bell outlets were opened in Spain and Cyprus in 2009, and in India in 2010.

International restaurants have required shifts in the traditional Taco Bell menu. In India, for instance, Taco Bell stores offer vegetarian and non-vegetarian options tailored to the Indian consumer. Offerings include potato and paneer burritos and a number of spicy "volcano" items, such as Volcano Burritos, Volcano Crunchwraps, Volcano Topped Nachos, Volcano Cake, and Volcano Tacos.

Today, Taco Bell is the nation's leading Mexican-style fast food restaurant chain, with more than $4.9 billion in systemwide sales. Taco Bell serves more than 55 million consumers each week in its 6,400 restaurants in the United States.

See also Architecture/Design; Burrito; Drive-Thrus; India; Kraft Foods; McDonald's; Mexican American Food; Mexico; Nachos; Tacos; Yum! Brands, Inc.

For Further Information:

Baldwin, Debra Lee. *Taco Titan: The Glen Bell Story*. Arlington, TX: Summit Publishing Group, 1999.

Jakle, John A., and Keith A. Sculle. *Fast Food: Roadside Restaurants in the Automobile Age*. Baltimore: Johns Hopkins University Press, 1999.

Smith, Andrew F. "Tacos, Enchiladas and Refried Beans: The Invention of Mexican-American Cookery." In Mary Wallace Kelsey and ZoeAnn Holmes, eds., *Cultural and Historical Aspects of Foods*. Corvallis: Oregon State University, 1999, 183–203; also at: http://food.oregonstate.edu/ref/culture/latinamerica/la_smith.html

Taco Bell Web site: www.tacobell.com

Taco Bueno

Taco Bueno is a small, fast-casual restaurant chain launched by Bill Waugh in Abilene, Texas, in 1967. It has a Tex-Mex menu, with its flagship product being tacos, but it also serves a variety of other items, including burritos, quesadillas, nachos, salads, and a pita sandwich. It prides itself on the fresh ingredients it uses in the food it serves. A few of its outlets have wireless digital menuboards that display nutritional and promotional information.

In 1981 Taco Bueno was sold to the British firm Unigate, and fifteen years later to CKE Restaurants. It was sold again to a private investment group in 2001. Taco Bueno began to franchise in 2005. Today it is owned by New York–based private equity firm Palladium Equity Partners. As of 2011, it had about 170 stores in Arkansas, Kansas, Louisiana, Missouri, Nebraska, New Mexico, Oklahoma, and Texas. It is headquartered in Farmers Branch, Texas.

See also CKE Restaurants; Fast Casual; Mexican American Food; Tacos

For Further Information:

Taco Bueno Web site: www.tacobueno.com.

Tacos

The taco was the staple of Cal-Mex food. The word "taco" meant a "wad" or "plug," purportedly "taken from the cotton used in ramming old-fashioned firearms." Colloquially, "taco" referred to a light meal or snack, or *antojitos*—little whimsies or small dishes. In Mexico, the word "taco" was a generic term like the English word "sandwich." Mexican tacos are basically any food rolled, folded, or fried into tortillas that are consumed by hand. The various fillings for tacos include chili sauce, beef (shredded or ground), chicken, pork, chorizo or sausage, egg, tomato, cheese, lettuce, guacamole, onions, and refried beans. Mexican tacos are usually soft shelled, unlike the U-shaped crisp fried tortillas served in many American Mexican restaurants and fast food outlets. The first-known English-language taco recipes appeared in California cookbooks beginning in 1914. The author, Bertha Haffner-Ginger, reported that tacos were "made by putting chopped cooked beef and chili sauce in tortilla made of meal and flour; folded, edges sealed together with egg; fried in deep fat, chile sauce served over it." Another Californian, Pauline Wiley-Kleemann,

Tacos. (Dreamstime.com)

featured six taco and tacquito recipes in her *Ramona's Spanish-Mexican Cookery*. These included recipes for Gorditos that came from Santa Nita or Xochimilco; Pork Tacos composed of snout, ears, jowls, kidneys, and liver; Cream Cheese Tacos; Egg Tacos; Mexican Tacos; and Tacquitos.

Not everyone was familiar with tacos by the 1930s. One author felt obligated to tell the reader that tacos were "the Mexican's Sandwich," and that they were composed "of roast meat or chicken, either sliced or minced but cheese and sweet fillings are rapidly gaining in popularity. The Mexican enjoys his Tacos and Hot Chocolate as does the American his Doughnuts and Coffee." The following year Blanche and Edna McNeill defined a taco as a "tidbit, or Mexican sandwich," which was a "much decorated, highly spiced tortilla with any filling." They offered recipes for making tacos filled with pork sausage and shrimp. Their recipe for Tacos de San Luis was based on a recipe developed by "old Carmen" from the Alameda in San Luis, Mexico. For thirty-five years Carmen made tacos by filling them with goat cheese, onion, and sausage. Just before the tacos were consumed, she poured hot lard over them. Taco recipes often appeared under the names for the Mexican locations from which they purportedly derived: Puebla-Style Tacos consisted of sausages, eggs, tomatoes, onions, peppers, and cream cheese; San Cristobal Tacos were filled with eggs, flour, sugar, and butter. Other taco recipes were named solely after their filling: Taco de Rajas were filled with sweet peppers. Perhaps unique in the Mexican American cookery traditions were the seafood tacos served in California.

See also Beef; Chipotle Mexican Grill; Mexican American Food; Taco Bell; Taco Bueno

For Further Information:

Smith, Andrew F. "Tacos, Enchiladas and Refried Beans: The Invention of Mexican-American Cookery." In Mary Wallace Kelsey and ZoeAnn Holmes, eds., *Cultural and Historical Aspects of Foods*. Corvallis: Oregon State University, 1999, 183–203, as at: http://food.oregonstate.edu/ref/culture/latinamerica/la_smith.html

Taffy

Taffy is an inexpensive chewy candy made from boiled sugar or molasses, and butter, combined with a wide variety of flavorings. The boiled mixture is removed from the heat just as it reaches the "hard ball" stage, and then it is cooled, placed on a hook and pulled, and stretched and folded by hand until stiff and it becomes the chewy confection. It originated in England in the late eighteenth century. The process of making it arrived in the United States with immigrants by the 1840s, and it promptly became a fad in East Coast cities. By the 1850s, it was sold in "every candy store" in New York, according to a contemporary source. In the early twentieth century it spread to Florida and the West Coast.

Saltwater Taffy

Atlantic City emerged as a seaside health resort, with many hotels serving thousands of annual visitors. John Ross Edmiston, a Pennsylvanian, sold postcards in his shop on the boardwalk in 1884. According to Edmiston, he hired a man named David Bradley, who brought in taffy as a sideline in the shop. Edmiston fired Bradley, but continued to sell the taffy. According to Edmiston's account, one night the tide came up and seawater filled the shop. When he opened in the morning, his taffy was covered with saltwater foam. He brushed off the salty residue and found that the pieces of candy were perfectly fine. This incident gave him the idea to give his candy a little extra seaside cachet, and he called it "saltwater taffy."

Edmiston entered his saltwater taffy into a contest at an agricultural fair in 1885. Despite the award he received, he left Atlantic City the following year. His store was taken over by an experienced confectioner, Joseph Fralinger, who retained the saltwater taffy name, perfected its formula, and expanded the product line by making the candy in a range of appealing pastel colors, various flavors, and diverse shapes. Customers loved Fralinger's taffy, and he opened additional stores in Atlantic City, Cape May, and Ocean City.

There is actually no difference between regular taffy and saltwater taffy. It was simply a marketing ploy—and a very successful one, at that. The name was picked up by other vendors in Atlantic City, and then borrowed by candy makers in other coastal towns from Florida to Massachusetts. By the 1920s, saltwater taffy had become a big business, with more than 450 companies manufacturing it. Today, saltwater taffy continues to be an important junk food on both the East and West Coasts. The largest manufacturer of saltwater taffy, however, is the Sweet Candy Company in Salt Lake City, Utah, which sells twenty-eight flavors, from banana to key lime to watermelon.

One advantage of taffy is that it can be variously shaped. Some taffies are long and flat, while others are compact and wrapped in wax paper. Taffy is used as an ingredient in a variety of candies. Bit-O-Honey is a slab of taffy with almond bits. Abba-Zaba is a taffy candy bar with a peanut butter center. Airheads, made by Perfetti Van Melle in Erlanger, Kentucky, are a taffy like candy that come in a variety of flavors, as are Tangy Taffy and Laffy Taffy manufactured by Nestlé.

See also Bit-O-Honey; Candy; Chewy Candy; Peanut Butter; Sweet Candy Company

For Further Information:

Almond, Steve. *Candyfreak*. Chapel Hill, NC: Algonquin Books of Chapel Hill, 2004. Annabelle Candy Company Web site: www.annabelle-candy.com

Richman, Alan. "People and Places: Pulling out Some Childhood Memories of Atlantic City Salt Water Taffy." *Bon Appétit* 41 (August 1, 1996): 30.

Smith, Andrew F. "A Seaside Tradition: A Longtime Beach-Town Favorite, Saltwater Taffy Has a History That's as Varied as Its Flavors." *Martha Stewart Living* (August 2008): 66–70.

Sweet Candy Company's Web site: www.sweetcandy.com

Tang

General Foods Corporation acquired the Perkins Products Company, maker of Kool-Aid, in 1953. It began experimenting with Kool-Aid, and the company came up with a powdered orange-flavored breakfast drink that was fortified with vitamins. In 1958 this new product was released under the brand name Tang. It did not become popular until the National Aeronautic and Space Administration (NASA) popularized it on their Gemini space flights in 1965. Although it is full of sugar, it was touted as a health drink that could substitute for soda. Today, the brand is owned by Kraft Foods. In addition to North America, Tang is marketed throughout Latin America, Eastern Europe, China, and India.

See also General Foods Corporation; Kool-Aid; Kraft Foods; Powdered Mixes; Soda/Soft Drinks; Sugars/Sweeteners

For Further Information:

Kraft Foods Web site: www.kraft.com

Tastee-Freez

In 1950 Leo Maranz invented a small freezer to make soft-serve ice cream. He approached Harry Axene, who had helped launch the Dairy Queen chain. The two formed a new Chicago-based chain, which they named Tastee-Freez. The company sold its freezers at cost to franchisees and made its profit on the sale of ice cream mix. In addition to its soft-serve ice cream, Tastee-Freez introduced other foods, such as its Big Tee Burgers. By 1956, the chain had 1,500 outlets in the United States.

One prominent early financial executive was Harry Sonneborn, who had gained a great deal of franchising experience while working with Tastee-Freez. In 1954 Sonneborn teamed up with Ray Kroc, and many consider him to be the co-founder of McDonald's.

In 1982 the DeNovo Corporation of Utica, Michigan, bought the Tastee-Freez brand and launched a program of store modernization. The majority of Tastee-Freez franchises serve a complete menu of fast food, including breakfast, lunch, and dinner. In 2003 Tastee-Freez became a part of Galardi Group, Inc., of Newport Beach, California, which also owns the hot dog chain Wienerschnitzel. It has about 350 outlets in 22 western states, and 2 in Panama. In addition, Tastee-Freez desserts are now served in many Wienerschnitzel outlets.

See also Dairy Queen; Drive-Thrus; Hot Dog; Ice Cream; Kroc, Ray; McDonald's; Wienerschnitzel

For Further Information:

Funderburg, Anne Cooper. *Chocolate, Strawberry, and Vanilla: A History of American Ice Cream*. Bowling Green, OH: Bowling Green State University Popular Press, 1995.

Jakle, John A., and Keith A. Sculle. *Fast Food: Roadside Restaurants in the Automobile Age*. Baltimore: Johns Hopkins University Press, 1999.

Langdon, Philip. *Orange Roofs, Golden Arches: The Architecture of American Chain Restaurants*. New York: Knopf, 1986.

Tastee-Freez Web site: www.tastee-freez.com

Tasti D-Lite

Tasti D-Lite was launched in 1987 in New York City. Its signature dish, a frozen dessert, was promoted as a healthy, low-fat, lower-calorie alternative to soft-serve ice cream. Independent tests conducted for *New York Magazine* and the New York Department of Consumer Affairs found higher fat and calorie content. Tasti D-Lite's popularity soared in 2004 with appearances on episodes of *Sex and the City* and *The Apprentice*.

Most of Tasti-D-Lite's outlets are in New York State. In 2007 Tasti D-Lite was acquired by SPG Partners, LLC, a private equity group. The company is headquartered in Franklin, Tennessee.

See also Ice Cream

For Further Information:

Tasti D-Lite Web site: www.tastidlite.com

Tater Tots

Tater Tots is a registered trademark for a commercial form of deep-fried hash browns formed into small cakes and sold frozen. They are made from potato shreds, which are left over from french fry production. They were invented in 1953 by Golden and F. Nephi Grigg of the Ore-Ida (derived from abbreviations of Oregon and Idaho) Company, which is now a subsidiary of the H. J. Heinz Company. They first became available in stores in 1954.

The fast food chain Sonic Drive-In features Tater Tots as a standard menu item, with cheese and/or chili toppings. Burger King serves Cheesy Tots, which are thumb-shaped shredded potatoes with mozzarella and cheddar cheese inside. Various other names have been used for Tater Tots. Cascadian Farms has produced an organic version, called Spud Puppies, and Taco Time International has made Mexi-Fries (flavored with Mexican-style spices or stuffed with cheese and diced jalapeno peppers) since the 1960s, and Taco Bell served similarly flavored Mexi-Nuggets. Manufacturers outside the United States have produced similar products. Potato Gems, for instance, are sold in Australia, New Zealand, and the United Kingdom, while Tasti Taters are produced by McCain Foods in Canada.

Tater tots. (Andrea Skjold | Dreamstime.com)

In 2004 Tater Tots were popularized in the film *Napoleon Dynamite.* The Idaho state legislature was so pleased that it passed a resolution offering special praise for the movie. Today, Tater Tots are commonly found in school cafeterias and lunch counters, as well as in supermarket frozen food aisles. Americans consume approximately 70 million pounds of Tater Tots per year. Heinz has extended the line to include other similar commercial products. The Ore-Ida Brand is the nation's leading marketer of frozen potatoes.

See also Burger King; French Fries; McCain Foods; School Food; Sonic; Supermarkets

For Further Information:

Ore-Ida Web site: www.oreida.com

Smith, Andrew F. *Potato: A Global History*. London: Reaktion Books, 2011.

Taxing Junk Food

Concerned about the increasing health risks of obesity, some health advocates in the United States and the United Kingdom have proposed taxes on junk foods to make them more expensive, and thereby decrease some consumption and use the revenue to fund anti-obesity efforts and recover the costs of treating illness caused or exacerbated by obesity. California enacted a snack tax law in 1991, but it was repealed within a year because of administrative and bureaucratic problems. In 1994 E. K. Battle and Kelly Brownell, director of the Rudd Center on Food Policy & Obesity, proposed levying what they called a "fat tax" (also called a sin tax) on junk food and fast food, based on the specific food's contribution to obesity. Similarly, in an article in the *American Journal of Public Health* (2000) Michael Jacobson and Kelly Brownell argued for a small tax on soft drinks and fast foods.

Advocates believe that higher prices will change some consumers' diets in the same way that increased cigarette and alcohol taxes and higher prices have discouraged smoking and alcohol consumption. These taxes have also raised money for health and education programs about the effects of smoking and drinking alcohol. In the same way, a junk food tax could discourage consumption of high calories and low-nutrient foods, and the revenues generated by the taxes could be devoted to educating youth about eating healthy food, covering costs of fitness programs (especially for youth), and helping pay medical expenses related to diseases and illnesses associated obesity.

The food industry strongly opposes junk food taxes. To fight such taxes, junk food manufacturers, soft drink companies, and restaurant associations have created several organizations, such as Americans against Food Taxes and the Center for Consumer Freedom, which spent heavily on television advertising campaigns opposing all measures on junk food taxes. They believe that the government should stay out of private behavior, and that it should not try to regulate what people eat or drink. J. Justin Wilson, a senior research analyst at the food industry–funded Center for Consumer Freedom, states that "the government doesn't have the right to social engineer," or "to protect us from ourselves." Other opponents have claimed that junk food taxes are regressive—they will disproportionately hurt the poor and minorities, who spend a larger proportion of their income on food.

Proponents of taxing junk food believe that obesity is a regressive disease that disproportionately affects poor and minority populations. While everyone must eat, junk food is not a necessary part of the diet and generally delivers many calories with little or no nutrition. If junk food taxes will decrease consumption of junk food, the poor will benefit most.

Others have proposed taxing people who are overweight. Advocates for this believe that overweight people are personally responsible for their weight owing to their eating habits, and this ends up costing the nation billions of dollars for health care and in lost wages.

Denmark has increased the tax on junk food, and some evidence suggests that obesity among younger Danish children is falling for the first time in sixty years. Adult obesity, however, has continued to increase. Other European nations are considering doing the same. In the United States, fat taxes have been considered by several cities and states. Reports have been prepared on taxing junk and fast food by several states and the Economic Research Service at the U.S. Department of

Agriculture. To date, no fat tax has been levied, although seven states have imposed special taxes or fees on soda drinks, and ten states exclude certain junk food from exemptions for taxes on food. According to a report of the White House Task Force on Childhood Obesity, "The effectiveness of a junk food tax could depend on its severity. Studies of current state-levied soda taxes suggest that they haven't had much impact on adolescent or adult weight, but experts studying the impact of tobacco taxes think higher junk food tax rates could reduce consumption."

See also Brownell, Kelly D.; Calories; Jacobson, Michael L.; Obesity; Rudd Center on Food Policy & Obesity; U.S. Department of Agriculture

For Further Information:

Brownell, Kelly D., and Katherine Battle Hogan. *Food Fight: The Inside Story of the Food Industry, America's Obesity Crisis, and What We Can Do about It.* Chicago: Contemporary Books, 2004.

Brownell, Kelly D., and Thomas R. Frieden. "Ounces of Prevention: The Public Policy Case for Taxes on Sugared Beverages." *New England Journal of Medicine* 360 (2009): 1805–8.

Chriqui, Jamie F., et al. "State Sales Tax Rates for Soft Drinks and Snacks Sold through Grocery Stores and Vending Machines, 2007." *Journal of Public Health Policy* 29 (July 2008): 226–49.

Kuchler, Fred, Abebayehu Tegene, and J. Michael Harris. *Taxing Snack Foods What to Expect for Diet and Tax Revenues.* Washington, D.C.: Economic Research Service, U.S. Dept. of Agriculture, 2004.

Lohman, Judith S. *Taxes on Junk Food.* Hartford, CT: Connecticut General Assembly, Office of Legislative Research, 2002.

TCBY

In 1981 TCBY, which reportedly stands for "The Country's Best Yogurt," was launched by Frank and Georgia Hickingbotham in Little Rock, Arkansas. By 1985, the company had 242 stores in three southern states; four years later, this had increased to 1,582 stores. Beginning in the 1990s, the company began to offer its products in A&W Restaurants and CITGO convenience stores. It is the largest seller of frozen yogurt in the United States. Its signature dish is 10–16 flavors of soft-serve frozen yogurt, but it also sells cakes, pies, smoothies, and other products. Although many of its products are low calorie and low fat, others have a large number of calories and are high in fat.

In 2000 the company was acquired by Mrs. Fields Famous Brands. As of 2011, the company had six hundred stores.

See also A&W; Cakes; Mrs. Fields Famous Brands; Pie; Smoothies; Yogurt

For Further Information:
TCBY Web site: www.tcby.com

Teen Hangouts

During the late nineteenth and early twentieth centuries, teenagers gathered at soda fountains where ice cream, sodas, and light foods were served. With the development of drive-ins in the 1920s, and with increased availability of automobiles at about the same time, youth began to congregate at drive-ins. Because many carhops were scantily clad females who worked mainly or exclusively for tips, young men frequented drive-ins to flirt with the carhops.

Teenage boys did not purchase much food, and they occupied space in the parking lot. Teenagers congregating at drive-ins were occasionally rowdy, and this scared away many families who would have purchased food.

Two restaurateurs who were particularly upset with this were the brothers Richard and Maurice McDonald, owners of a drive-in in a Los Angeles suburb. Their solution was to eliminate the carhops and create a self-service restaurant to reduce the number of teenagers that would hang out. Customers bought the food at windows and returned to their cars before consuming it. To discourage flirting, McDonald's hire only male employees. McDonald's target audience was suburban families, and they did not want teenagers at their establishments. Their new model worked precisely as planned, and virtually every fast food chain initially followed their example.

There were no indoor eating places at fast food establishments during the 1950s and early 1960s. This changed in 1967, when Burger King created an indoor dining area; McDonald's followed the next year with a new restaurant design that included indoor dining. Teen hangouts moved from drive-ins to malls, convenience stores, and video game parlors.

See also Automobiles; Burger King; Carhops; Convenience Stores; Drive-Ins; Ice Cream; McDonald's; Soda/Soft Drinks; Soda Fountains

For Further Information:

Jakle, John A., and Keith A. Sculle. *Fast Food: Roadside Restaurants in the Automobile Age*. Baltimore: Johns Hopkins University Press, 1999.

Langdon, Philip. *Orange Roofs, Golden Arches: The Architecture of American Chain Restaurants*. New York: Knopf, 1986.

Levenstein, Harvey. *Paradox of Plenty: A Social History of Eating in Modern America*. New York: Oxford University Press, 1993.

Schlosser, Eric. *Fast Food Nation: The Dark Side of the All-American Meal*. New York: Houghton Mifflin Company, 2001.

Schremp, Gerry. *Kitchen Culture: Fifty Years of Food Fads, From Spam to Spa Cuisine*. New York: Pharos Books, 1991.

Television

Television technology had been perfected by the late 1930s, but monetary and technological demands during World War II stopped early experimentation. When the war ended, television burst on the scene, but few Americans could afford to buy television sets, and the quality was poor.

In the 1950s the price for televisions declined and the disposable income of many Americans increased, so that most middle-class families could afford television sets. By 1956, 40 million television sets were in American homes. By the end of the decade, 86 percent of American homes possessed one.

Many television programs have aired programs highlighting junk food and fast food. The Food Network's *Unwrapped*, *Heavyweights*, and *Cupcake Wars* series; the History Channel's *Modern Marvels* series; the Travel Channel's *Man vs. Food*; and the Discovery Channel's *How Stuff Works* include one or more episodes on fast foods, junk foods, cereals, and soft drinks.

Advertising

Snack food manufacturers were quick to understand the importance of this new medium. Beginning in the 1940s, snack food manufacturers began advertising on television. Many companies targeted children's television programs to sell their products. Today, about 75 percent of food manufacturers' advertising budget is allocated for television.

Fast food chains were slow to take advantage of television advertising. This changed in 1960 when the McDonald's franchise in Washington, D.C., decided to sponsor a local children's television program called *Bozo's Circus.* Sales in Washington grew by a whopping 30 percent per year during the next four years. Previously, McDonald's franchisees had not developed television commercials. Using a simple rhyme, Willard Scott came up with the name "Ronald McDonald" for the company icon he portrayed in the first company television commercials broadcast in October 1963, which are viewable on YouTube.

The national McDonald's Corporation decided to sponsor the broadcast of the Macy's Thanksgiving Day Parade in 1965. Previously, fast food chains had not advertised on national television, and it was a risk because McDonald's major sales were in the summertime, not in November. The Thanksgiving Day promotion produced immediate nationwide results, and this convinced McDonald's to expend more funds targeting children, giving McDonald's an edge in the children's market.

By 1970, hundreds of millions of dollars of corporate funds were spent on child-oriented television advertising. By 1977 it was estimated that children under age six watched more than 25 hours of television per week, and they viewed about 20,000 commercials per year. Television advertising for junk foods and fast foods increasingly targeted children. Television promotions had succeeded in making

Ronald McDonald identifiable by fully 96 percent of American children, second only to Santa Claus.

Many studies have been conducted on junk food and fast food advertising on television. On average, American children spend three-and-a-half hours watching television every day. Between 2003 and 2007, children's and adolescents' exposure to fast food commercials increased. Toys, cereals, candy, and snacks account for more than three-quarters of all advertisements shown on the Saturday morning schedules of the major American television networks. Another study determined that exposure to television commercials for junk food was directly related to elevated body mass indexes among children and teens. Another study published in 2009 found that children and adults eating junk food while watching television consumed 45 percent more when exposed to food advertising. The study concluded that the increased consumption was "not related to reported hunger or other conscious influences, and what's more, those in the experiment were unaware that the ads had influenced them."

A 2010 study recorded the ads on three major networks, then evaluated the nutritional content of the products promoted in the ads. The researchers concluded that a diet consisting of observed food items would provide 2,560 percent of the recommended daily servings for sugars and 2,080 percent of the recommended daily servings for fat, while under-supplying twelve nutrients: iron, phosphorus, vitamin A, carbohydrates, calcium, vitamin E, magnesium, copper, potassium, pantothenic acid, fiber, and vitamin D.

Recent Developments

The massive influence of television advertising is of particular concern to those interested in childhood obesity. In 2006 the Committee on Communication of the American Academy of Pediatrics reviewed the large literature on the effects of food advertising on children and reported that American children were exposed to 40,000 commercials on television annually and about half are half food, especially sugared cereals and high-calorie snacks. Nearly 20 percent of fast food ads mentioned giveaway toys. Several studies document that young children request more junk food after viewing commercials. Another study correlated the amount of television viewed per week with requests for specific foods and with calorie intake. The committee believed that such advertisements may have contributed significantly to childhood and adolescent obesity and poor nutrition.

A report issued by the Institute of Medicine of the National Academies in 2006 indicated there is compelling evidence linking food advertising on television and increased childhood obesity. A study published in 2008 concluded that banning junk food advertising on children's programs would reduce the number of overweight children ages 3–11 by 18 percent, and the authors projected that this would reduce the number of overweight adolescents ages 12–18 by 14 percent.

A study published in 2007 focused on advertising on Nickelodeon, an American cable television network that is aimed at children 6–14 years old. It found that 88 percent of the advertisements were for junk foods. Of the food products promoted on Nickelodeon programs, 94 percent were junk foods.

In addition, Nickelodeon licensed the rights of characters, such as SpongeBob SquarePants and Dora the Explorer, for use on food packaging, and the study concluded that 60 percent of these placements promoted junk foods. Shortly after the study was conducted, Nickelodeon announced that it would stop licensing its characters to junk food companies and would license them to produce companies to encourage healthier diets for children.

Another study published in 2008 of commercials aired on children's television on Saturday morning found that 49 percent were for food; of those, 91 percent were for foods or beverages high in fat, sodium, or added sugars, and low in nutrients. The most commonly advertised food categories were ready-to-eat breakfast cereal and cereal bars, fast food restaurants, and snack foods. Cartoon characters were used in 74 percent of food ads, and toy or other giveaways were used in 26 percent of food advertisements.

Watching television is not just correlated with weight gain at the time, it is also a predictor of eating habits five years later. A longitudinal study in 2009 concluded that television viewing in middle and high school predicted poorer dietary intake five years later. The authors believed that "television viewing, especially during high school, may have long-term effects on eating choices and contribute to poor eating habits in young adulthood."

In 2006 several major companies agreed to voluntarily reduce their advertising of unhealthy food targeted at children and adolescents. In 2010 researchers acquired data from the Nielsen Company to assess trends in television food advertising from 2002 through 2008 among children and adolescents. The good news was that children's exposure to all food advertising declined by 12 percent from its peak in 2004. The bad news was that fast food advertising to both children and adolescents increased from 2002 through 2008. In 2008, preschoolers saw 56 percent more ads for Subway, 21 percent more ads for McDonald's, and 9 percent more ads for Burger King than they did in the previous year. The researchers called for continued monitoring of food marketing exposure to assess the impact of recent pledges by U.S. food companies to reduce unhealthy marketing to children.

See also Advertising; Cartoon Characters; Center for Science in the Public Interest (CSPI); Children's Food and Beverage Advertising Initiative (CFBAI); McDonald's; *Modern Marvels*; Rudd Center for Food Policy & Obesity; Subway; *Unwrapped*

For Further Information:

Barr-Anderson, Daheia, et al. "Does Television Viewing Predict Dietary Intake Five Years Later in High School Students and Young Adults?" *International Journal of Behavioral Nutrition and Physical Activity* 6, no. 7 (January 30, 2009), as at: www.ijbnpa.org/content/6/1/7

Batada, Ameena, and Margo G. Wootan. "Nickelodeon Markets Nutrition-poor Foods to Children." *American Journal of Preventive Medicine* 33, no. 1 (2007): 48–50.

Batada, Ameena, et al. "Nine Out of 10 Food Advertisements Shown During Saturday Morning Children's Television Programming Are for Foods High in Fat, Sodium, or Added Sugars, or Low in Nutrients." *Journal of the American Dietetic Association* 108, no.4 (April 2008): 673–78.

Committee on Communications. "Children, Adolescents, and Advertising." *Pediatrics* 118 (December 2006): 2563–69.

Consumers Union Education Services. *Selling America's Kids: Commercial Pressures on Kids of the 90's.* Mount Vernon, NY: Consumers Union, 1990.

Consumers Union Web site: www.consumersunion.org/other/sellingkids/index.htm

Food Marketing to Children and Youth: Threat or Opportunity? Report of the Institute of Medicine of the National Academies Web site: books.nap.edu

Harris, Jennifer L., et al. "Priming Effects of Television Food Advertising on Eating Behavior." *Health Psychology* 28, no. 4 (2009): 404–13.

Harris, Jennifer L., et al. "Trends in Television Food Advertising: Progress in Reducing Unhealthy Marketing to Young People?" New Haven, CT: Rudd Center for Food Policy & Obesity, 2010) at: www.yaleruddcenter.org/resources/upload/docs/what/reports/Rudd ReportTVFoodAdvertising_2.10.pdf

Jacobson, Michael F., and Bruce Maxwell. *What Are We Feeding Our Kids?* New York: Workman Publishing, 1994.

Mink, Michael, et al. "Nutritional Imbalance Endorsed by Televised Food Advertisements." *Journal of the American Dietetic Association* 110 (June 2010): 904–10.

Thomas, Dave

Wendy's founder R. David Thomas (1932–2002) was born in Atlantic City, New Jersey. Six weeks later, he was adopted by Tex and Auleva Thomas of Kalamazoo, Michigan. At the age of twelve he was hired for a job at a barbecue restaurant in Knoxville, Tennessee. Four years later, he dropped out of high school to work at the Hobby House Restaurant in Fort Wayne, Indiana. After a stint in the Army, he returned to Hobby House. In 1954 he married Lorraine Buskirk, and their daughter Melinda Lou was nicknamed Wendy. Thomas worked at many jobs, including one at Arthur Treacher's fast food restaurant. He became the operations manager for three hundred regional KFC outlets, and he met Harland Sanders, who was one of the greatest influences in his life, according to his 1991 autobiography, *Dave's Way.* In 1962 Thomas took over four failing KFC restaurants in Columbus, Ohio. He acquired additional KFC outlets but sold them back to the company in 1968. He used his profits to open the first Wendy's restaurant the following year. Thomas relinquished day-to-day control over Wendy's International in 1982, when he became senior chairman. In 1989 Thomas began appearing in Wendy's advertisements, and he became an instant media star. In 1993 Thomas went back to school; he completed his GED three years later. Thomas wrote two inspirational books, *Dave's Way* (1991) and *Dave Says—Well Done!* (1994). From the profits he earned through Wendy's, he and his wife gave large sums to charities. He died in 2002 at age sixty-nine.

See also Arthur Treacher's; Corporate Charities; KFC; Sanders, Harland; Wendy's

For Further Information:

Austin, Steven J. "America's Favorite 'Hamburger Cook," *Mississippi 55 & Fine*. May–October, 1994: 4–7.

Thomas, R. David. *Dave's Way: A New Approach to Old-Fashioned Success*. New York: G. P. Putnam's Sons, 1991.

Thomas, R. David. *Dave Says—Well Done! The Common Guy's Guide to Everyday Success*. Grand Rapids, MI: Zondervan, 1994.

3 Musketeers

In 1932 Mars, Inc., introduced the 3 Musketeers bar, which is a chocolate-flavored nougat covered with milk chocolate. Compared with the company's Snickers bar, 3 Musketeers is sweeter and has more chocolate flavor. The company claims that the chocolate bar was named after its original composition: three pieces and three flavors—vanilla, chocolate, and strawberry. When the price of strawberries rose, the company dropped them as an ingredient. At the time, Alexandre Dumas's novel *The Three Musketeers* was a children's favorite and Mars, Inc., has used musketeer characters from the book in its advertising.

The 3 Musketeers bar is one of the best-selling Mars products. It was so successful that the company has created a 3 Musketeers product line, including 3 Musketeers Chocolate Flavored Chews composed of sugar, corn syrup, processed cocoa powder, and other ingredients.

See also Advertising; Candy; Chocolate; Mars, Inc.; Nougat; Snickers; Sugars/Sweeteners

For Further Information:

Brenner, Joël Glenn. *The Emperors of Chocolate: Inside the Secret World of Hershey and Mars*. New York: Broadway Books, 2000.

Broekel, Ray. *The Great America Candy Bar Book*. Boston: Houghton Mifflin Company, 1982.

Pottker, Janice. *Crisis in Candyland: Melting the Chocolate Shell of the Mars Family Empire*. Bethesda, MD: National Press Books, 1995.

Richardson, Tim. *Sweets: A History of Candy*. New York: Bloomsbury, 2002.

3 Musketeers Web site: www.3musketeers.com

Tic Tacs

Tic Tacs, tiny, white-colored, mint-flavored candies in a small plastic container, were developed by the Ferrero Company, an Italian candy maker, in 1969. Their success in the United States was almost immediate. Grocery and convenience stores and many other foodservice operations began to sell them at their checkout counters. They were sugar-free and had fewer calories than did other breath mints, such as Breathsavers, produced by the Hershey Company, or Velamints, produced by the German company Ragold. New flavors and colors were added beginning in the 1970s. Today, a wide variety of Tic Tac flavors and colors are sold.

See also Convenience Stores; Ferrero Company; Hershey Company

For Further Information:

Dougherty, Philip H. "Advertising; Tic Tac's Turnaround." *New York Times*, April 19, 1982, as at: www.nytimes.com/1982/04/19/business/advertising-tic-tac-s-turnaround.html?sc p=1&sq=Advertising%3B+Tic+Tac%27s+Turnaround&st=nyt

Tic Tac USA Web site: tictacusa.com

Tim Hortons, Inc.

Tim Horton, a hall-of-fame Canadian hockey player, opened his first restaurant in Hamilton, Ontario, in 1964. It was known for its coffee—which was guaranteed to be served fresh—cappuccinos, doughnuts, and donut holes, but it quickly incorporated other items, such as a wide array of baked goods, specialty teas, sandwiches, soups, wraps, and ice cream. Tim Horton died in a car accident in 1974; at the time the company had forty franchises. It quickly expanded during the 1980s, and it became Canada's largest fast food operation.

In 1995 Tim Hortons merged with Wendy's, and it began to open outlets in the United States. In 2006 Tim Hortons was spun off from Wendy's and is today a publically traded company.

As of 2011, Tim Hortons had more than 3,670 systemwide restaurants, including 3,083 in Canada and about 587 outlets in the United States. The company has recently made an agreement to open more kiosks in Canadian Esso service stations. It is Canada's largest fast food chain and the fourth largest publically traded fast food chain in North America based on capitalization. It is headquartered in Oakdale, Ontario.

See also Canada; Coffee; Doughnuts/Donuts; Sandwiches; Service Stations; Wendy's

For Further Information:

Tim Hortons Web site: www.timhortons.com

Toblerone

In 1908 Theodore Tobler and his production manager, Emil Baumann, invented the Toblerone bar in Bern, Switzerland. It is an unusual triangular-shaped chocolate bar with almond and honey nougat. The name derives from Tobler (the name of the company and family) and *torrone*, an Italian nougat specialty. In 1970 the Tobler Company merged with the Jacobs Suchard Company of Switzerland, which became one of the largest chocolate companies in the world. In 1990 Kraft General Foods International acquired Jacobs Suchard, including the Toblerone brand. Today, Toblerone is sold in 120 countries (more countries than any other Kraft brand).

See also Chocolate; Kraft Foods

For Further Information:

Toblerone Web site: www.kraft.com/archives/brands/brands_toblerone.html

Toffee

Toffee probably originated in England in the mid-eighteenth century, when it was consumed mainly by children. It was made by caramelizing sugar or molasses, butter, and possibly orange, lemon, chocolate, or vanilla flavoring. From this basic recipe, two different candies emerged. If it were removed from the heat just as it reached the "hard ball" stage, cooled, placed on a hook and pulled, stretched, and folded by hand until stiff, it became the chewy confection we now call taffy. If the mixture were boiled to the "hard crack" stage, it became a hard candy—what is now called "toffee." It comes in a variety of textures, from semi-soft and sticky to hard. In the United States, English toffee is more buttery and it includes almonds. Today, toffee varieties often add other products, such as apples, bananas, chocolate, honeycomb, peanuts, and pecans. Toffee is also used in making other junk foods. Heath bars, Fiddle Faddle, Almond Roca, and peanut brittle include toffee as an ingredient, and toffee bits are frequently added to ice cream and sweet popcorn.

See also Candy; Heath Bar; Peanut Brittle; Sweet Popcorn; Taffy

Togo's

Togo's is a fast-casual restaurant chain that specializes in sandwiches. It was launched by a college student in 1971 in San Jose, California. As it offered sandwiches "to go," it was named Togo's, or so the story goes. In 1997 Allied Domecq Retailing USA, which included Baskin-Robbins and Dunkin' Donuts, acquired Togo's. This connection permitted the chain to open outlets in Baskin-Robbins and

Dunkin' Donuts outlets. In 2007 Togo's was sold to equity investors. Today, Togo's has 240 restaurants and the company is headquartered in San Diego.

See also Baskin-Robbins; Dunkin' Donuts; Fast Casual; Sandwiches

For Further Information:

Togo's Web site: www.togos.com

Tomatoes

Tomatoes are a common ingredient in fast food operations. Sliced tomatoes are used on hamburgers or in salads; diced tomatoes are used in tacos and other fast foods. Tomatoes are also converted into condiments, such as ketchup and salsa. About 80 percent of the processed tomatoes are grown in California, while the bulk of the fresh winter tomatoes are grown in Florida. Tomatoes that are to be used in canning, or for ketchup or bottled salsa, are all picked by machine. Fresh tomatoes, such as those sold in supermarkets or those used in making hamburgers and tacos, must be picked by hand. Farm workers who do the picking are mainly migrant workers, and several exposés about the working and living conditions of migrant farm workers have been produced. They are paid about 50 cents for every 32-pound bucket they fill. Workers earn an estimated $10,000 to $12,000 per year.

In 1996 the migrant workers formed the Coalition of Immokalee Workers (CIW), which attempted to change working and living conditions and pay for the tomato pickers. They were opposed by the Florida Tomato Growers Exchange, an industry lobby group whose members control 90 percent of the winter tomato crop. To gain visibility for the plight of the workers, in 2001 the CIW called for a national boycott of Taco Bell, one of the largest buyers of winter tomatoes. College, high school, and religious groups, including the National Council of Churches, joined the boycott against Taco Bell. In 2005 Taco Bell agreed to pay 1 cent more per pound for its tomatoes, provided that the money went to improving working and living conditions of the workers.

During the following five years, nine major food brands, including Yum! Brands (owner of Pizza Hut), McDonald's, Burger King, Whole Foods Market, and Subway, agreed to pay the 1 cent extra per pound, but the Florida tomato growers refused to participate. In November 2010 the growers finally agreed to a Fair Food Code of Conduct. Funds generated by this agreement will increase workers' pay to an estimated $17,000 per year and will be used to help educate farm laborers as to their rights and how to report violations, including sexual harassment of women workers, and it provides for a third-party system to help resolve disputes.

See also Anti-Unionization; Burger King; Condiments; Hamburger; Ketchup; McDonald's; Pizza Hut; Salads; Subway; Supermarkets; Taco Bell; Tacos; Yum! Brands, Inc.

For Further Information:

Smith, Andrew F. *The Tomato in America: Early History, Culture and Cookery*. Urbana: University of Illinois Press, 2001.

Tombstone Pizza

In the early 1960s, Joseph, Ronald, Frances, and Joan Simek owned the Tombstone Bar, a small country tavern across the street from a cemetery in Medford, Wisconsin. In 1962 they began making small pizzas for their customers, and they expanded to making frozen pizza in a small factory next to their tavern for distribution to other bars and taverns. Demand was high, so they opened factories in Medford and Sussex, Wisconsin. Kraft Foods bought the operation from the Simek family in 1986. During the 1990s, Tombstone Pizza became America's top-ranked frozen pizza, which was partly owing to television commercials. One particularly successful commercial aired in 1995, featuring an eighteenth-century French aristocrat who, for his last wish, asks for a Tombstone Pizza with cheese and pepperoni; a falling guillotine blade slices the pizza. In 2001 Kraft extended its Tombstone Pizza line with a Mexican-style pizza. In 2010 Kraft sold Tombstone to Nestlé.

See also Kraft Foods; Nestlé; Pizza, Frozen; Television

For Further Information:

Kraft Foods Web site: www.kraftfoods.com

Tommy's

Tommy's is a small, iconic hamburger chain that was launched by Tommy Koulax, the son of Greek immigrants, in 1946. Its first stand was a small one at Beverly and Rampart Boulevards in Los Angeles. It popularized the "chili-burger." It also sells a variety of other products, including chili-fries, hot dogs, breakfast burritos, and tamales. The clientele included movie stars as well as a number of international visitors. Koulax began to expand his operation in the 1960s, and as of 2011, it had thirty outlets, mainly in Southern California. Koulax died in 1992, but the company remains under family control.

See also Hamburgers

For Further Information:

Folkart, Burt A. "Tommy Koulax, Builder of Hamburger Chain, Dies." *Los Angeles Times*, May 29, 1992, as at: http://articles.latimes.com/1992-05-29/local/me-140_1_tommy-koulax

Original Tommy's World Famous Hamburgers Web site: www.originaltommys.com

Tootsie Roll Industries

In the late nineteenth century, the word "tootsie" was slang for a girl or sweetheart. Leo Hirschfeld, an Austrian immigrant, invented a number of machines, several related to making candy. In the 1890s he joined the firm that became Stern & Saalberg, a New York candy manufacturer. In 1908 Stern & Saalberg launched a new chocolate caramel that was small, log-shaped, and chewy. Supposedly Hirschfeld named the candy after his daughter, Clara, who was nicknamed Tootsie. Unlike other penny candy, the Tootsie Roll was individually wrapped. In 1917 the company was renamed the Sweets Company of America and it began advertising nationally. It extended its original Tootsie Roll line to include Tootsie, Nut Rolls, Tootsie Kisses, and Tootsie Caramels. In 1931 the company introduced the Tootsie Pop, which had a hard candy shell and a soft center on a stick. During the Depression, it ran into financial troubles, and the company was eventually acquired by William Rubin, owner of the company that supplied packaging to the Sweets Company of America.

During World War II, Tootsie Rolls were placed in soldiers' ration kits, mainly because the hard candy could survive various climatic conditions. After the war, the company was one of the first to target its advertising toward youth, by sponsoring popular children's television shows such as *Howdy Doody*, *Rin Tin Tin*, *Rocky & Bullwinkle*, and the *Mickey Mouse Club*.

The Sweets Company of America's name was changed to Tootsie Roll Industries in 1966, and the company began to expand its operations abroad, first into the Philippines and Southeast Asia, and later into Canada and Mexico. In 1991 Tootsie Roll Industries acquired the Charms Company, America's largest lollipop manufacturer and maker of Charms Blow Pop. Two years later, it acquired Warner-Lambert's chocolate and caramel division, which included Junior Mints, Sugar Daddy, Sugar Babies, and the Charleston Chew.

In 2004 Tootsie Roll Industries acquired Concord Confections, headquartered in Toronto, Canada, which was a leader in manufacturing gum, such as Double Bubble and Razzles. Tootsie Roll Industries is headquartered in Chicago.

See also Advertising; Caramels; Charleston Chew!; Chocolate; Junior Mints; Lollipops/Suckers; Razzles

For Further Information:

Brenner, Joël Glenn. *The Emperors of Chocolate: Inside the Secret World of Hershey and Mars*. New York: Broadway Books, 2000.

Broekel, Ray. *The Great America Candy Bar Book*. Boston: Houghton Mifflin Company, 1982.

Candy Professor Web site: candyprofessor.com

Richardson, Tim. *Sweets: A History of Candy*. New York: Bloomsbury, 2002.

Tootsie Roll Industries Web site: www.tootsie.com

Tostadas

Tostadas served in the United States derive from Mexican culinary traditions. They are composed of flat, hard, or toasted tortillas, either corn or wheat, with various toppings, such as cheese and beans. They are served in many Mexican American fast food chains, such as Del Taco and Taco Bell.

See also Del Taco; Mexican American Food; Taco Bell

For Further Information:

Smith, Andrew F. "Tacos, Enchiladas and Refried Beans: The Invention of Mexican-American Cookery." In Mary Wallace Kelsey and ZoeAnn Holmes, eds., *Cultural and Historical Aspects of Foods*. Corvallis: Oregon State University, 1999, 183–203.

Toys

America's first commercial confection, Cracker Jack, targeted children from its earliest days. The problem was how to reach children at a time before radio and television. The company advertised in children's magazines but it needed something better. Beginning in 1910, it began inserting into every package of Cracker Jack a coupon that could be redeemed for three hundred "varieties of handsome and useful articles, such as Watches, Jewelry, Silverware, Sporting Goods, Toys, Games, Sewing Machines and many other useful Household articles." Later, rather than spending time to fulfill the requests for coupon redemptions, the company took the radical step of including a children's toy in every package. This was so successful that within two years the company had inserted more than five hundred different toys in boxes. These toys were certainly one reason why Cracker Jack became America's top commercial confection and, shortly thereafter, became popular in other nations, as well. More than 23 billion toys have been given out since 1912.

McDonald's was the first fast food chain to discover the importance of toys. During the 1970s, the company concluded that its major target audience was children. To reach this audience, McDonald's developed the Happy Meal, which was launched in 1979. It linked with manufacturers to produce low-cost toys, which were then given away with children's meals. McDonald's also distributed more expensive toys, which it sold at a discount. In 1997 McDonald's launched a promotion that included a Teenie Beanie Baby in its Happy Meals. Customers waited in long lines to get Happy Meals with Teenie Beanie Babies inside. This campaign is considered one of the most successful promotions in the history of advertising. Before the promotion, McDonald's sold 10 million Happy Meals per month; during the promotion, Happy Meal sales increased to 100 million per month. It was so successful that McDonald's conducted a similar promotion the following year.

Toys are often related to movie tie-ins. For instance, in 2006 McDonald's offered toys based on characters from the new Walt Disney Pictures/Walden Media film *The Chronicles of Narnia: The Lion, the Witch and the Wardrobe* in Happy Meals and Mighty Kids Meals. Today, McDonald's is the nation's largest distributor of toys. Other fast food chains followed McDonald's lead and have given away or sold inexpensive toys along with their kids' meals.

Burger King has recently partnered with Marvel Enterprises, Inc., a subsidiary of the Walt Disney Company, to distribute Marvel-related merchandise—from toys based on Marvel's Super Hero Squad to Marvel movies, such as *Thor* and *Captain America—The First Avenger*.

Toys manufactured for junk food, fast food, and soda companies have become sought after as collectibles. Clubs have developed around them and many such toys are important sales items on the Internet.

In 2006 the fast food industry spent more than $360 million on toys to sell more than 1.2 billion meals to kids under the age of twelve. According to the Federal Trade Commission, these toy giveaways were the second highest youth expenditure by the industry after television advertising ($745 million).

As concern has grown about childhood obesity, critics have focused attention on the toys given away with non-nutritious kids' meals. In 2010 Santa Clara County passed an ordinance setting standards for restaurant toy giveaways. In November 2010 San Francisco's city supervisors voted to ban the inclusion of toys in fast food meals unless the meals contained fewer than six hundred calories, included vegetables and fruit, and met other nutritional standards. San Francisco's mayor vetoed the bill, claiming that "doing these types of toy bans is inappropriate, I don't think particularly effective, and I just think goes way too far in inserting government to try to be the decision-maker in someone's life as opposed to parents." The city supervisors thought otherwise and overrode the mayor's veto. Other cities are also considering banning toys.

In December 2010 the Center for Science in the Public Interest (CSPI) filed a class action lawsuit against McDonald's, claiming that the company used toys in its Happy Meals as "bait" used to lure children into gorging on "unhealthy junk food." Michael Jacobson, the executive director of CSPI, said "multi-billion-dollar corporations make parents' job nearly impossible by giving away toys and bombarding kids with slick advertising."

See also Advertising; Burger King; Center for Science in the Public Interest (CSPI); Cracker Jack; Happy Meals; Lawsuits; McDonald's; Movie Tie-ins; Obesity; Radio; Television

For Further Information:

Cross, Gary S. *Kids' Stuff: Toys and the Changing World of American Childhood.* Cambridge, MA: Harvard University Press, 1997.

Dobrow, Larry. "It's All about the Toys." *Advertising Age* 76 (July 25, 2005): S14.

Losonsky, Joyce, and Terry Losonsky. *McDonald's Happy Meal Toys around the World.* Atglen, PA: Schiffer Publishing, 1995.

Losonsky, Joyce, and Terry Losonsky. *McDonald's Pre-Happy Meal Toys from the Fifties, Sixties, and Seventies.* Atglen, PA: Schiffer Publishing, 1998.

Losonsky, Joyce, and Terry Losonsky. *The Encyclopedia of Fast Food Toys.* 2 vols. Atglen, PA: Schiffer Pub., 1999.

Marketing Food to Children and Adolescents: A Review of Industry Expenditures, Activities and Self-Regulation. Washington, D.C.: Federal Trade Commission, 2008, as at: www.ftc.gov/os/2008/07/P064504foodmktingreport.pdf

Markowski, Carol, Tom Hoder, Tom Schwartz, and Tom Tumbusch. *Tomart's Price Guide to Character & Promotional Glasses Including Pepsi, Coke, Fast-Food, Peanut Butter and Jelly Glasses; Plus Dairy Glasses & Milk.* Dayton, OH: Tomart Publications, 1990.

Piña, Ravi. *Cracker Jack Collectibles with Price Guide.* Atglen, PA: Schiffer Publishing, 1995.

Schlosser, Eric. *Fast Food Nation: The Dark Side of the All-American Meal.* New York: Houghton Mifflin Company, 2001.

Stoddard, Bob. *The Encyclopedia of Pepsi-Cola Collectibles.* Iola, WI: Krause Publications, 2002.

White, Larry. *Cracker Jack Toys: The Complete, Unofficial Guide for Collectors.* Atglen, PA: Schiffer Publishing, 1997.

Training

A major problem confronting the fast food industry has been the rapid turnover of employees, most of whom last only a few weeks or months before quitting. Fast food chains have consistently tried to routinize their operations into a system of very simple rules, such as what activities employees should perform and how they should greet customers. Strict regimentation creates standardized products and ways of operating. Work is broken into tasks that can be performed by an average worker with a minimum of training. The products are produced in assembly-line fashion, following the industrial model popularized by Henry Ford's automobile assembly-line methods.

Fast food chains have consistently tried to automate their operations so there is little need to train employees. Kitchens are full of buzzers and flashing lights that tell employees what to do. Computerized cash registers issue their own directions. Hence, new employees require little training, and when they leave there is not a great loss.

Fast food chains have spent considerable time training managerial staff. In 1949 ice cream maker Thomas Carvel of the Carvel Corporation launched the Carvel College of Ice Cream Knowledge (affectionately known as the Sundae School) to help franchisees understand the business. McDonald's followed a similar path when it established Hamburger University in 1961. This is a managerial training center that trains managers on how to deal with personnel issues, improve teamwork, and increase employee motivation. It promotes a common McDonald's culture. Those who complete the program receive a Degree in Hamburgerology. Later, Burger King established Whopper College in 1963 in Miami.

The critic Eric Schlosser reported in *Fast Food Nation* (2001) that fast food chains obtain funds from federal job training programs, even though the chains provide a minimum of training. He called for the elimination of these subsidies and tax breaks for fast food chains.

See also Burger King; Carvel Corporation; Fast Food; *Fast Food Nation*; Hamburger University; McDonald's

For Further Information:

Jakle, John A., and Keith A. Sculle. *Fast Food: Roadside Restaurants in the Automobile Age*. Baltimore: Johns Hopkins University Press, 1999.

Schlosser, Eric. *Fast Food Nation: The Dark Side of the All-American Meal*. New York: Houghton Mifflin Company, 2001.

Transfats

Transfats are commonly defined as hydrogenated vegetable oil. Transfats are unsaturated fats that studies have shown increase low-density lipoprotein (LDL), or "bad" cholesterol, and decrease high-density lipoprotein (HDL), or "good" cholesterol. Transfats increase the amount of saturated fat that raises blood cholesterol, clogs arteries, and increases the risk of heart disease. Transfats are commonly found in a wide variety of junk foods and fast foods, such as peanut butter, french fries, potato chips, commercial cookies, bakery goods, and microwave popcorn, which provide about 13 percent of transfat. In 2003 the FDA required food labels to include transfat content.

Transfats have generated lawsuits. Steven Joseph, a lawyer, became convinced that transfats were unhealthy. In 2003 he launched a campaign, "Ban Trans Fat: The Campaign to Ban Partially Hydrogenated Oils," and commenced lawsuits against Kraft and McDonald's over the presence of transfats in their foods. Joseph sought an injunction against Kraft for their use of transfats in Oreos. Kraft agreed to reduce or eliminate transfat from their products. McDonald's had previously announced that it would switch to a different frying oil, but it had not done so. Joseph sued McDonald's for failing to notify the public that the switch had not taken place. McDonald's agreed to pay $8.5 million, with some of the money going to the American Heart Association. In 2007 the Center for Science in the Public Interest (CSPI) brought suit against Burger King to stop using transfats; Burger King pledged to phase out transfats by November 1, 2008.

The Grocery Manufacturers Association reported that between 2002 and 2009, corporations have reformulated many products and the most commonly reported change has been reduction or elimination of transfats, followed by reducing or eliminating saturated fats. The World Health Organization confirmed that world-wide some companies have removed or reduced transfats from many popular foods. Several American companies have reported doing so. Au Bon Pain, for instance, has successfully eliminated transfats from its products. Frito-Lay has eliminated transfats from its Doritos, and Pepperidge Farm's Goldfish are now made without transfats. Other companies, such as the International House of Pancakes and KFC, have announced plans to cut transfats nationwide.

Products that are labeled "zero transfats," however, may contain transfats, as the United States Food and Drug Administrations has defined "0" as anything with less than 0.5 grams of transfats per serving. As dietary guidelines recommend consuming no more than 1.11 grams of transfats per day, it is difficult for even the most conscientious label readers to know if they have consumed more than this amount.

While it is good that many junk food manufacturers and fast food chains are eliminating transfats from their products, the same companies are often replacing the transfats with saturated fats and interesterified fat (IE), which also increases LDL and decreases HDL.

The reason why many fast food chains and junk food manufacturers continue to use transfats is that they are much cheaper than alternative unsaturated oils. Products with lower transfats and saturated fat cost more, and in junk food and fast food, lower-cost items sell more.

In 2005 McDonald's settled a lawsuit concerning its use of transfats in baked goods and the oil it used in deep-frying its french fries, agreeing to pay $7 million to the American Heart Association and to spend another $1.5 million for a public advertising campaign alerting the public to the dangers of transfats. In 2008 McDonald's began cooking its fries and other items with no transfat oil.

In 2007 New York City banned the use of most transfats in foods sold in restaurants and bakeries in the city. In 2010 California partially banned transfats, effective in 2011.

See also Au Bon Pain; Bakery Goods; Center for Science in the Public Interest (CSPI); Cookies; Fat, Dietary; Food and Drug Administration (FDA); French Fries; Frito-Lay; KFC; Pancakes; Peanut Butter; Popcorn; Potato Chips; World Health Organization (WHO)

For Further Information:

Ban Trans Fat; The Campaign to Ban Partially Hydrogenated Oils Web site: BanTrafsfat. com

Brandt, Eric J. "Deception of Trans Fats on Food and Drug Administration Food Labels: Proposed Revision to the Presentation of Trans Fats on Food Labels." *American Journal of Health Promotion* 25 (January/February 2011): 157–58.

Nishida1, C., and R. Uauy. "WHO Scientific Update on Health Consequences of Trans Fatty Acids." *European Journal of Clinical Nutrition* 63 (May 2009): S1–S4.

Stanfield, Maggie. *Transfats: The Killer in the Kitchen.* London: Souvenir, 2008.

World Health Organization Web site: www.who.int

Turkey Burgers

The turkey industry had a problem in the mid-twentieth century. Nearly 80 percent of the turkeys that they raised were sold in November and December for Thanksgiving and the Christmas holidays. In order to increase sales of turkey meat throughout the year, the industry began promoting a variety of other products, such as turkey bacon, sausages, and other processed food, that could be sold year-round, thus increasing profits.

One new turkey product was ground turkey, which was sold like hamburger. It could be used to make a variety of dishes, such as meatballs and turkey burgers. The advantage was that turkey burgers had less fat than did hamburgers. The disadvantage was that they were often dry and tasteless, and their beige color was unappetizing for those who loved hamburger. The industry solution was to add both white and dark meat—this combination added some color, fat, and calories, but turkey burger was still lower in fat than traditional hamburger.

Turkey burgers were discovered by home cooks and dieters during the 1970s and slowly became part of American cuisine. Restaurants began selling turkey burgers as a diet dish. Fast food chains caught on, and White Castle and Carl's Jr. have sold turkey burgers as part of their menus.

See also White Castle

For Further Information:

Smith, Andrew F. *The Turkey: An American Story*. Urbana: University of Illinois Press, 2009.

Twinkie Defense

At the 1979 trial of Daniel White, who admitted to the murders of San Francisco mayor George Moscone and supervisor Harvey Milk, White claimed that he should be absolved of his crime because of impaired mental capacity resulting from compulsive eating of too much junk food, such as Twinkies, candy bars, cupcakes, and Coke, which caused a chemical imbalance in his brain. White said he murdered because of his abnormally high blood sugar. This was a novel defense. White was still convicted, although he was given a relatively short sentence of five years. He served only two years of his sentence and was paroled. Called "the most hated man in San Francisco," White committed suicide in 1985.

In 1981 Congress outlawed the "Twinkie Defense." While many people are convinced that children's behavior is influenced by the large amounts of sweets they consume, little scholarly proof has been offered for this assertion.

See also Junk Foods; Sugars/Sweeteners; Twinkies

For Further Information:

Ettlinger, Steve. *Twinkies, Deconstructed*. New York: Hudson Street Press, March 2007.

Twinkies

In the 1920s the Continental Baking Company began making sponge cakes that were mainly used for strawberry shortcake. At the time, strawberries were only in season during the summer, and hence their shortcakes were sold only during that time. The company sought ideas for products that could be sold year-round. About 1930 Jimmy Dewar, a Chicago bakery manager working for Continental, came up with a banana creme–filled cake that could be sold year-round at the price of two for a nickle. Dewar claimed that he named the new product Twinkies after he saw an advertisement for the Twinkle Toe Shoe Company on a trip to St. Louis. Twinkies' popularity increased, such that they became the best-selling snack cake in the United States after World War II.

During World War II, it was difficult to acquire imported bananas. The Continental Baking Company substituted a vanilla creme filling, which has been used in Twinkies ever since. During the 1950s, the company advertised Twinkies extensively, particularly on children's television programs such as the *Howdy Doody Show*, and Twinkies sales greatly increased.

Hostess Twinkies. (AP/Wide World Photos)

Twinkies became a cultural icon. They have inspired a cartoon character (Twinkie the Kid) and have appeared in many movies, such as *Grease* (1978), *Ghostbusters* (1984), and *Sleepless in Seattle* (1993).

When health advocates argued for a tax on the sale of junk and fast foods, they called it a "fat tax" or a "Twinkie tax." Deep-Fried Twinkies became a cult favorite during the 1990s. In 1999 the White House Millennium Council selected Twinkies as one of the items to be preserved in the Nation's Millennium Time Capsule, representing "an object of enduring American symbolism." The manufacturer, Hostess, produces more than 500 million Twinkies a year.

See also Advertising; Cartoon Characters; Fast Food Diet; Hostess Brands; Twinkie Defense

For Further Information:

Ettlinger, Steve. *Twinkies, Deconstructed*. New York: Hudson Street Press, March 2007.

Gong, Leo. *The Twinkies Cookbook: An Inventive and Unexpected Recipe Collection from Hostess*. Berkeley, CA: 10 Speed Press, 2006.

Twinkies Web site: www.twinkies.com

Twitter

Twitter is a social media and blogging Web site created by Jack Dorsey in 2006. As of 2011, 1 billion tweets were posted each week. Virtually all fast food and junk food companies have a presence on Twitter.

According to the Rudd Center for Food Policy & Obesity, the fast food chains with the most Twitter followers in 2010 are Starbucks, Dunkin' Donuts, McDonald's, Taco Bell, Pizza Hut, Subway, KFC, Dominos, Wendy's, Dairy Queen, Burger King, and Sonic.

As many Twitter users are children and young adults, companies have used Twitter to promote their products. For instance, Fanta, a Coca-Cola brand, began offering $40 to adolescents to plug their products on Twitter and other social networking media.

See also Burger King; Dairy Queen; Domino's Pizza; KFC; McDonald's; Pizza Hut; Rudd Center for Food Policy & Obesity; Social Media; Sonic; Starbucks; Taco Bell; Wendy's

For Further Information:

Fitton, Laura, Michael Gruen, and Leslie Poston. *Twitter for Dummies*. Indianapolis, IN: Wiley Pub., Inc., 2009.

Funk, Tom. *Social Media Playbook for Business: Reaching Your Online Community with Twitter, Facebook, LinkedIn, and More*. Santa Barbara, CA: Praeger, 2011.

Miller, Michael. *Introduction to Social Networking*. Boston: Prentice Hall, 2011.

Rudd Center for Food Policy & Obesity FACTS Web site: fastfoodmarketing.org

Twitter Web site: twitter.com

U

Uniforms

During the 1970s, Billy Ingram, owner of White Castle, the nation's first fast food chain, faced many problems, one of which was the reputation of hamburger stands as being greasy, unclean, and unhealthy. To overcome these widespread perceptions, he required all employees to maintain strict standards of cleanliness. At first he did not require employees to wear uniforms, but he did require them to wear white shirts. Eventually, uniforms were required for all employees. The company supplied white wool caps, which shrank when they were washed. Then Ingram hit upon the idea of using white paper caps, which did not have to be washed and could be easily replaced. Over time, White Castle altered its uniforms to conform with changing fashions.

The pattern started by White Castle has been followed by other fast food chains. McDonald's, for instance, initially required all employees to be dressed in white. Its uniforms have remained standard, but they have shifted to specific uniforms for different outlets, thus reinforcing the image that the chain wished to convey. In addition to a clean appearance, uniforms give the outlet a semimilitary appearance, reflecting good management and excellent organization, and create an egalitarian working atmosphere untroubled by the latest fashions.

Many drive-ins also required uniforms, but they were just the opposite of those developed by White Castle and other fast food chains. Rather than being plain and white, drive-in uniforms were often gaudy and flamboyant. Carhops, for instance, were often required to wear bright uniforms, military-style caps, and pants with stripes down the side. Others were required to wear costumes similar to those worn by movie ushers. Still others dressed women in sexually suggestive majorette costumes with white boots and abbreviated skirts.

See also Carhops; Drive-Ins; Hamburger; McDonald's; White Castle

For Further Information:

Jakle, John A., and Keith A. Sculle. *Fast Food: Roadside Restaurants in the Automobile Age*. Baltimore: Johns Hopkins University Press, 1999.

Langdon, Philip. *Orange Roofs, Golden Arches: The Architecture of American Chain Restaurants*. New York: Knopf, 1986.

Unilever

Unilever was formed in 1930, when the Dutch margarine company Margarine Unie merged with British soap maker Lever Brothers. The resulting Anglo-Dutch multinational corporation has acquired many food companies. In the United States, these include Ben & Jerry's, Slim-Fast, Hellmann's, Birds Eye, Good Humor, Breyers, and Gold Bond Ice Cream, makers of Popsicles and Good Humor, Dove, and Klondike bars.

See also Ben & Jerry's; Breyers; Dove Bar; Good Humor; Ice Cream; Klondike Bars

For Further Information:
Unilever Web site: www.unilever.com

United Kingdom

American soft drinks, cereal, and junk food companies have been operating in the United Kingdom since the early twentieth century. By 1936, Coca-Cola had expanded to the United Kingdom. Coca-Cola tried to introduce its Dasani water into the United Kingdom in 2002, and the campaign flopped.

Fast Food

McDonald's was not the first American hamburger chain in England. That honor goes to the Wimpy Grill. In 1953 its founder, Eddie Gold, offered the UK rights to Joseph Lyons and Co., of London, which had operated a chain of tearooms called Lyons Corner Houses since 1894. On a trial basis, Lyons opened a Wimpy counter in its Coventry Street Corner House in London. It was perfect timing on Lyons' part. The American military had introduced hamburger culture into Britain during World War II. By the early 1950s, beef rationing had ended and the British public was open to a new, inexpensive food from America. When Lyons offered Wimpy burgers at the Ideal Home Exhibition in 1954, they sold an average of ten thousand burgers a week. Lyons finalized the arrangement with Gold and began opening Wimpy restaurants. Unlike the fast food chains that were developing in the United States, Wimpy served their burgers on a plate, with cutlery, and orders were delivered to the table by waiters. In 1957 Lyons created a subsidiary company, called Pleasure Foods, Ltd., to franchise Wimpy Bars throughout the United Kingdom.

The Wimpy chain did well and hundreds of outlets were opened. In 1958 Gold and Lyons created Wimpy International to promote the chain outside of the United States and the United Kingdom. During the following decades, Wimpy outlets were opened in other countries, but its greatest success outside of the United States and the United Kingdom was in South Africa, where the company opened its first outlet in Durban in 1967. The chain has thrived in South Africa ever since.

McDonald's opened its first restaurant in London in 1974. McCafés are separate areas within McDonald's restaurants that sell pastries, premium coffee, mocha frappes, and cappuccinos. Its intent was to compete with the wildly successful Starbucks franchises, but the McCafé was less expensive. McDonald's slowly introduced McCafés into its restaurants in Europe. Store revenues jumped an estimated 20–25 percent with the addition of a McCafé. As of 2011, there were about 1,200 McCafés and more are in the planning stage.

Burger King also opened restaurants in the United Kingdom. In 1989 the company was acquired by the British conglomerate Grand Metropolitan and its successor, Diageo. Burger King's operations were expanded throughout the United Kingdom. Not every new menu item introduced by Burger King has been successful. Its limited edition Sprout Surprise Whopper, with a fried brussels sprout patty and Emmental cheese, introduced into select stores England in 2010, was not a success. Other innovations were successful. A London Burger King developed the Dessert Bar, which serves BK Fusions ice cream, brownies, cakes, cookies, and muffins as a way to compete with Starbucks and the McCafés developed by McDonalds.

See also Burger King; Cereals; Coca-Cola Company; Coffee; Europe; Hamburger; McCafé; McDonald's; Soda/Soft Drinks; Wimpy

For Further Information:

Royle, Tony. *Working for McDonald's in Europe: The Unequal Struggle?* New York: Routledge, 2001.

Smith, Andrew F. *Hamburger: A Global History*. London: Reaktion Books, 2008.

Vidal, John. *McLibel: Burger Culture on Trial*. New York: The New Press, 1997.

Unwrapped

Unwrapped is a television series on the Food Network, hosted by Marc Summers, which first aired in June 2001. It revels in "the magic and secrets of America's best loved food and drink." The show leads viewers on behind-the-scenes tours of factories and other food facilities. It has programs about a number of junk foods and fast foods, including candy, candy corn, candy canes, cotton candy, Bosco chocolate syrup, bubblegum, cereal, peanut butter, and french fries. Many programs have featured commercial mass-produced products, which generally has generated positive consumer feedback and awareness for the featured products.

See also Candy; Candy Canes; Cereals; Chocolate Beverages; Cotton Candy; French Fries; Peanut Butter; Television

For Further Information:

Food Network Web site: www.foodnetwork.com

Urban Blight

Fast food chains are not the cause of urban blight, but they have contributed to it. During the 1920s, drive-in restaurants targeted customers driving automobiles. Drive-ins were usually constructed on the outskirts of cities where land prices were lower and automobile traffic was high, thus contributing to urban sprawl. Because automobiles sped along at a fast clip, drive-ins developed gaudy architecture and large signs to attract motorists. Citizens objected to these outlandish structures and promotions and considered them eyesores; these complaints have continued ever since.

After World War II, Americans began leaving inner cities and moving into suburbs. This movement created challenges and opportunities for fast food chains. Those fast food chains that had targeted inner cities, such as White Castle and White Tower, confronted a major loss of customers and a significant increase in crime and vagrancy. Without a large customer base, many fast food establishments in inner cities closed and their buildings deteriorated.

Other fast food chains, such as McDonald's and Burger King, initially targeted the suburbs. Some municipalities objected to them because of their architecture. McDonald's, for instance, was criticized because of the arches bursting through their roofs, and others considered the slanted roofs to be eyesores. Likewise, others objected to Burger King's handlebars on their roofs. Both McDonald's and Burger King redesigned their outlets to appear less gaudy in hopes of quashing criticism. However, the concerns do not just rest with the design of particular outlets; the massive collections of fast food outlets that have spread along highways passing through cities are considered objectionable, as well.

In addition, fast food chains have greatly contributed to the trash that is generated by their patrons. Of the garbage along city streets and highways, it is estimated that 40 percent comes from fast food chains.

See also Architecture/Design; Automobiles; Burger King; Crime; Drive-Ins; McDonald's; White Castle; White Tower

For Further Information:

Langdon, Philip. *Orange Roofs, Golden Arches: The Architecture of American Chain Restaurants.* New York: Knopf, 1986.

U.S. Department of Agriculture (USDA)

The Bureau of Agriculture was established in 1862; in 1889 the Bureau was upgraded to the U.S. Department of Agriculture (USDA), with cabinet rank. The USDA is one of the largest federal agencies; it administers thousands of programs related to food and agriculture and has sponsored extensive research to help farmers improve their crops. Critics have claimed that USDA programs have strongly supported factory farms and large commercial concerns at the expense of small, independent family farms.

The USDA also has responsibilities for food safety and nutrition. In 1906 Congress passed the Meat Inspection Act on the same day that it passed the Pure Food and Drug Act. The Meat Inspection Act required the Department of Agriculture to inspect cattle, chickens, sheep, goats, swine, and horses before they were slaughtered and processed into products for human consumption. The USDA was also authorized to set sanitary standards established for slaughterhouses and meat-processing plants.

Inspection

The USDA's Food Safety Inspection Service (FSIS) is charged with ensuring that all meat, poultry, and egg products in the United States are safe to consume and are accurately labeled. This includes all food products that contain more than 2–3 percent meat products. All other food products are regulated by the Food and Drug Administration (FDA). There are several ways by which unsafe or improperly labeled meat and poultry products are detected, including (a) those uncovered by the company that manufactured or distributed the food; (b) FSIS test results that indicate that the products are adulterated or misbranded; (c) when FSIS field inspectors discover unsafe or improperly labeled foods; or (d) when epidemiological data from local, state, or federal sources (such as the FDA or the Centers for Disease Control and Prevention) reveal unsafe, unwholesome, or inaccurately labeled food. When problems are discovered, manufacturers or distributors initiate a food recall to protect the public. If a company refuses to recall its products, then the FSIS has the legal authority to detain and seize those products. Once a recall has been issued, FSIS conducts effectiveness checks to verify that the product is removed from commerce. Critics believe that the FSIS has not met its responsibilities, in part because it does not have the funds necessary to properly inspect and test food. Recently, the USDA has increased inspection of meat and poultry facilities.

Organic Food

As concerns were raised with the use of pesticides, chemical fertilizers, hormones, and food additives, some Americans sought alternative systems of agriculture and food processing. What emerged was organic food. The problem was that there were many different definitions of the term "organic." The 1990 Farm Bill passed by the U.S. Congress contained the Organic Foods Production Act, which set national standards for how organic food must be produced, handled, and labeled. Organic foods could not include synthetic fertilizers or pesticides. The bill also established the National Organic Standards Board, which issues a list of prohibited substances, such as synthetic fertilizer and antibiotics, that cannot be used in organic food. After twelve years of work by the National Organic Standards Board, the National

Organic Program (NOP) took effect in October 2002; it is administered by the USDA. Today, many junk foods contain the organic label.

Dietary Guidelines

In the interest of promoting better eating habits among Americans, the Department of Agriculture and the Department of Health and Human Services jointly disseminated the *Dietary Guidelines for Americans* in 1980. They have been regularly updated every five years. Because of an increase in heart disease in America, in 1992 the USDA unveiled the Food Pyramid, which broke from the recommendations of the previous food charts to emphasize consumption of more complex carbohydrates and less animal protein, fat, and sugar. The latest *Dietary Guidelines for Americans* was released in 2010. It was concerned with issues related to overweight and obesity. To reduce the incidence and prevalence of overweight and obesity, it recommended that Americans reduce "overall calorie intake and [increase] physical activity." The report also recommended that Americans "significantly reduce intake of foods containing added sugars and solid fats because these dietary components contribute excess calories and few, if any, nutrients. In addition, reduce sodium intake and lower intake of refined grains, especially refined grains that are coupled with added sugar, solid fat, and sodium."

SNAP and School Food

The largest component of the USDA's budget is food connected with poverty programs, such as the Supplemental Nutrition Assistance Program (SNAP), which provides support to needy households and to those making the transition from welfare to work. In these programs, the USDA sets standards for what can be acquired by recipients through the program.

The USDA also administers school meal programs, such as the School Breakfast Program, the National School Lunch Program, and the Summer Food Service Program. For these programs, the USDA sets nutritional standards for those meals and controls the types of food offered or sold in school cafeterias during the time that these meals are being served. While the USDA has banned "Foods of Limited Nutritional Value" (some junk foods) at school meal times, the ban does not include candy bars, soda, potato chips, cookies, and most other high-fat snack foods. A 2010 study funded by the USDA found that banning all junk food in schools resulted in an 18 percent reduction in overweight or obese students, and recommended that the sale of junk food during meals be banned.

See also Factory Farms; Food and Drug Administration (FDA); Food Labeling; Nutrition; Nutritional Guidelines; Organic Junk Foods; School Food

For Further Information:

Dietary Guidelines for Americans for 2010 Web site: www.cnpp.usda.gov/DGAs2010-DGACReport.htm

Food Safety and Inspection Service Web site: www.fsis.usda.gov

Kennedy, Patricia, Mary McGarvey, and Bree Dority. "Marketing Foods and Beverages in Schools: The Effect of School Food Policy on Students' Overweight Measures." *Journal of Public Policy and Marketing* 29 (Fall 2010): 277–79.

Nestle, Marion. *Safe Food: Bacteria, Biotechnology, and Bio-Terrorism*. Berkeley: University of California Press, 2003.

Nestle, Marion. *Food Politics: How the Food Industry Influences Nutrition and Health*. Rev. ed. Berkeley: University of California Press, 2007.

Schlosser, Eric. *Fast Food Nation: The Dark Side of the All-American Meal*. New York: Houghton Mifflin Company, 2001.

U.S. Department of Agriculture Web site: www.usda.gov

Utz Quality Foods

Utz Quality Foods, Inc., is a privately held company based in Hanover, Pennsylvania, that makes potato chips, kettle chips, tortilla chips, pretzels, pork rinds, popcorn, and cheese curls in the mid-Atlantic region. It was launched by Bill and Salie Utz in 1921, when they began to make and sell homemade potato chips, and they slowly expanded their distribution network and the number of products that they made. In 1936 they acquired an automatic chip fryer, which greatly increased their production of potato chips. In the 1970s the company added pretzels and popcorn to their growing list of products. During the following decade, they added kettle chips, cheese curls, and corn chips. Today, Utz's distribution is mainly on the East Coast from Maine to Florida.

Snyder's of Hanover and Utz began merger talks in 2009, but later abandoned discussions after questions were raised by the Federal Trade Commission. In 2011 the company acquired Zappe Endeavors, a Cajun snack foods firm in Gramercy, Louisiana. Utz remains a family-owned business. It is headquartered in Hanover, Pennsylvania, and it is one of America's largest privately owned snack food companies. It produces one million pounds of potato chips each week.

See also Cheese-Flavored Snacks; Kettle Foods; Popcorn; Pork Rind; Potato Chips; Pretzels; Snyder's of Hanover

For Further Information:
Utz Quality Food Web site: www.utzsnacks.com

V

Valentine's Day Candies

Valentine's Day is celebrated on February 14, traditionally in honor of a saint killed in Roman times. It was a popular holiday in medieval Europe. Precisely when candy became the traditional gift given on Valentine's Day is unclear. In the 1860s Richard Cadbury introduced the first Valentine's Day box of chocolates in England. One of the earliest American Valentine's Day candies was invented by the one of the predecessors of the New England Confectionery Company (NECCO), which began manufacturing Conversation Hearts in the 1860s. These heart-shaped candies were renamed Sweethearts in 1902. By the twenty-first century, NECCO produced about 8 billion Sweethearts each year, and virtually all are sold within six weeks before Valentine's Day. They are the best-selling Valentine's Day candy in the world.

Valentine's Day candy. (Dreamstime.com)

By tradition, males give chocolates to their sweethearts, mothers, or wives on Valentine's Day. It is promoted as a day of love, and candies have reflected this dimension. Chemicals found in small amounts in chocolate are anandamide, serotonin, endorphins, and phenylethylamine (PEA); in the human brain these chemicals create positive feelings. The aphrodisiac effect of chocolate has been greatly exaggerated in advertisement imagery in order to increase sales.

According to the National Confectioners Association, Americans spent $935 million for Valentine's Day in 2010.

See also Candy; Chocolate; National Confectioners Association; New England Confectionery Company (NECCO); Seasonal Candy

For Further Information:

National Confectioners Association Web site: www.candyusa.com

Santino, Jack. *New Old-Fashioned Ways: Holidays and Popular Culture*. Knoxville: The University of Tennessee Press, 1996.

Vanilla

Vanilla is a common flavoring used in ice cream and junk foods. The vanilla plant is native to southern Mexico, Central America, and the West Indies. The source of its distinctive flavor is the "bean"—the long, flat, slender, seed pod, which is odorless when picked. The distinctive vanilla aroma only develops when the pod is properly cured. In pre-Columbian times, the Totonac people discovered that beans left in the sun became fragrant, and they sold great quantities of them to the Aztecs, who called them *tlilxochitl*, or black flower. The first European to make mention of vanilla was Bernal Díaz, a soldier in the army of the explorer Hernan Cortéz, who conquered Mexico in the early sixteenth century. Díaz recorded that vanilla beans were added to ground cacao beans to make a frothy and fragrant, though bitter, drink that was the delight of the Aztec nobility. The Spanish called the newly discovered product *vainilla*, which means "little pod." Cortéz sent vanilla and cacao beans to Spain, where they were among the first New World foods to be adopted in the Old World. Large quantities of vanilla beans were shipped to Europe, where people readily took up the habit of drinking chocolate beverages flavored with vanilla. Vanilla was in such demand that repeated unsuccessful attempts were made to grow the plants in greenhouses in Europe. The reason for this, which was not understood until the nineteenth century, is that vanilla's natural pollinators are the Melipona bees and other insects native to Mexico. As these insects did not thrive outside of southern Mexico, this region was the only supplier of vanilla beans until the nineteenth century.

Charles Morren of Liège, Belgium, experimented with artificial fertilization; he succeeded in 1836. The French grew vanilla on their islands in the Indian Ocean. Five years after Morren's discovery, Edmond Albius, a former slave on the island of Réunion, uncovered a better way of pollinating the flowers, which greatly increased productivity. Vanilla growing expanded to other tropical French islands, including Madagascar and Tahiti.

Joseph Burnett, a Boston chemist, figured out how to make extract from vanilla beans, and he began bottling and selling it in 1847. The extract was easier to ship and store than the whole beans, and the extract was pale brown in color, making it useful for flavoring white or light-colored sauces. In 1874 German chemists synthesized vanillin, the dominant flavor component of vanilla beans. While synthetic vanillin does not have the full flavor of natural vanilla, its production did greatly lower the cost of vanilla-like flavoring for home and commercial use.

By the late nineteenth century, vanilla was an important ingredient in American recipes for sauces, ice cream, baked goods, and beverages. Aside from the Joseph Burnett Company, vanilla extract was produced by many other firms, including the C. F. Sauer Company of Richmond, Virginia, and the J. R. Watkins Company of Winona, Minnesota.

As the price of vanilla and vanillin declined, the flavoring was used in a much wider range of foods and dishes, including custards, puddings, cakes, candies, cookies, meringues, macaroons, pies, and soft drinks. In the 1870s soda fountain proprietors began using vanilla as a flavoring, and the cream soda was invented. In addition to cookery, vanilla also became an important ingredient in making perfume and other scent-based commercial products.

Vanilla manufacturers produced cookbooklets filled with recipes to encourage the use of their products. The first non-commercial vanilla cookbook was published in 1986 by Patricia Rain. She has subsequently promoted vanilla cookery throughout the United States and is referred to as the "Vanilla Queen." Today, the largest culinary use of vanilla is in the making of ice cream. Until the mid-twentieth century, vanilla was America's favorite ice cream flavor, followed by chocolate. Although no longer America's favorite flavor of ice cream, vanilla remains important. The largest American manufacturer of vanilla extract and vanillin is McCormick & Company of Baltimore.

See also Cakes; Ice Cream; Pie; Soda/Soft Drinks

For Further Information:

Rain, Patricia. *Vanilla: The Cultural History of the World's Favorite Flavor and Fragrance*. New York: Penguin, 2004.

Vegetarian/Vegan

The term "vegetarian" was used in the United States by the 1830s, but it was popularized by the Vegetarian Society of the United Kingdom at their first meeting in 1847, and by the American Vegetarian Society at its inaugural meeting in 1850. During the latter part of the nineteenth century, the Seventh-Day Adventist Church strongly encouraged its members to become vegetarians for health reasons. John Harvey Kellogg, a Seventh-Day Adventist, became director of the Battle Creek sanitarium in Michigan, and he promoted vegetarianism throughout his entire life. He invented cold cereal, such as Kellogg's Corn Flakes, as an alternative to the traditional breakfast of eggs and bacon. As part of his efforts to create an alternative to butter made from cow's milk, he invented peanut butter, which became popular during the early twentieth century. Peanut butter has been an important ingredient in many confections.

Vegetarianism has been variously defined, but it is generally considered the practice of not eating meat, poultry, or fish. Ovo vegetarians also do not eat eggs and lacto vegetarians do not eat dairy products. The word "vegan" was coined by Donald Watson, the founder of the Vegan Society, in 1944. A vegan eats neither meat nor meat byproducts, eggs, or dairy products.

Vegetarianism became particularly popular in the late twentieth century. In 1960 there were an estimated 2 million vegetarians in the United States; by 1990, there were more than 6 million. Part of this growth can be attributed to the organizing efforts of the North American Vegetarian Society, which was founded in 1974, and the publication of several vegetarian magazines, such as *Vegetarian Times.*

Vegetarians have opposed fast food sales of meat, fish, or poultry, as well as products that have been made with nonvegetarian byproducts. Vegetarians have challenged fast food operations, such as the way large-scale suppliers raise and slaughter animals. They have also opposed certain food preparation practices, such as using animal products in making french fries. Vegetarians have influenced fast food chains. McDonald's, for instance, which once used animal byproducts in the oils used to cook french fries, has discontinued the practice. Some vegetarians have taken stronger action, as in 1999 when some vegetarians set fire to a McDonald's in Antwerp, Belgium, in protest.

Vegetarians have also influenced the selection of ingredients in junk foods. In 2007 Mars in the United Kingdom announced that several of its products, including the Mars Bar, Maltesers, and Twix, would in the future be made with rennet, a product derived from the stomach linings of mammals, and therefore these products would not be vegetarian. Alternative non-animal products had been used previously, but Mars had decided not to continue using them. Vegetarians complained and Mars reversed its decision.

Vegetarian Fast Food

Many fast food chains now offer vegetarian meals, such as veggie burgers and salads. In addition, many vegetarian products are now sold in stores. For instance, in 1993 Max Shondor, a Florida-based natural food restaurateur, introduced soy-based Boca Burgers; he subsequently expanded his line to include other flavors, meatless breakfast patties, and nuggets. Similar products are now sold in some fast food chains. Meatless burgers ("veggie burgers") get their substance and texture from soy protein, starchy vegetables, fruit slices, beans, or nuts. The Hula Burger, for instance, complete with sliced pineapple, cheese, and no meat on a bun was developed in Cincinnati for Catholics to eat on Fridays and during Lent.

See also French Fries; Lawsuits; Mars, Inc.; McDonald's; Nuts; Suppliers

For Further Information:

Goldstein, Myrna Chandler, and Mark A. Goldstein. *Controversies in Food and Nutrition; A Reference Guide.* 2nd ed. Westport, CT: Greenwood Press, 2009.

Schlosser, Eric. *Fast Food Nation: The Dark Side of the All-American Meal.* New York: Houghton Mifflin Company, 2001.

Vending Machines

Vending machines are an important source of junk foods. Machines can be placed virtually everywhere; they are typically available twenty-four hours a day, and they require no employees to make transactions. The junk foods that vending machines typically sell are cakes, candy, coffee, cookies, crackers, gum, ice cream, soda, salty snacks, and other junk foods. Some machines also sell fast foods, including french fries and hamburgers.

History

Coin-operated vending machines were developed in the United Kingdom in the 1880s. They initially sold postcards. The Thomas Adams Gum Company began selling gum in vending machines on New York's elevated train platforms in 1888. Previously, penny candy, gum, and peanuts had been sold in glass jars by grocers. Coin-operated machines offered the means to sell junk foods in many places without the need for a sales force. Vending machines took off nationally in 1901, when F. W. and H. S. Mills debuted penny-in-the-slot machines in Chicago. The following year, Horn and Hardart Automat opened a restaurant in Philadelphia that sold food, such as sandwiches and coffee, solely from vending machines. The company opened other stores throughout the East Coast. By the end of the decade, there were 30,000 machines selling penny candy, peanuts, and gum across America. During the early 1920s, vending machines began dispensing soft drinks into cups.

By 1926, there was a vending machine for every one hundred people in America. These machines generated $1 million per day. At that time, the largest single operator was William Wrigley, who installed ten thousand slot machines in the New York City subway system. Bottled beverages, such as Coca-Cola, were sold in vending machines by the 1930s.

Vending machines were also the core of automats, which dispensed more substantial food. These types of machines were also placed in offices and public areas. They sold sandwiches, pies, coffee, candy, ice cream, and soda. In 1965 soft drinks in cans were dispensed from vending machines. In 1981 talking vending machines were introduced; five years later, the first vending machines that accepted credit/debit cards were introduced. Wireless transmission between vending machines and warehouses began service in 1993. Annually, vending machines do more than $21 billion in business, and many different products are sold in them. It is estimated that Coca-Cola products alone are sold in 1.4 million vending machines. In 2009 Coca-Cola Company introduced the "Freestyle" machine, a touchscreen soda fountain, which features more than one hundred different Coca-Cola drink products and custom flavors. Beginning in late 2010, Freestyle machines have begun to be distributed to select locations across the United States.

Many states tax the foods and beverages sold through vending machines, and these taxes are often higher than for the same items purchased in grocery stores. This has led some observers to claim that this difference is indicative of a "disfavored" tax status attributed to vended items.

Controversies

Vending machines became controversial when they were placed on public school campuses. Studies indicate that a large percentage of high schools in America have vending machines, while slightly more than 50 percent of the middle schools and only about 16 percent of the elementary schools have food/beverage vending machines. In 2006 Faerie Films released a documentary film titled *Vending Machine*, which examined health issues as seen from the viewpoint of teenagers who have been targeted by fast food and junk food manufacturers. Research conducted at the University of Michigan Medical School has indicated that 22 percent of the children and adolescents in the study purchased foods in vending machines during the day. The students who consumed vending machine food mainly consumed candies, snack chips, crackers, cookies, cakes, ice cream, and nondiet soda. They consumed significantly more sugar, and much lower sodium, dietary fiber, B vitamins, and iron intakes than those students who did not consume food from school vending machines. As a result, students who consumed vended machine items, concluded the study, are more likely to develop poor diet quality, and access to vending machines may also be associated with being overweight and obese.

Owing to concern with child and adolescent overweight and obesity, efforts are under way to remove vending machines selling sugar-added beverages and junk foods from schools. In 2004 the Center for Science in the Public Interest (CSPI) released a report that said school vending machines were responsible for "dispensing junk," owing to all the high-calorie, sugar-filled products they offered. Centers for Disease Control reports that across thirty-four states, the percent of secondary schools that ditched non-nutritious snacks increased to 64 percent in 2008. This figure was up from 46 percent in 2006. By 2010, the American Beverage Association estimated that there was an 88 percent reduction in beverage calories sold through vending machines in schools. The Health Care Reform Act passed in March 2010 requires vending machines to list nutritional information for each product.

Healthy Food

As Americans have become more concerned about the nutritional content of the foods they eat, operators have begun to sell more healthy fare, such as fresh fruit, gluten-free snacks, and organic yogurt. Others sell baked chips, nutrition bars, oatmeal, smoothies, salads, and yogurt, as well as 100-Calorie Snack Packs of Oreos, Cheez-Its, Chips Ahoy!, Rold Gold pretzels, and Wheat Thins. In 2010 carrot farmers teamed up with a vending machine operator to sell baby carrots in high schools. It was accompanied by a massive advertising campaign.

With the passage of the Healthy, Hunger-Free Kids Act in 2010, vending machine operators are scrambling to add more healthy fare with fewer calories, less sodium and fat, and more healthy foods, such as bottled water, milk, diet drinks, and fruit juices without added sugar.

Vending machine operations is a $50 billion industry in the United States. Of this, Americans spend approximately $21 billion every year buying food and beverages from vending machines.

See also Automats, Cafeterias, Diners, and Lunchrooms; Cakes; Candy; Chips Ahoy!; Coca-Cola Company; Coffee; French Fries; Gum; Ice Cream; 100-Calorie Snack Packs; Oreos; Peanuts; Penny Candy; Pie; Pretzels; Salads; Sandwiches; Smoothies, Soda/Soft Drinks; Yogurt

For Further Information:

American Beverage Association Web site: www.ameribev.org

The Automatic Vending Machine Industry: Its Growth and Development. Washington, D.C.: U.S. Government Printing Office, 1962.

Chriqui, Jamie F., et al. "State Sales Tax Rates for Soft Drinks and Snacks Sold through Grocery Stores and Vending Machines, 2007." *Journal of Public Health Policy* 29 (July 2008): 226–49.

Kakarala, Madhuri, Debra R. Keast, and Sharon Hoerr. "Schoolchildren's Consumption of Competitive Foods and Beverages, Excluding à la Carte." *Journal of School Health* 80, no. 9 (September 2010): 429–35.

National Automatic Merchandising Association Web site: www.vending.org

Vernor's Ginger Ale

In 1866 James Vernor, a Detroit pharmacist, introduced Vernor's Ginger Ale, which is considered the first commercial carbonated soft drink. In 1896 Vernor established his own soda fountain, and he began selling the extract to drugstores in other cities, such as Buffalo, Toledo, and Cleveland. Today, Vernor's brand is owned by PepsiCo.

See also PepsiCo; Soda/Soft Drinks; Soda Fountains

For Further Information:

Rouch, Lawrence L. *The Vernor's Story: From Gnomes to Now*. Ann Arbor: University of Michigan Press, 2003.

Violence

In addition to crime, fast food chains have been subjected to violence owing to various political, economic, and social causes. An activist French farmer, José Bové, became upset in 1999 with tariffs placed on importation of Roquefort cheese into the United States, which he and fellow farmers made. As a result, he and his group, the radical Confédération Paysanne, decided to retaliate by bulldozing a local McDonald's restaurant under construction in Millau, France. He declared that his action was a challenge to globalism. When he went on trial, 30,000 people demonstrated on his behalf, carrying signs saying "Non à McMerde." Bové was convicted and served three months in a French prison. Subsequently, he and his supporters destroyed research plots with genetically modified crops in Brazil and have participated in demonstrations (some of which have turned violent) against globalization of food.

In addition to violent protests against globalism, fast food chains have been subjected to violence owing to international events and causes. In 1979 Marxist guerrillas blew up a McDonald's outlet in San Salvador and announced that their act was intended as a blow against "imperialist America." When American aircraft accidentally bombed the Chinese embassy in Belgrade during the war in Yugoslavia in 1999, Chinese students ransacked the McDonald's in Beijing. During the American bombing of Afghanistan in 2001, Pakistan's KFC outlets were trashed. In 1996 a KFC in Bangalore, India, was looted by farmers who believed that the company threatened their agricultural practices. Anarchists destroyed a McDonald's in Copenhagen in 1995 and regularly protest at McDonald's locations in Paris and London. Bombs have destroyed McDonald's restaurants in St. Petersburg, Russia; Athens, Greece; and Rio de Janeiro, Brazil. Vegetarians set fire to McDonald's in Antwerp in 1999, and a McDonald's in London was trashed, also in 1999. In 2000 a bomb was set off in a McDonald's restaurant in Breton, France, killing a twenty-seven-year-old employee; five activists belonging to Emgann, a group considered a front for the Breton Revolutionary Army, were arrested in connection with that action. In 2001 five hundred enraged Hindus ransacked a McDonald's in Bombay, India, and smeared cow dung all over a statue of Ronald McDonald because they wrongly thought that french fries served at Indian restaurants were being fried in beef tallow. In 2002 the McDonald's in Bali, Indonesia, was bombed by Indonesian terrorists. When American troops attacked Iraq in 2003, protests were held in many cities, and McDonald's was again the target of demonstrators. In Moscow, a McDonald's restaurant was destroyed by a bomb in 2003.

In 2005 a bomb destroyed a KFC restaurant in Karachi, Pakistan. Members of the Balochistan Liberation Army, an ethnic Baloch group in the Balochistan province, claimed responsibility and the suspects who were apprehended were members of that group.

Another cause of violence in fast food outlets has been crime. In 2001 a bomb was set off in a Xian, China, McDonald's restaurant that killed two people. Two years later, a man was convicted of the bombing; prior to the bombing, he had sent threatening letters to the management, extorting money.

In 2006 Pakistani rioters burned down a KFC in the wake of the controversy over a Danish cartoon's depiction of the Prophet Muhammad. KFC became the focus of potential violence in January 2011, when rumor swept the Egyptian crowds demonstrating against the Egyptian president that the protesters were being given chicken from KFC. The protesters believed that this was a deliberate attempt by others to discredit them.

See also Crime; French Fries; Genetically Modified Food; KFC; McDonald's; Ronald Mc-Donald; Vegetarian/Vegan

For Further Information:

Bové, José, François Dufour, and Gilles Luneau. *The World Is Not for Sale: Farmers Against Junk Food.* New York: Verso, 2001.

Schlosser, Eric. *Fast Food Nation: The Dark Side of the All-American Meal.* New York: Houghton Mifflin Company, 2001.

W

Waffles

The contents of waffles are similar to that of pancake batter, but waffles require waffle irons to be made. Waffles are traditionally consumed with a number of sweeteners, including powdered sugar, jam, butter, Nutella, honey, chocolate, ice cream, fruit, whipped cream, or syrup, and they usually are high in calories. In the early 1950s Eggo Food Products, Inc., introduced frozen waffles, which at the time was a risky venture, as refrigerators with freezers were just coming into use in American homes and most grocery stores had limited freezer space. The advantage of frozen waffles was they were convenient and easily prepared. All consumers had to do was simply place the frozen waffles in toasters, and within a few minutes breakfast was served. As kids could do this by themselves, they became an immediate success with children.

Dozens of different frozen waffles are now sold in most grocery stores and supermarkets. The target consumers for frozen waffles are mainly children. Companies that make frozen waffles have targeted children with their advertising and have extended their product lines to include a wide variety of other products, such as waffle sticks with dips in cups.

Some companies now produce waffle brands with improved nutritional components, such as those high in fiber or with whole grains and fewer calories. Despite the diversity of frozen waffles today, the Eggo brand controls a large percentage of the frozen waffle market. It is now owned by the Kellogg Company, which has kept its sales up by a series of clever advertising campaigns, such as the one that made famous the line, "L'eggo my Eggo."

Waffles are also specialty items in a number of casual restaurant chains, such as Waffle House and the International House of Pancakes (IHOP); Dunkin' Donuts claims to have introduced the first fast food breakfast sandwich made with waffles.

See also Dunkin' Donuts; Kellogg Company; Supermarkets

For Further Information:

Eggo Web site: www.leggomyeggo.com

Walmart

Walmart was launched in Bentonville, Arkansas, by Sam Walton in 1962. The discount department store expanded aggressively in the United States and then abroad. It had become the largest retail chain store in the world by the 1990s. In that same decade, Walmart began selling bulk-purchased groceries at reduced prices. Walmart's SuperCenters and their volume division, Sam's Club (a membership outlet), have been highly efficient in selling goods at reduced prices. Walmart had virtually no sales of food in 1993; by 2001 it was the second-largest food retailer in America. Today the company is the largest seller of groceries in the world. Walmart went from selling $66.5 billion in groceries in 2004, to $135 billion four years later, which was more than the next three chains combined.

Walmart is the largest seller of junk food in the United States. It has, however, also joined other corporations in pledging to reduce 1 trillion calories from their products in the United States by the end of 2015, in an effort to stem obesity in America.

See also Junk Foods; Supermarkets

For Further Information:

Fishman, Charles. *The Wal-Mart Effect: How the World's Most Powerful Company Really Works—and How It's Transforming the American Economy.* New York: Penguin Press, 2006.

Lichtenstein, Nelson. *The Retail Revolution: How Wal-Mart Created a Brave New World of Business.* New York: Metropolitan Books, 2009.

Loveless, Ronald L., and Brian Rouff, ed. *Walmart Inside Out.* Las Vegas, NV: Stephens Press, 2011.

Walmart Web site: www.walmart.com

Walnettos

Walnettos are chewy, caramel-walnut candies that were first introduced by the J. N. Collins Company of Minneapolis, Minnesota, in 1919. They became one of the top candies purchased at movie theaters throughout the United States. This candy is made by Walnettos, Inc., headquartered in Cudahy, California.

See also Candy; Movie Theaters; Nuts

For Further Information:

Walnettos Web site: www.walnettosinc.com

Waste

According to the Environmental Protection Agency, there are 3,091 active landfills in the United States and more than 10,000 old municipal landfills. The waste in the landfills has become a major concern for environmentalists.

Fast Food Waste

Fast food outlets produce a large amount of disposable materials, such as paper bags, coffee, and soda cups, much of which does not end up in the outlets' garbage containers. As drive-thru windows now generate an estimated 70 percent of the sales in many outlets, much of the litter ends up on streets and other locations. A number of cities, such as Oakland, California, charge fast food outlets (and food distributors) a litter fee based on gross sales. This fee is intended to keep the streets, sidewalks, and public spaces clean and sanitary. Other communities and states are considering similar fees.

Fast food chains package their foods in disposable paper bags, wrappers, and cardboard and Styrofoam containers. Fast food outlets therefore do not have to clean utensils, ceramic cups, plates, or serving dishes. Although paper, plastic, and foam products cost money, they are not as expensive as the stolen and broken dishes that prevailed before the fast food industry shifted to disposable packaging. Many Americans believe that fast food generates vast amounts of trash. However, studies have consistently shown that fast food establishments are responsible for less than 1 percent of landfill volumes. The problem with fast food trash has been the customers who toss their refuse onto highways and streets, making it highly visible. Fast food establishments have placed trash containers in convenient locations so they can be easily used. Chains have also encouraged customers to "put trash in its place." Also, most fast food chains have installed trash compactors in each outlet to limit the volume of trash generated at the outlet. To counteract the bad public relations, many fast food chains have contributed to local activities, such as sponsoring highway cleanups.

In addition to the waste generated at the fast food outlets, a great deal of secondary waste is generated by fast food suppliers, and this is a serious problem. Feedlots and slaughterhouses, for instance, produce vast amounts of waste, which greatly contribute to pollution.

A large volume of trash is generated by the soda industry. It is estimated that 44 billion soft drink cans and bottles are thrown into landfills annually. Many municipalities and states have required deposits on all bottles, and others have enacted laws requiring recycling. Soda manufacturing and bottling companies have opposed such laws, but because they found that they generate much more money from people who fail to redeem deposits than they lose on the recycling, they now strongly support such efforts.

Some fast food and junk food companies have greatly reduced the amount of waste in their operations. For many companies, the goal is zero waste going to landfills. To do this, they have reduced waste through composting, recycling, and other practices. PepsiCo, for instance, claims to have reduced its landfill waste by 88 percent since 2008. It plans to achieve zero waste to landfills by 2020. Other companies have set similar goals.

See also PepsiCo; Soda/Soft Drinks; Suppliers

For Further Information:

Schlosser, Eric. *Fast Food Nation: The Dark Side of the All-American Meal.* New York: Houghton Mifflin Company, 2001.

Schlosser, Eric, and Charles Wilson. *Chew On This: Everything You Don't Want to Know about Fast Food.* Boston: Houghton Mifflin, 2006.

Water

Water contains no calories, fat, or sodium. It is an essential for life, and therefore is not a junk food. However, it is a component in many junk foods, such as soft drinks, ice cream, Kool-Aid, sports drinks, energy drinks, sugary fruit juices, and diet drinks.

Historically water, especially in urban areas, was polluted. It could not be consumed without boiling. It was not until the late nineteenth century that sanitation systems improved to the point where water could be safely consumed throughout most of the United States. Until then, most Americans—men, women, and children—consumed alcoholic beverages, and many Americans became alcoholics.

As the health and social consequences of alcoholism became apparent, many Americans joined together to promote temperance and Prohibition. Simultaneously with the rise of the temperance movement was the rise of soft drinks. Initially, many soft drinks were invented by pharmacists and were sold in drugstores at counters. As the temperance movement picked up steam, soft drinks and other nonalcoholic beverages, such as canned fruit juice and Kool-Aid, became important components of American life.

Recently companies have released vitamin, or fortified, water. One such company was Fuze Beverage, formed in 2000 in Englewood Cliff, New Jersey. It makes energy, tea, and vitamin-enriched beverages. It was purchased for $250 million by the Coca-Cola Company in 2007.

Another such company is Energy Brands, headquartered in Whitestone, New York. It operates under the name of Glacéau. The company was founded in 1996, and it was acquired by the Coca-Cola Company in 2007 for $4.1 billion. Its Smartwater contained no calories, was enhanced with electrolytes, and was marketed as a sports drink. As one reviewer noted, Smartwater was better to consume than sugary sodas, but it would be much less expensive to just drink water and take vitamins.

Energy Brands also produces Fruitwater, a flavored version of Smartwater but sweetened with fructose. It comes in raspberry, peach, grape, and lime flavors. The company also produces Vitaminwater, which contains some nutrients, but its main ingredient is sugar (33 grams per twenty-ounce bottle). Vitaminwater was advertised as a product that would keep the consumer as "healthy as a horse" and would bring about a "healthy state of physical or mental being." Advertisements also claimed that Vitaminwater "may reduce the risk of age-related eye disease."

The Center for Science in the Public Interest (CSPI) filed a class action lawsuit against Coca-Cola, claiming that Vitaminwater's marketing claims were likely to mislead consumers. CSPI's lead litigator proclaimed that Vitaminwater was "no more than non-carbonated soda, providing unnecessary added sugar and contributing to weight gain, obesity, diabetes, and other diseases." In July 2010 a federal judge ruled against Coke, stating that its advertising violated the Food and Drug Administration's regulations.

The two leading brands of vitamin-enriched waters are Coca Cola's Vitaminwater and Pepsi's SoBe Lifewater. Lifewater contains 50 calories per serving, and each bottle contains 2.5 servings. As most people consume the entire bottle, that means there are 125 calories in a bottle of Lifewater. Coca-Cola's thirty-two-ounce Vitaminwater XXX contains 4 servings, each with 50 calories.

See also Coca-Cola Company; Diet Soda; Energy Drinks; Ice Cream; Kool-Aid; Soda/Soft Drinks; Sports Drinks

For Further Information:

Center for Science in the Public Interest Web site: www.cspinet.org/new/201007231.html

Glacéau's Web site: www.glaceau.com

Wendy's

Dave Thomas worked for KFC and Arthur Treacher's before he opened his first Wendy's restaurant in 1969 in Columbus, Ohio. Thomas believed that Americans wanted larger hamburgers than those offered by other chains, so he created a square beef patty, which probably was influenced by White Castle's square patty. He charged 55 cents for the large sandwich, which was a risk because at that time McDonald's charged 18 cents for its hamburgers. Wendy's claimed that Thomas' Old Fashioned Hamburger could be ordered in 256 different ways. Thomas concentrated on young adults for customers, as opposed to the children whom other chains targeted. He correctly judged the willingness of young adults to purchase a more expensive hamburger.

Beginning in 1970, Thomas expanded his operation in other cities in Ohio. In 1972 the first out-of-state Wendy's was opened in Indianapolis. Wendy's went

Wendy's meal. (AP/Wide World Photos)

from 9 outlets in 1972 to 1,818 six years later. Wendy's went public in 1975. One reason for Wendy's early success was the drive-thru windows that were installed in 1971. Their advantage was that less space had to be used for parking lots or indoor eating space. McDonald's and Burger King followed Wendy's example.

In addition to hamburgers and french fries, Wendy's has diversified its menu to include chicken sandwiches, the Frosty (similar to a milkshake), baked potatoes, and chili. The salad bar was added in 1979. In September 1986 Wendy's introduced the Big Classic, which was a quarter-pound hamburger on a Kaiser-style bun.

Wendy's, like other fast food chains, has advertised extensively on television. In 1984 the company launched its famous "Where's the Beef?" commercial. Later that year, the phrase ended up being used by Walter Mondale in his presidential campaign against Ronald Reagan. Dave Thomas appeared in Wendy's advertisements beginning in 1989.

Global

Wendy's is the third-largest hamburger chain, with more than 6,600 outlets in the United States and 34 other countries. Since June 2009, the company has made agreements with franchisees to open outlets in the Caribbean, Middle East, North Africa, Russia, Singapore, and Turkey. It opened its first franchise in Argentina in 2010, and planned to add 50 more outlets in future years. Wendy's opened its first outlet in Russia in 2011. It is aggressively seeking opportunities to expand in Brazil, China, and Japan.

Wendy's was acquired by the company that owned Arby's in 2008, thus creating Wendy's/Arby's Group, Inc.

See also Advertising; Arby's; Burger King; Chicken; Drive-Thrus; French Fries; Hamburger; McDonald's; Sandwiches; Thomas, Dave; Wendy's/Arby's Group, Inc.

For Further Information:

Jakle, John A., and Keith A. Sculle. *Fast Food: Roadside Restaurants in the Automobile Age*. Baltimore: Johns Hopkins University Press, 1999.

Thomas, R. David. *Dave's Way: A New Approach to Old-Fashioned Success*. New York: G. P. Putnam's Sons, 1991.

Thomas, R. David. *Dave Says—Well Done! The Common Guy's Guide to Everyday Success*. Grand Rapids, MI: Zondervan, 1994.

YouTube Wendy's Advertisement "Where's the Beef?" as at: www.youtube.com/watch?v=Ug75diEyiA0&feature=related

Wendy's/Arby's Group, Inc.

In 2008 the company that owned Arby's purchased Wendy's and changed its name to Wendy's/Arby's Group, Inc. As of 2011, there were 3,719 Arby's and 6,625 Wendy's restaurants in operation in the United States and in 21 other countries and territories. It was the third-largest U.S. fast food company in the world with more than 10,334 restaurants in 24 countries. In 2011 the company decided to focus solely on selling hamburgers and decided to sell off Arby's to a private equity firm. As it did so, Wendy's planned to remodel its stores, expand abroad, and add new products to its menu.

See also Arby's; Wendy's

For Further Information:
Wendy's/Arby's Web site: www.wendysarbys.com

Whataburger

Harmon Dobson founded Whataburger in Corpus Christi, Texas, in 1950. Its flagship products are large, made-to-order quarter-pound hamburgers. It also serves fajitas, fries, shakes, and sodas. Breakfast items include taquitos and pancakes.

There are seven hundred Whataburger outlets in ten states from Arizona to Florida. All restaurants are open twenty-four hours a day. Whataburger remains controlled by the Dobson family that launched the chain. It is headquartered in San Antonio, Texas.

See also Breakfast Fast Food; Hamburger; Milkshakes, Malts, and Ice Cream Sodas; Pancakes; Regional Fast Foods;

For Further Information:
Whataburger Web site: www.whataburger.com

Wheat

Wheat originated in the Middle East and was introduced into North America by colonists in the seventeenth century. Wheat is one of the most important staples in

American food, and it is an important ingredient in many fast foods and junk foods, as cheap flour is a basic building block for both of these industries. It ends up in the buns for hamburgers and hot dogs, the crust for pizza, the bread for subs and sandwiches, and the dough for cookies, pastries, and baked goods. Although some flours are enriched with vitamins and minerals, most are just high in calories and low in nutrition.

During the 1970s, the federal government began to establish minimum price supports for major staples, such as wheat. This meant that farmers could grow as much wheat as they wanted, and the federal government guaranteed them a profit. Farmers greatly expanded their wheat production and the price fell, which is one reason why so many junk foods and fast foods include flour as ingredients.

Researchers examining the reasons for the increase in obesity in America have concluded that inexpensive grains, such as wheat, have contributed about 46 percent of the increase in calories that Americans consume. Some health food advocates have argued for an end to agricultural subsidies for wheat in hopes of improving the health of America. As wheat prices rise, proponents advocate, Americans would consume less flour and more fruits and vegetables, which do not receive subsidies and would become more competitive with junk foods and fast foods.

As some people are allergic to gluten, a composite protein found in processed wheat and related grains, some fast food chains now offer gluten-free items on their menu.

See also Bakery Goods; Cookies; Food Allergies; Hamburger; Hot Dog; Pizza; Sandwiches

For Further Information:

Wallinga, David. "Agricultural Policy and Childhood Obesity: A Food Systems and Public Health Commentary." *Health Affairs* 29 (March 2010): 405–10.

White Castle

In 1916 J. Walter "Walt" Anderson, a short-order cook in a diner in Wichita, Kansas, purchased an old shoe repair building, which he converted into a hamburger stand. He sold his burgers for a nickle apiece, which his customers (mainly workers) could afford. At the time, hamburgers were commonly sold on the street, but they did not have a particularly good reputation. The ground beef was frequently overcooked and tasteless, and everyone was worried about its composition. Anderson's burgers were different. His secret was to make thin, square patties that permitted quick cooking. To ensure freshness, he arranged for beef and square buns to be delivered twice a day, and sometimes more often. To make sure that customers knew what was in his hamburgers, he ground his own beef where

White Castle. (AP/Wide World Photos)

customers could watch him do so through glass windows. It was so successful that he opened three additional stands, all with carry-out service. Additional stands were opened, and in 1920 customers proclaimed Anderson to be the "King of the Hamburger."

Anderson wanted to expand his operation even further, but he needed a partner with money. In 1921 he went into business with Edgar Waldo "Billy" Ingram, a real estate and insurance man who liked what Anderson had accomplished. Ingram also believed that Anderson's operation could be greatly improved. The new joint venture was renamed White Castle. Ingram designed a new structure, complete with turrets, that imitated the Chicago Water Tower, which was one of the few structures to survive the Chicago fire of 1871. It was a symbol of permanence, which was quite different from the image of other low-cost hamburger stands that dotted the nation at the time. The dominant color of the new outlets was white, which was intended to represent purity and cleanliness. This new design was successful and White Castle expanded to Omaha, Kansas City, and St. Louis by 1924. In 1925 the company sold more than 84,000 hamburgers.

White Castle initially served only coffee, hamburgers, Coca-Cola, and pie, but this menu expanded over the years. Employees were required to observe high standards of cleanliness and had to wear uniforms. At first, Ingram made arrangements with local butchers to produce a particular meat product. As White Castle became larger, he established meat-processing plants, paper suppliers, and bun-baking operations to produce consistent products.

Anderson sold his portion of the operation to Ingram, who continued to expand it, particularly in urban areas near mass-transit stops across the street from large factories. As White Castle expanded in various regions, it was possible for the company to advertise over a broad area, thus increasing the sales. White Castle advertised in newspapers and through radio. It offered a single slogan for all outlets: "Sell 'em by the Sack."

By 1931, the company owned 131 outlets. The Depression was not a major problem. The company restructured its operation by closing unprofitable outlets and opening new operations in more profitable areas. Because it sold its products at a low price, White Castle food was a luxury that Americans with jobs could afford. The company streamlined its operations further, and hamburgers were sold at an increasing rate. The company also advertised in newspapers and included coupons for reduced prices. The company also experimented with new products, such as milkshakes, which it decided not to continue because they took so long to make and the equipment frequently broke down and was difficult for operators to fix. White Castle management also believed that milkshakes ruined customer's appetites for hamburgers, the company's flagship product. In 1935 White Castle sold 40 million hamburgers.

During World War II, White Castle did face serious problems owing to labor shortages and the lack of meat, which was rationed during the war. Likewise, sugar was also rationed and Coca-Cola was in short supply. Ingram sought new potential products. One was the fried-egg sandwich. Eggs were fried in a metal ring and were then served on a bun, much like McDonald's Egg McMuffin. Potatoes were another product that White Castle experimented with during the war. Potatoes were inexpensive, plentiful, and were not rationed. White Castle began serving french fries, which previously had not been served at many fast food operations.

White Castle continued to sell french fries after the war, but they were discontinued because many managers believed that deep-frying in hot grease was dangerous for operators, and it was difficult for operators to know when the fries were properly cooked. In the 1950s technological improvements made it possible for french fries to be easily and safely prepared, and so they were returned to the menu. Milkshake equipment also improved during the 1950s, so White Castle resumed selling them. In 1958 they test-marketed a King Size hamburger to compete with the increasing popularity of the Bob's Big Boy. It was not a success.

White Castle was confronted with a series of problems. Suburbs developed and highways permitted workers easy access to cities. As the number of automobiles sold skyrocketed during the 1940s and 1950s, car owners began frequenting drive-ins. Most White Castle outlets were located in urban areas, and many outlets did not have parking lots. Another problem was the crime that affected inner cities; many White Castles were open twenty-four hours a day and were frequent targets of robbers late at night. In addition, many inner-city establishments became havens for the homeless. Many used White Castle's restrooms to bathe and left messes, destroying White Castle's reputation for cleanliness. Finally, racial unrest hit the inner cities. Most Americans became wary of eating at White Castle, and by the 1960s there were only ninety White Castle outlets left.

In 1968 White Castle began a new construction program, locating many outlets in suburbs. While it could not compete with large chains such as McDonald's or Burger King, it could compete with smaller chains. Recently, White Castle has developed new partnerships with other chains, such as Church's Chicken, which has expanded White Castle's operations.

The White Castle system that Ingram developed had important differences from previous hamburger operations. Its formula had five components: efficiency and economy (5-cent hamburgers), limited menu, mass volume, standardization, and simplification of processes of preparing the food; prominent locations (near mass-transit stops); uniform and distinctive architecture (the white castle); aggressive expansion of outlets; and pleasant settings, which were especially good places for women and children. These characteristics, somewhat altered, became the basis for each subsequent fast food chain.

White Castle changed American culture dramatically. Hamburgers became one of America's most important foods during the 1920s, in part owing to White Castle. Customer surveys indicated that they liked the taste of the hamburger, the low price, the quality of all the products served, the cleanliness of the outlets, and the convenience. That this system has survived for more than eighty years (even though throughout much of its history it was a small, family-owned business) is a credit to its model, which was duplicated by other fast food chains, such as McDonald's. Most fast food chains today are based on variations of the White Castle system. As a result of this system, millions of fast food hamburgers are sold, not only in the United States, but throughout the world.

As of 2011, there were more than four hundred White Castle outlets, mainly in the Midwest, Tennessee, and New York. The company is headquartered in Columbus, Ohio.

See also Architecture/Design; Automobiles; Big Boy; Burger King; Church's Chicken; Coffee; French Fries; Hamburger; Radio; Slogans/Jingles; Soda/Soft Drinks; Uniforms; White Tower

For Further Information:

Hirshorn, Paul, and Steven Izenour. *White Towers*. Cambridge, MA: MIT Press, 1979.

Hogan, David Gerald. *Selling 'em by the Sack: White Castle and the Creation of American Food*. New York: New York University Press, 1997.

Ingram, Billy. *All this from a 5-cent Hamburger! The Story of the White Castle System*. New York: Newcomen Society in North America, 1964.

Jakle, John A., and Keith A. Sculle. *Fast Food: Roadside Restaurants in the Automobile Age*. Baltimore: Johns Hopkins University Press, 1999.

YouTube "White Castle Commercial," as at: www.youtube.com/watch?v=CKbfcObtgiU

White Tower

In the 1920s John E. Saxe, his son Thomas E. Saxe, and an associate, Daniel J. O'Connell, examined White Castle outlets in Minneapolis and concluded that fast food was an excellent idea and that White Castle had the right approach. In 1926 they opened their first White Tower restaurant near Marquette University in Milwaukee. It was an imitator of White Castle. Like White Castle, White Tower located its outlets at subway, trolley, and bus stops frequented by workers going to or from large factories. It specialized in 5-cent hamburgers, which were almost the same as White Castle's, but also sold ham sandwiches, doughnuts, pies, and beverages. The buildings were similar. White Tower's slogan, "Take Home a Bagful," was a take-off on White Castle's "Sell 'em by the Sack." Like White Castle restaurants, White Tower outlets were white to assure customers of the purity and cleanliness of their restaurants. Unlike White Castle, White Tower franchised its operation and the chain expanded steadily throughout the Midwest. In the late 1920s White Tower was one of the largest hamburger chains in America. In 1929 White Castle sued White Tower for trademark infringement, and the court ruled in favor of White Castle. White Tower was ordered to change its name and all resemblances to White Castle in its architecture and slogans. White Tower maintained its name by paying White Castle a large sum of money. After World War II, the chain began to falter as urban areas decayed and the suburbs began siphoning off the middle class. By 1979, White Tower had only eighty outlets, all of which were owned by Tombrock Corporation. White Tower slowly disappeared thereafter.

See also Architecture/Design; Automobiles; Beverages; Coffee; Doughnuts/Donuts; Hamburger; Pie; Radio; Sandwiches; Slogans/Jingles; Soda/Soft Drinks; Uniforms; White Castle

For Further Information:

Funderburg, Anne Cooper. *Sundae Best: A History of Soda Fountains*. Bowling Green, OH: Bowling Green State University Popular Press, 2002.

Hirshorn, Paul, and Steven Izenour. *White Towers*. Cambridge, MA: MIT Press, 1979.

Hogan, David Gerald. *Selling 'em by the Sack: White Castle and the Creation of American Food*. New York: New York University Press, 1997.

Levenstein, Harvey. *Paradox of Plenty: A Social History of Eating in Modern America*. New York: Oxford University Press, 1993.

Wienerschnitzel

Glen Bell, then an owner of a small chain of Mexican restaurants called El Taco, convinced John Galardi, a commissary manager for the company, to launch his own fast food chain in 1961. Bell invested in it and helped develop the idea. Martha Bell,

Glen's wife, supplied the name, Der Wienerschnitzel. It derived from the traditional Austrian veal dish, *wiener schnitzel*, which has nothing to do with hot dogs. The "Der" was removed from the name in 1977. In 1961 the first outlet, featuring hot dogs, corn dogs, and chili dogs, opened in Newport Beach, California. Galardi's first stand was flat-roofed, but he switched to an A-frame structure in which customers actually drove through the middle of the building. The chain's mascot is a hot dog that runs away from people who want to eat him. Wienerschnitzel remains privately owned; its parent company, the Galardi Group Franchise & Leasing, Inc., is headquartered in Newport Beach. Wienerschnitzel is the largest hot dog chain, with more than 360 outlets in 10 states and Guam. In 2005 the company co-branded with Tastee-Freez, so that its menu now includes Taste-Freez items.

See also Architecture/Design; Branding; Corn Dogs; Hot Dog; Tastee-Freez

For Further Information:

Jakle, John A., and Keith A. Sculle. *Fast Food: Roadside Restaurants in the Automobile Age*. Baltimore: Johns Hopkins University Press, 1999.

Langdon, Philip. *Orange Roofs, Golden Arches: The Architecture of American Chain Restaurants*. New York: Knopf, 1986.

Wimpy

Elzie Crisler Segar, a syndicated cartoonist for the King Features, created the Popeye the Sailor Man comics in 1929. In 1931 Segar introduced J. Wellington Wimpy, a fat cartoon character who loved to eat hamburgers. Wimpy was either too cheap or too poor to pay for them, and so he tried to con others into buying them for him. His immortal phrase was, "I'd gladly pay you tomorrow for a hamburger today." The term "Wimpy" became synonymous with "hamburger" in the United States and later in the United Kingdom. This association was so close that it spawned Wimpy's Grills, a hamburger chain that was launched in 1934 by Edward Vale Gold of Chicago. The chain thrived in the United States for a decade, and at its height had about 1,500 outlets. It featured a 10-cent hamburger, which was expensive for the time, as well as sandwiches made with roasted and toasted meats.

In 1953 its founder, Eddie Gold, offered the UK rights to Joseph Lyons and Co., of London, which had operated a chain of tearooms called Lyons Corner Houses since 1894. On a trial basis, Lyons opened a Wimpy counter in its Coventry Street Corner House in London. It was perfect timing on Lyons' part. The American military had introduced hamburger culture into Britain during World War II. By the early 1950s, beef rationing had ended and the British public was open to a new, inexpensive food from America. When Lyons offered Wimpy burgers at the Ideal Home Exhibition in 1954, they sold an average of ten thousand burgers a week. Lyons finalized the arrangement with Gold and began opening Wimpy restaurants. Unlike the fast food chains that were developing in the United States, Wimpy served their burgers on a plate, with cutlery, and orders were delivered to the table by waiters. In 1957 Lyons created a subsidiary company called Pleasure Foods, Ltd., to franchise Wimpy Grills throughout the United Kingdom.

In the United States, Wimpy Grills languished. When Gold died in 1977, only six outlets remained. In the United Kingdom, on the other hand, the Wimpy chain did well and hundreds of outlets were opened. McDonald's opened its first restaurant in London in 1974. To combat this new competition, Wimpy began advertising extensively, including on children's television programs in 1976. But McDonald's rapidly expanded throughout the UK, and by the end of the century it had more than one thousand outlets throughout the British Isles.

Faced with heavy competition from McDonald's, Lyons sold the UK Wimpy's outlets to United Biscuit, who in turn sold them to Grand Metropolitan. Subsequently, Grand Metropolitan acquired Pillsbury, which owned Burger King. Grand Metropolitan concluded that Burger King was a more efficient operation, and it converted many Wimpy Grills into Burger King restaurants. By 1998, Wimpy's franchises had declined to 280 counter-service outlets in the United Kingdom. In 2002 investors acquired Wimpy International. Despite the changes in ownership, Wimpy's has continued to innovate its menu. The Beanburger was introduced in 1987, as was the Quorn Burger, a vegetarian alternative to the hamburger, in 1997. Competition from McDonald's and other fast food chains has greatly diminished the number of Wimpy outlets, but the company is the oldest surviving hamburger chain in the United Kingdom.

In 1958 Gold and Lyons created Wimpy International to promote the chain outside of the United States and the United Kingdom. During the following decades, Wimpy outlets were opened in other countries, but its greatest success outside of the United States and the United Kingdom was in South Africa, where the company opened its first outlet in Durban in 1967. The chain has thrived in South Africa ever since.

See also Cartoon Characters; Hamburger; Pillsbury; South Africa; United Kingdom

For Further Information:

Hogan, David Gerald. *Selling 'em by the Sack: White Castle and the Creation of American Food*. New York: New York University Press, 1997.

Winchell's Donut House

In 1948 Verne H. Winchell founded Winchell's Donut House in Temple City, a suburb of Los Angeles. It sold mainly doughnuts and coffee, but it later expanded into a variety of menu items, including breakfast sandwiches, specialty coffees, ices, and juices. From Los Angeles, the chain spread northward to San Francisco, Portland, Seattle, and east to Phoenix and Denver. The company merged with the Denny's restaurant chain twenty years later. The trend toward healthier foods caused serious problems for doughnut sales beginning in the 1980s, and many outlets closed.

Many Winchell's franchises were sold to Cambodian immigrants, who established a special economic niche for themselves. By 1985, 80 percent of California's doughnut shops were Cambodian-owned.

Winchell's has expanded its product line. It now includes seventy different varieties of doughnuts, croissants, cinnamon rolls, bagels, and muffins, as well as beverages including coffee, frozen cappuccinos, fruit juices, and soda. In celebration of its fiftieth anniversary in 1998, Winchell's in Pasadena, California, created the world's largest doughnut, weighing five thousand pounds and measuring ninety-five feet in diameter.

Today, Winchell's is owned by Yum-Yum Donuts, a small chain of about 64 outlets in California. As of 2011, Winchell's Donut House chain had about 170 stores, mainly in 12 western states, as well as in Guam, Saipan, and Saudi Arabia. Winchell's and Yum-Yum Donuts are headquartered in the City of Industry, a suburb of Los Angeles.

See also Coffee; Doughnuts/Donuts; Soda/Soft Drinks

For Further Information:

Jakle, John A., and Keith A. Sculle. *Fast Food: Roadside Restaurants in the Automobile Age*. Baltimore: Johns Hopkins University Press, 1999.

Mullins, Paul R. *Glazed America: A History of the Doughnut*. Gainesville: University Press of Florida, 2008.

Winchell's Donut's Web site: www.winchells.com

Wing Zone

Wing Zone was created in 1991 by Matt Friedman and Adam Scott. Its flagship product is hot Buffalo wings. They also sell other items, including teriyaki, potato wedges, sandwiches, and salads.

As of 2011, the Wing Zone had about one hundred outlets in twenty-three states. They also have outlets in Panama, the Bahamas, and are considering opening restaurants in Japan. The company is headquartered in Atlanta.

See also Buffalo Wings; Chicken; Chicken Wings; Potatoes; Salads; Sandwiches

For Further Information:

Wing Zone Web site: www.wingzone.com

Wonka Brand

In 1964 Roald Dahl wrote *Charlie and the Chocolate Factory*, a story about a poor boy who wins a tour in a candy factory. The book was an immediate children's best seller. A movie based on the book, *Willy Wonka & the Chocolate Factory*, was released in 1971, directed by Mel Stuart. Breaker Confections of Chicago bought the rights to use the Willy Wonka name for its candies. In 1976 Breaker released the Everlasting Gobstopper, a jawbreaker, which Wonka had invented "for children who are given very little pocket money." Everlasting Gobstoppers, as reported in *Charlie and the Chocolate Factory*, could be put "in your mouth and you can suck it and suck it and suck it and suck it and it will never get any smaller!"

Breaker was acquired by Sunmark Companies of St. Louis, and Sunmark changed the name to Willy Wonka Brand in 1980. Sunmark was acquired by Rowntree's of York, a British chocolate company. Rowntree's was acquired by Nestlé in 1988. The name of the brand was changed to the Willy Wonka Candy Factory in 1993; five years later, Nestlé released Wonka Bars, the only candy other than Gobstoppers that were specifically mentioned in *Charlie and the Chocolate Factory*. Nestlé combined several candies acquired by the company under the Wonka brand name, including Bottle Caps, Pixy Stix, Nerds, Fun Dip, and Laffy Taffy.

Sales of Wonka Bars dropped off in 2000 and Nestlé planned to discontinue them. Then, director Tim Burton acquired the movie rights to *Charlie and the Chocolate Factory* and announced his plans to remake the 1971 film. Nestlé jumped at the chance for product placement in the movie. It provided hundreds of candy bars and thousands of props, and engaged in a massive promotional campaign promoting the movie and its own candy. It supplied 30,000 retailers, including Walmart, Target, Barnes & Noble, grocery stores, and Warner Bros. movie theaters, with special in-store promotions, and manufactured 60 million candy bars. The placement of Nestlé chocolates in the movie and the massive advertising campaign relaunched the brand. The new movie was a tremendous success, as was the sale of Nestlé candies featuring a cartoon likeness of Willy Wonka.

Wonka chocolate bar. (AP/Wide World Photos)

See also Bottle Caps; Movie Theaters; Nestlé; Pixy Stix; Rowntree's of York

For Further Information:

Lehu, Jean-Marc. *Branded Entertainment: Product Placement and Brand Strategy in the Entertainment Business*. Philadelphia, PA: Kogan Page, 2009.

Nestle USA Web site: www.Nestleusa.com

Wonka Web site: www.wonka.com

World Health Organization (WHO)

The World Health Organization (WHO), formed in 1948, is a specialized agency of the United Nations. Its purpose is to combat disease and promote health throughout the world. WHO is headquartered in Geneva, Switzerland.

WHO collects and disseminates statistics about the state of disease and health. For the past decade, the agency has become particularly concerned with diet, overweight, and obesity worldwide. According to WHO: "Obesity has reached epidemic proportions globally, with more than 1 billion adults overweight—at least 300 million of them clinically obese—and is a major contributor to the global burden of chronic disease and disability." It blames poor eating for the rising levels of obesity, pointing to "increased consumption of more energy-dense, nutrient-poor foods with high levels of sugar and saturated fats." It concludes that diets that contain large amounts of fat, sugar, or salt contribute to chronic diseases such as diabetes, heart disease, and cancers, which cause 60 percent of all deaths worldwide. Other studies conducted by WHO have examined the serious negative consequences of consuming transfats. It recommends that countries adopt policies that promote low-fat, high-fiber foods; daily physical exercise of at least thirty minutes; greater consumption of fruit and vegetables; and a move away from animal saturated fats to unsaturated, vegetable oil–based fats.

In 2004 WHO adopted a plan to improve diets and physical activity. In 2010 delegates to WHO agreed to reduce children's consumption of junk food and soft drinks by asking member states to restrict advertising and marketing. It specifically recommended making schools and playgrounds free from all forms of marketing of junk food and sugary drinks. In 2011 WHO urged member nations to reduce exposure of children to such marketing. WHO reports that Coca-Cola, Mexico's Grupo Bimbo, General Mills, Kellogg, Kraft, McDonald's, Mars, Nestle, PepsiCo, Unilever, and the World Federation of Advertisers have signed a code of conduct in which they have promised not to market their unhealthy items to children younger than age twelve.

WHO arranged for a meeting of heads of state for September 19–20, 2011, at the United Nations in New York, to discuss restrictions on advertisements for unhealthy foods.

See also Fast Food; Junk Foods; Marketing to Children; Obesity

For Further Information:

Nishida, C., and R. Uauy. "WHO Scientific Update on Health Consequences of Trans Fatty Acids." *European Journal of Clinical Nutrition* 63 (May 2009): S1–S4.

World Health Organization Web site: www.who.int/en

Wrigley Co.

In 1891 William Wrigley Jr. moved to Chicago and began selling soap. To increase sales, he gave away gum to his customers. His gum was a hit, and so he decided to make and sell it. In 1893 he began manufacturing Juicy Fruit and Spearmint gums. Wrigley's gum was packaged in small containers with five sticks each, and they were distributed though confectioners and grocery stores. At the time, Wrigley was just one of hundreds of gum manufacturers in the United States.

Wrigley began promoting his gum through advertisements, and he began to expand his operation. He was the first American gum manufacturer to begin selling his products abroad, first in Canada (1910), and then in the United Kingdom (1911) and Australia (1915). In 1927 he opened up a factory in London. He also continued to create new products and innovate their distribution. For instance, the company released its Doublemint gum in 1914. Wrigley sold his gum through vending machines, and in the 1920s he purchased the rights to ten thousand machines in the New York City subways.

During World War II, the Wrigley Co. was contracted to pack K-rations for soldiers. It inserted a stick of chewing gum in every ration. The company has continued to develop new gums; it introduced its Freedent Gum (designed to not stick to dentures) in 1977 and Extra Sugarfree Gum in 1984. Two years later, it introduced Hubba Bubba Bubble Gum.

Wrigley has engaged in extensive advertising. Its jingle "Double your pleasure, double your fun" for Doublemint Gum was rated by *Advertising Age* in 2001 as one of the top ten advertising jingles of the twentieth century.

Wrigley has factories in 40 other countries and its gum is distributed in 180 countries. It is the top-selling gum in China. The company is the world's largest maker of chewing and bubble gum; its headquarters are in Chicago. It has acquired other confections, such as LifeSavers. In 2008 the company was acquired by Mars, Inc.

See also Advertising; Gum; LifeSavers; Slogans/Jingles; Vending Machines

For Further Information:

Hendrickson, Robert. *The Great American Chewing Gum Book*. Radnor, PA: Chilton Book Company, 1976.

Redclift, Michael R. *Chewing Gum: The Fortunes of Taste*. New York: Routledge, 2004.

Y

Yogurt

Yogurt is a sour fermented product made from milk, commonly used in the Middle East and India; today, it is commonly sold in the United States as a semi-solid, often-flavored food. The lactic-acid bacilli was isolated at the Pasteur Institute by a Russian scientist named Elie Metchnikoff, who believed that regularly consuming it would prolong a person's life. After World War I, yogurt began to be commercialized by Isaac Carasso in Barcelona, Spain. He formed Danone, which thrived in Europe until World War II. Carasso immigrated to the United States and launched Dannon in 1942. Today, yogurt is made from milk that has been fermented with bacteria. Because plain yogurt is sour, most commercial brands add flavorings and colorings.

Yogurt was a fringe food until the 1970s, when it was promoted as a health food. Although yogurt companies do have plain and low-calorie lines, critics claim that many products are filled with sugar (240 calories per container), and some brands have begun to add candy. A full-fat yogurt can contain up to 16 grams of saturated fat. As one critic noted, many brands of yogurt contain more sugar than junk food.

Common brands of yogurt for sale in the United States are Dannon; Yoplait, made by General Mills; Light n' Lively, made by Kraft Foods; Weight Watchers; and Breyers. Yogurt has developed a number of other lines, such as frozen yogurt, yogurt drinks, and portable yogurt (GoGurt) in a tube.

For a variety of reasons, the sale of yogurt has doubled recently. Reasons for this increase include its purported health value and a trend toward global flavors, such as Greek yogurt and Icelandic yogurt. Perhaps most important has been the emergence of self-serve frozen yogurt shops. Yogurt sales are expected to expand further in the future.

See also Danone/Dannon; TCBY; Yogurt, Frozen; Yoplait

Greek-Style Yogurt

Greek-style yogurt has recently become the rage. It is thicker and usually higher in protein than regular yogurt. Stonyfield Farm, owned by Group Danone, released its Oikos brand yogurt in 2007, and in 2011 Kraft Foods launched its Athenos Greek yogurt brand.

For Further Information:

Chandan, Ramesh C. *Manufacturing Yogurt and Fermented Milks*. Ames, IA: Blackwell Pub., 2006.

Yogurt, Frozen

Frozen yogurt originated in New England in the 1970s. It is a dessert that includes yogurt culture as an ingredient. It tends to be less sweet than ice cream and lower in fat. It has a healthy image largely owing to yogurt's healthy image, and it is frequently considered a diet food. TCBY is one of the larger companies that sell frozen yogurt.

Frozen yogurt is sold by a number of small chains. Pinkberry, for instance, sells Swirly Goodness, a premium frozen yogurt. Tutti Frutti has about one hundred outlets in California, Virginia, Georgia, Texas, Hawaii, Indonesia, Vietnam, Philippines, Tahiti, and Mexico. Healthy Fast Food, with about ten outlets, sells U-SWIRL Frozen Yogurt.

See also Danone/Dannon; TCBY; Yogurt; Yoplait

For Further Information:

Hoffman, Mable, and Gar Hoffman. *Ice Cream & Frozen Yogurt*. Tucson, AZ: Fisher Books, 2000.

Kaldunski, Shelly. *Sweet Scoops: Ice Cream, Gelato, Frozen Yogurt, Sorbet, and More*. San Francisco, CA: Weldon Owen, Inc., 2011.

TCBY Web site: www.tcby.com

U-SWIRL Web site: www.U-SWIRL.com

Yoplait

In 1965 two French dairy co-ops, Yola and Coplait, merged, becoming Yoplait. Its first franchise was licensed in Switzerland in 1969. Since then, the co-op has expanded to fifty other countries. In the United States, General Mills is licensed to sell Yoplait yogurt and other products, such as smoothies, whips, and delights. General Mills also markets Trix Yogurt,

Yoplait. (AP/Wide World Photos)

based on their breakfast cereal of the same name. Yoplait's Fiber One, a new introduction, is a fifty-calorie yogurt with five grams of fiber and zero grams of fat. Yoplait is the second-largest seller of fresh dairy products in the world.

See also Danone/Dannon; General Mills; Smoothies; Yogurt

For Further Information:
Yoplait (USA) Web site: www.yoplaitusa.com

York Peppermint Patties

York Peppermint Patties are flat, round, dark chocolates with peppermint creme inside. They were formulated and launched in 1940 by the York Cone Company, which mainly manufactured ice cream cones. The company had been founded in 1920 in York, Pennsylvania; it mainly distributed its product in the northeast, Ohio, Indiana, and Florida. In 1972 the company was acquired by Peter Paul, which expanded production and aggressively promoted it nationally beginning in 1975. Peter Paul was sold to Cadbury in 1978 and, ten years later, the Hershey Company acquired York Peppermint Patties when it purchased the confectionery operations of Cadbury Schweppes in the United States. It is one of the best-selling candies in the United States.

See also Cadbury; Candy; Chocolate; Hershey Company; Peter Paul Candy Company

For Further Information:
York Peppermint Pattie Web site: www.hersheys.com/products/details/york.asp

YouTube

YouTube, a video-sharing Web site, was launched in 2005 by Chad Hurley, Steve Chen, and Jawed Karim in San Bruno, California. It was acquired by Google in 2006. YouTube is one of the most visited Web sites on the Internet. Virtually every fast food and junk food company has a presence on YouTube, including advertisements and promotional offers. YouTube also has spoofs, exposés, and videos uploaded by opponents of fast food and junk food.

McDonald's produced three computer videos in 2010 to promote fruit and vegetables: "Crave my Fave," "Fruit is Fun," and "Yummivore," which stars a cartoon character who loves healthy food, all of which are on the McDonald's YouTube Web site. These have not received many visits. According to the Rudd Center for Food Policy & Obesity, as of June 2010, the fast food companies that have the most uploads on YouTube are, in descending order: Starbucks, Dominos, and Taco Bell.

See also Advertising; Domino's Pizza; Internet; Marketing to Children; Rudd Center for Food Policy & Obesity; Social Media; Starbucks; Taco Bell

For Further Information:

Lacy, Sarah. *The Stories of Facebook, YouTube & Myspace: The People, the Hype and the Deals Behind the Giants of Web 2.0.* Richmond, UK: Crimson, 2008.

YouTube "Early Burger King Commercial," as at: www.youtube.com/watch?v=YLMJFX WhtVg&feature=related

YouTube "Rare First Ever Ronald McDonald Commercial," as at: www.youtube.com/watch?v=QIuXv7Y8QA4&feature=related

YouTube "Ronald McDonald Commercial from the 1970s," as at: www.youtube.com/watch?v=bnP8vfR9Ph4&feature=related

YouTube Web site: www.youtube.com

Yum! Brands, Inc.

Beginning in the 1970s, PepsiCo began acquiring several fast food restaurant chains, including KFC, Pizza Hut, and Taco Bell, as an adjunct to its soda business. It required that those chains serve only Pepsi-Cola. Other fast food chains, such as McDonald's, saw PepsiCo as a competitor and refused to sell PepsiCo products. PepsiCo finally concluded that it would be in the company's interest to spin off its restaurant businesses. Accordingly, in 1997 Tricon Global Restaurants, Inc., was founded as an independent, publicly traded company. In 2002 Tricon announced the acquisition of Yorkshire Global Restaurants and its two brands, Long John Silver's and A&W All-American Food. Tricon changed its name to Yum! Brands, Inc., in 2003.

Globalization

Yum! Brands is the world's largest fast food restaurant system, and it is rapidly expanding outside the United States. In 2009 Yum! Brands opened more than 1,400 new restaurants around the world. In 2010 it opened more than 4 new restaurants each day.

In 2007 Yum! Brands began to raise money to fight world hunger. Since then, the company has raised $85 million for the United Nations World Food Programme and other hunger relief agencies. The company also has an extensive program to make its restaurants more energy efficient and its containers more environmentally friendly.

Yum! Brands has more than 3,900 restaurants—mainly KFC and Pizza Hut—in China, where the company plans to add an additional 500 units in 2011, and a total of 16,000 more restaurants by 2020. Yum! Brands also acquired a major interest in other restaurant chains in China who operate similar franchises to KFC, such as Little Sheep, a Mongolian Hot Pot chain with 480 outlets. It is also rapidly expanding elsewhere in Asia, including India, Indonesia, Malaysia, and Vietnam, and it has targeted Africa, where it already has a 44 percent market share in South Africa.

Corporate

Yum! Brands, Inc., is based in Louisville, Kentucky. In 2009 it generated revenues of nearly $11 billion. As of 2011, it was the world's largest fast food restaurant system, with more than 37,000 restaurants, of which 23,000 are located in the United States and 14,000 are located in 110 other countries. It operates in seven divisions: KFC-U.S., Pizza Hut-U.S., Taco Bell-U.S., Long John Silver's-U.S., A&W Restaurants-U.S., Yum Restaurants International, and Yum Restaurants China. In 2011 Yum! Brands announced that it intended to sell Long John Silver's and A&W Restaurants, which were not able to expand abroad, so that it could focus on KFC, Pizza Hut, and Taco Bell. In September 2011 Yum! Brands reached agreement to sell A&W Restaurants-U.S. and Long John Silver's-U.S. to franchisees.

See also A&W; China; KFC; Long John Silver's; PepsiCo; Pizza Hut; Taco Bell

For Further Information:
Yum! Brands Web site: www.yum.com

Z

Zotz

Zotz are hard candies with a fizzy, sour center. Zotz Fizz Power Candies were introduced in 1968, seven years before Pop Rocks. The popularity of Zotz with children was immediate; sales skyrocketed. As other fizzy candy began to be sold, Zotz sales declined. Unlike many other fizzy candies, Zotz candies have survived, and today are America's best-selling fizzy candies.

Zotz are manufactured by G. B. Ambrosoli, a family-owned company headquartered in Como, Italy. In the United States, Zotz are distributed by Andre Post, Inc., of Old Saybrook, Connecticut. Zotz come in six flavors: lemon, orange, grape, cherry, watermelon, and sour apple.

See also Candy; Pop Rocks

For Further Information:

Andre Post Web site: www.andreprost.com

Glossary

Addiction   Addiction is the persistent, compulsive use of a substance regardless of its negative consequences.

Antibiotics   Antibiotics are drugs that kill or retard the growth of bacteria. They have had a tremendous positive effect in preventing or treating disease in humans and are generally considered safe.

Aspartame   Marketed under the names NutraSweet and Equal, aspartame is an artificial sweetener that was discovered in 1965. It was first authorized to enter the U.S. market in 1974. Numerous allegations have been made against aspartame, none of which have been conclusively proven.

Batch Processing   Some junk foods are made by batch processing, where they are manufactured in small individual batches as opposed to processing them through the more common continuous-flow machines. As batch processing is more costly, junk foods made this way are more expensive.

Blood Pressure   Blood pressure (BP) is the force exerted by the contraction of the heart on the walls of blood vessels, especially arteries. BP varies between a maximum (systolic) and a minimum (diastolic). Normal BP is 120 (systolic) and 80 (diastolic). BP is influenced by a variety of factors, including health, age, gender, height, and physical condition. High blood pressure is called hypertension. It is defined as a BP at 140 (systolic) and 90 (diastolic) or higher.

Body Mass Index   Body Mass Index (BMI) is a statistical ratio of weight to height. It is calculated by dividing a person's height in inches (squared) by their weight in pounds. BMI is a simple test that correlates with fatness. A BMI of 18.5 or less is underweight; a BMI of 18.5 to 24.9 is healthy; and a BMI of 25 to 29.9 is overweight. Obesity is medically defined as a BMI over 30. Studies have shown that individuals who have a BMI between 25 and 30 have a 13 percent greater chance of an early death when compared with those with BMIs of 18.5 to 24.9. Those with BMIs over 40 are considered morbidly obese and their chance for an early death is 250 percent.

Bundling   Bundling is the practice of joining related products together for the purpose of selling them as a single unit.

Caffeine   Caffeine is a bitter alkaloid that is metabolized in the liver. It is a mild stimulant commonly found naturally in cocoa, coffee beans, tea leaves, and kola nuts. It appears in many junk foods, including chocolate, coffee, tea, colas, power and sports drinks, and energy bars. Consumed in small doses it can increase alertness, relieve drowsiness, and improve coordination. In large doses it can cause anxiety, insomnia, nervousness, and hypertension. Caffeine is a diuretic. It can relieve some head-aches, and hence it is found in many pain relievers.

Calorie   In the 1890s, chemist Wilbur O. Atwater analyzed the nutri-tional components of food (proteins, fats, and carbohydrates) and measured the caloric value of each of the groups. In the early 1900s, Russell Chittenden, a chemist at Yale University, took Atwater's idea of assessing food in terms of calories—the amount of heat required to raise the temperature of 1 gram of water 1° Centigrade—and applied it not only to energy taken in but to energy burned in exercise. Calorie counting was born. Lulu Hunt Peters' book, *Diet and Health, with Key to the Calories* (1917), advocated calorie counting as a method of weight reduction. It introduced the so-called scientific prin-ciple that calorie control equated weight control. Those who were unable to control their weight were judged to have no self-discipline, and obesity became a sign of moral weakness.

Carbohydrates   Carbohydrates are one of the major dietary components. Their primary function is to provide energy for the body. The most important carbohydrates include simple sugars, starches, glycogens, and fiber. Complex carbohydrates are ultimately broken down into simple sugars that the body can easily metabolize.

Carbonation   Carbonation occurs when carbon dioxide (CO_2) gas is dissolved in a liquid. This creates the "fizz" in soft drinks, beer, cham-pagne, and sparkling mineral water.

Chains   Chains are multiple restaurants owned by the same company or franchisers.

Cholesterol, Blood The body manufactures cholesterol in the form of dietary cholesterol, and high levels of blood cholesterol increase risk of heart disease. Cholesterol travels in the blood in little packages of fat and protein called lipoproteins. Cholesterol in high-density lipoproteins (HDL) is the so-called good cholesterol; cholesterol in low-density lipoproteins (LDL) is bad because it is headed for the artery walls.

Cholesterol, Dietary Dietary cholesterol is a crystalline substance found in animal tissues. The body normally synthesizes it in the liver. Its level in the bloodstream can be influenced by heredity and the consumption of certain foods. Cholesterol can cause atherosclerotic plaque and heart disease.

Class Action Lawsuit A class action lawsuit is a legal action undertaken by one or more plaintiffs with a common interest in a matter.

Co-Branding Co-branding is the displaying of more than one brand name on a product or location; the marketing or distribution of co-branded products or services; or a co-branding arrangement with potential benefits to be gained for both sides.

Continuous Processing Continuous processing is a common way of manufacturing food, as opposed to batch processing. Continuous processing is more efficient and is less costly than batch processing. Most large food manufacturers have installed continuous processing machines that process their products with little human intervention.

Electrolytes Electrolytes are sodium and potassium salts that are lost owing to exercise and other causes. Sports drinks with electrolytes are used to replenish the body's water and electrolyte levels after dehydration caused by exercise, diaphoresis, diarrhea, vomiting, or starvation. Giving pure water at such times is not the best way to restore fluid levels because it dilutes the salts inside the body's cells and interferes with their chemical functions.

Encroachment Encroachment is the awarding of a new franchise or the opening of a company store too close to an existing franchise.

Experimental Design An experimental design is a research plan in which the selection of subjects, their assignment to groups, their exposure to various treatments, and the recording of observations are all controlled by the researcher as much as possible.

Extruding Extruding is the process wherein hot foods are forced through an extruder and then puff up when they hit cool air.

Fat, Dietary   There are five major types of dietary fats: saturated, unsaturated, polyunsaturated, monounsaturated, and partially hydrogenated vegetable oil. Saturated fats are saturated with hydrogen atoms. In the United States they are mainly found in dairy products, meat, poultry, and vegetable shortenings made with coconut oil, palm oil, and/or palm kernel oil. Saturated fats can raise blood cholesterol levels, whereas unsaturated fats do not. Polyunsaturated fat molecules are missing hydrogen atoms. Sources of polyunsaturated fats are corn oil, cottonseed oil, safflower oil, soybean oil, and sunflower oil, as well as some fish oils, margarines, mayonnaise, almonds, and pecans. Monounsaturated fats are dietary fats with one double-bonded carbon in the molecule; they are commonly found in poultry, shortening, meat, dairy products, and olive and canola oils. Partially hydrogenated vegetable oils are harder and more stable than other oils. Companies mix them with hydrogen, which increases the amount of saturated fat and creates transfat, which raises blood cholesterol.

Food Allergy   An allergy is an immunological reaction to proteins in food. There are eight common foods that trigger this response: eggs, wheat, peanuts, milk, tree nuts, soy, fish, and crustaceans. Contact with allergens can have a wide range of effects, such as itching, swelling, rash, spreading hives, vomiting, diarrhea, breathing difficulties, and in the most severe cases, death. Food allergies are distinct from food intolerances. Allergic reactions to food usually occur within thirty minutes of ingesting or exposure to the allergen.

Food Intolerance   A food intolerance (food sensitivity or food hypersensitivity) is a common disorder caused by the inability to properly digest or fully process certain foods, which can lead to a wide range of symptoms affecting the skin, respiratory tract, or gastrointestinal tract. Reactions to food intolerances may be delayed up to forty-eight hours after ingestion or contact with the food. Food intolerances are usually difficult to diagnose, as they mimic many other diseases.

Fondant   Fondant is a sweet, creamy sugar paste used as a filling or for coating candies, cakes, and pastries as icing. It is composed of gelatin, confectioner's sugar, and water. It is a very smooth and malleable icing that dries hard. Bon bons are candies that frequently have fondant fillings.

Franchise

A franchise is the authorization granted to an individual or group by a company to sell its products or services in a particular area.

Fructose

Fructose is a monosaccharide sugar occurring in many fruits, vegetables, and honey. It is commonly used as a sweetener in food because it is much sweeter than glucose. When chemically combined with glucose, fructose forms sucrose, or common table sugar.

Glucose

Glucose is a simple monosaccharide sugar that occurs naturally in many plants and animal tissue. It is the most important energy source for the body's cells. Several hormones, including insulin, control glucose levels in the blood. Glucose is also referred to as dextrose, especially in the food industry. When chemically combined with fructose, glucose forms sucrose, or common table sugar.

Hazard Analysis & Critical Control Points

Hazard Analysis & Critical Control Points (HACCP) is defined by the Food and Drug Administration as "a management system in which food safety is addressed through the analysis and control of biological, chemical, and physical hazards from raw material production, procurement and handling, to manufacturing, distribution and consumption of the finished product." It is employed in the retail and food service industry to detect and avoid potential health problems related to the food they prepare and sell.

Herbicides

Herbicides, or weedkillers, are pesticides used to kill specific plants but leave the desired crop relatively unharmed. The use of chemical herbicides since the 1940s has greatly increased agricultural production. Concerns have been raised about the effects of chemical herbicides on farm workers and on wild animal populations. In addition, small amounts of some chemical herbicides find their way into foods, and concerns have been expressed about the effects on consumers. In the United States, the Environmental Protection Agency is responsible for setting pesticide tolerances.

High-Fructose Corn Syrup

High-fructose corn syrup (HFCS) is a sweetener made by refining corn starch into glucose, which is then converted into fructose. It is much sweeter than sucrose (common table sugar). It is used extensively in junk foods, especially baked goods and sugary beverages, such as soda.

Hormones   Hormones are chemicals produced by a cell or gland in one part of the body that regulate other cells and organs. Hormones may alter the body's growth, reproduction, functioning, digestion, and metabolism.

Insulin   Insulin is a protein hormone made by the pancreas that regulates the level of glucose in the blood. It permits cells to store or use glucose for energy. In Type 1 diabetes the pancreas does not produce enough insulin. In Type 2 diabetes the pancreas produces insulin, but the cells throughout the body do not respond normally to it, which causes glucose levels in the blood to rise.

Junk Food   Junk foods are defined as those high in calories, fat, caffeine, sugar, and/or salt, with little nutritional value.

Leadership in Energy and Environmental Design   Leadership in Energy and Environmental Design (LEED) is a program offered by the U. S. Green Building Council that certifies buildings that promote "environmentally responsible, profitable and healthy places to live and work." Many fast food chains have begun to open LEED certified outlets, including Dunkin' Donuts, Subway, McDonald's, Arby's, and Starbucks.

Longitudinal Study   A longitudinal study is one that examines a group of individuals at regular intervals over a relatively long period of time, typically five, ten, or even more years.

Maltose   Maltose is a disaccharide composed of two glucose residues. It is used as a nutrient and sweetener, particularly in China, where historically it has been extracted from sorghum grass.

MSG   MSG (Monosodium glutamate) is a common food additive found in many junk foods. It is considered a flavor enhancer. Some people are allergic to it, but it is generally considered harmless for most people.

Nougat   Nougat is a chewy or hard confection made from sugar or honey; nuts such as almonds, walnuts, or pistachios; and occasionally fruit. Flavorings are added to produce nougats with different tastes. Nougats are used in the manufacture of many confections, including 3 Musketeers candy bars.

Obesity   Obesity is a chronic condition characterized by excessive body fat. There are several different methods of determining obesity. A man is considered obese when his weight is 20 percent or more above the maximum recommended weight for his height (25 percent for women). A method of calculating obesity is the Body Mass Index (BMI), where obesity is defined as a BMI over 30.

Pesticides   Pesticides are substances intended for preventing, destroying, or controlling any pest, including plants or animals causing harm during or otherwise interfering with the production, processing, storage, transport, or marketing of food. In the United States, the Food and Drug Administration (FDA) was responsible for regulating pesticides until 1969, when the Environmental Protection Agency (EPA) was created. Since then, the EPA is responsible for setting pesticide tolerances.

Private Equity Firm   A private equity firm acquires and manages companies, usually through partnerships with the management of the acquired company. A private group does not have publicly traded stock and is not listed on stock exchanges.

Proteins   Proteins are molecules composed of one or more amino acids. Twenty-two amino acids have been identified as necessary for health; fourteen of these the body metabolizes, and eight essential amino acids need to be consumed from food. Proteins are essential to building, maintaining, and repairing body tissue, such as skin, internal organs, bones, and muscle. Proteins often function as enzymes, hormones, and antibodies. They are commonly found in many foods, such as eggs, cheese, meat, poultry, and fish.

QSR   Quick-service restaurant (QSR) is the term used by many companies as an alternative to the term "fast food," which has pejorative connotations.

rBGH   In March 1990 the U.S. Food and Drug Administration approved the use of bioengineered recombinant chymosin in cheesemaking. Chymosin served as a substitute for rennet, an enzyme traditionally scraped from the lining of calves' stomachs. Today, about 90 percent of American hard cheese contains this transgenic enzyme, and little controversy surrounded this application of bioengineering. But controversy swirled around the next decision when, three years later, the FDA approved Monsanto's application for recombinant bovine growth hormone (rBGH), also known as recombinant bovine somatotropin (rBST), which increases lactation in dairy cows by 10 to 20 percent. This transgenic hormone, marketed under the name Posilac, is in regular use in many non-organic dairies. The concerns raised relate to animal welfare, the fear that the hormone will contaminate local water supplies, and potential harm to the health of those who consume milk produced by cows injected with rGBH/rBST. Others have dismissed the concerns and have pointed to the environmental advantages of having fewer cows produce more milk. More than 120 studies have shown that "rBST poses no risk to human health." Whatever the debate, Monsanto estimates that one-third of all dairy cows in America are injected with Posilac. In August 2008, Monsanto announced the sale of Posilac to Eli Lilly and Company's subsidiary, Elanco Animal Health, for $300 million.

Saccharin

Saccharin is an artificial sweetener that was invented by a graduate student at Johns Hopkins University in 1879. This became the foundation for the megacorporation Monsanto. The long-term safety of saccharin was challenged in 1977, and the FDA placed a moratorium on its use until more studies were conducted. The ban was lifted in 1991, but by that time virtually all diet soda production had shifted to using aspartame.

Serotonin

Serotonin is neurotransmitter that permits nerve impulses. It is derived from tryptophanin. An imbalance of serotonin may affect moods, sleep, and appetite. Medications that influence serotonin levels are employed to treat depression.

Stress

Stress is a physical, mental, or emotional state that causes bodily or mental tension. It may be caused by social pressures and anxiety, and it may contribute to overeating, especially overeating of junk foods and fast foods.

Sucrose

Sucrose (common table sugar) is a crystalline disaccharide composed of one molecule each of fructose and glucose. It is found in many plants, but it is extracted mainly from sugarcane and sugar beets. It is widely used as a sweetener and preservative.

Sugar

Common sugars include sucrose, fructose, and glucose. All three are simple carbohydrates, easily absorbed and converted by the body into energy. Sucrose is the most adaptable for culinary purposes, and it has been used for hundreds of years as a preservative and sweetener. It is also used as an aid to the fermentation of beer and wine, and because it encourages yeast growth it has been used in baking. It is present in all green plants, but it exists in sufficient quantities to be viable for commercial extraction only in sugarcane and sugar beets. Refined sugar has no nutritional value (no minerals, vitamins, protein, or fiber), other than providing calories.

Tie-In

A tie-in is an association between two publicity campaigns in the form of a theme common to both, or an advertisement that appears in two different media.

Whole grains   Whole grain flours are cereal grains that contain more germ and bran after milling. They are higher in dietary fiber and other nutrients than other refined grains, which contain only the endosperm. Whole grains may reduce the risk of heart disease and improve digestion.

Selected Bibliography

Aaseng, Nathan. *Business Builders in Sweets and Treats*. Minneapolis: Oliver Press, 2005.

Alfino, Mark, John S. Caputo, and Robin Wynyard, eds. *McDonaldization Revisited: Critical Essays on Consumer Culture*. Westport, CT: Greenwood Press, 1998.

Allen, Gary, and Ken Albala, eds. *The Business of Food: Encyclopedia of Food and Drink Industries*. Westport, CT: Greenwood Press, 2007.

Allen, Lawrence L. *Chocolate Fortunes: The Battle for the Hearts, Minds, and Wallets of China's Consumers*. New York: American Management Association, 2010.

Almond, Steve. *Candyfreak*. Chapel Hill, NC: Algonquin Books of Chapel Hill, 2004.

Amos, Wally, with Leroy Robinson. *The Famous Amos Story: The Face That Launched a Thousand Chips*. Garden City, NY: Doubleday, 1983.

Anderson, Michael, and David Matsa. "Are Restaurants Really Supersizing America?" *American Economic Journal: Applied. Economics* 2, no. 2 (May 2010): 164–78.

Aronson, Marc, and Marina Bidhos. *Sugar Changed the World: A Story of Magic, Spice, Slavery, Freedom and Science*. Boston: Houghton Mifflin Harcourt, 2010.

Avise, John. *The Hope, Hype & Reality of Genetic Engineering: Remarkable Stories from Agriculture, Industry, Medicine, and the Environment*. New York: Oxford University Press, 2004.

Balinska, Maria. *The Bagel: The Surprising History of a Modest Bread*. New Haven, CT, and London: Yale University Press, 2008.

Bernstein, Charles, and Ron Paul. *Winning the Chain Restaurant Game: Eight Key Strategies*. New York: John Wiley & Sons, 1994.

Bishop, Marlene R., ed. *Chocolate, Fast Foods, and Sweeteners: Consumption and Health*. New York: Nova Science Publishers, 2010.

Boas, Max, and Steve Chain. *Big Mac: The Unauthorized Story of McDonald's.* New York: Mentor Books, The New American Library, 1977.

Borushek, Allan. *Calorie, Fat & Carbohydrate Counter; Plus 200 Fast-Food Chains & Restaurants.* Costa Mesa, CA: Family Health Publications, 2010.

Bové, José, François Dufour, and Gilles Luneau. *The World Is Not for Sale: Farmers Against Junk Food.* New York: Verso, 2001.

Bowers, Q. David. *The Moxie Encyclopedia.* Vestal, NY: Vestal Press, 1985.

Bradley, John. *Cadbury's Purple Reign: The Story Behind Chocolate's Best-Loved Brand.* Hoboken, NJ: John Wiley, 2008.

Branen, Alfred Larry, et al. *Food Additives.* 2nd ed. New York: Marcel Dekker, 2002.

Bray, George. *The Battle of the Bulge: A History of Obesity Research.* Pittsburgh, PA: Dorrance Pub. Co., 2007.

Brenner, Joël Glenn. *The Emperors of Chocolate: Inside the Secret World of Hershey & Mars.* New York: Broadway Books, 2000.

Broekel, Ray. *The Great America Candy Bar Book.* Boston: Houghton Mifflin Company, 1982.

Broekel, Ray. *The Chocolate Chronicles.* Lombard, IL: Wallace-Homestead Book Company, 1985.

Brookes, Graham, and Peter Barfoot. *GM Crops: The First 10 Years—Global Socio-Economic and Environmental Impacts.* Brief 36. Dorchester, UK: International Service for the Acquisition of Agro-Biotech Applications, 2006.

Brownell, Kelly D., and Katherine Battle Horgen. *Food Fight: The Inside Story of the Food Industry, America's Obesity Crisis, and What We Can Do About It.* Chicago: Contemporary Books, 2004.

Burhans, Dirk E. *Crunch!: A History of the Great American Potato Chip.* Madison, WI: Terrace Books, 2008.

Burstein, John. *Snack Attack: Unhealthy Treats, Junk Food.* New York: Crabtree Pub., 2008.

Butko, Brian. *Klondikes, Chipped Ham & Skyscraper Cones: The Story of Isaly's.* Mechanicsburg, PA: Stackpole Books, 2001.

Cadbury, Deborah. *Chocolate Wars: The 150-Year Rivalry Between the World's Greatest Chocolate Makers.* New York: PublicAffairs, 2010.

Cahn, William. *Out of the Cracker Barrel: From Animal Crackers to ZuZu's.* New York: Simon and Schuster, 1969.

Campos, Paul. *The Obesity Myth: Why America's Obsession with Weight Is Hazardous to Your Health.* New York: Gotham Books, 2004.

Cardello, Hank, and Doug Garr. *Stuffed: An Insider's Look at Who's (Really) Making America Fat.* New York: Ecco, 2009.

Carlson, Laurie Winn. *Cattle: An Informal Social History*. Chicago: Ivan R. Dee, 2001.

Cartensen, Laurence W. "The Burger Kingdom: Growth and Diffusion of McDonald's Restaurant's in the United States, 1955–1978." In George O. Carney, ed., *Fast Food, Stock Cars, and Rock 'N' Roll: Place and Space in American Pop Culture*. Lanham, MD: Rowman & Littlefield Publishers, 1995.

Chen, Joanne. *The Taste of Sweet: Our Complicated Love Affair with Our Favorite Treats*. New York: Crown Publishers, 2008.

Christeson, William, Amy Dawson Taggart, and Soren Messner-Zidell. *Too Fat to Fight: Retired Military Leaders Want Junk Food out of America's Schools; a Report by Mission: Readiness*. Washington, D.C.: Mission: Readiness, 2010.

Clark, Taylor. *Starbucked: A Double Tall Tale of Caffeine, Commerce, and Culture*. New York: Little, Brown and Co., 2007.

Coe, Sophie D., and Michael D. Coe. *The True History of Chocolate*. New York: Thames and Hudson, Inc., 1996.

Cohen, Gerald Leonard, Barry Popik, and David Shulman. *Origin of the Term "Hot Dog."* Rolla, MO: G. Cohen, 2004.

Cohon, George. *To Russia with Fries*. Toronto: McFarlane, 1997.

Consumers Union Education Services. *Selling America's Kids: Commercial Pressures on Kids of the 90's*. Mount Vernon, NY: Consumers Union, 1990. Consumers Union Web site: www.consumersunion.org/other/sellingkids/index.htm

Consumers Union Education Services. *Captive Kids: A Report on Commercial Pressures on Kids at School*. Yonkers, NY: Consumers Union, 1998.

Conza, Tony. *Success: It's a Beautiful Thing: Lessons on Life and Business from the Founder of Blimpie International*. New York: Wiley, 2000.

Culbertson, William L. *A Sweet Century: The 100-Year History of Spangler Candy Company and the Spangler Family, Bryan, Ohio*. Bryan, OH: Spangler Candy Co., 2006.

Currie, Janet M. *The Effect of Fast Food Restaurants on Obesity*. Cambridge, MA: National Bureau of Economic Research, 2009.

D'Antonio, Michael. *Hershey: Milton S. Hershey's Extraordinary Life of Wealth, Empire, and Utopian Dreams*. New York: Simon & Schuster, 2006.

Darden, Robert. *Secret Recipe: Why KFC Is Still Cooking after 50 Years*. nl: Tapestry Press, 2004.

Décasy, Gyula. *Hamburger for America and the World: A Handbook of the Transworld Hamburger Culture*. Vol. 3 of the Transworld Identity Series. Bloomington, IN: EUROPA, European Research Association, 1984.

Edge, John T. *Hamburgers and Fries: An American Story*. New York: G. P. Putnam's Sons, 2005.

Ellis, Harry E. *Dr Pepper: King of Beverages Centennial Edition*. Dallas: Dr Pepper Company, 1986.

Emerson, Robert L. *Fast Food: The Endless Shakeout*. New York: Lebhar-Friedman Books, 1979.

Emerson, Robert L. *The New Economics of Fast Food*. New York: Van Nostrand Reinhold, 1990.

Enrico, Roger, and Jesse Kornbluth. *The Other Guy Blinked: How Pepsi Won the Cola Wars*. New York: Bantam, 1986.

Espejo, Roman, ed. *Fast Food*. Detroit, MI: Greenhaven Press, 2009.

Ettlinger, Steve. *Twinkies, Deconstructed*. New York: Hudson Street Press, March 2007.

Facella, Paul, and Adina M. Genn. *Everything I Know about Business I Learned at McDonald's: The 7 Leadership Principles That Drive Break Out Success*. New York: McGraw-Hill, 2009.

Fast Food Advertising Characters: Burger King Characters, McDonald's Characters, Colonel Sanders, McDonaldland, the Burger King, Brooke Burke. nl: General Books, 2010.

Feldman, Stanley A., and Vincent Marks, eds. *Panic Nation: Unpicking the Myths We're Told about Food and Health*. London: Blake, 2005.

Finklestein, Eric A. *The Fattening of America: How the Economy Makes Us Fat, If It Matters, and What to Do about It*. Fort Lee, NJ: Wiley, 2008.

Food Advertising Characters: Beverage Advertising Characters, Burger King Characters, Cereal Advertising Characters. nl: General Books, 2010.

Friedman, Lauri S., ed. *Fast Food*. Detroit, MI: Greenhaven Press, 2010.

Fuller, Linda K. *Chocolate Fads, Folklore & Fantasies: 1,000+ Chunks of Chocolate Information*. New York: Haworth Press, 1994.

Funderburg, Anne Cooper. *Chocolate, Strawberry, and Vanilla: A History of American Ice Cream*. Bowling Green, OH: Bowling Green State University Popular Press, 1995.

Funderburg, Anne Cooper. *Sundae Best: A History of Soda Fountains*. Bowling Green, OH: Bowling Green State University Popular Press, 2002.

Furgang, Adam. *Carbonated Beverages: The Incredibly Disgusting Story*. New York: Rosen Central, 2011.

Goldstein, Myrna Chandler, and Mark A. Goldstein. *Food and Nutrition Controversies Today: A Reference Guide*. 2nd ed. Westport, CT: Greenwood Press, 2009.

Gould, William. *Business Portraits: McDonald's.* Lincolnwood, IL: VGM Career Horizons, 1996.

Grivetti, Louis, and Howard-Yana Shapiro. *Chocolate: History, Culture, and Heritage.* Hoboken, NJ: Wiley, 2009.

Gupta, B. S., and Uma Gupta, eds. *Caffeine and Behavior: Current Views and Research Trends.* Boca Raton, FL: CRC Press, 1999.

Harris, Jennifer L., et al. "Fast Food FACTS: Evaluating Fast Food Nutrition and Marketing to Youth." New Haven, CT: Rudd Center for Food Policy & Obesity, 2010, as at: www.fastfoodmarketing.org/media/FastFoodFACTS_Report.pdf

Haugen, David M. *How Does Advertising Impact Teen Behavior?* Detroit, MI: Greenhaven Press, 2008.

Hays, Constance L. *The Real Thing; Truth and Power at the Coca-Cola Company.* New York: Random House, 2005.

Heath, Richard J., with Ray Elliott. *Bittersweet: The Story of the Heath Candy Co.* 2nd ed. West Frankfort, IL: New Authors Publications, 1995.

Heimann, Jim. *Car Hops and Curb Service: A History of American Drive-In Restaurants, 1920–1960.* San Francisco: Chronicle Books, 1996.

Heller, Richard F., and Rachael F. Heller. *Carbohydrate-Addicted Kids: Help Your Child or Teen Break Free of Junk Food and Sugar Cravings—for Life!* New York: HarperCollins, 1997.

Helstosky, Carol. *Pizza: A Global History.* London: Reaktion Books, 2008.

Hendrickson, Robert. *The Great American Chewing Gum Book.* Radnor, PA: Chilton Book Company, 1976.

Henriques, Gary, and Audre DuVall. *McDonald's Collectibles: Identification and Value Guide.* Paducah, KY: Collector Books, nd.

Hirshorn, Paul, and Steven Izenour. *White Towers.* Cambridge, MA: MIT Press, 1979.

Hogan, David Gerard. *Selling 'em by the Sack: White Castle and the Creation of American Food.* New York: New York University Press, 1997.

Holechek, Jim. *Henry Perky: The Shredded Wheat King.* New York: iUniverse, Inc., 2007.

Ingram, Billy. *All This from a 5-Cent Hamburger! The Story of the White Castle System.* New York: Newcomen Society in North America, 1964.

Jacobson, Michael F. *Liquid Candy: How Soft Drinks are Harming Americans' Health.* 2nd ed. Washington, D.C.: Center for Science in the Public Interest, 2005.

Jacobson, Michael F., and Sarah Fritschner. *Fast-Food Guide.* 2nd ed. New York: Workman Publishing, 1991.

Jacobson, Michael F., and Bruce Maxwell. *What Are We Feeding Our Kids?* New York: Workman Publishing, 1994.

Jakle, John A., and Keith A. Sculle. *Fast Food: Roadside Restaurants in the Automobile Age.* Baltimore: Johns Hopkins University Press, 1999.

Kahn, E. J., Jr. *The Big Drink: The Story of Coca-Cola.* New York: Random House, 1960.

Kant, Ashima K. "Consumption of Energy-Dense, Nutrient-Poor Foods by Adult Americans: Nutritional and Health Implications. The Third National Health and Nutrition Examination Survey, 1988–1994." *American Journal of Clinical Nutrition* 72 (October, 2000): 929–36.

Keller, Kathleen. *Encyclopedia of Obesity.* Los Angeles: Sage Publications, 2008.

Kerr, Jim. *Diet and Obesity.* Mankato, MN: Sea-to-Sea Publications, 2010.

Kimmerle, Beth. *Chocolate: The Sweet History.* Portland, OR: Collectors Press, 2005.

Kimmerle, Beth. *Candy: The Sweet History.* Portland, OR: Collectors Press, Inc., 2003.

Kimmerle, Beth. *Sweet Times: 100 Years of Making Confections Better: A PMCA Retrospective.* Bethlehem, PA: PMCA, 2007.

Kincheloe, Joe L. *The Sign of the Burger: McDonald's and the Culture of Power.* Philadelphia: Temple University Press, 2002.

Kiple, Kenneth F., and Kriemhid Conee Ornelas, eds. *The Cambridge World History of Food.* Two volumes. New York: Cambridge University Press, 2000.

Kraig, Bruce. *Hot Dog: A Global History.* London: Reaktion Books, 2009.

Kroc, Ray, with Robert Anderson. *Grinding It Out: The Making of McDonald's.* Chicago: Henry Regnery Company, 1977.

Langdon, Philip. *Orange Roofs, Golden Arches: The Architecture of American Chain Restaurants.* New York: Knopf, 1986.

Lankford, Ronnie D., ed. *Junk Food.* Detroit, MI: Greenhaven Press, 2010.

Lee, Paula Young, ed. *Meat, Modernity, and the Rise of the Slaughterhouse.* Durham, NH: University of New Hampshire Press.

Leidner, Robin. *Fast Food, Fast Talk: Service Work and the Routinization of Everyday Life.* Berkeley: University of California Press, 1993.

Levi, Jeffrey, Laura M. Segal, Rebecca St. Laurent, and Serena Vinter. *F as in Fat: How Obesity Threatens America's Future, 2010.* Washington, D.C.: Trust for America's Health, 2010, as at: www.healthyamericans.org/reports/obesity2010/Obesity2010Report.pdf

Levine, Ed. *Pizza: A Slice of Heaven. The Ultimate Pizza Guide and Companion.* New York: Universe Publishing, 2005.

Levinson, Marc. *The Great A&P and the Struggle for Small Business in America.* New York: Hill and Wang, 2011.

Libal, Autumn. *Fats, Sugars, and Empty Calories: The Fast Food Habit.* Philadelphia: Mason Crest Publishers, 2006.

Liu, Warren. *KFC in China: Secret Recipe for Success.* Singapore; Hoboken, NJ: Wiley, 2008.

Losonsky, Joyce, and Terry Losonsky. *McDonald's Pre-Happy Meal Toys from the Fifties, Sixties, and Seventies.* Atglen, PA: Schiffer Publishing, 1998.

Losonsky, Terry, and Joyce Losonsky. *McDonald's Happy Meal Toys around the World.* Atglen, PA: Schiffer Publishing, 1995.

Louis, J. C., and Harvey Yazijian. *The Cola Wars: The Story of the Global Corporate Battle between the Coca-Cola Company and PepsiCo.* New York: Everest House, 1980.

Love, John F. *McDonald's Behind the Arches.* Revised and updated. New York: Bantam Books, 1995.

Magee, David. *Moon Pie: Biography of an Out-of-This-World Snack.* Lookout Mountain, TN: Jefferson Press, 2007.

Marketing Food to Children and Adolescents: A Review of Industry Expenditures, Activities and Self-Regulation. Washington, D.C.: Federal Trade Commission, 2008, as at: www.ftc.gov/os/2008/07/P064504foodmktingreport.pdf

Martin, Milward W. *Twelve Full Ounces.* 2nd ed. New York: Holt, Rinehart and Winston, 1969.

Mattern, Joanne. *Robert Cade: Gatorade Inventor.* Edina, MN: ABDO Pub. Co., 2011.

Matz, Samuel A. *Snack Food Technology.* 3rd ed. New York: AVI Van Nostrand Reinhold, 1993.

McLamore, James W. *The Burger King: Jim McLamore and the Building of an Empire.* New York: McGraw-Hill, 1998.

McNeil, Cameron L. *Chocolate in Mesoamerica: A Cultural History of Cacao.* Gainesville: University Press of Florida, 2006.

Mercola, Joseph, and Ben Lerner. *Generation XL: Raising Healthy, Intelligent Kids in a High-Tech, Junk-Food World.* Nashville, TN: Thomas Nelson, 2007.

Mercuri, Becky. *American Sandwich: Great Eats from All 50 States.* Layton, UT: Gibbs Smith, 2004.

Michelli, Joseph. *The Starbucks Experience: 5 Principles for Turning Ordinary into Extraordinary.* New York: McGraw-Hill, 2007.

Miller, Henry I. *The Frankenfood Myth: How Protest and Politics Threaten the Biotech Revolution.* Westport, CT: Praeger, 2004.

Minich, Deanna, *An A-Z Guide to Food Additives: Never Eat What You Can't Pronounce*. San Francisco, CA: Conari Press, 2009.

Mintz, Sidney. "Fast Food Nation: What the All-American Meal Is Doing to the World." *Times Literary Supplement*, September 14, 2001, 7–9.

Monaghan, Tom, with Robert Anderson. *Pizza Tiger*. New York: Random House, 1986.

Moore, John. *Tribal Knowledge: Business Wisdom Brewed from the Grounds of Starbucks Corporate Culture*. Chicago: Kaplan, 2006.

Morton, Marcia, and Frederic Morton. *Chocolate: An Illustrated History*. New York: Crown Publishers, 1986.

Moss, Sarah, and Alexander Badenoch. *Chocolate: A Global History*. London: Reaktion Books, 2009.

Motz, George. *Hamburger America; One Man's Cross-Country Odyssey to Find the Best Burgers in the Nation*. Philadelphia, PA: Running Press, 2008.

Nestle, Marion. *Safe Food: Bacteria, Biotechnology, and Bioterrorism*. Berkeley: University of California Press, 2003.

Newman, Jerry M. *My Secret Life on the McJob: Lessons from behind the Counter Guaranteed to Supersize Any Management Style*. New York: McGraw-Hill, 2007.

Nottingham, Stephen. *Genescapes: The Ecology of Genetic Engineering*. London and New York: ZED Books, 2002.

Off, Carol. *Bitter Chocolate: The Dark Side of the World's Most Seductive Sweet*. New York: New Press, 2008.

Oliver, J. Eric. *Fat Politics: The Real Story behind America's Obesity Epidemic*. New York: Oxford University Press, 2005.

Organisation for Economic Co-Operation and Development. *Obesity and the Economics of Prevention: Fit not Fat*. Paris: OECD, 2010.

Otis, Caroline Hall. *The Cone with the Curl on Top: Celebrating Fifty Years 1940–1990*. Minneapolis, MN: International Dairy Queen, 1990.

Ozersky, Josh. *Hamburgers: A Cultural History*. New Haven, CT: Yale University Press, 2008.

Pendergrast, Mark. *For God, Country and Coca-Cola*. New York: Scribner's, 1993.

Pendergrast, Mark. *Uncommon Grounds: The History of Coffee and How It Transformed Our World*. New York: Basic Books, 1999.

Perman, Stacy. *In-N-Out Burger: A Behind-the-Counter Look at the Fast-Food Chain that Breaks All the Rules*. New York: Collins Business, 2009.

Petrini, Carlo. *Terra Madre: Forging a New Global Network of Sustainable Food Communities*. White River Junction, VT: Chelsea Green Pub., 2009.

Piehl, Norah, ed. *Should Junk Food Be Sold in Schools?* Detroit, MI: Greenhaven Press, 2011.

Pollan, Michael. *The Botany of Desire: a Plant's-Eye View of the World*. New York: Random House, 2001.

Pollan, Michael. *The Omnivore's Dilemma: A Natural History of Four Meals*. New York: Penguin, 2006.

Pollan, Michael. *In Defense of Food: An Eater's Manifesto*. New York: The Penguin Press, 2008.

Popkin, Barry. *The World Is Fat: The Fads, Trends, Policies, and Products That Are Fattening the Human Race*. New York: Avery, Penguin, 2009.

Poppendieck, Janet. *Free for All: Fixing School Food in America*. Berkeley: University of California Press, 2010.

Potter, Frank N. *The Moxie Mystique*. Virginia Beach, VA: Donning Company, 1981.

Pottker, Janice. *Crisis in Candyland: Melting the Chocolate Shell of the Mars Family Empire*. Bethesda, MD: National Press Books, 1995.

Powell, Marilyn. *Ice Cream, the Delicious History*. Woodstock and New York: Overlook Press, 2007.

Pringle, Peter. *Food, Inc.: Mendel to Monsanto—The Promises and Perils of Biotech Harvest*. New York: Simon & Schuster, 2003.

Quinzio, Jeri. *Of Sugar and Snow: A History of Ice Cream Making*. Los Angeles: University of California Press, 2009.

Redclift, Michael R. *Chewing Gum: The Fortunes of Taste*. New York: Routledge, 2004.

Richardson, Tim. *Sweets: A History of Candy*. New York: Bloomsbury, 2002.

Ritzer, George. *The McDonaldization of Society*. Rev. ed. Thousand Oaks, CA: Pine Forge Press, 1996.

Ritzer, George. *The McDonaldization Thesis: Explorations and Extensions*. Thousand Oaks, CA: Sage Publications, 1998.

Ritzer, George, and Elizabeth Malone. "Globalization Theory: Lessons from the Exportation of McDonaldization and the New Means of Consumption." *American Studies* 41 (Summer–Fall, 2000): 97–99.

Ritzer, George, ed., *McDonaldization: The Reader*. 2nd ed. Thousand Oaks, CA: Pine Forge Press, 2006.

Ritzer, George. *The McDonaldization of Society 5*. Los Angeles, CA: Pine Forge Press, 2008.

Ritzer, George. *The McDonaldization of Society*. 6th ed. Thousand Oaks, CA: Pine Forge Press, an imprint of Sage Publications, 2010.

Roden, Steve, and Dan Goodsell. *Krazy Kid's Food! Vintage Food Graphics*. Köln, Germany: Taschen, 2002.

Rodengen, Jeffrey L. *The Legend of Dr. Pepper/Seven-Up*. Ft. Lauderdale, FL: Write Stuff Syndicate, 1995.

Rosenblum, Mort. *Chocolate: A Bittersweet Saga of Dark and Light*. New York: North Point Press, 2005.

Rothblum, Esther, and Sondra Solovay, eds. *The Fat Studies Reader*. New York: New York University Press, 2009.

Rouch, Lawrence L. *The Vernor's Story: From Gnomes to Now*. Ann Arbor: University of Michigan Press, 2003.

Royle, Tony. *Working for McDonald's in Europe: The Unequal Struggle?* New York: Routledge, 2001.

Royle, Tony, and Brian Towers. *Labour Relations in the Global Fast Food Industry*. New York: Routledge, 2002.

Rubin, Charles J., David Rollert, John Farago, Rick Stark, and Jonathan Etra. *Junk Food*. New York: Dell Publishing Company, 1980.

Rudolph, Marv. *Pop Rocks: The Inside Story of America's Revolutionary Candy*. Sharon, MA: Specialty Publishers, 2006.

Santino, Jack. *New Old-Fashioned Ways: Holidays and Popular Culture*. Knoxville: The University of Tennessee Press, 1996.

Schlosser, Eric. *Fast Food Nation: The Dark Side of the All-American Meal*. New York: Houghton Mifflin Company, 2001.

Schlosser, Eric, and Charles Wilson. *Chew on This: Everything You Don't Want to Know about Fast Food*. Boston: Houghton Mifflin Co., 2006.

Schrepfer, Susan R., and Phillip Scranton, eds. *Industrializing Organisms: Introducing Evolutionary History*. New York and London: Routledge, 2004.

Schultz, Howard, and Dori Jones Yang. *Pour Your Heart into It: How Starbucks Built a Company One Cup at a Time*. New York: Hyperion, 1997.

Seago, Alex. "Where Hamburgers Sizzle on an Open Grill Night and Day: Global Pop Music and Americanization in the Year 2000." *American Studies* 41 (Summer–Fall, 2000), as at: https://journals.ku.edu/index.php/amerstud/article/view/3105

Seixas, Judith S. *Junk Food—What It Is, What It Does*. New York: Greenwillow Books, 1984.

Simon, Bryant. *Everything but the Coffee: Learning about America from Starbucks*. Berkeley: University of California Press, 2009.

Sinatra, Stephen T., and Jim Punkre. *The Fast Food Diet: Lose Weight and Feel Great Even If You're Too Busy to Eat Right*. Hoboken, NJ: John Wiley, 2006.

Smart, Barry, ed. *Resisting McDonaldization*. Thousand Oaks, CA: Sage Publications, 1999.

Smith, Andrew F. *Popped Culture: The Social History of Popcorn in America*. Columbia: University of South Carolina Press, 1999.

Smith, Andrew F. "Tacos, Enchiladas and Refried Beans: The Invention of Mexican-American Cookery." In Mary Wallace Kelsey and ZoeAnn Holmes, eds., *Cultural and Historical Aspects of Foods*. Corvallis: Oregon State University, 1999, 183–203; also at: http://food.oregonstate.edu/ref/culture/latinamerica/la_smith.html

Smith, Andrew F, ed. *Oxford Encyclopedia of Food and Drink in America*. New York: Oxford University Press, 2004.

Smith, Andrew F. *Peanuts: The Illustrious History of the Goober Pea*. Urbana: University of Illinois Press, 2006.

Smith, Andrew F. *Hamburger: A Global History*. London: Reaktion Books, 2008.

Smith, Andrew F, ed. *The Oxford Companion to American Food and Drink*. New York: Oxford University Press, 2009.

Smith, Andrew F. *Eating History: Thirty Turning Points in the Making of American Cuisine*. New York: Columbia University Press, 2009.

Smith, Andrew F. *Drinking History: Fifteen Beverages That Changed America*. New York: Columbia University Press, forthcoming.

Smith, Andrew F. *Sugar: A Global History*. London: Reaktion Books, forthcoming.

Snack Food Association. *Fifty Years: A Foundation for the Future*. Alexandria, VA: Snack Food Association, 1987.

Snack Food Association. *Who's Who in the Snack Food Industry*. Alexandria, VA: Snack Food Association, 1996.

Spitznagel, Eric. *The Junk Food Companion: The Complete Guide to Eating Badly*. New York: Plume/Penguin Group, 1999.

Spurlock, Morgan. *Don't Eat This Book: Fast Food and the Supersizing of America*. New York: G. P. Putnam's Sons, 2005.

Spurlock, Morgan, and Jeremy Barlow. *Supersized: Strange Tales from a Fast-Food Culture*. Milwaukie, OR: Dark Horse Books, 2011.

Striffler, Steve. *Chicken: The Dangerous Transformation of America's Favorite Food*. New Haven, CT: Yale University Press, 2005.

Talwar, Jennifer Parker. *Fast Food, Fast Track: Immigrants, Big Business, and the American Dream*. Boulder, CO: Westview Press, 2002.

Tannock, Stuart. *Youth at Work: The Unionized Fast-Food and Grocery Workplace.* Philadelphia: Temple University Press, 2001.

Taubes, Gary. *Good Calories, Bad Calories: Challenging the Conventional Wisdom on Diet, Weight Control, and Disease.* New York: Alfred A. Knopf, 2007.

Tennyson, Jeffrey. *Hamburger Heaven: The Illustrated History of the Hamburger.* New York: Hyperion, 1993.

The Twinkies Cookbook: An Inventive and Unexpected Recipe Collection. Berkeley, CA: 10 Speed Press, 2006.

Thomas, R. David. *Dave's Way: A New Approach to Old-Fashioned Success.* New York: G. P. Putnam's Sons, 1991.

Thomas, R. David. *Dave Says—Well Done! The Common Guy's Guide to Everyday Success.* Grand Rapids, MI: Zondervan, 1994.

Thomas, R. David, and Michael Seid. *Franchising for Dummies.* Foster City, CA: IDG Books Worldwide, 2000.

Thorner, Marvin Edward. *Convenience and Fast Food Handbook.* Westport, CT: AVI Publishing Company, 1973.

Ukers, William H. *All About Coffee.* 2nd ed. New York: The Tea and Coffee Trade Journal Company, 1935.

Untermeyer, Louis. *A Century of Candymaking 1847–1947: The Story of the Origin and Growth of New England Confectionery Company.* Boston: The Barta Press, 1947.

Vaccaro, Pamela J. *Beyond the Ice Cream Cone: The Whole Scoop on Food at the 1904 World's Fair.* St. Louis, MO: Enid Press, 2004.

Vidal, John. *McLibel: Burger Culture on Trial.* New York: The New Press, 1997.

Volpe, Tina. *The Fast Food Craze: Wreaking Havoc on Our Bodies and Our Animals.* Kagel Canyon, CA: Canyon Publishing, 2005.

Warner, Deborah Jean. *Sweet Stuff: An American History of Sweeteners to Sugar to Sucralose.* Washington, DC: Smithsonian Institutional Press, 2011.

Warshaw, Hope S. *Guide to Healthy Fast-Food Eating.* Alexandria, VA: American Diabetes Association, 2006.

Watson, James L., ed. *Golden Arches East: McDonald's in East Asia.* Stanford, CA: Stanford University Press, 1997.

Watson, Stephanie. *Fast Food.* New York: Rosen Pub. Group, 2008.

Weber, Karl, ed. *Food, Inc.: How Industrial Food Is Making Us Sicker, Fatter and Poorer—and What You Can Do about It.* New York: PublicAffairs, 2009.

Weinberg, Bennett Alan, and Bonnie K. Bealer. *The World of Caffeine: The Science and Culture of the World's Most Popular Drug.* New York: Routledge, 2001.

Weiss, Laura. *Ice Cream: A Global History*. London: Reaktion Books, 2011.

Williams, Meredith. *Tomart's Price Guide to McDonald's Happy Meal Collectibles*. Revised and updated. Dayton, OH: Tomart Publications, 1995.

Winchell, Lawrence, ed. *Drive-In Management Guidebook*. New York: Harcourt Brace, 1968.

Winter, Ruth. *A Consumer's Dictionary of Food Additives; Descriptions in Plain English of More than 12,000 Ingredients Both Harmful and Desirable Found in Foods*. New York: Three Rivers Press, 2009.

Yates, Donald, and Elizabeth Yates, eds. *American Stone Ginger Beer & Root Beer Heritage, 1790 to 1920; Written by Numerous Authors and Historians*. Homerville, OH: Donald Yates Publishers, 2003.

Yu, Er. "Foreign Fast Foods Gobble Up Chinese-Style Fast Foods." *Chinese Sociology & Anthropology* 31 (Summer 1999): 80–87.

Resource Guide

CDs, DVDs, Films, and Videos

The Adventures of Fat Albert and the Cosby Kids. With Bill Cosby. (Alexandria, VA: Time-Life Video, 2002), DVD.

American Eats: History on a Bun. Hosted by Peter Schillinger, Alan Goldberg, and Pamela Wolfe, producer/writers. (Atlas Media Corporation for the History Channel, 1999).

Armstrong, Franny. *McLibel: Two People Who Wouldn't Say Sorry.* (Oley, PA: Bullfrog Films, 2005), film.

Big Mac: Inside the McDonald's Empire. (Princeton, NJ: Films for the Humanities and Sciences, 2007), film.

Biography. "Ray Kroc, Fast Food McMillionaire." Written and produced by Greg Weinstein. (History Television Productions, A&E Television Network, 1996).

Crayhon, Robert. *Junk Food Nation.* Pennsauken, NJ: Manufactured and printed by Disc Makers, 1998, CD.

Fast Food Survival Guide. With a teaching guide. (Lake Zurich, IL: Learning Seed, 2005), videocassette.

Food, Inc. Directed by Robert Kenner. (Magnolia Home Entertainment, 2009), DVD.

The Future of Food. Documentary film. (Distributor: Cinema Libre Studio, 2005).

How to Create a Junk Food. With Julia Child. With a teaching guide. (Boston: WGBH. Released by Coronet, 1988), videocassette.

Junk Food: Nothing to Snickers About. Cambridge Career Products; Cambridge Educational; Motion Masters Film & Video Production. (Charleston, WV: Cambridge Educational, 1991).

Junk Food & Nutrition. With Phil Donahue. Produced by Multi-Media Entertainment, Inc. (Princeton, NJ: Films for the Humanities & Sciences, Inc., 1988), videocassette.

Junk Food Junkie: The Effects of Diet on Health. (Mt. Kisco, NY: Guidance Associates; Indianapolis: distributed by the Indiana Department of Education, 1990), videocassette.

Junk Food Wars. (Lawrenceville, NJ: Cambridge Educational, 2006).

Killer at Large: Why Obesity Is America's Greatest Threat. (New York: Disinformation Company, 2009).

King Corn. Documentary produced by Aaron Woolf, 2006.

McLibel. Documentary directed by Franny Armstrong, 2005.

Nikkel, Evelyn. *Junk Food vs. the Right Stuff.* (Des Moines: Iowa Dept. of Management, 2001), videocassette.

Super Size Me. Directed by Morgan Spurlock. (Goldwyn Films, 2004).

Vending Machine. A documentary film released by Fairie Films, an independent film company located in Aliso Viejo, California. The film examines the lives of teenagers who have been targeted by junk food and fast food manufacturers. The film focuses on nutrition and health issues. Web site: www.vending-machinemovie.com

Organizations

American Beverage Association
1101 Sixteenth Street NW
Washington, D.C. 20036
Phone: (202) 463-6732
Web site: www.ameribev.org

Center for Science in the Public Interest (CSPI)
1875 Connecticut Avenue NW
Number 300
Washington, D.C. 20009
Phone: (202) 332-9110
Web site: www.cspinet.org

Let's Move
Web site: www.letsmove.gov

National Confectioners Association
1101 Thirtieth Street NW
Suite 200
Washington, D.C. 20007
Phone: (202) 534-1440
Web site: www.candyusa.com

National Restaurant Association
1200 Seventeenth Street NW
Washington, D.C. 20036
Phone: (202) 331-5900
Web site: www.restaurant.org

People for the Ethical Treatment of Animals (PETA)
501 Front Street
Norfolk, VA 23510
Web site: www.peta.org

Physicians Committee for Responsible Medicine
5100 Wisconsin Avenue NW
Suite 400
Washington, D.C. 20016
Phone: (202) 686-2210
Web site: www.pcrm.org

Rudd Center for Food Policy & Obesity
Yale University
309 Edwards Street
New Haven, CT 06511
Phone: (203) 432-6700
Web site: www.yaleruddcenter.org

Slow Food U.S.A.
Phone: (718) 260-8000
Web site: www.slowfoodusa.org

Snack Food Association
1600 Wilson Boulevard
Suite 650
Arlington, VA 22209
Phone: (703) 836-4500
Web site: www.sfa.org

Television Series

Food Wars, as at: www.travelchannel.com/TV_Shows/Food_Wars

Heavyweights, as at: www.foodnetwork.com/heavyweights/index.html

Man v. Food, as at: www.travelchannel.com/TV_Shows/Man_V_Food

Modern Marvels, as at: www.history.com/shows/modern-marvels

Web sites
California Healthy Kids Resource Center
A project funded in part by the state's Department of Education, it maintains an impressive collection of health education materials for preschool through twelfth grade.
www.hkresources.org

California Project LEAN
Funded in part by the California Department of Health Services, under Bright Ideas, it maintains an inspiring array of successful examples of healthy eating and physical activity strategies in schools. Case studies include how the San Francisco Unified School District developed policies to rid schools of soda and junk food in 2003.
www.californiaprojectlean.org

CSPI Nutrition Site for Children
www.smart-mouth.org

Farm to School
Programs in each state connect schools with local farms to serve healthy meals and provide health and nutrition education, all the while supporting small, local farmers.
www.farmtoschool.org

Feingold Association of the United States
Web site dedicated to helping youth and adults apply dietary techniques for better health.
health.www.feingold.org

Food Is Elementary
Authored by Cornell-trained food education expert Antonia Demas, this program teaches about food and nutrition.
www.foodstudies.org

McSpotlight
Web site focusing on the legal issues surrounding the McLibel court case in the United Kingdom from the defendants' point of view.
www.mcspotlight.org

No Junk Food
A resource for those interested in promoting a healthier environment for youth.
www.nojunkfood.org

Nutrition.gov

The U.S. Department of Agriculture Web site that covers nutritional information. *www.nutrition.gov*

Super Size Me

The Web site for Morgan Spurlock's film about the effects of eating fast food. *www.supersizeme.com*

Index

Boldface page numbers indicate main entries in the Encyclopedia.

About the Author

Andrew F. Smith has taught food studies at the New School University in Manhattan since 1995. He is the author or editor of nineteen books, including *Hamburger: A Global History* and *Potato: A Global History*, and he serves as the editor in chief for the *Oxford Encyclopedia of Food and Drink in America*. He has written more than three hundred articles in academic journals, popular magazines, and newspapers, and he has been regularly interviewed on radio and television, including National Public Radio, the History Channel, and the Food Network. He has served as historical consultant to several television series, including PBS's *What We Eat and Why*, the Food Network's *Heavyweights*, the History Channel's *American Eats*, and Discovery's *How Stuff Is Made*. For more about him, visit his Web site: www .andrewfsmith.com.